Blackstone's Police Manual

Crime

Blackstone's Police Manual

Volume 1

Crime

2024

Paul Connor

Cert Ed (FE), PG Cert Ed (ODE), LLB

Consultant Editor: Paul Connor

OXFORD
UNIVERSITY PRESS

OXFORD
UNIVERSITY PRESS

Great Clarendon Street, Oxford, OX2 6DP,
United Kingdom

Oxford University Press is a department of the University of Oxford.
It furthers the University's objective of excellence in research, scholarship, and education by publishing worldwide. Oxford is a registered trade mark of Oxford University Press in the UK and in certain other countries

First Edition published in 1998
Twenty-sixth Edition published in 2023

Published in the United States of America by Oxford University Press
198 Madison Avenue, New York, NY 10016, United States of America

British Library Cataloguing in Publication Data
Data available

CIP data is on file at the Library of Congress

ISBN 978-0-19-889063-8

DOI: 10.1093/law/9780198890638.001.0001

Printed in the UK by
Bell & Bain Ltd., Glasgow

Foreword for 2024 Blackstone's Police Manuals

As the Chief Executive of the College of Policing, the professional body for policing, I am pleased to provide the foreword for *Blackstone's Police Manuals 2024*.

The role of the College is to set standards, provide training and share good practice for policing nationally. Practitioner knowledge is at the heart of everything we do, and we use evidence of *what works*, to make a difference in fighting crime and protecting the public.

Attention has intensified on the challenges of policing because of shocking tragedies, violence and abuse committed by police officers and, as a result, public trust in policing is declining. It has never been more important than now, that knowledge and standards are the cornerstones of the policing profession. Blackstone's Manuals are the definitive reference source for all who are involved in police law and procedure and those seeking to progress or specialise in a role. They are widely used in the professional development of police officers and staff in a variety of roles.

Whilst Oxford University Press produce these titles independently, the College develops, maintains and tests standards to ensure suitability for promotion by producing a comprehensive and relevant syllabus. The Blackstone's Manuals are the official study guide for the College's National Police Promotion Framework that underpins the national legal examination, which candidates must pass, to be promoted to the ranks of sergeant and inspector.

If you are using these Manuals as a reference guide for continuous professional development, thank you for your commitment. If you are using the Manuals as a professional reference to ensure your work is of the highest possible standards, thank you for your dedication and, finally, if you are referencing these books to study for promotion or progression into a specialist role, I wish you every success.

Chief Constable Andy Marsh QPM
Chief Executive, College of Policing

Preface

Many readers of the *Blackstone's Police Manuals* are studying for promotion examinations, either to the rank of sergeant or inspector. To assist in this process, the Manuals not only provide the reader with the law in statute form but also numerous examples of the law in action, offering pragmatic explanations to sometimes complex legal issues (particularly in the 'Keynote' sections). This enables practically minded individuals to make the connection between the law on the streets and the law as it is applied and interpreted by the courts.

All the Manuals include explanatory keynotes and case law examples, providing clear and incisive analysis of important areas. As well as covering basic law and procedure, they take full account of the PACE Codes of Practice and human rights implications. They can also be used as a training resource for police probationers, special constables and PCSOs, or as an invaluable reference tool for police staff of all ranks and positions.

Oxford University Press are always happy to receive any useful written feedback from readers on the content and style of the Manual, especially from those involved in or with the criminal justice system. Please email this address with any comments or queries: police@oup.com.

The law is stated as at 1 June 2023.

Acknowledgements

Blackstone's Police Manuals have become a firmly established 'household name' in the context of police law, particularly to candidates studying for the police promotion examinations.

The production of the Manuals could not be accomplished without the professional participation of a great many people in a variety of capacities.

Many thanks to the production, editorial and marketing team at Oxford University Press, particularly Fiona Briden, Jordan Burke and Stuart Johnson.

Thanks must also go to the team of legal checkers and the staff of the College of Policing for their work in reviewing the 2024 editions.

And last, but by no means least, I thank my wife, whose continued whole-hearted support and understanding for me and my work has been, and continues to be, the primary reason you are reading these words.

Paul Connor

Contents

Table of Cases xv
Table of Statutes xxi
Table of Secondary Legislation xxix
Table of Codes of Practice xxxi
Table of Home Office Circulars xxxi
Table of International Treaties and Conventions xxxi
How to use this Manual xxxiii
Police Promotion Examinations Candidate Handbook Information xxxv

1.1 *Mens Rea* (State of Mind) 1
1.1.1 Introduction 1
1.1.2 Intent 1
1.1.3 Recklessness 3
1.1.4 Malice 4
1.1.5 Wilfully 5
1.1.6 Dishonestly 5
1.1.7 Knowing 5
1.1.8 Belief 5
1.1.9 Negligence 5
1.1.10 Strict Liability 6
1.1.11 Transferred *Mens Rea* 6

1.2 *Actus Reus* (Criminal Conduct) 7
1.2.1 Introduction 7
1.2.2 Voluntary Act 7
1.2.3 Automatism 7
1.2.4 Coincidence with *Mens Rea* 8
1.2.5 Omissions 8
1.2.6 Causal Link or Chain of Causation 9
1.2.7 Intervening Act 10
1.2.8 Principals and Accessories 11
1.2.9 Corporate Liability 14
1.2.10 Vicarious Liability 15

1.3 Incomplete Offences 16
1.3.1 Introduction 16
1.3.2 Encouraging or Assisting Crime 16
1.3.3 Conspiracy 19
1.3.4 Attempts 21
1.3.5 Impossibility 23

1.4 General Defences 24
1.4.1 Introduction 24
1.4.2 Inadvertence and Mistake 24
1.4.3 Duress 25
1.4.4 Duress of Circumstances 26

1.4.5	Defence of Self, Others or Property	27
1.4.6	Police Officers	30
1.4.7	Infancy	31
1.5	**Homicide**	**32**
1.5.1	Introduction	32
1.5.2	Murder	32
1.5.3	Voluntary Manslaughter and 'Special Defences'	33
1.5.4	Involuntary Manslaughter	36
1.5.5	Causing or Allowing a Child or Vulnerable Adult to Die or Suffer Serious Physical Harm	38
1.5.6	Encouraging or Assisting Suicide	39
1.5.7	Solicitation of Murder	40
1.6	**Misuse of Drugs**	**42**
1.6.1	Introduction	42
1.6.2	Classification	42
1.6.3	Possession	44
1.6.4	Supplying	48
1.6.5	Possession with Intent to Supply	50
1.6.6	Supply of Articles	51
1.6.7	Production of a Controlled Drug	52
1.6.8	Cultivation of Cannabis	52
1.6.9	General Defence under Section 28	53
1.6.10	Regulated Possession and Supply of Controlled Drugs	55
1.6.11	Occupiers, etc.	56
1.6.12	Community Protection Notices	57
1.6.13	Assisting or Inducing Offence Outside United Kingdom	57
1.6.14	Incitement	57
1.6.15	Travel Restriction Orders	57
1.6.16	Police Powers	58
1.6.17	Psychoactive and Intoxicating Substances	60
1.7	**Firearms and Gun Crime**	**62**
1.7.1	Introduction	62
1.7.2	Definitions—Firearm, Ammunition and Imitation Firearm	62
1.7.3	Categories of Firearms and Related Offences	65
1.7.4	Section 1 Firearm	65
1.7.5	Restrictions on Transfer of Firearms	66
1.7.6	Imitation Firearm Offences	67
1.7.7	Prohibited Weapon	69
1.7.8	General Exemptions	71
1.7.9	Criminal Use of Firearms	73
1.7.10	Further Firearms Offences	77
1.7.11	Police Powers	78
1.7.12	Possession or Acquisition of Firearms by Convicted Persons	79
1.8	**Weapons—SERGEANT'S SYLLABUS ONLY**	**81**
1.8.1	Introduction	81
1.8.2	Having Offensive Weapon in Public Place	81
1.8.3	Threatening with Offensive Weapon in Public	84
1.8.4	Having Bladed or Pointed Article in Public Place	84

1.8.5 Offences and Powers Relating to School Premises 86
1.8.6 Trespassing with Weapon of Offence 88
1.8.7 Manufacture and Sale of Weapons 89
1.8.8 Possession of Offensive Weapons in Private 90
1.8.9 Knives 90

1.9 Racially and Religiously Aggravated Offences 93
1.9.1 Introduction 93
1.9.2 Offences Covered by the Legislation 93
1.9.3 'Racially or Religiously Aggravated' 94

1.10 Non-fatal Offences Against the Person 99
1.10.1 Introduction 99
1.10.2 Assault 99
1.10.3 Battery 100
1.10.4 Assault or Battery? 101
1.10.5 Consent 101
1.10.6 Assault Offences 103
1.10.7 Other Assault Offences 109
1.10.8 Threats to Kill 111
1.10.9 Strangulation or Suffocation 112

1.11 Offences Involving the Deprivation of Liberty 114
1.11.1 Introduction 114
1.11.2 False Imprisonment 114
1.11.3 Kidnapping 114
1.11.4 Slavery, Servitude and Forced or Compulsory Labour 115

1.12 Sexual Offences 119
1.12.1 Introduction 119
1.12.2 Anonymity 119
1.12.3 Rape 120
1.12.4 Assault 125
1.12.5 Causing Sexual Activity without Consent 128
1.12.6 Rape and Other Offences Against Children Under 13 128
1.12.7 Child Sex Offences 129
1.12.8 Abuse of Position of Trust 134
1.12.9 Familial Child Sex Offences 135
1.12.10 Offences Involving Photographs and Images of Children 137
1.12.11 Sexual Exploitation of Children 143
1.12.12 Possession of a Paedophile Manual 146
1.12.13 Offences Outside the United Kingdom 147
1.12.14 Sexual Offences Against People with a Mental Disorder 147
1.12.15 Offences Relating to Prostitution 150
1.12.16 Preparatory Offences 153
1.12.17 Sex with an Adult Relative 155
1.12.18 Other Sexual Offences 156
1.12.19 Possession of Extreme Pornographic Images 159
1.12.20 Disclosing or Threatening to Disclose Private Sexual Photographs/Films 161

1.13 Child Protection 164
1.13.1 Introduction 164
1.13.2 Child Abduction 164

1.13.3	Child Cruelty	167
1.13.4	Police Powers under the Children Act 1989	168
1.14	**Theft and Related Offences**	**173**
1.14.1	Introduction	173
1.14.2	Theft	173
1.14.3	Robbery	183
1.14.4	Blackmail	185
1.14.5	Burglary	186
1.14.6	Aggravated Burglary	190
1.14.7	Taking a Conveyance without Consent	193
1.14.8	Aggravated Vehicle-taking	195
1.14.9	Interfering with Vehicles	197
1.14.10	Going Equipped	197
1.14.11	Handling Stolen Goods	198
1.14.12	Retaining a Wrongful Credit	203
1.14.13	Making Off without Payment	204
1.14.14	Proceeds of Crime	205
1.15	**Fraud**	**209**
1.15.1	Introduction	209
1.15.2	Fraud	209
1.15.3	Gain and Loss	209
1.15.4	Fraud by False Representation	210
1.15.5	Fraud by Failing to Disclose	211
1.15.6	Fraud by Abuse of Position	212
1.15.7	Possession or Control of Articles for Use in Frauds	212
1.15.8	Making or Supplying Articles for Use in Frauds	213
1.15.9	Obtaining Services Dishonestly	213
1.15.10	False Accounting	214
1.16	**Criminal Damage**	**216**
1.16.1	Introduction	216
1.16.2	Simple Damage	216
1.16.3	Aggravated Damage	219
1.16.4	Arson	220
1.16.5	Threats to Destroy or Damage Property	221
1.16.6	Having Articles with Intent to Destroy or Damage Property	222
1.16.7	Contamination or Interference with Goods	223
Index		225

Table of Cases

Adams v DPP [2002] EWHC 438 (Admin) 1.6.3.3
Alphacell Ltd v Woodward [1972] AC 824 .... 1.2.7, 1.2.9
Andrews v DPP [1937] AC 576 .... 1.5.4.1
Assange v Sweden [2001] EWHC 2489 (Admin) 1.12.3.3
Atkins v DPP [2000] 1 WLR 1427 .... 1.12.10.2
Attorney-General v Able [1984] QB 795 .... 1.2.8
Attorney-General for Northern Ireland v Gallagher [1963] AC 349 .... 1.1.2.2
Attorney-General's Reference (No. 1 of 1975) [1975] QB 773 .... 1.2.8
Attorney-General's Reference (No. 1 of 1983) [1985] QB 182 .... 1.14.2.8
Attorney-General's Reference (No. 1 of 2020) [2020] EWCA Crim 1665 .... 1.12.4.3
Attorney-General's Reference (No. 3 of 1992) [1994] 1 WLR 409 .... 1.3.4.2
Attorney-General's Reference (No. 3 of 1994) [1998] AC 245 .... 1.5.2
Attorney-General's Reference (No. 3 of 2003) [2005] QB 73 .... 1.1.5
Attorney-General's Reference (No. 4 of 2004), sub nom Attorney-General v D [2005] EWCA Crim 889 .... 1.9.3.6
Attorney-General's Reference (No. 6 of 1980) [1981] QB 715 .... 1.10.5.1, 1.10.6.5

B (A Minor) v DPP [2000] 2 AC 428 .... 1.1.10
B & S v Leathley [1979] Crim LR 314 .... 1.14.5.2
Barlow Clowes International (in liq) v Eurotrust International Ltd [2006] 1 All ER 333 .... 1.1.6, 1.3.3.2, 1.14.2.2, 1.14.11.2, 1.14.12, 1.14.13, 1.15.4, 1.15.10
Behrendt v Burridge [1976] 3 All ER 285 .... 1.12.15.5
Biggs v R (2003) 12 December, unreported 1.14.2.3
Blackburn v Bowering [1994] 1 WLR 1324 .... 1.10.7.2
Blake v DPP [1993] Crim LR 586 .... 1.16.2.6
Blayney v Knight (1974) 60 Cr App R 269 .... 1.14.7
Bliss v Lilley (1862) 32 LJMC 3 .... 1.14.6.1
Boggeln v Williams [1978] 1 WLR 873 .... 1.14.2.1
Brooker v DPP [2005] EWHC 1132 (Admin) 1.8.4
Brown v DPP (1992) The Times, 27 March 1.7.7.1
Bryan v Mott (1976) 62 Cr App R 71 .... 1.8.2.1, 1.8.2.5

C v DPP [2001] EWHC Admin 1093 .... 1.8.2.5
Cafferata v Wilson [1936] 3 All ER 149 .... 1.7.2.1
Candish v DPP [2022] EWHC 842 (Admin) 1.14.2
Clements v DPP [2005] EWHC 1279 (Admin) 1.16.5
Collins v Wilcock [1984] 1 WLR 1172 .... 1.10.7.2
Commission for Racial Equality v Dutton [1989] QB 783 .... 1.9.3.6

Daly v Cannon [1954] 1 WLR 261 .... 1.14.10
Davis v Alexander (1970) 54 Cr App R 398 .... 1.8.2.5
Davis v Lisle [1936] 2 KB 434 .... 1.10.7.2
Dawes v DPP [1995] 1 Cr App R 65 .... 1.14.8
Dawkins v Crown Suppliers (Property Services Agency) [1993] ICR 517 .... 1.9.3.7
Doodeward v Spence (1908) 6 CLR 406 .... 1.14.2.5
DPP v Armstrong [2000] Crim LR 379 .... 1.3.2.1, 1.6.14
DPP v Gregson (1993) 96 Cr App R 240 .... 1.8.4.1
DPP v H [1997] 1 WLR 1406 .... 1.1.10
DPP v Hynde [1998] 1 WLR 1222 .... 1.8.2.5
DPP v J [2002] EWHC 291 (Admin) 1.14.2.9
DPP v L [1999] Crim LR 752 .... 1.10.7.2
DPP v M [2004] EWHC 1453 (Admin) 1.9.3.6
DPP v Majewski [1977] AC 443 .... 1.1.2.2
DPP v McFarlane [2002] EWHC 485 (Admin) 1.9.3.1
DPP v Meaden [2003] EWHC 3005 (Admin) 1.6.16.1
DPP v Morgan [1976] AC 182 .... 1.4.2
DPP v Newbury [1977] AC 500 .... 1.5.4.1
DPP v Pal [2000] Crim LR 756 .... 1.9.3.6
DPP v Patterson [2004] EWHC 2744 (Admin) 1.8.2.1
DPP v Ray [1974] AC 370 .1.14.13
DPP v Rogers [1998] Crim LR 202 .... 1.4.4
DPP v Santana-Bermudez [2003] EWHC 2908 (Admin) 1.10.3
DPP v Smith [1961] AC 290 .... 1.10.6.3
DPP v Smith (Ross Michael) [2006] EWHC 94 (Admin) 1.10.6.3
DPP v Spriggs [1994] RTR 1.14.7
DPP v Taylor [1992] QB 645 .... 1.10.4
DPP v Woods [2002] EWHC 85 (Admin) 1.9.3.1

Eden District Council v Braid [1998] COD 259 .... 1.4.3
Edwards v Ddin [1976] 1 WLR 942 .... 1.14.2.6, 1.14.13
Edwards v Toombs [1983] Crim LR 43 .... 1.15.10
Evans v Hughes [1972] 1 WLR 1452 .... 1.8.2.2

Fagan v Metropolitan Police Commissioner [1969] 1 QB 439 .... 1.2.4, 1.10.2, 1.10.3
Field v R [2021] EWCA Crim 380 .... 1.2.7
Flack v Baldry [1988] 1 WLR 393 .... 1.7.7.1
Foster v DPP [2004] EWHC 2955 (Admin) 1.13.2.3

Green v DPP (1991) 155 JP 816 .... 1.10.7.3
Green v Moore [1982] QB 1044 .... 1.10.7.3

H v CPS [2010] EWHC 1374 (Admin) 1.10.5.11
Hambleton v Callinan [1968] 2 QB 427 .... 1.6.3.6
Hardman v Chief Constable of Avon and Somerset [1986] Crim LR 330 .... 1.16.2.1
Harriot v DPP [2005] EWHC 965 (Admin) 1.8.4
Harris v DPP [1993] 1 WLR 82 .... 1.8.4
Haystead v Chief Constable of Derbyshire [2000] 3 All ER 890 .... 1.10.3
Hepburn v Chief Constable of Thames Valley [2002] EWCA Civ 1841 .... 1.6.16.1
Hewitt v DPP [2002] EWHC 2801 (QB) 1.4.2
Hill v Baxter [1958] 1 QB 277 .... 1.2.3
Hinchcliffe v Sheldon [1955] 1 WLR 1207 .... 1.10.7.3
Houghton v Chief Constable of Greater Manchester Police (1987) 84 Cr App R 319 .... 1.8.2.2
Houghton v Smith [1975] AC 476 .... 1.14.11.1
Hui Chi-ming v The Queen [1992] 1 AC 34 .... 1.2.8
Hulme v DPP [2006] EWHC 1347 (Admin) 1.12.14.2

Idrees v DPP [2011] EWHC 624 (Admin) 1.15.4
Ingleton v Dibble [1972] 1 QB 480 .... 1.10.7.3

Jaggard v Dickinson [1981] QB 527 .... 1.1.2.2, 1.16.2.6
JH Walker v Hussain [1996] ICR 291 .... 1.9.3.7
Johnson v Youden [1950] 1 KB 544 .... 1.2.8.1

K v DPP [2006] EWHC 2183 (Admin) 1.7.2.4, 1.7.9.2
Kenlin v Gardiner [1967] 2 QB 510 .... 1.10.6.5
King-Ansell v Police [1979] 2 NZLR 531 .... 1.9.3.6
Knuller (Publishing, Printing and Promotions) Ltd v DPP [1973] AC 435 .... 1.12.18.1

Langley v Liverpool City Council and Chief Constable of Merseyside [2005] EWCA Civ 1173 .... 1.13.4
Lawrence v Metropolitan Police Commissioner [1972] AC 626 .... 1.14.2.3
Ledger v DPP [1991] Crim LR 439 .... 1.10.7.3
Liverpool Society for the Prevention of Cruelty to Children v Jones [1914] 3 KB 813 .... 1.13.3
Logdon v DPP [1976] Crim LR 121 .... 1.10.2.1
Low v Blease [1975] Crim LR 513 .... 1.14.5.3
Lynch v DPP [2001] EWHC 882 (Admin) 1.8.4.1

Malnik v DPP [1989] Crim LR 451 .... 1.8.2.2
Mandla v Dowell Lee [1983] 2 AC 548 .... 1.9.3.6
Martin Edward Pace & Simon Peter Rogers v R [2014] EWCA Crim 186 .... 1.14.11.2
McCann v United Kingdom (1996) 21 EHRR 97 .... 1.4.5.1
McNally v R [2013] EWCA Crim 1051 .... 1.12.3.2, 1.12.3.3
Mepstead v DPP [1996] COD 13 .... 1.10.7.2
Metropolitan Police Commissioner v Wilson [1984] AC 242 .... 1.14.5.3
Moores v DPP [1992] QB 125 .... 1.12.15.4

National Coal Board v Gamble [1959] 1 QB 11 .... 1.2.8.1
National Employers' Mutual Insurance Association Ltd v Jones [1990] 1 AC 24 .... 1.14.2.3
National Rivers Authority v Alfred McAlpine Homes (East) Ltd [1994] 4 All ER 286 .... 1.2.10
Norfolk Constabulary v Seekings and Gould [1986] Crim LR 167 .... 1.14.5.2
Northern Joint Police Board v Power [1997] IRLR 610 .... 1.9.3.6

Ohlson v Hylton [1975] 1 WLR 724 .... 1.8.2.2, 1.8.2.3
O'Leary v Allied Domecq (2000) 29 August, unreported (Case No 950275-79) 1.9.3.6
Osman v United Kingdom (2000) 29 EHRR 245 .... 1.4.5.1
Oxford v Moss (1979) 68 Cr App R 183 .... 1.14.2.4

P v DPP [2012] EWHC 1657 (Admin) 1.14.3
Palmer v The Queen [1971] AC 814 .... 1.4.5.3
Parry v DPP [2004] EWHC 3112 (Admin) 1.9.3.1, 1.9.3.2
Plowden v DPP [1991] Crim LR 850 .... 1.10.7.2
Price v DPP [1996] CLY 1469 .... 1.7.7.3

R v Abdullahi [2006] EWCA Crim 2060 .... 1.12.7.4
R v Abu Hamza [2007] QB 659 .... 1.5.7
R v Adomako [1995] 1 AC 171 .... 1.5.4.2
R v Ahmad [2012] EWCA Crim 959 .... 1.5.7
R v Akhtar [2015] EWCA Crim 176 .... 1.8.2.5
R v Ali [2012] EWCA Crim 934 .... 1.8.2.5
R v Allen [1988] Crim LR 698 .... 1.1.2.2
R v Altham [2006] EWCA Crim 7 .... 1.4.4
R v Ambler [1979] RTR 217 .... 1.14.7.7
R v Anderson [1966] 2 QB 110 .... 1.2.8.2
R v Andrews [2002] EWCA Crim 3021 .... 1.6.4
R v Archer [2011] EWCA Crim 2252 .... 1.11.3
R v Armstrong [1989] Crim LR 149 .... 1.5.4.1
R v Ashton [2007] EWCA Crim 234 .... 1.7.2.2
R v Asmelash [2013] EWCA Crim 157 .... 1.5.3.2
R v Atakpu [1994] QB 69 .... 1.14.2.3, 1.14.3
R v Auguste [2003] EWCA Crim 3929 .... 1.6.11
R v B [2006] EWCA Crim 2945 .... 1.12.3.2
R v Bain [2005] EWCA Crim 7 .... 1.10.6.5
R v Baker [1997] Crim LR 497 .... 1.4.3
R v Ball [1983] 1 WLR 801 .... 1.14.11.4
R v Barnes [2004] EWCA Crim 3246 .... 1.10.5.1
R v Bassett [2008] EWCA Crim 1174 .... 1.12.18.2
R v Bateman (1925) 19 Cr App R 8 .... 1.5.4.2
R v Becerra (1976) 62 Cr App R 212 .... 1.2.8
R v Bentham [1973] QB 357 .... 1.7.9.1
R v Bentham [2005] UKHL 18 .... 1.7.2.4, 1.14.6.1
R v Bentley (1850) 4 Cox CC 406 .... 1.4.2
R v Berry [1996] 2 Cr App R 226 .... 1.13.2.4
R v Best (1980) 70 Cr App R 21 .... 1.6.2.2
R v Bett [1999] 1 WLR 2109 .... 1.6.11
R v Bevans (1988) 87 Cr App R 64 .... 1.14.4.1
R v Bewley [2012] EWCA Crim 1457 .... 1.7.2.1
R v Bingham [2013] 2 Cr App R 307 .... 1.12.3.6
R v Birmingham [2002] EWCA Crim 2608 .... 1.10.6.4
R v Blaue [1975] 1 WLR 1411 .... 1.2.7
R v Bloxham [1983] 1 AC 109 .... 1.14.11.2
R v Bogacki [1973] QB 832 .... 1.14.7.3
R v Bounekhla [2006] EWCA Crim 1217 .... 1.12.4.4
R v Bow (1977) 64 Cr App R 54 .... 1.14.7.5
R v Bowden [2001] QB 88 .... 1.12.10.2
R v Bowles [2004] EWCA Crim 1608 .... 1.3.4.1
R v Boyesen [1982] AC 768 .... 1.6.3.6
R v Bradish [2004] EWCA Crim 1340 .... 1.7.9.4
R v Brightling [1991] Crim LR 364 .... 1.4.2
R v Bristol Magistrates' Court, ex parte E [1999] 1 WLR 390 .... 1.16.2
R v Brooks (1983) 76 Cr App R 66 .... 1.14.13
R v Brown [1985] Crim LR 212 .... 1.14.5.1
R v Brown [1993] 2 WLR 556 .... 1.10.9
R v Brown [1994] 1 AC 212 .... 1.10.5.1, 1.10.5.2
R v Brown and Ciarla [1995] Crim LR 328 .... 1.7.9.1
R v Bryce [2004] EWCA Crim 1231 .... 1.2.6, 1.2.8
R v Buckfield [1998] Crim LR 673 .... 1.7.2.1
R v Buckingham (1976) 63 Cr App R 159 .... 1.16.6
R v Buckley (1979) 69 Cr App R 371 .... 1.6.4
R v Bundy [1977] 1 WLR 914 .... 1.14.10
R v Butler [1988] Crim LR 695 .... 1.8.2.5
R v Byrne [1960] 2 QB 396 .... 1.5.3.1
R v Cairns [1999] 2 Cr App R 137 .... 1.4.4
R v Cakmak [2002] EWCA Crim 500 .... 1.16.5
R v Calhaem [1985] QB 808 .... 1.2.8
R v Campbell [1991] Crim LR 268 .... 1.3.4.1
R v Carey [2006] EWCA Crim 17 .... 1.5.4.1
R v Chahal [2010] EWHC 439 (Admin) 1.8.4.1
R v Champ [1981] 73 Cr App R 367 .... 1.6.8
R v Chan-Fook [1994] 1 WLR 689 .... 1.10.6.3
R v Chatwood [1980] 1 WLR 874 .... 1.6.2
R v Cheshire [1991] 3 All ER 670 .... 1.2.7
R v Chrastny [1991] 1 WLR 1381 .... 1.3.3.1
R v Church [1966] 1 QB 59 .... 1.5.4.1

R v Clancy [2012] EWCA Crim 8 .... 1.8.2.2
R v Clarke [1986] 1 WLR 209 .... 1.7.7.2
R v Clear [1968] 1 QB 670 .... 1.14.4.2
R v Clouden [1987] Crim LR 65 .... 1.14.3
R v Clowes (No. 2) [1994] 2 All ER 316 .... 1.14.2.7
R v Coffey [1987] Crim LR 498 .... 1.14.2.9
R v Cogan [1976] QB 217 .... 1.12.3
R v Coid [1998] Crim LR 199 .... 1.6.11
R v Coley [2013] EWCA Crim 223 .... 1.2.3
R v Collier [2004] EWCA Crim 1411 .... 1.12.10.4
R v Collins [1973] QB 100 .... 1.14.5.1
R v Coney (1882) 8 QBD 534 .... 1.2.8
R v Constanza [1997] 2 Cr App R 492 .... 1.10.2.1, 1.10.2.3
R v Cooke [1986] AC 909 .... 1.3.3.2
R v Cooper [1994] Crim LR 531 .... 1.12.3.2
R v Corbett [1996] Crim LR 594 .... 1.2.7
R v Cort [2003] EWCA Crim 2149 .... 1.11.3
R v Court [1989] AC 28 .... 1.12.4.2
R v Cremin [2007] EWCA Crim 666 .... 1.7.7.3
R v Cruikshank [2001] EWCA Crim 98 .... 1.16.7
R v Cunningham [1957] 2 QB 396 .... 1.1.3
R v D [1984] AC 778 .... 1.11.3
R v Da Silva [2006] EWCA Crim 1654 .... 1.14.14.3
R v Dalby [1982] 1 WLR 425 .... 1.5.4.1
R v Daubney (2000) 164 JP 519 .... 1.8.4
R v Davis (1823) Russ & Ry 499 .... 1.14.5.1
R v Davis (1989) 88 Cr App R 347 .... 1.14.2.4, 1.14.2.6
R v Davis [1998] Crim LR 564 .... 1.8.4
R v Dawson (1977) 64 Cr App R 170 .... 1.14.3
R v Dawson (1985) 81 Cr App R 150 .... 1.5.4.1
R v Day (1845) 1 Cox CC 207 .... 1.10.3
R v Deegan [1998] 2 Cr App R 121 .... 1.8.4
R v Dempsey (1986) 82 Cr App R 291 .... 1.6.3.8, 1.6.4
R v Densu [1998] 1 Cr App R 400 .... 1.8.2.2
R v Denton [1981] 1 WLR 1446 .... 1.16.2.6
R v Devonald [2008] EWCA Crim 527 .... 1.12.3.6
R v Deyemi [2007] EWCA Crim 2060 .... 1.7.7.3
R v Dias [2001] EWCA Crim 2986 .... 1.2.7, 1.6.4
R v Dica [2004] EWCA Crim 1103 .... 1.10.6.4, 1.12.3.2
R v Dietschmann [2003] UKHL 10 .... 1.5.3.1
R v Donovan [1934] 2 KB 498 .... 1.10.6.5
R v Dooley [2005] EWCA Crim 3093 .... 1.12.10.2
R v Downes [1984] Crim LR 552 .... 1.6.5
R v Dubar [1994] 1 WLR 1484 .... 1.14.2.7
R v Dudley [1989] Crim LR 57 .... 1.16.3
R v Duffus [1994] 158 JP 224 .... 1.14.11.4
R v Dunne (1998) 162 JP 399 .... 1.1.7
R v Dyke [2001] EWCA Crim 2184 .... 1.14.2.6
R v Dytham [1979] QB 722 .... 1.2.5
R v El-Faisal [2004] EWCA Crim 343 .... 1.5.7
R v El-Hakkaoui [1975] 1 WLR 396 .... 1.7.9.1
R v El-Mashta [2010] EWCA Crim 2595 .... 1.15.5
R v Ellames [1974] 1 WLR 1391 .... 1.14.10
R v Emmanuel [1988] Crim LR 347 .... 1.8.4.1
R v Evans (1977) 64 Cr App R 237 .... 1.6.13
R v Farr [1982] Crim LR 745 .... 1.6.7
R v Fazal [2010] 1 WLR 694 .... 1.14.14.4
R v Fellows [1997] 1 Cr App R 244 .... 1.12.10.3
R v Fiak [2005] EWCA Crim 2381 .... 1.16.2.1
R v Fisher [2004] EWCA Crim 1190 .... 1.4.3, 1.7.9.4
R v Forde (1985) 81 Cr App R 19 .... 1.6.16.2
R v Formosa; R v Upton [1991] 2 QB 1.7.7.1, 1.8.2.5
R v Forsyth [1997] 2 Cr App R 299 .... 1.14.11.2
R v Forsyth [2001] EWCA Crim 2926 .... 1.6.3.2
R v G [2010] EWCA Crim 1693 .... 1.12.7.7
R v G and R [2003] UKHL 50 .... 1.1.3, 1.1.3.1
R v Garwood [1987] 1 WLR 319 .... 1.14.4.2
R v Geary (Michael) [2010] EWCA Crim 1925 .... 1.14.14.5
R v Geddes [1996] Crim LR 894 .... 1.3.4.1
R v Georgiades [1989] 1 WLR 759 .... 1.7.9.1
R v Giles [2003] EWCA Crim 1287 .... 1.8.4
R v Gilks [1972] 1 WLR 1341 .... 1.14.2.8
R v Gingell [2000] 1 Cr App R 88 .... 1.14.11.2
R v Golding [2014] EWCA Crim 889 .... 1.10.6.4
R v Goluchowski [2006] EWCA Crim 1972 .... 1.7.9.2
R v Gomez [1993] AC 442 .... 1.14.2.3
R v Goodfellow (1986) 83 Cr App R 23 .... 1.5.4.1
R v Goodward [1992] Crim LR 588 .... 1.6.4.1
R v Gotts [1992] 2 AC 412 .... 1.4.3
R v Graham [1970] 1 WLR 113 .... 1.6.3.6
R v Graham [1982] 1 WLR 294 .... 1.4.3
R v Graham [1997] 1 Cr App R 302 .... 1.14.2.3
R v Greenfield [1984] 78 Cr App R 179 .... 1.6.5
R v Greensmith [1983] 1 WLR 1124 .... 1.6.2
R v Greig [2010] EWCA Crim 1183 .... 1.15.4
R v Griffiths [1966] 1 QB 589 .... 1.3.3.1
R v Griffiths (1974) 60 Cr App R 14 .... 1.14.11.2
R v Grout [2011] EWCA Crim 299 .... 1.12.5
R v Gullefer [1990] 1 WLR 1063 .... 1.3.4.1
R v H [2005] EWCA Crim 732 .... 1.12.4.3, 1.12.4.4
R v H [2008] EWCA Crim 1202 .... 1.12.5
R v Hale (1979) 68 Cr App R 415 .... 1.14.2.3, 1.14.3
R v Hall [1973] QB 126 .... 1.14.2.7
R v Hancock [1986] AC 455 .... 1.1.2, 1.5.2.1
R v Hanrahan [2004] EWCA Crim 2943 .... 1.8.2.4
R v Harris [1968] 1 WLR 769 .... 1.6.4
R v Harris [1996] 1 Cr App R 369 .... 1.6.7
R v Harrison [1970] Crim LR 415 .... 1.14.10
R v Harrison [2007] EWCA Crim 2976 .... 1.12.10.2
R v Harvey (1981) 72 Cr App R 139 .... 1.14.4.3
R v Harvey [2010] EWCA Crim 1317 .... 1.2.7
R v Hatton (2005) EWCA Crim 2951 .... 1.1.2.2
R v Haye [2002] EWCA Crim 2476 .... 1.6.5
R v Hayles [1969] 1 QB 364 .... 1.13.3
R v Heath [2000] Crim LR 109 .... 1.4.3
R v Henderson [2016] EWCA Crim 965 .... 1.8.4
R v Hendy-Freegard [2007] EWCA Crim 1236 .... 1.11.3
R v Hill (1989) 89 Cr App R 74 .... 1.16.2.6
R v Hinks [2001] 2 AC 24 .... 1.14.2.3
R v Hobson [1998] 1 Cr App R 31 .... 1.5.3.1
R v Hollinshead [1985] AC 975 .... 1.3.3.2
R v Howard (1965) 1 WLR 13 .... 1.12.3.2
R v Howe [1987] AC 417 .... 1.4.3
R v Howells [1977] QB 614 .... 1.7.8
R v Hughes (1985) 81 Cr App R 344 .... 1.6.4.1
R v Hughes [2013] 2 All ER 613 .... 1.14.8
R v Hussain [2005] EWCA Crim 1866 .... 1.3.3.2
R v Hutchins [1988] Crim LR 379 .... 1.11.3
R v ICR Haulage Ltd [1944] KB 551 .... 1.3.3.1
R v Ireland [1998] AC 147 .... 1.10.2.1, 1.10.2.2, 1.10.2.3, 1.10.3, 1.10.6.4
R v Jackson [2000] 1 Cr App R 97 .... 1.6.4.1
R v Jacobs [2001] 2 Cr App R (S) 38 .... 1.9.3.4
R v Jakeman (1983) 76 Cr App R 223 .... 1.2.4
R v Jheeta [2007] EWCA Crim 1699 .... 1.12.3.6
R v Jogee [2016] UKSC 8 .... 1.2.8.2
R v Jolie [2003] EWCA Crim 1543 .... 1.8.4.1
R v Jones [1979] CLY 411 .... 1.14.6

R v Jones [1990] 1 WLR 1057 .... 1.3.4.2
R v Jones (Margaret) [2004] EWCA Crim 1981 .... 1.4.4, 1.16.2.6
R v Jones and Smith [1976] 1 WLR 672 .... 1.14.5.1
R v Jordan (1956) 40 Cr App R 152 .... 1.2.7
R v Josephs (1977) 65 Cr App R 253 .... 1.6.11
R v Kanwar [1982] 1 WLR 845 .... 1.14.11.2
R v Kayani [1997] 2 Cr App R (S) 313 .... 1.5.7
R v Kelleher [2003] EWCA Crim 2846 .... 1.16.2.6
R v Kelly (1993) 97 Cr App R 245 .... 1.14.6
R v Kelly [1999] QB 621 .... 1.14.2.5, 1.14.2.6
R v Kelt [1977] 1 WLR 1365 .... 1.7.9.4
R v Kennedy [2007] UKHL 38 .... 1.2.7, 1.5.4.1
R v Kenning [2008] EWCA Crim 1534 .... 1.3.3.1
R v Khan [1990] 1 WLR 813 .... 1.3.4.2
R v Khan [1998] Crim LR 830 .... 1.2.5
R v Kingston [1995] 2 AC 355 .... 1.1.2.2
R v Kite [1996] 2 Cr App R (S) 295 .... 1.2.9
R v Klass [1998] 1 Cr App R 453 .... 1.14.6
R v Klineberg [1999] 1 Cr App R 427 .... 1.14.2.7
R v Kohn (1979) 69 Cr App R 395 .... 1.14.2.3, 1.14.2.4
R v Konzani [2005] EWCA Crim 706 .... 1.10.6.4, 1.12.3.2
R v Kousar [2009] EWCA Crim 139 .... 1.6.3.3
R v Krause (1902) 66 JP 121 .... 1.5.7
R v Kray [1998] EWCA Crim 3211 .... 1.6.4.1, 1.6.5
R v Lamb [1967] 2 QB 981 .... 1.5.4.1
R v Lambert [2002] 2 AC 545 .... 1.6.3
R v Land [1999] QB 65 .... 1.12.10.3
R v Latif [1996] 1 WLR 104 .... 1.2.7
R v Latimer (1886) 17 QBD 359 .... 1.1.11
R v Law [1999] Crim LR 837 .... 1.7.7
R v Lawrence [1982] AC 510 .... 1.5.4.1
R v Lawrence [2020] EWCA Crim 971 .... 1.12.3.3
R v Leather [1993] Crim LR 516 .... 1.13.2.3
R v Lee [2001] 1 Cr App R 19 .... 1.4.2
R v Leeson [2000] 1 Cr App R 233 .... 1.6.5
R v Lester (1955) 39 Cr App R 157 .... 1.14.10
R v Lipman [1970] 1 QB 152 .... 1.5.4.1
R v Lloyd (1989) 11 Cr App R (S) 36 .... 1.10.5.1
R v Lorimer [2003] EWCA Crim 721 .... 1.8.2.2
R v Maginnis [1987] AC 303 .... 1.6.4
R v Mallett [1978] 1 WLR 820 .... 1.15.10
R v Manning (1871) LR 1 CCR 338 .... 1.14.5.2
R v Marriott [1971] 1 WLR 187 .... 1.6.3.5
R v Marsh [2011] EWCA Crim 3190 .... 1.10.6.4
R v Marshall [1998] 2 Cr App R 282 .... 1.14.2.4
R v Martin [1989] 1 All ER 652 .... 1.4.4
R v Martin (1993) 14 Cr App R (S) 645 .... 1.10.8
R v Matthews [2003] EWCA Crim 813 .... 1.8.4.1
R v May (1990) 91 Cr App R 157 .... 1.12.18.1
R v Mayling [1963] 2 QB 717 .... 1.12.18.1
R v McAuley [2010] EWCA Crim 2130 .... 1.8.4.1
R v McCalla (1988) 87 Cr App R 372 .... 1.8.2.2
R v McDonnell [1966] 1 QB 233 .... 1.3.3.1
R v McGee [2012] EWCA Crim 613 .... 1.6.11
R v McGowan [1990] Crim LR 399 .... 1.6.9
R v McHugh (1993) 97 Cr App R 335 .... 1.14.2.9
R v McKechnie [1992] Crim LR 194 .... 1.2.6
R v McNally [2013] EWCA Crim 1051 .... 1.12.3.2
R v Metcalfe [1971] Crim LR 112 .... 1.14.10
R v Miller [1954] 2 QB 282 .... 1.10.6.3
R v Miller [1983] 2 AC 161 .... 1.2.5
R v Misalati [2017] EWCA Crim 2226 .... 1.10.6.1
R v Misra and Srivastava [2004] EWCA Crim 2375 .... 1.5.4.2
R v Mitchell [1992] Crim LR 723 .... 1.6.4.1
R v Mitchell (1999) 163 JP 75 .... 1.2.8
R v Moloney [1985] AC 905 .... 1.1.2, 1.5.2.1
R v Monteiro [2014] EWCA Crim 747 .... 1.8.4
R v MS [2021] EWCA Crim 600 .... 1.3.4.1
R v Murphy [2002] EWCA Crim 1587 .... 1.6.3.8
R v Nedrick [1986] 1 WLR 1025 .... 1.1.2
R v Nelson [2001] QB 55 .... 1.7.9.5
R v Nicklin [1977] 1 WLR 403 .... 1.14.11.2
R v Norton [1977] Crim LR 478 .... 1.7.9.1
R v O and H [2010] EWCA Crim 2233 .... 1.15.10
R v O'Grady [1987] QB 995 .... 1.1.2.2
R v Pace [2014] EWCA Crim 186 .... 1.14.14.4
R v Pagett (1983) 76 Cr App R 279 .... 1.5.4.1
R v Pannell (1983) 76 Cr App R 53 .... 1.7.7.2
R v Panton [2001] EWCA Crim 611 .... 1.6.4
R v Park (1988) 87 Cr App R 164 .... 1.14.11
R v Patel [2012] EWCA Crim 2172 .... 1.10.8
R v Paul (Benjamin) [1999] Crim LR 79 .... 1.7.4.2, 1.7.7.4
R v Pawlicki [1992] 1 WLR 827 .... 1.7.9.4, 1.14.6
R v Peacock [1973] Crim LR 639 .... 1.8.2.2
R v Pearce [1973] Crim LR 321 .... 1.14.7.3
R v Peart [1970] 2 QB 672 .... 1.14.7.1
R v Peaston (1979) 69 Cr App R 203 .... 1.6.3.1
R v Pembliton (1874) LR 2 CCR 119 .... 1.1.11
R v Phipps (1970) 54 Cr App R 300 .... 1.14.7.1
R v Pittwood (1902) 19 TLR 37 .... 1.2.5
R v Porter [2006] EWCA Crim 560 .... 1.12.10.2
R v Preddy [1996] AC 815 .... 1.14.12
R v R [2007] EWCA Crim 3312 .... 1.8.2.5
R v Rahman (1985) 81 Cr App R 349 .... 1.11.2
R v Rapier (1980) 70 Cr App R 17 .... 1.8.2.5
R v Reid [1992] 1 WLR 793 .... 1.2.5
R v Reynolds [1988] Crim LR 679 .... 1.5.3.1
R v Richardson [1999] QB 444 .... 1.10.5.1
R v Robert Millar (Contractors) Ltd [1970] 2 QB 54 .... 1.2.9
R v Roberts (1971) 56 Cr App R 95 .... 1.2.7
R v Roberts [2003] EWCA Crim 2753 .... 1.8.4
R v Robinson [1977] Crim LR 173 .... 1.14.3
R v Rogers [2005] EWCA Crim 2863 .... 1.9.3.6
R v Rostron; R v Collinson [2003] EWCA Crim 2206 .... 1.14.2.6
R v Rowley [1991] 1 WLR 1020 .... 1.12.18.1
R v Russell (1991) 94 Cr App R 351 .... 1.6.7
R v Ryan [1996] Crim LR 320 .... 1.14.5.1
R v Sakalauskas [2014] 1 All ER 1231 .... 1.15.7
R v Salih [2007] EWCA Crim 2750 .... 1.7.9.1
R v Searle [1971] Crim LR 592 .... 1.6.3.3, 1.6.3.5
R v Self [1992] 1 WLR 657 .... 1.10.7.1
R v Sharp [1987] QB 853 .... 1.4.3
R v Shephard (1919) 2 KB 125 .... 1.5.7
R v Shepherd (1987) 86 Cr App R 47 .... 1.4.3
R v Shivpuri [1987] AC 1 .... 1.3.5
R v Shwan Faraj [2007] EWCA Crim 1033 .... 1.11.2
R v Simpson [1983] 1 WLR 1494 .... 1.8.2.5
R v Singh [1999] Crim LR 582 .... 1.2.5
R v Smith [1959] 2 QB 35 .... 1.2.7
R v Smith (Ivor) [1995] Crim LR 940 .... 1.6.5
R v Smith and Jayson [2002] EWCA Crim 683 .... 1.12.10.2
R v Snooks [1997] Crim LR 230 .... 1.8.2.5
R v Solanke [1970] 1 WLR 1 .... 1.10.8
R v Spanner [1973] Crim LR 704 .... 1.8.2.1
R v Steer [1988] AC 111 .... 1.16.3

R v Stoddart [1998] 2 Cr App R 25 .... 1.7.9.4
R v Stokes [1983] RTR 59 .... 1.14.7.5
R v Stone [1977] QB 354 .... 1.2.5
R v Strong (1989) The Times, 26 January 1990 .... 1.6.3.3
R v Sundhers [1998] Crim LR 497 .... 1.15.10
R v Sweeney (1986) 8 Cr App R (S) 419 .... 1.5.3.3
R v Szewczyk [2019] EWCA Crim 1811 .... 1.8.4
R v T [1999] 163 JP 349 .... 1.12.10.3
R v Tabassum [2000] 2 Cr App R 328 .... 1.10.5.1, 1.12.4.2
R v Tait [1990] 1 QB 290 .... 1.10.8
R v Tan [1983] QB 1053 .... 1.12.15.4
R v Tao [1977] QB 141 .... 1.6.11
R v Taylor [1996] 10 Archbold News 2 .... 1.14.3
R v Taylor [2001] EWCA Crim 2263 .... 1.6.5
R v Taylor [2016] 1 WLR 500 .... 1.14.8
R v Thomas (1976) 63 Cr App R 65 .... 1.6.11
R v Thorpe [1987] 1 WLR 383 .... 1.7.2.1
R v Titus [1971] Crim LR 279 .... 1.7.7.1
R v Toomer [2001] 2 Cr App R (S) 8 .... 1.12.10.2
R v Tucker [2016] EWCA Crim 13 .... 1.8.2.5
R v Turner [2006] EWCA Crim 63 .... 1.12.18.2
R v Turner (No. 2) [1971] 1 WLR 901 .... 1.14.2.6
R v Tyrrell [1894] 1 QB 710 .... 1.2.8, 1.3.2.1
R v Vann and Davis [1996] Crim LR 52 .... 1.7.10.1
R v Vasili [2011] EWCA Crim 615 .... 1.8.2.5
R v Veasey [1999] Crim LR 158 .... 1.8.2.3
R v Velumyl [1989] Crim LR 299 .... 1.14.2.9
R v Vincent [2001] 1172 EWCA Crim 295 .... 1.14.13
R v Walker [1996] 1 Cr App R 111 .... 1.12.18.1
R v Walker [2006] EWCA Crim 1907 .... 1.12.6
R v Walkington [1979] 1 WLR 1169 .... 1.14.5.2, 1.14.5.4
R v Waller [1991] Crim LR 381 .... 1.7.7.3
R v Warner (1970) 55 Cr App R 93 .... 1.14.2.9
R v Waterfield [1964] 1 QB 164 .... 1.10.7.2
R v Waugh (1986) The Times, 1 October 1.10.7.3
R v Webster and Warwick [1995] 2 All ER 168 .... 1.16.3
R v Wellard [1978] 1 WLR 921 .... 1.11.3
R v Welsh [1971] RTR 478 .... 1.14.2.5
R v White [2001] EWCA Crim 216 .... 1.9.3.7
R v Whybrow (1951) 35 Cr App R 141 .... 1.3.4.2
R v Willer (1986) 83 Cr App R 225 .... 1.4.4
R v Williams [1992] 1 WLR 380 .... 1.2.7
R v Williams [2006] EWCA Crim 1650 .... 1.7.2.4
R v Williams [2011] EWCA Crim 232 .... 1.6.7
R v Williams (Roy) [2001] 1 Cr App R 23 .... 1.14.2.4
R v Williamson (1978) 67 Cr App R 35 .... 1.8.2.5
R v Willoughby [2004] EWCA Crim 3365 .... 1.16.4
R v Wilson [1997] QB 47 .... 1.10.5.2
R v Witchelo (1992) 13 Cr App R (S) 371 .... 1.16.7
R v Woollin [1999] 1 AC 82 .... 1.1.2
R v Wright [1994] Crim LR 55 .... 1.6.5
R v X [1994] Crim LR 827 .... 1.6.4
R v Young [1984] 1 WLR 654 .... 1.6.9.1
R v Zaman [2002] EWCA Crim 1862 .... 1.14.4
R (On the Application of Hilton) v Canterbury Crown Court [2009] EWHC 2867 (Admin) 1.8.4.1
R (On the Application of Nicolaou) v Redbridge Magistrates' Court [2012] EWHC 1647 (Admin) 1.13.2.1
R (On the Application of the Royal Borough of Windsor and Maidenhead) v East Berkshire Justices [2010] EWHC 3020 (Admin) 1.8.9.1
R (DPP) v Glendinning (2005) EWHC 2333 (Admin) 1.10.7.3
R (F) v DPP [2013] EWHC 945 (Admin) 1.12.3.3
R Cruickshank Ltd v Chief Constable of Kent Constabulary [2002] EWCA Civ 1840 .... 1.14.11.3
Read v Coker (1853) 138 ER 1437 .... 1.10.2.4
Read v Donovan [1947] KB 326 .... 1.7.2.1
Rice v Connolly [1966] 2 QB 414 .... 1.10.7.3
Roe v Kingerlee [1986] Crim LR 735 .... 1.16.2.1
Ross v Collins [1982] Crim LR 368 .... 1.7.10.1
Royal Brunei Airlines Sdn Bhd v Tan [1995] 3 All ER 97 .... 1.1.6, 1.3.3.2, 1.14.2.2, 1.14.11.2, 1.14.12, 1.14.13, 1.15.4, 1.15.10
Rubie v Faulkner [1940] 1 KB 571 .... 1.2.8
Ruddock v The Queen [2016] UKPC 7 .... 1.2.8.2

S v S (Chief Constable of West Yorkshire Police Intervening) [1998] 1 WLR 1716 .... 1.13.4.3
Scott v Metropolitan Police Commissioner [1975] AC 819 .... 1.3.3.2
Smith v Hughes [1960] 2 All ER 859 .... 1.12.15.5
Smith v Mellors and Soar (1987) 84 Cr App R 279 .... 1.2.8.1
Southern Water Authority v Pegrum [1989] Crim LR 442 .... 1.2.7
Stewart v United Kingdom (1985) 7 EHRR CD 453 .... 1.4.5.1
Street v DPP [2003] EWHC 86 (Admin) 1.7.10.1
Sullivan v Earl of Caithness [1976] QB 966 .... 1.7.7.3
Sweet v Parsley [1970] AC 132 .... 1.6.11

T v DPP [2003] EWHC 266 (Admin) 1.10.6.3
Taylor v Chief Constable of Kent [1981] 1 WLR 606 .... 1.6.11
Taylor v DPP [2006] EWHC 1202 (Admin) 1.9.3.5
Tesco Stores Ltd v Brent London Borough Council [1993] 1 WLR 1037 .... 1.2.9
Tesco Supermarkets Ltd v Nattrass [1972] AC 153 .... 1.2.9
Treacy v DPP [1971] AC 537 .... 1.14.4.2, 1.15.4
Tuberville v Savage (1669) 1 Mod Rep 3 .... 1.10.2.4

Wai Yu-Tsang v The Queen [1992] 1 AC 269 .... 1.3.3.2
Warner v Metropolitan Police Commissioner [1969] 2 AC 256 .... 1.6.3.2
Weisz v Monahan [1962] 1 All ER 664 .... 1.12.15.5
Whittaker v Campbell [1984] QB 318 .... 1.14.7.1
Willmot v Atack [1977] QB 498 .... 1.10.7.3

Yip Chiu-Cheung v The Queen [1995] 1 AC 111 .... 1.3.3.1

Table of Statutes

Academies Act 2010
s. 1B ... 1.8.5.1, 1.8.8
Accessories and Abettors Act 1861
s. 8 ... 1.2.8
Anti-social Behaviour Act 2003
s. 43 ... 1.16.2
Anti-social Behaviour, Crime and Policing Act 2014
Pt 4 ... 1.6.12
s. 110 ... 1.7.12
s. 116 ... 1.12.11.3
s. 116(3) ... 1.12.11.3
s. 116(4)–(6) ... 1.12.11.3
s. 116(8) ... 1.12.11.3
s. 118(1) ... 1.12.11.3
s. 118(2) ... 1.12.11.3
s. 118(2)(a) ... 1.12.11.3
s. 176(5) ... 1.14.2
s. 176(6) ... 1.14.2
Assaults on Emergency Workers (Offences) Act 2018 ... 1.10.6.2
s. 2(2) ... 1.10.6.2
s. 2(3) ... 1.10.6.2
s. 3(2) ... 1.10.6.2
s. 3(3) ... 1.10.6.2
British Nationality Act 1981
Pt. 4 ... 1.11.4.2
Child Abduction Act 1984
Pt. 1 ... 1.7.9.5
s. 1 ... 1.3.4.1, 1.13.2.1, 1.13.2.2
s. 1(1) ... 1.13.2.1
s. 1(2) ... 1.13.2.1
s. 1(3) ... 1.13.2.1
s. 1(3)(a) ... 1.13.2.1
s. 1(4)–(5) ... 1.13.2.2
s. 1(5)(c) ... 1.13.2.2
s. 1(5A) ... 1.13.2.2
s. 2 ... 1.13.2.2, 1.13.2.4
s. 2(1) ... 1.13.2.4
s. 2(1)(a) ... 1.13.2.2
s. 2(1)(b) ... 1.13.2.2
s. 2(3) ... 1.13.2.4
s. 2(3)(a) ... 1.13.2.4
s. 4(2) ... 1.13.2.1
s. 5 ... 1.13.2.1
Children Act 1989 ... 1.13.2.1
Pt II ... 1.13.2.1
s. 8(1) ... 1.13.2.1
s. 21 ... 1.13.4
s. 31(9) ... 1.13.4
s. 31(10) ... 1.13.4
s. 34 ... 1.13.4.1
s. 44 ... 1.13.4, 1.13.4.1
s. 44(4) ... 1.13.4.1
s. 46 ... 1.13.4, 1.13.4.1, 1.13.4.2
s. 46(1) ... 1.13.4
s. 46(1)(a) ... 1.13.4
s. 46(1)(b) ... 1.13.4
s. 46(2) ... 1.13.4
s. 46(3) ... 1.13.4.1
s. 46(3)(e) ... 1.13.4.1
s. 46(4) ... 1.13.4.1
s. 46(5) ... 1.13.4.1
s. 46(6) ... 1.13.4
s. 46(7) ... 1.13.4.1
s. 46(8) ... 1.13.4.1
s. 46(9)(a) ... 1.13.4.1
s. 46(9)(b) ... 1.13.4.1
s. 46(10) ... 1.13.4.1
s. 47(1)(b) ... 1.13.4.1
s. 49 ... 1.13.4.2
s. 50 ... 1.13.4.2
s. 50(3) ... 1.13.4.2
s. 50(7)(b) ... 1.13.4.2
s. 51 ... 1.13.4
s. 102 ... 1.13.4.2
s. 102(3) ... 1.13.4.2
s. 105 ... 1.13.4
Children and Young Persons Act 1933 ... 1.7.12
s. 1 ... 1.1.5, 1.13.3
s. 1(1) ... 1.13.3
s. 1(2) ... 1.13.3
s. 1(2)(b) ... 1.13.3
s. 1(2A) ... 1.13.3
s. 1(3)(b) ... 1.13.3
s. 17 ... 1.13.3
s. 50 ... 1.4.7
Civil Partnership Act 2004 ... 1.3.3.1
Civil Partnerships, Marriages and Deaths (Registration etc.) Act 2019 ... 1.3.3.1
Consumer Protection Act 1987
s. 11 ... 1.6.17
Coroners and Justice Act 2009 ... 1.5.4
s. 54 ... 1.5.3.2
s. 54(1)(b) ... 1.5.3.2
s. 54(1)(c) ... 1.5.3.2
s. 54(2) ... 1.5.3.2
s. 54(3) ... 1.5.3.2
s. 55 ... 1.5.3.2
s. 55(6) ... 1.5.3.2
s. 62 ... 1.12.10.5, 1.12.12
s. 62(1) ... 1.12.10.5
s. 62(4) ... 1.12.10.5
s. 62(5) ... 1.12.10.5
s. 62(6) ... 1.12.10.5
s. 63 ... 1.12.10.5
s. 64 ... 1.12.10.5
s. 65 ... 1.12.10.5
s. 65(5) ... 1.12.10.5
s. 65(6) ... 1.12.10.5
Sch. 12 ... 1.5.6.1
Corporate Manslaughter and Corporate Homicide Act 2007 ... 1.2.9
s. 20 ... 1.5.4.2

Crime and Courts Act 2013
s. 43 .... 1.4.5.4
Crime and Disorder Act 1998 .... 1.9.1, 1.9.3.6
s. 28 .... 1.9.2, 1.9.3, 1.9.3.6, 1.9.3.7, 1.10.6.5
s. 28(1) 1.9.3.9
s. 28(1)(a) 1.9.3.1, 1.9.3.2, 1.9.3.3, 1.9.3.4, 1.9.3.6, 1.9.3.8
s. 28(1)(b) 1.9.3.3, 1.9.3.4, 1.9.3.5, 1.9.3.8
s. 28(2) 1.9.3.6, 1.9.3.8
s. 28(3) 1.9.3.9
s. 28(4) 1.9.3.6
s. 29 .... 1.9.3.1, 1.10.6.5
s. 29(1)(a) 1.10.6.4
s. 29(1)(b) 1.10.6.3
s. 29(1)(c) 1.10.6.1
s. 30(1) 1.16.2
s. 30(3) 1.9.3.4
Criminal Attempts Act 1981 .... 1.3.5, 1.14.11.2, 1.15.2
s. 1 .... 1.3.4
s. 1(1) 1.3.4.2, 1.14.7
s. 1(3) 1.3.4.2, 1.3.5
s. 1(4) 1.14.7
s. 3 .... 1.3.4
s. 4(1) 1.3.4
s. 9 .... 1.14.9
Criminal Damage Act 1971
s. 1 .... 1.7.9.5
s. 1(1) 1.1.3.3, 1.9.2, 1.16.2, 1.16.4
s. 1(2) 1.16.3
s. 1(3) 1.16.4
s. 2 .... 1.16.5
s. 2(a) 1.16.5
s. 3 .... 1.16.6
s. 3(b) 1.16.6
s. 5 .... 1.1.2.2, 1.16.2.4, 1.16.2.6, 1.16.3
s. 5(2) 1.16.2.5, 1.16.5
s. 5(2)(a) 1.16.2.4, 1.16.2.5, 1.16.2.6
s. 5(2)(b) 1.16.2.4, 1.16.2.6
s. 5(3) 1.16.2.6
s. 5(4) 1.16.2.6
s. 5(5) 1.16.2.6
s. 6 .... 1.16.6
s. 10(1) 1.16.2.2
s. 10(2) 1.16.2.3
Criminal Evidence (Amendment) Act 1997
s. 1 .... 1.12.10.3
s. 2 .... 1.12.10.3
Criminal Justice Act 1967
s. 8 .... 1.1.2
Criminal Justice Act 1987
s. 12 .... 1.3.3.2
Criminal Justice Act 1988 .... 1.8.2.5, 1.12.10.1
s. 39 .... 1.9.2, 1.10.4, 1.10.6.1, 1.10.6.3
s. 40 .... 1.10.6.1
s. 139 .... 1.8.4, 1.8.5.1, 1.8.5.6, 1.8.9.1
s. 139(1) 1.8.4, 1.8.5.2, 1.8.5.4
s. 139(4)–(5) 1.8.4.1
s. 139A(1) 1.8.5.2, 1.8.5.4
s. 139A(2) 1.8.5.3, 1.8.5.4
s. 139A(4)(b) 1.8.5.4
s. 139AA 1.8.5, 1.8.5.1
s. 139B 1.8.5.5
s. 141 .... 1.7.9.6, 1.8.7.1, 1.8.8
s. 141(1) 1.8.7, 1.8.8
s. 141(4) 1.8.7
s. 141(5)–(7) 1.8.7.1, 1.8.8
s. 141(8)–(11) 1.8.7.1
s. 141(1A) 1.8.8
s. 141(1C) 1.8.8
s. 141(7A) 1.8.8
s. 141(8A) 1.8.8
s. 141(11A) 1.8.7.1
s. 141(11B) 1.8.7.1
s. 141(11C) 1.8.7.1
s. 141A 1.7.9.6, 1.8.9.1
s. 141A(1) 1.8.9.1
s. 141A(2)(a) 1.8.9.1
s. 141A(4) 1.8.9.1
s. 160 .... 1.12.10.2, 1.12.10.3, 1.12.10.4, 1.12.10.5, 1.12.12, 1.12.13
s. 160(2) 1.12.12
s. 160(2)(b) 1.12.10.4
s. 160(4) 1.12.10.4
s. 160A 1.12.10.4
Criminal Justice Act 1991
s. 80(1) 1.10.6.2
s. 90(1) 1.7.9.5
Criminal Justice Act 2003
s. 145 .... 1.10.6.5
Criminal Justice and Courts Act 2015
s. 33 .... 1.12.20, 1.12.20.1, 1.12.20.2
s. 33(2A) 1.12.10.1
s. 33(3)–(6) 1.12.20.2
s. 34(4) 1.12.20.1
s. 34(5) 1.12.20.1
s. 35(2) 1.12.20.1
s. 35(3) 1.12.20.1
s. 35(3)(c) 1.12.20.1
Criminal Justice and Immigration Act 2008
s. 63 .... 1.12.12, 1.12.19
s. 63(1) 1.12.19
s. 63(4) 1.12.19
s. 63(5) 1.12.19
s. 63(8) 1.12.19
s. 63(9) 1.12.19
s. 64 .... 1.12.19
s. 65 .... 1.12.19
s. 66 .... 1.12.19
s. 76 .... 1.4.5.2, 1.4.5.3, 1.4.5.4, 1.4.5.5
s. 76(2)(aa) 1.4.5.5
s. 76(3) 1.4.5.3
s. 76(5) 1.4.5.3
s. 76(6) 1.4.5.3, 1.4.5.5
s. 76(7) 1.4.5.3
Criminal Justice and Police Act 2001 .... 1.6.15
s. 33 .... 1.6.15
s. 33(3) 1.6.15
s. 34 .... 1.6.15
s. 35 .... 1.6.16
s. 35(5)(a) 1.6.16
s. 36 .... 1.6.16
s. 36(3) 1.6.16
s. 37 .... 1.6.16
Criminal Justice and Public Order Act 1994
s. 13(1) 1.7.9.5
sch. 1, para. 1 .... 1.10.6.2

Criminal Law Act 1967 .... 1.4.5
s. 3 .... 1.4.5.1
s. 3(1) 1.4.5.2, 1.4.5.3, 1.4.5.5
Criminal Law Act 1977
s. 1 .... 1.3.3.1
s. 1(1) 1.3.3.1
s. 2(2) 1.3.3.1
s. 8(1) 1.8.6
s. 8(2) 1.8.6
s. 12 .... 1.8.6
s. 65 .... 1.10.8
sch. 12 .... 1.10.8
Domestic Abuse Act 2021
s. 71(2) 1.10.5.3
s. 71(5) 1.10.5.3
Domestic Violence, Crime and Victims Act 2004
s. 5 .... 1.2.5, 1.5.5
s. 5(1) 1.5.5
s. 5(3) 1.5.5
s. 5(4)(a) 1.5.5
s. 5(4)(b) 1.5.5
s. 5(5) 1.5.5
s. 5(6) 1.5.5
Education Act 1996
s. 4 .... 1.8.5.1, 1.8.8
s. 550AA 1.8.5.6
s. 550ZA 1.8.5.6
s. 550ZA(1)–(2) 1.8.5.6
s. 550ZA(3) 1.8.5.6
s. 550ZC 1.8.5.6
Equality Act 2010 .... 1.9.3.6
Family Law Act 1986
s. 33 .... 1.13.4.3
Firearms Act 1968 .... 1.7.1, 1.14.6.1, 1.14.10
ss. 1–5 .... 1.7.8
s. 1 .... 1.7.4, 1.7.4.2, 1.7.5
s. 1(4) 1.7.4
s. 3 .... 1.7.5
s. 3(1) 1.7.5
s. 3(3) 1.7.5
s. 4(3) 1.7.6
s. 4(4) 1.7.4.2
s. 4A 1.7.6
s. 5 .... 1.7.2.3, 1.7.7, 1.7.7.1, 1.7.7.2, 1.7.7.3, 1.7.7.4
s. 5(1) 1.7.7.1, 1.7.7.2
s. 5(1)(aba) 1.7.7.4
s. 5(1)(b) 1.7.7.4
s. 5(1)(c) 1.7.7.4
s. 5(1A) 1.7.7.1
s. 5(1A)(g) 1.7.2.3
s. 5A 1.7.7.4
s. 7(1) 1.7.8
s. 8 .... 1.7.5
s. 8(1) 1.7.8
s. 9 .... 1.7.5
s. 9(2) 1.7.5
s. 10 .... 1.7.7.4
s. 11 .... 1.7.8
s. 11(1) 1.7.8
s. 11(2) 1.7.8
s. 11(4) 1.7.8
s. 11(6) 1.7.8
s. 11A 1.7.8
s. 16 .... 1.7.9.1
s. 16A 1.7.9.2
s. 17 .... 1.3.4, 1.7.9.3
s. 17(1) 1.7.9.3
s. 17(2) 1.7.9.5
s. 17(4) 1.7.9.3
s. 18(1) 1.7.9.4, 1.7.11
s. 18(2) 1.7.9.4, 1.7.11
s. 19 .... 1.7.10.1
s. 20 .... 1.7.11
s. 20(1) 1.7.10.2
s. 20(2) 1.7.10.2
s. 20(3) 1.7.10.2
s. 21 .... 1.7.12
s. 21(2A) 1.7.12
s. 21(3) 1.7.12
s. 21(3A) 1.7.12
s. 21(5) 1.7.12.1
s. 21(6) 1.7.12
s. 24A 1.7.6.1
s. 26A 1.7.4.2
s. 32A–32C 1.7.4.2
s. 33 .... 1.7.5
s. 47 .... 1.7.9.4, 1.7.10.2, 1.7.11
s. 47(2) 1.7.11
s. 47(3) 1.7.11
s. 47(4) 1.7.11
s. 48(1) 1.7.11.1
s. 48(2) 1.7.11.1
s. 48(3) 1.7.11.1
s. 57 .... 1.7.2.1, 1.7.2.4
s. 57(1) 1.7.2.1
s. 57(1)(b) 1.7.2.1
s. 57(1)(c) 1.7.2.1
s. 57(1B) 1.7.2.1
s. 57(1D) 1.7.2.1
s. 57(2) 1.7.2.3
s. 57(4) 1.7.4.2, 1.7.5, 1.7.7.4, 1.7.10.1
s. 57(6)(a) 1.7.4.3
s. 57(6)(b) 1.7.10.1
s. 57A 1.7.2.1
s. 57A(2) 1.7.2.1
s. 57A(3) 1.7.2.1
s. 58 .... 1.7.7.4
s. 58(2) 1.7.8
sch. 1 .... 1.7.9.5
Firearms Act 1982 .... 1.7.2.4
s. 1 .... 1.7.2.4, 1.7.4.2
s. 2 .... 1.7.2.4, 1.7.4.2
Firearms (Amendment) Act 1988
s. 6(1) 1.7.4.3
s. 6(2) 1.7.4.3
s. 7 .... 1.7.4.1
s. 8 .... 1.7.2.2
s. 8(a) 1.7.2.2
s. 15(1) 1.7.8
s. 17 .... 1.7.8
Firearms (Amendment) Act 1997 .... 1.7.5
s. 2 .... 1.7.7.4
s. 3 .... 1.7.7.4
s. 4(1) 1.7.7.4
s. 4(2) 1.7.7.4
s. 5(a) 1.7.7.4

s. 5(b) ... 1.7.7.4
s. 6 ... 1.7.7.4
s. 7(4) ... 1.7.7.4
s. 8 ... 1.7.7.4
ss. 32–35 ... 1.7.5
s. 32(2)(a) ... 1.7.5
s. 32(2)(b) ... 1.7.5
s. 32(2)(c) ... 1.7.5
s. 33(2) ... 1.7.5
ss. 34–35 ... 1.7.5
s. 44(1) ... 1.7.4.2
Fraud Act 2006 ... 1.14.2.6, 1.15.1
s. 1 ... 1.14.11.1, 1.14.12, 1.15.2
s. 2 ... 1.14.11.2, 1.15.3, 1.15.4
s. 2(1)(a) ... 1.15.4
s. 2(5) ... 1.15.4
s. 3 ... 1.15.3, 1.15.4, 1.15.5
s. 4 ... 1.15.4, 1.15.6
s. 5 ... 1.15.3
s. 6 ... 1.15.7
s. 7 ... 1.15.7, 1.15.8
s. 8 ... 1.15.7
s. 11 ... 1.15.9
s. 17 ... 1.15.10
s. 17(1)(b) ... 1.15.10
Further and Higher Education Act 1992
s. 85AA ... 1.8.5.6
s. 85B ... 1.8.5.6
s. 91 ... 1.8.5.1, 1.8.8
Gambling Act 2005 ... 1.14.2.8
Homicide Act 1957 ... 1.5.4
s. 2 ... 1.5.3.1
s. 4 ... 1.5.3.3
s. 4(3) ... 1.5.3.3
Human Tissue Act 2004 ... 1.11.4.2
Immigration and Asylum Act 1999
s. 147 ... 1.10.6.2
Knives Act 1997
s. 1 ... 1.8.9.2
s. 1(1) ... 1.8.9.2, 1.8.9.4
s. 1(3) ... 1.8.9.2
s. 1(4) ... 1.8.9.2
s. 2 ... 1.8.9.3
s. 2(1) ... 1.8.9.4
ss. 3–4 ... 1.8.9.3
s. 3(2) ... 1.8.9.4
s. 4(2) ... 1.8.9.4
s. 4(3) ... 1.8.9.3
s. 5 ... 1.8.9.4
s. 5(4) ... 1.8.9.3
s. 10 ... 1.8.9.2
Law Reform (Year and a Day Rule) Act 1996
s. 1 ... 1.5.2.2
s. 2 ... 1.5.2.2
Legal Aid, Sentencing and Punishment of Offenders Act 2012
s. 143 ... 1.10.6.5
Magistrates' Courts Act 1980
s. 22 ... 1.16.2
s. 22A ... 1.14.2
s. 44 ... 1.2.8
s. 127 ... 1.14.7
Mental Health Act 1983
s. 1(2) ... 1.12.14.1
Misuse of Drugs Act 1971 ... 1.4.4, 1.6.1, 1.6.2.1, 1.6.10, 1.6.16
Pts I–III ... 1.6.2
s. 3 ... 1.6.2.1, 1.6.16
s. 4 ... 1.6.2.1, 1.6.5
s. 4(1) ... 1.6.4.1
s. 4(2) ... 1.6.7, 1.6.9, 1.6.16
s. 4(3) ... 1.6.4.1, 1.6.4.2, 1.6.9, 1.6.15
s. 4(3)(b) ... 1.6.4.1
s. 4A ... 1.6.4.2
s. 4A(5) ... 1.6.4.2
s. 4A(6) ... 1.6.4.2
s. 4A(7) ... 1.6.4.2
s. 4A(8) ... 1.6.4.2
s. 5 ... 1.6.3.7
s. 5(2) ... 1.6.3.7, 1.6.9, 1.13.3
s. 5(2A) ... 1.6.3.7
s. 5(3) ... 1.6.2.1, 1.6.5, 1.6.9
s. 5(4) ... 1.6.3.8
s. 5(4)(a) ... 1.6.3.8
s. 5(4)(b) ... 1.6.3.8
s. 6 ... 1.6.8
s. 6(2) ... 1.6.9
s. 8 ... 1.6.11
s. 8(a) ... 1.6.11
s. 8(b) ... 1.6.11
s. 8(d) ... 1.6.11
s. 9 ... 1.6.9
s. 9A ... 1.6.6
s. 19 ... 1.6.14, 1.6.16
s. 20 ... 1.6.13
s. 23 ... 1.6.3.4, 1.6.16.1
s. 23(4) ... 1.6.16.2
s. 28 ... 1.6.4.1, 1.6.9
s. 28(2) ... 1.6.9.1, 1.6.9.2
s. 28(3) ... 1.6.9.2
s. 28(3)(a) ... 1.6.9.2, 1.6.9.3
s. 28(3)(b) ... 1.6.9.2
s. 28(3)(b)(i) ... 1.6.9.2
s. 28(3)(b)(ii) ... 1.6.9.3
s. 36 ... 1.6.13
s. 37 ... 1.6.2.2, 1.6.7
s. 37(1) ... 1.6.4.1, 1.6.8
s. 37(3) ... 1.6.3.1
Sch. 2 ... 1.6.2
Modern Slavery Act 2015 ... 1.11.1
Pt. 1 ... 1.11.4
Pt. 2 ... 1.11.4
s. 1 ... 1.11.4.1
s. 1(1) ... 1.11.4.1
s. 1(2) ... 1.11.4.1
s. 1(3) ... 1.11.4.1
s. 1(5) ... 1.11.4.1
s. 2 ... 1.11.4.2
s. 3 ... 1.11.4.2
s. 3(2) ... 1.11.4.2
s. 3(3) ... 1.11.4.2
s. 3(3)(b) ... 1.11.4.2
s. 3(3)–(6) ... 1.11.4.1
s. 3(4) ... 1.11.4.2
s. 3(5) ... 1.11.4.1, 1.11.4.2
s. 3(6) ... 1.11.4.1, 1.11.4.2
s. 4 ... 1.11.4.2
s. 5(2) ... 1.11.4.2

s. 5(3) ... 1.11.4.2
s. 12 ... 1.11.4.2
National Health Services Act 2006
s. 1(1) ... 1.10.6.2
National Health Service (Wales) Act 2006
s. 1(1) ... 1.10.6.2
Offences Against the Person Act 1861
s. 4 ... 1.5.7
s. 9 ... 1.5.2
s. 16 ... 1.10.8
s. 18 ... 1.1.4, 1.7.9.5, 1.10.5.3, 1.10.6.2, 1.10.6.4, 1.10.6.5, 1.12.3.2, 1.14.5.3, 1.14.5.5
s. 20 ... 1.1.2.1, 1.1.3.3, 1.1.4, 1.7.9.5, 1.9.2, 1.10.5.2, 1.10.5.3, 1.10.6.4, 1.10.6.5, 1.12.3.2, 1.14.5.5
s. 23 ... 1.6.4
s. 38 ... 1.4.2, 1.10.7.1
s. 39 ... 1.10.6.4
s. 47 ... 1.1.2.2, 1.7.9.5, 1.9.2, 1.10.5.2, 1.10.5.3, 1.10.6.2, 1.10.6.3, 1.10.6.4
Police Act 1996
s. 89 ... 1.7.9.5, 1.10.7.2, 1.10.7.3
s. 89(1) ... 1.10.7.2
s. 89(2) ... 1.10.7.3
Police, Crime, Sentencing and Courts Act 2022 ... 1.12.18.3
Police and Criminal Evidence Act 1984
s. 1 ... 1.16.6
Powers of Criminal Courts (Sentencing) Act 2000
s. 90 ... 1.5.2
Prevention of Crime Act 1953 ... 1.8.4, 1.8.5.6, 1.8.7.1
s. 1(1) ... 1.8.2, 1.8.2.3
s. 1(4) ... 1.8.2.4, 1.8.2.5
s. 1A ... 1.8.3, 1.8.5.1
Proceeds of Crime Act 2002 ... 1.6.2.1, 1.14.14.1, 1.14.14.6
s. 327 ... 1.14.14.1, 1.14.14.3, 1.14.14.4, 1.14.14.6
s. 327(1)(c) ... 1.14.11.4
s. 327(2) ... 1.14.11.4, 1.14.11.5
s. 328 ... 1.14.14.1, 1.14.14.3, 1.14.14.4, 1.14.14.5
s. 328(1) ... 1.14.14.5
s. 329 ... 1.14.11.2, 1.14.14.1, 1.14.14.3, 1.14.14.4, 1.14.14.6
s. 329(1) ... 1.14.14.6
s. 329(1)(b) ... 1.14.14.6
s. 329(1)(c) ... 1.14.14.6
s. 329(2)(c) ... 1.14.14.6
s. 340 ... 1.14.14.2, 1.14.14.6
s. 340(2) ... 1.14.14.2
s. 340(3) ... 1.14.14.3
s. 340(4) ... 1.14.14.2
s. 340(9) ... 1.14.14.3
Protection from Harassment Act 1997
s. 2 ... 1.9.2
s. 2A ... 1.9.2
s. 4 ... 1.9.2
s. 4A ... 1.9.2
s. 7 ... 1.2.8.1
Protection of Children Act 1978 ... 1.12.10.1, 1.12.16.2
s. 1 ... 1.12.10.3, 1.12.11.3, 1.12.12, 1.12.13
s. 1(1)(a) ... 1.12.10.2, 1.12.10.3
s. 1(1)(b) ... 1.12.10.3
s. 1(1)(c) ... 1.12.10.3
s. 1A ... 1.12.10.3
s. 1A(4) ... 1.12.10.3
s. 1A(5) ... 1.12.10.3
s. 1A(6) ... 1.12.10.3
s. 1B ... 1.12.10.3
s. 2(3) ... 1.12.10.3
s. 7 ... 1.12.10.2
s. 7(8) ... 1.12.10.3
Psychoactive Substances Act 2016 ... 1.6.17
s. 2 ... 1.6.17
s. 2(2) ... 1.6.17
s. 2(3) ... 1.6.17
s. 5 ... 1.6.17
s. 59(2)(b) ... 1.6.17
Public Order Act 1986
s. 4 ... 1.9.2, 1.9.3.1
s. 4A ... 1.9.2
s. 5 ... 1.9.2
s. 5(1)(a) ... 1.9.3.5
s. 38 ... 1.16.7
s. 38(1) ... 1.16.7
s. 38(1)(a)–(d) ... 1.16.7
s. 38(1)(b) ... 1.16.7
s. 38(2) ... 1.16.7
s. 38(6) ... 1.16.7
Race Relations Act 1976 ... 1.9.3.6
Restriction of Offensive Weapons Act 1959
s. 1(1) ... 1.8.7
Road Traffic Act 1988 ... 1.5.4.1
s. 3ZB ... 1.14.8
s. 5 ... 1.1.10
s. 6(6) ... 1.2.5
s. 170 ... 1.2.5, 1.14.8
s. 185(1)(c) ... 1.14.9
Road Traffic Offenders Act 1988
s. 34 ... 1.14.8
Sale of Goods Act 1979 ... 1.14.2.6
Serious Crime Act 2007
s. 44 ... 1.3.2, 1.3.2.1
s. 45 ... 1.3.2, 1.3.2.1
s. 46 ... 1.3.2, 1.3.2.1
s. 49(1) ... 1.3.2.1
s. 49(3) ... 1.3.2.1
s. 50 ... 1.3.2.1
s. 51 ... 1.3.2.1
s. 65 ... 1.3.2.1
Serious Crime Act 2015
s. 69 ... 1.12.12
s. 69(1) ... 1.12.12
s. 69(2) ... 1.12.12
s. 69(8) ... 1.12.12
s. 75A ... 1.10.9
s. 75A(2) ... 1.10.9
s. 75A(3) ... 1.10.9
s. 75A(3)(b) ... 1.10.9
s. 75B ... 1.10.9
Sexual Offences Act 1956
s. 33A ... 1.12.15.4
s. 33A(1) ... 1.12.15.4
ss. 34–36 ... 1.12.15.4
Sexual Offences Act 2003 ... 1.2.8, 1.12.1, 1.12.3.2, 1.12.3.6, 1.12.4.2, 1.12.4.4, 1.12.7, 1.12.14, 1.12.15.1
Pt. 1 ... 1.11.4.2, 1.12.2, 1.12.7.7, 1.12.12, 1.12.16.2
ss. 1–4 ... 1.12.6, 1.12.13
ss. 1–13 ... 1.12.11.3
s. 1 ... 1.7.9.5, 1.12.1, 1.12.3, 1.12.3.4
s. 1(2) ... 1.12.2, 1.12.3
s. 2 ... 1.7.9.5, 1.12.3.4, 1.12.4.1
s. 2(1) ... 1.12.4.1

s. 2(2) 1.12.4.1
s. 3 1.12.2, 1.12.3.4, 1.12.4.3, 1.12.4.4
s. 3(1) 1.12.4.3
s. 3(2) 1.12.4.3
s. 4 1.7.9.5, 1.12.3.4, 1.12.3.6, 1.12.5
s. 4(1) 1.12.5
s. 4(2) 1.12.5
s. 4(4)(a)–(d) 1.7.9.5
ss. 5–8 1.12.6
ss. 5–13 1.12.7.6
ss. 5–19 1.12.13
s. 5 1.7.9.5, 1.12.1
s. 6 1.7.9.5
s. 6(1) 1.12.2
s. 8 1.7.9.5, 1.12.6
s. 8(2)(a)–(d) 1.7.9.5
ss. 9–12 1.12.7.5, 1.12.8
s. 9 1.12.7.1
s. 9(1) 1.12.7.1
s. 10 1.12.7.2
s. 10(1) 1.12.7.2
ss. 11–12 1.12.7.8
s. 11 1.12.7.3, 1.12.7.4
s. 11(1) 1.12.7.3
s. 12 1.12.7.4
s. 12(1) 1.12.7.4
s. 13 1.12.7.5
s. 13(1) 1.12.7.5
s. 14 1.12.7.6
s. 14(1) 1.12.7.6
s. 14(2) 1.12.7.6
s. 14(3) 1.12.7.6
s. 15 1.12.7.7
s. 15(1) 1.12.7.7
s. 15(1)(a)(iii) 1.12.7.7
s. 15A 1.12.4.2, 1.12.7.4, 1.12.7.8
s. 15A(1) 1.12.7.8
s. 15A(2) 1.12.7.8
ss. 16–19 1.12.8, 1.12.11.3
s. 21 1.121.8
s. 21(2) 1.12.8
s. 21(3) 1.12.8
s. 21(4) 1.12.8
s. 21(5) 1.12.8
s. 22A(1) 1.12.8
s. 23 1.12.8
s. 24 1.12.8
ss. 25–26 1.12.9, 1.12.11.3, 1.12.13
s. 25 1.12.9.1
s. 25(1) 1.12.9.1
s. 25(2) 1.12.9.1
s. 25(3) 1.12.9.1
s. 26 1.12.9.2
s. 26(1) 1.12.9.2
s. 26(2) 1.12.9.2
s. 26(3) 1.12.9.2
s. 27 1.12.9.1
ss. 30–41 1.12.11.3, 1.12.13
s. 30 1.7.9.5, 1.12.1, 1.12.14.2, 1.12.14.4
s. 30(1) 1.12.14.2
s. 30(2) 1.12.14.2
s. 31 1.7.9.5, 1.12.14.3
s. 31(1) 1.12.14.3
s. 31(3)(a)–(d) 1.7.9.5
s. 32 1.12.14.4
s. 32(1) 1.12.14.4
s. 32(1)(c)(i) 1.12.14.4
s. 33 1.12.14.5
s. 33(1) 1.12.14.5
s. 34 1.12.14.2
s. 35 1.12.14.2
s. 36 1.12.14.4
s. 37 1.12.14.5
ss. 47–50 1.12.11, 1.12.11.3, 1.12.13
s. 47 1.12.11.1
s. 47(1) 1.12.11.1
s. 47(2) 1.12.11.1
ss. 48–50 1.12.11.2
s. 48 1.12.15.2
s. 48(1) 1.12.11.2
s. 48(1)(b) 1.12.11.2
s. 49(1) 1.12.11.2
s. 49(1)(b) 1.12.11.2
s. 50(1) 1.12.11.2
s. 50(1)(b) 1.12.11.2
s. 51(2) 1.12.11.2, 1.12.15.1, 1.12.15.4
s. 51(3) 1.12.11.2
s. 51A 1.12.15.5
s. 52 1.12.15.2
s. 52(1) 1.12.15.2
s. 53(1) 1.12.15.2
s. 53A 1.12.15.3
s. 54 1.12.15.2
s. 61 1.12.11.3, 1.12.13, 1.12.16.1
s. 61(1) 1.12.16.1
s. 62 1.12.13, 1.12.16.2, 1.12.16.3
s. 62(1) 1.12.16.2
s. 62(2) 1.12.16.2
s. 63 1.12.13, 1.12.16.3
s. 63(1) 1.12.16.3
s. 63(2) 1.12.16.3
s. 64 1.12.2, 1.12.17
s. 64(1) 1.12.17
s. 65 1.12.2, 1.12.17
s. 65(1) 1.12.17
ss. 66–67 1.12.11.3
s. 66 1.12.18.1
s. 67 1.12.18.2
s. 67(2) 1.12.18.2
s. 67(4) 1.12.18.2
s. 67A 1.12.18.3
s. 67A(1)–(2) 1.12.18.3
s. 67A(2A)–(2B) 1.12.18.3
s. 67A(3A) 1.12.18.3
s. 68 1.12.18.2
s. 71 1.12.2, 1.12.4.2, 1.12.18.4
s. 71(1) 1.12.18.4
s. 72 1.12.13
s. 72(1) 1.12.13
s. 73(2) 1.12.7
s. 74 1.12.3.2, 1.12.3.3, 1.12.3.6
s. 75 1.12.3.1, 1.12.3.4, 1.12.3.5
s. 75(1) 1.12.3.5
s. 75(2) 1.12.3.5
s. 76 1.11.3.1, 1.12.3.3, 1.12.3.4, 1.12.3.6
s. 76(2) 1.12.3.6
s. 77 1.12.3.5
s. 78 1.12.4.2, 1.12.5, 1.12.7.8, 1.12.16.1

s. 78(b) 1.12.4.4
s. 79(2) 1.12.3.1
s. 79(3) 1.12.3.1
s. 79(4) 1.12.7.4, 1.12.14.5
s. 79(5) 1.12.7.4, 1.12.14.5, 1.12.18.2
s. 79(7) 1.12.7.3, 1.12.14.4
s. 79(8) 1.12.4.4
s. 79(9) 1.12.3
sch. 2 .... 1.12.13
Sexual Offences (Amendment) Act 1992
s. 1 .... 1.12.2
Street Offences Act 1959
s. 1 .... 1.12.15.5
s. 1(2A) 1.12.15.5
Suicide Act 1961
s. 2 .... 1.5.6
s. 2(2) 1.5.6
s. 2(4) 1.5.6
s. 2A 1.5.6.1
s. 2A(1) 1.5.6.1
s. 2A(2) 1.5.6.1
s. 2A(3) 1.5.6.1
Terrorism Act 2000
s. 19 .... 1.2.5
Theft Act 1968 .... 1.7.9.5, 1.14.5.1, 1.16.2, 1.16.2.3
s. 1 .... 1.14.2, 1.14.3, 1.14.5.3, 1.14.10
s. 1(1) 1.14.2
s. 2 .... 1.1.6, 1.4.2, 1.14.2.1, 1.14.2.2
s. 2(1) 1.14.2.1
s. 2(1)(a) 1.14.3
s. 2(1)(b) 1.14.2.1
s. 2(1)(c) 1.14.2.1
s. 2(2) 1.14.2.1
s. 3 .... 1.14.2.3, 1.14.13
s. 3(1) 1.14.2.3
s. 3(2) 1.14.2.3
s. 3(3) 1.14.13
s. 4 .... 1.14.2.4
s. 4(1) 1.14.2.4
s. 4(2) 1.14.2.4
s. 4(3) 1.14.2.4
s. 4(4) 1.14.2.4
s. 5 .... 1.14.2.6
s. 5(1) 1.14.2.6
s. 5(2) 1.14.2.6
s. 5(3) 1.14.2.7
s. 5(4) 1.14.2.8
s. 6 .... 1.14.2.9
s. 6(1) 1.14.2.9
s. 6(2) 1.14.2.9
s. 8 .... 1.14.2, 1.14.3
s. 8(1) 1.14.3
s. 9 .... 1.14.5.1, 1.14.10
s. 9(1)(a) 1.1.2, 1.1.2.1, 1.14.5, 1.14.5.1, 1.14.5.3, 1.14.5.5, 1.14.6
s. 9(1)(b) 1.3.4, 1.14.5, 1.14.5.5, 1.14.6
s. 9(4) 1.14.5.2
s. 10 .... 1.14.6, 1.14.6.1
s. 10(1) 1.14.6, 1.14.6.1
s. 12 .... 1.14.7, 1.14.7.7, 1.14.10
s. 12(1) 1.1.2.1, 1.14.7, 1.14.8
s. 12(5) 1.14.7.4
s. 12(6) 1.14.7.4, 1.14.7.7
s. 12(7) 1.14.7.4
s. 12A 1.14.8, 1.14.8.1
s. 12A(2)(b) 1.14.8
s. 12A(3) 1.14.8.1
s. 12A(8) 1.14.8
s. 13 .... 1.14.2.5
s. 21 .... 1.14.3, 1.14.4, 1.14.11.1
s. 21(1) 1.14.4.3
s. 22 .... 1.1.7, 1.1.8, 1.14.2, 1.14.11, 1.14.11.2
s. 22(1) 1.14.11
s. 24 .... 1.14.11.1, 1.14.11.5
s. 24(1) 1.14.11.1
s. 24(2) 1.14.11.1
s. 24(3) 1.14.11.1
s. 24(4) 1.14.11.1, 1.14.12
s. 24(5) 1.14.11.1
s. 24A 1.14.11.1, 1.14.12
s. 24A(2A) 1.14.12
s. 24A(8) 1.14.11.1, 1.14.12
s. 25 .... 1.14.10
s. 25(1) 1.14.10
s. 25(3) 1.14.10
s. 26 .... 1.14.11.3
s. 27 .... 1.14.11.4
s. 27(3)(a) 1.14.11.4
s. 27(3)(b) 1.14.11.4
s. 27(4) 1.14.11.5
s. 27(5) 1.14.11.5
s. 30(4) 1.14.2, 1.16.2
s. 30(4)(a) 1.14.2, 1.16.2
s. 34 .... 1.14.4.1
s. 34(2) 1.14.4.1
s. 34(2)(b) 1.14.11.1
Vehicles (Crime) Act 2001 .... 1.14.7
Violent Crime Reduction Act 2006 .... 1.7.6.1
s. 28(1) 1.7.9.6
s. 28(3) 1.7.9.6
s. 29(13) 1.7.9.6
s. 29(14)(a) 1.7.9.6
ss. 36–41 .... 1.7.6.1
s. 36 .... 1.7.6.1
s. 38 .... 1.7.6.1
s. 38(1) 1.7.6.1
s. 38(3) 1.7.6.1
s. 39 .... 1.7.6.1
s. 40 .... 1.7.6.1
War Crimes Act 1991 .... 1.5.2

Table of Secondary Legislation

Cigarette Lighter Refill (Safety) Regulations 1999 (SI 1999/1844)
- reg. 2 .... 1.6.17

Criminal Justice Act 1988 (Offensive Weapons) Order 1988 (SI 1988/2019) 1.8.7.1

Criminal Justice Act 1988 (Offensive Weapons) (Exemption) Order 1996 (SI 1996/3064) 1.8.9.1

Misuse of Drugs Regulations 2001 (SI 2001/3998) 1.6.10
- reg. 4 .... 1.6.10
- reg. 5 .... 1.6.10
- reg. 6 .... 1.6.10
- reg. 6(5)–(7) 1.6.10
- Sch. 2 .... 1.6.10

Misuse of Drugs (Amendments) (Cannabis and Licence Fees) (England, Wales and Scotland) Regulations 2018 (SI 2018/1055) 1.6.10

Misuse of Drugs and Misuse of Drugs (Safe Custody) (Amendment) Regulations 2007 (SI 2007/2154) 1.6.10

Violent Crime Reduction Act 2006 (Realistic Imitation Firearms) Regulations 2007 (SI 2007/2606) 1.7.6.1

Table of Codes of Practice

PACE Code of Practice Code A........... 1.6.16.1, 1.7.11, 1.8.5.5

Table of Home Office Circulars

Home Office Circular 17/2008.. 1.13.4

Table of International Treaties and Conventions

European Convention on Human Rights
Art. 2..................................... 1.4.5, 1.4.5.1, 1.4.5.2, 1.4.5.5
Art. 2(a)–(c) 1.4.5.1
Art. 4... 1.11.4.1
Art. 8.. 1.6.5, 1.10.5.2
Art. 9... 1.6.5

How to use this Manual

Volume numbers for the Manuals

The 2024 *Blackstone's Police Manuals* each have a volume number as follows:

Volume 1: *Crime*
Volume 2: *Evidence and Procedure*
Volume 3: *General Police Duties*

The first digit of each paragraph number in the text of the Manuals denotes the Manual number. For example, chapter 2.3 is chapter 3 of the *Evidence and Procedure* Manual and chapter 3.3 is chapter 3 of the *General Police Duties* Manual.

All index entries and references in the Tables of Legislation and the Table of Cases, etc. refer to paragraph numbers instead of page numbers, making information easier to find.

Material outside the scope of the police promotion examinations syllabus—blacklining

These Manuals contain some information which is outside the scope of the police promotion examinations. A full black line down the margin indicates that the text beside it is excluded from Inspectors' examinations.

Length of sentence for an offence

Where a length of sentence for an offence is stated in this Manual, please note that the number of months or years stated is the maximum number and will not be exceeded.

Any feedback regarding content or other editorial matters in the Manuals can be emailed to police@oup.com.

Police Promotion Examinations Candidate Handbook Information

The rules and syllabus for the police promotion examinations system are defined within the Candidate Handbook published by College of Policing Selection and Assessment on behalf of the Police Promotion Examinations Board (PPEB). The Candidate Handbook is published annually each September, and applies to all police promotion assessments scheduled for the calendar year following its publication. For example, the September 2024 Candidate Handbook would apply to all police promotion assessments held during 2024.

The document provides details of the law and procedure to be tested within the National Police Promotion Framework Step 2 Legal Examination, and also outlines the rules underpinning the police promotion examination system.

All candidates who are taking a police promotion examination are strongly encouraged to familiarise themselves with the Candidate Handbook during their preparation. The police promotion examination rules apply to candidates undertaking the National Police Promotion Framework.

The document can be downloaded from the Development Section of the College of Policing website, which can be found at <https://www.college.police.uk>. Electronic versions are also supplied to all force examination officers.

If you have any problems obtaining the Candidate Handbook from the above source, please contact your force examination officer.

Usually, no further updates to the Candidate Handbook will be issued during its year-long lifespan. However, in exceptional circumstances, the College of Policing (on behalf of the PPEB) reserves the right to issue an amended syllabus prior to the next scheduled annual publication date.

For example, a major change to a key area of legislation or procedure (e.g. the Codes of Practice) during the lifespan of the current Candidate Handbook would render a significant part of the current syllabus content obsolete. In such circumstances, it may be necessary for an update to the syllabus to be issued, which would provide guidance to candidates on any additional material which would be examinable within their police promotion examinations.

In such circumstances, an update to the Candidate Handbook would be made available through the College of Policing website, and would be distributed to all force examination contacts. The College of Policing will ensure that any syllabus update is distributed well in advance of the examination date, to ensure that candidates have sufficient time to familiarise themselves with any additional examinable material. Where possible, any additional study materials would be provided to candidates free of charge.

Please note that syllabus updates will only be made in exceptional circumstances; an update will not be made for every change to legislation included within the syllabus. For further guidance on this issue, candidates are advised to check regularly the College of Policing website, or consult their force examination officer, during their preparation period.

1.1 *Mens Rea* (State of Mind)

1.1.1 Introduction

Any analysis of law begins with an examination of *mens rea* (state of mind) and *actus reus* (criminal conduct). These concepts are fundamental to understanding all offences and the idea of criminal liability generally.

Mens rea alone will not amount to an offence; thinking about committing a crime is not committing a crime. In fact, the default position is that the application of the mind is essential for liability to exist as acts (or omissions) alone cannot amount to a crime unless they are accompanied by '*mens rea*' at the time of the act (or omission).

It is therefore vital to consider, among others, what is meant by terms such as 'intent' and 'recklessness'.

1.1.2 Intent

'Intent' is a word often used in relation to consequences. If a defendant intends something to happen, he/she wishes to bring about a consequence. In some offences, say burglary under s. 9(1)(a) of the Theft Act 1968, the defendant's *intention* may be very clear; he/she may enter a house as a trespasser *intending* to steal property inside.

However, there will often be consequences following a defendant's actions that he/she did not *intend* to happen. What if, in the above burglary, the householder came across the burglar and suffered a heart attack? It might be reasonable to suggest that it was the defendant's behaviour that had brought about the situation (**see chapter 1.2**). The defendant, however, may argue that, although he/she intended to break in and steal, there had never been any *intention* of harming the occupant. At this point, you might say that the defendant should have thought about that before breaking into someone else's house. This brings in the concept of *foresight*, a concept that has caused the courts some difficulty over the years—for several reasons.

First, there is the Criminal Justice Act 1967 which says (under s. 8) that a court/jury, in determining whether a person has committed an offence:

- shall not be bound in law to infer that he intended or foresaw a result of his actions by reason only of its being a natural and probable consequence of those actions; but
- shall decide whether he did intend or foresee that result by reference to all the evidence, drawing such inferences from the evidence as appear proper in the circumstances.

Secondly, there is the body of case law which has developed around the area of 'probability', culminating in two cases in the House of Lords (*R* v *Moloney* [1985] AC 905 and *R* v *Hancock* [1986] AC 455). Following those cases, it is settled that foresight of the probability of a consequence does not amount to an intention to bring that consequence about, *but may be evidence of it.*

So you cannot claim that a defendant *intended* a consequence of his/her behaviour simply because it was virtually certain to occur. What you can do is to put evidence of the defendant's foresight of that probability before a court, which may infer an intention from it. Such an argument would go like this:

- at the time of the criminal act there was a *probability* of a consequence;
- the greater the probability of a consequence, the more likely it is that the defendant *foresaw* that consequence;

- if the defendant foresaw that consequence, the more likely it is that the defendant *intended* it to happen.

Whether or not a defendant intended a particular consequence will be a question of fact left to the jury (or magistrate(s) where appropriate). In murder cases (**see chapter 1.5**), where death or serious bodily harm was a *virtual certainty* from the defendant's actions and he/she had appreciated that to be the case, the jury *may* infer that the defendant intended to bring about such consequences (*R* v *Nedrick* [1986] 1 WLR 1025). Therefore, where the defendant threw a three-month-old baby down onto a hard surface in a fit of rage, the jury *might* have inferred both that death/serious bodily harm was a virtual certainty from the defendant's actions and that he must have appreciated that to be the case; they should therefore have been directed by the trial judge accordingly (*R* v *Woollin* [1999] 1 AC 82).

Finally, the relevant intent may have been formed, not of the defendant's own volition, but influenced in some way by other external factors. An example is where the defendant's thinking is affected by duress (as to which, **see para. 1.4.5**).

1.1.2.1 Offences of 'Specific' and 'Basic' Intent

Crimes of 'specific' intent are only committed where the defendant is shown to have had a particular intention to bring about a specific consequence at the time of the criminal act. Murder is such a crime as is burglary with intent (Theft Act 1968, s. 9(1)(a)). The common feature with these offences is that the *intention* of the offender is critical—without that intent, the offence does not exist.

Other criminal offences require no further proof of anything other than the 'basic' intention to bring about the given circumstances. For example, the offence of maliciously wounding or inflicting grievous bodily harm (Offences Against the Person Act 1861, s. 20) or taking a conveyance (Theft Act 1968, s. 12(1)).

The important difference between offences of specific and basic intent is that, in the case of the latter, *recklessness* will often be enough to satisfy the mental element.

Whether an offence is one of 'specific' or 'basic' intent connects to the issues around voluntary or involuntary intoxication.

1.1.2.2 Intoxication: Voluntary or Involuntary

Intoxication potentially removes the necessary *mens rea* required for a defendant to commit an offence (intoxication is not a defence—if it were, a significant proportion of criminal behaviour would go unpunished).

Intoxication can be divided into two categories; voluntary intoxication (you got yourself in that condition) and involuntary intoxication (you are not responsible for getting in that condition). The distinction is important when considering whether the offence alleged is one of 'specific' or 'basic' intent.

Where an offence is a specific intent offence, such as murder, defendants who were voluntarily intoxicated at the time the offence was committed may be able to show they were so intoxicated that they were incapable of forming the *mens rea* required for the offence. An individual who is voluntarily intoxicated *would not* be able to say this if accused of an offence of basic intent as the courts have accepted that a defendant is still capable of forming basic intent even when completely inebriated (*DPP* v *Majewski* [1977] AC 443).

Where the offence is a basic intent offence, such as s. 47 assault, defendants who were involuntarily intoxicated (perhaps because their drink had been spiked) at the time of the offence may be able to say that they lacked the *mens rea* for that basic intent offence.

KEYNOTE

Therefore, voluntary intoxication can be raised in answer to a charge of an offence of specific intent but not basic intent; involuntary intoxication can be raised in answer to a charge of both specific and basic intent.

If defendants simply misjudge the amount or strength of intoxicants which they take, this will not be regarded as involuntary intoxication (*R* v *Allen* [1988] Crim LR 698). So if a defendant knowingly drinks beer but is unaware that the beer has been laced with vodka, this will still be 'voluntary' intoxication. Similarly, if defendants can be shown to have actually formed the required *mens rea* necessary for the offence, intoxication (voluntary or involuntary) will not be available as a drunken intent is still an 'intent' (*R* v *Kingston* [1995] 2 AC 355).

The source of the intoxication can be drink or drugs. In the latter case, however, the courts will consider the known effects of the drug in deciding whether or not defendants had formed the required degree of *mens rea*; the characteristics of the drugs will be relevant in determining whether defendants behaved recklessly in taking them.

Where the defendant forms a 'mistaken belief' based on the fact that he/she is intoxicated, that belief may sometimes be raised as a defence. In cases of criminal damage where a defendant has mistakenly believed that the property being damaged is his/her own property, and that mistaken belief has arisen from the defendant's intoxicated state, the courts have accepted the defence under s. 5 of the Criminal Damage Act 1971 (*Jaggard* v *Dickinson* [1981] QB 527) (**see chapter 1.16**). However, this appears to be confined to the wording of that particular statute and the courts have refused to accept similar defences of mistaken, drunken belief (e.g. in *R* v *O'Grady* [1987] QB 995, where a defendant charged with murder could not rely on a mistake induced by his own voluntary intoxication and claim 'self-defence'), or where the defendant mistakenly believed that the victim of a rape was consenting to sexual intercourse. The Court of Appeal has confirmed that the decision in *O'Grady* also applies to manslaughter (*R* v *Hatton* [2005] EWCA Crim 2951).

If defendants become intoxicated in order to gain false courage to go and commit a crime, they will not be able to claim a defence of intoxication *even if the crime is one of specific intent*. This is because they have already formed the intent required and the intoxication is merely a means of plucking up 'Dutch' courage to carry it out (*Attorney-General for Northern Ireland* v *Gallagher* [1963] AC 349).

1.1.3 Recklessness

Recklessness is a state of mind that is relevant to a large number of crimes and is essentially concerned with unjustified risk-taking. Following the case of *R* v *G and R* [2003] UKHL 50, the approach taken to the interpretation of the word 'reckless' is that it will be 'subjective'.

The requirements of subjective recklessness can be found in the case of *R* v *Cunningham* [1957] 2 QB 396 and are satisfied in situations where *the defendant* foresees the consequences of his/her actions as being probable or even possible. In *G*, the House of Lords held that a person acts recklessly with respect to:

- a circumstance when he/she is *aware* of a risk that it exists or will exist;
- a result when he/she is *aware* of the risk that it will occur;

and it is, in the circumstances known to him/her, *unreasonable* to take that risk.

To establish recklessness, therefore, requires consideration of the degree of risk that is actually foreseen by the defendant of which he/she is aware and whether it was reasonable.

1.1.3.1 Awareness

Here we are concerned with what was going on in the mind of the defendant—were they aware of the risk? For example, in *G* the defendants were two children (aged 11 and 12) who set fire to some newspapers in the rear yard of a shop premises whilst camping out. The children put the burning papers under a wheelie bin and left them, expecting the small fire to burn itself out on the concrete floor of the yard. In fact, the fire spread causing around £1,000,000 of damage. The children were convicted of criminal damage under the former law ('objective' recklessness) on the basis that the fire would have been obvious to any reasonable bystander. The convictions were quashed by the House of Lords who reinstated the general subjective element described above. A reasonable bystander might well have been aware of the risk of such activity—the children were not.

1.1.3.2 Reasonableness

The risk a defendant is aware of may be small but that does not automatically mean that it is reasonable to take that risk. Each situation will be decided on its own merits, but whether the risk is reasonable or not will be decided by the court—not the defendant. What this does is to introduce an objective element into the recklessness equation but, even though that is the case, it must be stressed that recklessness is still subjective—the key question is whether the defendant was aware of the risk.

1.1.3.3 Different Crime = Different Risk

Depending on the crime, the nature of the risk the defendant needs to be aware of will change. For example, to commit an offence under s. 20 of the Offences Against the Person Act 1861 (wounding or inflicting grievous bodily harm (**see chapter 1.10**)), the defendant must unlawfully and recklessly wound or inflict grievous bodily harm on the victim. Here 'recklessness' means that the defendant was aware of the risk that *some harm* would befall the victim. If we consider simple criminal damage under s. 1(1) of the Criminal Damage Act 1971 (**see chapter 1.16**), then the risk the defendant would need to be aware of to be reckless is that property belonging to another would be damaged or destroyed.

1.1.4 Malice

The term 'malice' is particularly relevant to ss. 18 and 20 of the Offences Against the Person Act 1861 (offences relating to grievous bodily harm/wounding). It *should not* be considered as one relating to ill will, spite or wickedness. 'Malice' requires either the actual intention to cause the relevant harm or at least foresight of the risk of causing *some harm* (though not the extent of the harm) to a person.

EXAMPLE

D throws a coin at V thinking that this will result in a small cut to V's forehead (so D has foresight that some harm, albeit minor, will befall V as a result of D's actions). The coin actually strikes V in the eye, causing V serious injury and the loss of sight in the eye.

It does not matter that the harm that D foresaw was minor compared to the resultant harm caused to V. D has committed a s. 20 grievous bodily harm offence because D has behaved 'maliciously'—D saw the risk of some harm befalling V but went on to take the risk anyway.

1.1.5 Wilfully

'Wilfully' is mentioned in offences such as child cruelty (s. 1 of the Children and Young Persons Act 1933). The term 'wilfully' should not be understood in a literal sense as meaning 'deliberate' or 'voluntary'. It is taken to mean intentionally or recklessly (subjective) (*Attorney-General's Reference (No. 3 of 2003)* [2005] QB 73).

1.1.6 Dishonestly

The expression 'dishonesty' is defined for certain purposes in s. 2 of the Theft Act 1968. However, it has also been extended by common law decisions of the courts (as per the decision in *Barlow Clowes* and *Royal Brunei Airlines*) and it is critical, in dealing with offences requiring proof of dishonesty (such as theft or fraud), that you identify the nature of the state of mind required and the ways in which it can be proved/disproved. For a full discussion of this concept, **see chapter 1.14**.

1.1.7 Knowing

The term 'knowing' is relevant to several offences such as s. 22 of the Theft Act 1968 (handling stolen goods). One *knows* something if one is absolutely sure that it is so. Since it is difficult to be absolutely sure of anything, it has to be accepted that a person who feels 'virtually certain' about something can equally be regarded as 'knowing' it (*R* v *Dunne* (1998) 162 JP 399).

1.1.8 Belief

The degree of certainty required to be experienced by an accused to create a 'belief' would appear to be the same for 'knowing'—the difference is that knowing something implies correctness of belief whereas a 'belief' could turn out to be mistaken. This is how 'belief' has been interpreted by the courts for the purposes of handling stolen goods (s. 22 of the Theft Act 1968) where it has been stressed that there is a need to distinguish belief from recklessness or suspicion and that it is not sufficient that an accused believed it to be more probable than not that the goods were stolen.

1.1.9 Negligence

Negligence is generally concerned with the defendant's compliance with the standards of reasonableness of ordinary people. The concept of negligence focuses on the consequences of the defendant's conduct rather than demanding proof of a particular state of mind at the time and ascribes some notion of 'fault' or 'blame' to the defendant who must be shown to have acted in a way that runs contrary to the expectations of the reasonable person.

The most important common law criminal offence that can be committed by negligence is manslaughter (manslaughter by gross negligence). Other offences that can be committed by negligence do not usually contain the word itself but attract that test in relation to the mental element (for example, offences involving standards of driving).

1.1.10 Strict Liability

Some offences are said to be offences of 'strict liability'. This expression generally means that there is little to prove beyond the act itself; however, in most cases it is more accurate to say that there is no need to prove *mens rea* in relation to one particular aspect of the behaviour. There have been isolated instances in which the courts have held that an offence does not require any *mens rea* to be proved. For example, in *DPP* v *H* [1997] 1 WLR 1406 it was stated that the offence of driving with excess alcohol, contrary to the Road Traffic Act 1988, s. 5 (**see *General Police Duties*, chapter 3.22**) did not require proof of any *mens rea*.

Situations where strict liability is imposed are usually to enforce statutory regulation (e.g. road traffic offences), particularly where there is some social danger or concern presented by the proscribed behaviour.

As a general rule, however, there is a presumption that *mens rea* is required for a criminal offence unless Parliament clearly indicates otherwise (*B (A Minor)* v *DPP* [2000] 2 AC 428). This rule should be borne in mind, not only when approaching the rest of the material in this Manual, but also when considering criminal law in general.

1.1.11 Transferred *Mens Rea*

The state of mind required for one offence can, on occasions, be 'transferred' from the original target or victim to another. *This only operates if the crime remains the same*. In other words, a defendant cannot be convicted if he/she acted with the *mens rea* for one offence but commits the *actus reus* of another offence. In *R* v *Latimer* (1886) 17 QBD 359, the defendant lashed out with his belt at one person but missed, striking a third party instead. As it was proved that the defendant had the required *mens rea* when he swung the belt, the court held that the same *mens rea* could support a charge of wounding against any other victim injured by the same act. If the *nature of the offence* changes, then this approach will not operate. Therefore if a defendant is shown to have thrown a rock at a crowd of people intending to injure one of them, the *mens rea* required for that offence cannot be 'transferred' to an offence of criminal damage if the rock misses that person and breaks a window instead (*R* v *Pembliton* (1874) LR 2 CCR 119).

The issue of transferred *mens rea* can be important in relation to the liability of accessories (as to which, **see chapter 1.2**). If the principal's intentions are to be extended to an accessory, it must be shown that those intentions were either contemplated and accepted by that person at the time of the offence or that they were 'transferred'.

EXAMPLE

A person (X) encourages another (Y) to assault Z. Y decides to attack a different person instead. X will not be liable for that assault because it was not contemplated or agreed by X. If, however, in trying to assault Z, Y happens to injure a third person inadvertently, then 'transferred *mens rea*' may result in X being liable for those injuries even though X had no wish for that person to be so injured.

1.2 *Actus Reus* (Criminal Conduct)

1.2.1 Introduction

Having considered *mens rea* (state of mind), the next key element is that of the *actus reus* (criminal conduct). Many statutory offences describe the sort of behaviour that will attract liability, but there are some important general rules that also need to be considered.

For a person to be found guilty of a criminal offence you must show that he/she:

- acted in a particular way;
- failed to act in a particular way (omissions); or
- brought about a state of affairs.

This is the *actus reus* of an offence, i.e. the behavioural element of an offence. When proving the required *actus reus*, you must show:

- that the defendant's conduct was voluntary; and
- that it occurred while the defendant still had the requisite *mens rea*.

1.2.2 Voluntary Act

This can best be understood by considering that a voluntary act is something *done* by the defendant, whereas an involuntary act is something that *happens* to a defendant. You must show that a defendant acted or omitted to act 'voluntarily'; that is, by the operation of free will.

If a person is shoved into a shop window, he/she cannot be said to be guilty of criminal damage even though he/she was the immediate physical cause of the damage. Similarly, if a person was standing in front of a window waiting to break it and someone came up and pushed that person into the window, the presence of the requisite *mens rea* would still not be enough to attract criminal liability for the damage. In each case, the person being pushed could not be said to be acting of his/her own volition in breaking the window and therefore could not perform the required *actus reus*.

This aspect of voluntariness is also important when defendants have lost control of their own physical actions. Reflexive actions are generally not classed as being willed or voluntary, hence the (limited) availability of the 'defence' of automatism (**see para. 1.2.3**).

Likewise, the *unexpected* onset of a sudden physical impairment (such as severe cramp when driving, actions when sleepwalking) can also render any linked actions 'involuntary'. If the onset of the impairment could reasonably have been foreseen (e.g. where someone is prone to blackouts), the defendant's actions may be said to have been willed in that he/she could have prevented the loss of control or at least avoided the situation (e.g. driving) which allowed the consequences to occur.

1.2.3 Automatism

Strictly speaking, automatism is not a 'defence'; it is an absence of a fundamental requirement for any criminal offence; namely, the 'criminal conduct' (*actus reus*). Criminal conduct must be voluntary and willed; it follows that if defendants have *total* loss of control over their actions, they cannot be held liable for those actions and there may be grounds to claim a defence of automatism. This view was confirmed in *R* v *Coley* [2013] EWCA Crim 223, where it was said that the question is not whether the accused is acting consciously or not but whether there is a 'complete destruction of voluntary control'. The best example of this defence is one where a swarm of bees flies into a car causing a reflex action by the driver resulting in an accident (an example given in *Hill* v *Baxter* [1958] 1 QB 277). As the driver's actions are involuntary and not sufficient to support a criminal charge, the defence of automatism would be available. Other examples might include a person inadvertently dropping and damaging property when suddenly seized by cramp or discharging a firearm as a result of an irresistible bout of sneezing.

If the loss of control is brought about by voluntary intoxication or by insanity, the defence becomes narrower.

1.2.4 Coincidence with *Mens Rea*

It must be shown that the defendant had the requisite *mens rea* at the time of carrying out the *actus reus*. However, there is no need for that 'state of mind' to remain unchanged throughout the entire commission of the offence. If a person (X) poisons another (Y) intending to kill Y at the time, it will not alter X's criminal liability if X changes his mind immediately after giving the poison or even if X does everything he can to halt its effects (*R* v *Jakeman* (1983) 76 Cr App R 223).

Conversely, if the *actus reus* is a continuing act, as 'appropriation' is (**see chapter 1.14**), it may begin without any particular *mens rea* but the required 'state of mind' may come later while the *actus reus* is still continuing. If this happens, whereby the *mens rea* 'catches up' with the *actus reus*, the offence is complete at the first moment that the two elements (*actus reus* and *mens rea*) unite.

For example, in a case where a motorist was directed to pull his car over to the kerb by a police officer and drove it onto the officer's foot, there was no proof that he did so deliberately. However, it was clear that he deliberately left it there after the officer told him what he had done. His conviction for assaulting the officer was upheld by the Divisional Court on the basis that there was an ongoing act, which became a criminal assault once the motorist became aware of it (*Fagan* v *Metropolitan Police Commissioner* [1969] 1 QB 439).

1.2.5 Omissions

Most criminal offences require a defendant to carry out some positive act before liability can be imposed. Ordinarily, there is no liability for a failure (or omission) to act unless the law specifically imposes such a DUTY on a person.

EXAMPLE

A sees B drowning and is able to save him by holding out his hand. A abstains from doing so in order that B may be drowned, and B is drowned. A has committed no offence.

Although A may have failed to save B, he did no positive act to cause B's death and, under English law, A has done nothing wrong.

However, although criminal conduct is most often associated with *actions*, occasionally liability is brought about by a failure to act. Most of the occasions where failure or omission will attract liability are where a **DUTY** *to act* has been created. Such a **DUTY** can arise from a number of circumstances, the main ones being:

D Dangerous situation created by the defendant. For example, in *R* v *Miller* [1983] 2 AC 161 the defendant was 'sleeping rough' and entered a building and fell asleep on a mattress while smoking a cigarette. When he awoke, he saw the mattress was smouldering but instead of calling for help or doing anything about the smouldering mattress, he simply moved into another room in the building and fell asleep. The mattress caught fire and the fire spread to the rest of the building. The defendant was convicted of arson, not for starting the fire but for failing to do anything about it.

U Under statute, contract or a person's public 'office'. Examples would include:

- Statute—a driver who is involved in a damage or injury accident fails to stop at the scene of the accident (s. 170 of the Road Traffic Act 1988), a driver who fails to co-operate with a preliminary test procedure (s. 6(6) of the Road Traffic Act 1988) or a person who does not disclose information in relation to terrorism (s. 19 of the Terrorism Act 2000).
- Contract—a crossing keeper omitted to close the gates (a job that was part of his contractual obligations) at a level crossing and a person was subsequently killed by a passing train (*R* v *Pittwood* (1902) 19 TLR 37).
- Public office—whilst on duty, a police officer stood aside and watched as a man was beaten to death outside a nightclub. The officer then left the scene, without calling for assistance or summoning an ambulance. For this, the officer was convicted of the common law offence of misconduct in a public office (*R* v *Dytham* [1979] QB 722).

T Taken it upon him/herself—the defendant voluntarily undertakes to care for another who is unable to care for him/herself as a result of age, illness or infirmity and then fails to care for that person. For example, in *R* v *Stone* [1977] QB 354 the defendant accepted a duty to care for her partner's mentally ill sister who subsequently died from neglect.

Y Young person—in circumstances where the defendant is in a parental relationship with a child or a young person, i.e. an obligation exists for the parent to look after the health and welfare of the child and he/she does not do so.

Whether or not there is a sufficient proximity between the defendant and the victim brought about by a duty to act will be a question of law (*R* v *Singh* [1999] Crim LR 582 and *R* v *Khan* [1998] Crim LR 830).

Having established such a duty, you must also show that the defendant has *voluntarily* omitted to act as required or that he/she has not done enough to discharge that duty. If a defendant is unable to act (e.g. because someone else has stopped him/her) or is incapable of doing more because of his/her own personal limitations (e.g. a child is drowning in a river but the parent is unable to save the child because of an inability to swim), the *actus reus* will *not* have been made out (*R* v *Reid* [1992] 1 WLR 793).

Some statutory offences are specifically worded to remove any doubt as to whether they can be committed by omission as well as by a positive act (e.g. causing or allowing a child or vulnerable adult to die or suffer serious physical harm under s. 5 of the Domestic Violence, Crime and Victims Act 2004).

1.2.6 Causal Link or Chain of Causation

Once the *actus reus* has been proved, you must then show a *causal link* between it and the relevant consequences. That is, you must prove that the consequences would not have happened 'but for' the defendant's act or omission.

In a case of simple criminal damage, it may be relatively straightforward to prove this causal link: a defendant throws a brick at a window and the window is broken by the brick hitting it; the window would not have broken 'but for' the defendant's conduct. Where the link becomes more difficult to prove is when the defendant's behaviour triggers other events or aggravates existing circumstances. For example, in *R* v *McKechnie* [1992] Crim LR 194 the defendant attacked the victim, who was already suffering from a serious ulcer, causing him brain damage. The brain damage (caused by the assault) prevented doctors from operating on the ulcer which eventually ruptured, killing the victim. The Court of Appeal, upholding the conviction for manslaughter, held that the defendant's criminal conduct (the assault) had made a significant contribution to the victim's death even though the untreated ulcer was the actual cause of death.

In some cases, a significant delay can occur between the acts which put in train the criminal consequences. An example is where a defendant transported an accomplice to a place near to the victim's house some 13 hours before the accomplice shot and killed the victim. Despite the delay and despite the fact the accomplice had not fully made up his mind about the proposed shooting at the time he was dropped off by the defendant, there was no intervening event that diverted or hindered the planned murder (*R* v *Bryce* [2004] EWCA Crim 1231).

1.2.7 Intervening Act

The causal link can be broken by a new intervening act provided that the 'new' act is 'free, deliberate and informed' (*R* v *Latif* [1996] 1 WLR 104).

If a drug dealer supplies drugs to another person who then kills him/herself by taking an overdose, the dealer cannot, without more, be said to have *caused* the death. Death would have been brought about by the deliberate exercise of free will by the user (*R* v *Kennedy* [2007] UKHL 38 (**see para. 1.5.4.1**)). The supplier is unlikely to be held liable for *causing* death in such a case unless he/she actually takes a more active part in the administering of the drug (*R* v *Dias* [2001] EWCA Crim 2986). The position may be different if the victim *does not* make an informed choice. In *Field* v *R* [2021] EWCA Crim 380, the defendant tricked the victim into drinking a large quantity of whisky which, in conjunction with the drugs the defendant had previously given him, caused or substantially contributed to his death. Distinguishing *Kennedy*, the Court of Appeal upheld the trial judge's direction that 'if it is proved that, with the intent to kill, D gave V the drink then, even if V agreed to it, it would be open to you to conclude that the giving was a cause of death, unless V's decision was informed in that he knew that the drink being offered to him was intended to cause his death'. The Court of Appeal stated that the case could be compared to one in which a weak swimmer is deliberately lured to his death by a false promise of rescue should the need arise.

It is foreseeable that the victim of an attack or accident may require medical treatment, but it is also foreseeable that his/her injuries may be misdiagnosed or that treatment may not be carried out correctly. This is one reason why incorrect medical treatment is hardly ever categorised by the courts as amounting to an intervening act. For example, in *R* v *Smith* [1959] 2 QB 35 two soldiers were fighting each other when one stabbed the other with a bayonet. Other soldiers carried the injured man to a medical centre, dropping him twice on the way. An overworked doctor failed to notice that one of the injured man's lungs had been pierced and the treatment the soldier received 'might well have affected his chances of recovery'. This did not, however, break the chain of causation as the original injury was still the operating and substantial cause of death. An *exceptional* case is *R* v *Jordan* (1956) 40 Cr App R 152, where the defendant had stabbed the deceased, who was taken to hospital for treatment. The deceased received treatment for the injuries and recovered so that the original injury brought about by the stabbing had almost totally healed. At this time, there was a mix-up resulting in the administration of a drug (terramycin) after the deceased had shown he was intolerant to it (treatment described as 'palpably wrong' by the court). The court concluded that it was the medical treatment that had caused the death and not the stab wound. *R* v *Jordan* has been described as a very particular case, depending on its exact facts. In *Smith*, the death could still be attributed to the wound inflicted by being stabbed with a bayonet, whereas in *Jordan* the wound had largely healed and the mistreatment of the deceased was the sole cause of death. Furthermore, the mistreatment was so bizarre as to be unforeseeable. Had the victim in *Jordan* died from the first dose of antibiotics, a conviction for murder would almost certainly be upheld. This is apparent from the case of *R* v *Cheshire* [1991] 3 All ER 670, in which the victim was shot with a shotgun causing injury to his hip. As part of his emergency treatment, a tracheotomy was carried out. Whilst the gunshot wounds healed, there were complications regarding the tracheotomy which caused the victim to die. The defendant was convicted regarding the death as the complications were still a natural consequence of his original act (the shooting). The basic rule is that an intervening act will not generally break the causal link/chain of causation.

There is also a rule which says defendants must 'take their victims as they find them'. This means that if victims have a particular characteristic, such as a very thin skull or a very nervous disposition, which makes the consequences of an act against them much more acute, that is the defendant's bad luck. An example of this principle can be seen in *R* v *Harvey* [2010] EWCA Crim 1317 where, during a 'domestic tiff', the offender threw a television remote control at his wife, which hit her behind the ear. Unknown to anyone, she had an unusual weakness of the vertebral artery, which ruptured and caused her death. Save for the death, the offence charged would have been one of battery. Such characteristics (e.g. where an assault victim died after refusing a blood transfusion on religious grounds (*R* v *Blaue* [1975] 1 WLR 1411)) will not break the causal link.

Actions by the victim will sometimes be significant in the chain of causation, such as where a victim of a sexual assault was injured when jumping from her assailant's car in an attempt to escape (*R* v *Roberts* (1971) 56 Cr App R 95). Where such actions take place, the victim's behaviour will not necessarily be regarded as introducing a new intervening act. If the victim's actions are those which might reasonably be anticipated from any victim in such a situation, there will be no new and intervening act and the defendant will be responsible for the consequences flowing from them. So, in *R* v *Corbett* [1996] Crim LR 594, the defendant was convicted of manslaughter when a man he was assaulting was struck and killed by a car as he attempted to escape. If, however, the victim's actions are done entirely of his/her own volition or where those actions are, in the words of Stuart-Smith LJ, 'daft' (*R* v *Williams* [1992] 1 WLR 380), they will amount to a new intervening act and the defendant cannot be held responsible for them.

An 'act of God' or other exceptional natural event may break the chain of causation leading from the defendant's initial act, if it was the sole immediate cause of the consequences in question. Such an event must be 'of so powerful a nature that the conduct of the defendant was not a cause at all, but was merely a part of the surrounding circumstances' (*Southern Water Authority* v *Pegrum* [1989] Crim LR 442). If the defendant attacks his/her victim and leaves him slowly dying of his injuries, then the chain of causation may be broken if the victim is ultimately killed by a lightning bolt or a falling tree, rather than the original injuries. In contrast, routine hazards, such as seasonal rain or cold winter nights, would not have such an effect (*Alphacell Ltd* v *Woodward* [1972] AC 824).

1.2.8 Principals and Accessories

Once you have established the criminal conduct and the required state of mind, you must identify what degree of involvement the defendant had.

There are two ways of attracting criminal liability for an offence: either as a *principal* or an *accessory* (accessories can also be referred to as *secondary parties*).

A principal offender is one whose conduct has met all the requirements of the particular offence. An accessory is someone who helped in or brought about the commission of the offence. If an accessory 'aids, abets, counsels or procures' the commission of an offence, he/she will be treated by a court in the same way as a principal offender for an indictable offence (Accessories and Abettors Act 1861, s. 8) or for a summary offence (Magistrates' Courts Act 1980, s. 44). The expression 'aid, abet, counsel and procure' is generally used in its entirety when charging a defendant, without separating out the particular element that applies. Generally speaking, the expressions mean as follows:

- aiding = giving help, support or assistance;
- abetting = inciting, instigating or encouraging.

Each of these would usually involve the presence of the secondary party at the scene (unless, for example, part of some pre-arranged plan):

- counselling = advising or instructing;
- procuring = bringing about.

These last two activities would generally be expected to take place before the commission of the offence. These are purely guides by which to separate the elements of this concept and will not necessarily apply in all cases.

If an accessory is present at the scene of a crime when it is committed, his/her presence may amount to encouragement which would support a charge of aiding or abetting if he/she was there as part of an agreement in respect of the principal offence. This would not be the case if a person was simply passing by and watched the offence. It is not an offence to do so, as the ordinary citizen is not under a duty to prevent an offence occurring and failing to do so will not create liability as an accomplice (*R* v *Coney* (1882) 8 QBD 534).

What of the situation where the accessory is not present during the substantive offence? The position can be summarised as follows:

Where the principal (P) relies on acts of the accessory (D) which assist in the preliminary stages of a crime later committed in D's absence, it is necessary to prove *intentional assistance by D* in acts which D knew were steps taken by P towards the commission of the crime. Therefore the prosecution must prove:

- an act done by D;
- which *in fact* assisted the later commission of the offence;
- that D did the act deliberately realising that it was capable of assisting the offence;
- that D, at the time of doing the act, contemplated the commission of the offence by P; and
- that, when doing the act, D intended to assist P.

(*R* v *Bryce* [2004] EWCA Crim 1231.)

'Counselling' an offence requires no causal link (*R* v *Calhaem* [1985] QB 808). As long as the principal offender is aware of the 'counsellor's' advice or encouragement, the latter will be guilty as an accessory, even if the principal would have committed the offence anyway (*Attorney-General* v *Able* [1984] QB 795).

However, if you are trying to show that a defendant *procured* an offence, you must show a causal link between his/her conduct and the offence (*Attorney-General's Reference (No. 1 of 1975)* [1975] QB 773).

If the principal cannot be traced or identified, the accessory may still be liable (*Hui Chiming* v *The Queen* [1992] 1 AC 34). Similarly, an accessory may be convicted of procuring an offence even though the principal is acquitted or has a defence for his/her actions. This is because the principal often supplies the *actus reus* for the accessory's offence. If the accessory also has the required *mens rea*, the offence will be complete and should not be affected by the fact that there is some circumstance or characteristic preventing the principal from being prosecuted.

Additionally, if the accessory had some responsibility and the actual ability to control the actions of the principal, his/her failure to do so may attract liability (e.g. a driving instructor who fails to prevent a learner driver from driving without due care and attention (*Rubie* v *Faulkner* [1940] 1 KB 571)).

It is possible for an accomplice to change his/her mind before the criminal act is carried out. However, the exact requirements for making an effective 'withdrawal' before any liability is incurred are unclear. Evidence such as how far the proposed plan had proceeded before the withdrawal, and the amount/nature of any help or encouragement already given by the accessory, will be relevant. Simply fleeing at the last moment because someone was approaching would generally not be enough. In the absence of some overwhelming supervening event, an accessory can only avoid liability for assistance rendered to the principal offender towards the commission of the crime by acting in a way that amounts to the *countermanding* of any earlier assistance, such as a withdrawal from the common purpose. Repentance alone will not be enough (*R* v *Becerra* (1976) 62 Cr App R 212 and *R* v *Mitchell* (1999) 163 JP 75).

A person whom the law is intended to protect from certain types of offence cannot be an accessory to such offences committed against them. For example, a girl under 16 years of age is protected (by the Sexual Offences Act 2003 (**see chapter 1.12**)) from people having sexual intercourse with her. If a 15-year-old girl allows someone to have sexual intercourse with her, she cannot be charged as an accessory to the offence (*R* v *Tyrrell* [1894] 1 QB 710).

1.2.8.1 State of Mind for Accessories

Generally, the state of mind (*mens rea*) which is needed to convict an accessory is: 'proof of intention to aid as well as of knowledge of the circumstances' (*National Coal Board* v *Gamble* [1959] 1 QB 11 at p. 20). Whether there was such an intention to aid the principal is a question of fact to be decided in the particular circumstances of each case. The requirement for proof of intention to aid means that the wider notions of recklessness and negligence are not enough to convict an accessory.

The *minimum* state of mind required of an accessory to an offence is set out in *Johnson* v *Youden* [1950] 1 KB 544. In that case, the court held that before anyone can be convicted of aiding and abetting an offence, he/she must at least know the essential matters that constitute that offence. Therefore the accessory to an offence of drink/driving (**see *General Police Duties*, chapter 3.22**) must at least have been aware that the 'principal' (the driver) had been drinking (*Smith* v *Mellors and Soar* (1987) 84 Cr App R 279).

Occasionally statutes will make specific provision for the state of mind and/or the conduct of accessories and principals. An example can be found in s. 7 of the Protection from Harassment Act 1997 (**see *General Police Duties*, chapter 3.12**).

1.2.8.2 Joint Enterprise and 'Parasitic Accessory Liability'

A joint criminal enterprise exists where two (or more) people embark on the commission of an offence by one or both (or all) of them. It is a joint enterprise because all the parties have a common goal—that an offence will be committed.

KEYNOTE

As the parties to a joint enterprise share a combined purpose, each would be liable for the consequences of the actions of the other in the pursuit of their joint enterprise (but see below for such liability when the nature of the offence changes). This is the case even if the consequences of the joint enterprise are a result of a mistake. For example, two offenders (A and B) agree to carry out a burglary on a particular house. Offender A leads the way but makes an error and mistakenly breaks into the wrong house. This error by offender A will not prevent offender B being guilty as an accomplice to the burglary offence.

Parasitic Accessory Liability

What happens when one party goes beyond that which was agreed or contemplated by the other? This particular narrower area of secondary responsibility is described as 'parasitic accessory liability'.

EXAMPLE

Two men (A and B) agree to carry out an offence of theft. During the course of the offence, the owner of the property subject of the offence appears and tries to prevent the offence taking place. Offender A produces a flick-knife and stabs the victim, causing grievous bodily harm. Offender B had no idea that offender A had a flick-knife and had never contemplated the use of violence during the theft offence.

The actions of offender A are a departure from the nature and type of crime that was envisaged by offender B who did not know that A possessed a flick-knife; it is an act so fundamentally different from that originally contemplated by B that B is most unlikely to be liable for the injuries caused to the victim (*R* v *Anderson* [1966] 2 QB 110).

The situation would alter if offender B knew that offender A possessed the flick-knife and encouraged A to use the flick-knife. Here, offender B could be convicted of a wounding offence if it can be proved that he had *intended* to assist or encourage the wounding offence. *Foresight* that the wounding might occur is simply evidence (albeit sometimes strong evidence) of intent to assist or encourage. It is a question for the jury in every case whether the intention to assist or encourage is shown—a person is not to be taken to have had an intention merely because of foreseeability. This was the ruling in *R* v *Jogee* [2016] UKSC 8 and *Ruddock* v *The Queen* [2016] UKPC 7. In *Jogee* and *Ruddock*, the court made it clear that the ruling:

- did not affect the law that a person who joins in a crime which any reasonable person would realise involves a risk of harm, and death results, is at least guilty of manslaughter. Manslaughter cases can vary in their gravity, but may be very serious and the maximum sentence is life imprisonment (**see para. 1.5.4**);
- does not affect the rule that a person who intentionally encourages or assists in the commission of a crime is as guilty as the person who physically commits it;
- did not alter the fact that it is open to a jury to infer intentional encouragement or assistance, for example from weight of numbers in a combined attack, whether more or less spontaneous or planned, or from knowledge that weapons are being carried. It is commonplace for juries to have to decide what inferences they can properly draw about intention from an accused person's behaviour and what he/she knew.

1.2.9 Corporate Liability

Companies which are 'legally incorporated' have a legal personality of their own and they can commit offences. There are difficulties associated with proving and punishing criminal conduct by companies. However, companies have been prosecuted for offences of strict liability (*Alphacell Ltd* v *Woodward* [1972] AC 824), offences requiring *mens rea* (*Tesco Supermarkets Ltd* v *Nattrass* [1972] AC 153) and offences of being an 'accessory' (*R* v *Robert Millar (Contractors) Ltd* [1970] 2 QB 54). There are occasions where the courts will accept that the knowledge of certain employees will be extended to the company (*Tesco Stores Ltd* v *Brent London Borough Council* [1993] 1 WLR 1037).

Clearly, there are some offences that would be conceptually impossible for a legal corporation to commit (e.g. some sexual offences) but, given that companies can be guilty as accessories (*Robert Millar*), they may well be capable of aiding and abetting such offences even though they could not commit the offence as a principal.

A company (OLL Ltd) has also been convicted, along with its managing director, of manslaughter (*R* v *Kite* [1996] 2 Cr App R (S) 295). Companies can be prosecuted for such offences under the terms of the Corporate Manslaughter and Corporate Homicide Act 2007.

1.2.10 Vicarious Liability

The general principle in criminal law is that liability is *personal*. There are, however, occasions where liability can be transmitted *vicariously* to another.

The most frequent occasions are cases where a statutory duty is breached by employees in the course of their employment (*National Rivers Authority* v *Alfred McAlpine Homes (East) Ltd* [1994] 4 All ER 286), or where a duty is placed upon a particular individual, such as a licensee, who delegates some of his/her functions to another. The purpose behind this concept is generally to prevent individuals or organisations from evading liability by getting others to carry out unlawful activities on their behalf.

1.3 Incomplete Offences

1.3.1 Introduction

There are circumstances where defendants are interrupted or frustrated in their efforts to commit an offence, perhaps as a result of police intervention or as a result of things not going as the defendants had hoped. In these cases, the defendant's conduct may be dealt with using incomplete offences.

It should be noted that most incomplete offences *cannot* be mixed, and that most *cannot* be attempted. For instance, you *cannot* conspire to aid and abet, neither can you attempt to conspire. There are, as ever, limited exceptions to this rule.

1.3.2 Encouraging or Assisting Crime

The common law offence of inciting an offence was abolished by the Serious Crime Act 2007. Incitement was replaced by the offences under ss. 44, 45 and 46 of the Act.

KEYNOTE

Any references in existing legislation to 'incitement' are to be read as references to the offences in ss. 44, 45 and 46, i.e. to be read as 'encouraging or assisting an offence'.

OFFENCE: **Intentionally Encouraging or Assisting an Offence—*Serious Crime Act 2007, s. 44***

• Triable in the same way as the anticipated offence • Where the anticipated offence is murder, the offence is punishable by life imprisonment • In any other case, a person is liable to any penalty for which he/she would be liable on conviction of the anticipated offence

The Serious Crime Act 2007, s. 44 states:

(1) A person commits an offence if—
(a) he does an act capable of encouraging or assisting in the commission of an offence; and
(b) he intends to encourage or assist its commission.
(2) But he is not to be taken to have intended to encourage or assist the commission of an offence merely because such encouragement or assistance was a foreseeable consequence of his act.

KEYNOTE

Section 44 involves the defendant intentionally encouraging or assisting an offence. To commit the offence, the defendant must actually do an act capable of encouraging or assisting the commission of an offence and intend to encourage or assist in its commission.

EXAMPLE

D might supply P with a weapon with the intent that P will use it to kill or seriously injure another person. Alternatively, D might simply offer verbal encouragement to P to commit the offence.

The defendant must intend to encourage or assist in the commission of the 'anticipated' offence.

EXAMPLE

D gives P a baseball bat and intends P to use it to inflict a minor injury on V. However, P uses the baseball bat to attack V and intentionally kills V—D would not be liable for encouraging or assisting murder, unless he also believes or is reckless as to whether V will be killed.

OFFENCE: **Encouraging or Assisting an Offence Believing it will be Committed—*Serious Crime Act 2007, s. 45***

• Triable in the same way as the anticipated offence • Where the anticipated offence is murder, the offence is punishable by life imprisonment • In any other case, a person is liable to any penalty for which he/she would be liable on conviction of the anticipated offence

The Serious Crime Act 2007, s. 45 states:

A person commits an offence if—
(a) he does an act capable of encouraging or assisting in the commission of an offence; and
(b) he believes—
  (i) that the offence will be committed; and
  (ii) that his act will encourage or assist its commission.

KEYNOTE

This covers the situation where the defendant may not intend that a particular offence is committed, but he/she believes both that it will be committed and that his/her act will encourage its commission. For example, D supplies a weapon to P believing P is going to commit murder with the weapon but being quite indifferent as to whether or not P will do so as it is D's sole concern to make a profit from the sale of the weapon.

OFFENCE: **Encouraging or Assisting Offences Believing One or More will be Committed—*Serious Crime Act 2007, s. 46***

• Triable on indictment • Where the reference offence is murder, the offence is punishable with life imprisonment • In any other case, a person is liable to any penalty for which he he/she would be liable on conviction of the reference offence

The Serious Crime Act 2007, s. 46 states:

(1) A person commits an offence if—
  (a) he does an act capable of encouraging or assisting the commission of one or more of a number of offences: and
  (b) he believes—
    (i) that one or more of those offences will be committed (but has no belief as to which); and
    (ii) that his act will encourage or assist the commission of one or more of them.
(2) It is immaterial for the purposes of subsection (1)(b)(ii) whether a person has any belief as to which offence will be encouraged or assisted.

KEYNOTE

This covers a situation where D may not intend that a particular offence is committed but believes that one or more offences will be committed and that his/her act will encourage or assist the commission of one or more of those offences.

EXAMPLE

D drives P to the home of V knowing that P is going to harm V but not knowing whether this will take the form of an assault on V or the murder of V.

1.3.2.1 General Issues

In respect of each offence (ss. 44, 45 and 46), D must merely do an act that is capable of encouraging or assisting the commission of an offence(s). Section 49(1) of the Act states that offences can be committed regardless of whether or not the encouragement or assistance has the effect which the defendant intended or believed it would have.

EXAMPLE

D, a surgeon, wishes to sexually assault his patients whilst they are unconscious under anaesthetic. To do so, D will need the cooperation of his assistant, V. D puts his idea to V while they are having a drink in a pub, intending to encourage V to take part in the offences. V is outraged and wants nothing to do with D's plan. The fact that V is not remotely interested in D's plan and is not encouraged to take part in it will not alter the fact that D has committed an offence under s. 44 of the Act.

An 'act' may take a number of different forms, including a course of conduct or a failure to discharge a duty. It includes threatening another person or putting pressure on another person to commit the offence (s. 65).

What of the situation where, rather than approaching others, an undercover police officer is approached to take part in a proposed offence?

In relation to this activity, s. 49(1) would still apply as there is no need for the person encouraged to have any intention of going on to commit the offence. In a case involving incitement (the predecessor of these offences), the Divisional Court held that there is no requirement for 'parity of *mens rea*' between the parties (*DPP* v *Armstrong* [2000] Crim LR 379). In that case, the defendant had approached an undercover police officer asking him to supply child pornography. At his trial, the defendant argued that as the officer in reality had no intention of supplying the pornography, there was no offence of incitement. On appeal by the prosecutor, the Divisional Court held that incitement, like conspiracies and attempts, was an auxiliary offence where criminal liability was attributed to the defendant where the full offence had not been committed. Consequently, the intent of the person incited (in this case, an undercover police officer) was irrelevant.

A person can be convicted of more than one of these offences (s. 44, 45 or 46) in relation to the same act (s. 49(3)).

Section 50 of the Act sets out that it will be a defence to the offences under ss. 44, 45 and 46 if the person charged acted reasonably; that is, in the circumstances he/she was aware of, or in the circumstances he/she reasonably believed existed, it was reasonable to act as he/she did.

Section 51 limits liability by setting out in statute the common law exception established in *R* v *Tyrrell* [1894] 1 QB 710. A person cannot be guilty of the offences in ss. 44, 45 and 46 if, in relation to an offence that is a 'protective' offence, the person who does the act capable of encouraging or assisting that offence falls within the category of persons that offence was designed to protect and would be considered as the victim.

EXAMPLE

D is a 12-year-old girl and encourages P, a 40-year-old man, to have sex with her. P is not interested and does not attempt to have sex with D. D cannot be liable of encouraging or assisting child rape despite the fact that it is her intent that P has sexual intercourse with a child under 13 (child rape) because she would be considered the 'victim' of that offence had it taken place, and the offence of child rape was enacted to protect children under the age of 13.

1.3.3 Conspiracy

Conspiracies can be divided into statutory and common law conspiracies.

1.3.3.1 Statutory Conspiracy

OFFENCE: **Statutory Conspiracy—*Criminal Law Act 1977, s. 1***

> • Triable on indictment • Where conspiracy is to commit murder, an offence punishable by life imprisonment or any indictable offence punishable with imprisonment where no maximum term is specified—life imprisonment • In other cases, sentence is the same as for completed offence

The Criminal Law Act 1977, s. 1 states:

> (1) Subject to the following provisions of this Part of this Act, if a person agrees with any other person or persons that a course of conduct shall be pursued which, if the agreement is carried out in accordance with their intentions, either—
> (a) will necessarily amount to or involve the commission of any offence or offences by one or more of the parties to the agreement; or
> (b) would do so but for the existence of facts which render the commission of the offence or any of the offences impossible,
> he is guilty of conspiracy to commit the offence or offences in question.

KEYNOTE

A charge of conspiracy can be brought in respect of an agreement to commit indictable or summary offences. Conspiracy is triable only on indictment even if it relates to a summary offence (in which case the consent of the DPP will be required). Offences of conspiracy are committed at the time of the agreement; it is immaterial whether or not the substantive offence is ever carried out.

Agreeing with Another

For there to be a conspiracy, there must be an agreement—a 'meeting of minds'. Therefore there must be at least two people (two minds) involved. Consequently, A cannot be guilty of a conspiracy with B (if B is the only other party to the agreement) if B intends to frustrate or sabotage it; there would not be a 'meeting of minds' in terms of an agreement to carry out an offence.

Each conspirator must be aware of the overall common purpose to which they all attach themselves. If one conspirator enters into *separate* agreements with different people, each agreement is a separate conspiracy (*R* v *Griffiths* [1966] 1 QB 589).

A person can be convicted of conspiracy even if the actual identity of the other conspirators is unknown.

A defendant *cannot* be convicted of a statutory conspiracy if the only other party to the agreement is:

- his/her spouse or civil partner;
- a person under the age of criminal responsibility, i.e. under 10 years of age;
- the intended victim (Criminal Law Act 1977, s. 2(2)).

A husband and wife can both be convicted of a statutory conspiracy if they conspire with a third party (not falling into the above categories) (*R* v *Chrastny* [1991] 1 WLR 1381).

A person is not guilty of statutory conspiracy if the only other person with whom he/she agrees is their civil partner. A civil partnership is a legally recognised union available to both same-sex couples and opposite-sex couples (under the Civil Partnership Act 2004 and the Civil Partnerships, Marriages and Deaths (Registration etc.) Act 2019).

A corporation may be a party to a conspiracy (*R* v *ICR Haulage Ltd* [1944] KB 551), but a company and one of its directors cannot be the only parties to a conspiracy because there can be no 'meeting of minds' (*R* v *McDonnell* [1966] 1 QB 233).

The 'end product' of the agreement must be the commission of an offence by *one or more of the parties to the agreement*. Once agreed upon, any failure to bring about the end result or an abandoning of the agreement altogether will not prevent the statutory conspiracy being committed. An agreement to aid and abet an offence of conspiracy is not, in law, capable of constituting a statutory conspiracy under s. 1(1) of the Criminal Law Act 1977 (*R* v *Kenning* [2008] EWCA Crim 1534).

What if a defendant enters into an agreement with another person to commit an offence but that other person is in fact a police officer? Under normal circumstances, forming an agreement with another person to carry out an offence is a conspiracy. If, however, one of only two conspirators is an undercover officer who has no intention of going through with the agreement, there is a strong argument that there can be no 'true' conspiracy as the only other person had no intention of going through with the plan (*Yip Chiu-Cheung* v *The Queen* [1995] 1 AC 111). In conspiracies, the intention of at least two parties *is* the basis of the whole offence. So, in cases where the only other 'conspirator' is a police officer, encouraging an offence may be a more appropriate charge.

1.3.3.2 Common Law Conspiracies

OFFENCE: **Conspiracy to Defraud—*Common Law***

- Triable on indictment • 10 years' imprisonment and/or a fine

Conspiracy to defraud involves:

> ... an agreement by two or more [persons] by dishonesty to deprive a person of something which is his or to which he is or would or might be entitled [or] an agreement by two or more by dishonesty to injure some proprietary right [of the victim] ...
>
> (*Scott* v *Metropolitan Police Commissioner* [1975] AC 819)

KEYNOTE

This offence has been endorsed by senior judges as representing an effective means of dealing with multiple defendants engaged in a fraudulent course of conduct.

The common law offence of conspiracy to defraud can be divided into two main types. The first is contained in the case of *Scott*, the second involves a dishonest agreement to deceive another into acting in a way that is contrary to his/her duty (*Wai Yu-Tsang* v *The Queen* [1992] 1 AC 269).

Although the requirement for an agreement between at least two people is the same, this offence is broader than statutory conspiracy. There is no requirement to prove that the end result would amount to the commission of an *offence*, simply that it would result in depriving a person of something under the specified conditions or in injuring his/her proprietary right.

You must show *intent* to defraud a victim (*R* v *Hollinshead* [1985] AC 975).

You must also show that a defendant was dishonest as set out in *Barlow Clowes* and *Royal Brunei Airlines* (see para. 1.14.2.3).

Clearly, there will be circumstances where the defendant's behaviour will amount to both a statutory conspiracy and a conspiracy to defraud. The Criminal Justice Act 1987, s. 12 makes provision for such circumstances and allows the prosecution to choose which charge to prefer.

Examples of common law conspiracies to defraud include:

- Buffet car staff selling their own home-made sandwiches on British Rail trains thereby depriving the company of the opportunity to sell their own products (*R* v *Cooke* [1986] AC 909).
- Directors agreeing to conceal details of a bank's trading losses from its shareholders (*Wai Yu-Tsang*).
- Making unauthorised copies of commercial films for sale (*Scott*).

- Marketing devices to falsify gas or electric meters enabling customers (who were not party to the conspiracy) to defraud their gas and electric suppliers (*Hollinshead*).

A further example can be found in *R* v *Hussain* [2005] EWCA Crim 1866, where the defendant pleaded guilty to conspiracy to defraud after a widespread abuse of the postal voting system. In that case, the defendant, an official Labour Party candidate, collected uncompleted postal votes from households and completed them in his own favour.

1.3.4 Attempts

The Criminal Attempts Act 1981, s. 1 states:

(1) If, with intent to commit an offence to which this section applies, a person does an act which is more than merely preparatory to the commission of the offence, he is guilty of attempting to commit the offence.

...

(2) A person may be guilty of attempting to commit an offence to which this section applies even though the facts are such that the commission of the offence is impossible.

(3) In any case where—

(a) apart from this subsection a person's intention would not be regarded as having amounted to an intent to commit an offence; but

(b) if the facts of the case had been as he believed them to be, his intention would be so regarded,

then, for the purposes of subsection (1) above, he shall be regarded as having had an intent to commit that offence.

(4) This section applies to any offence which, if it were completed, would be triable in England and Wales as an indictable offence, other than—

(a) conspiracy (at common law or under section 1 of the Criminal Law Act 1977 or any other enactment);

(b) aiding, abetting, counselling, procuring or suborning the commission of an offence;

(ba) an offence under section 2(1) of the Suicide Act 1961 (c 60) (encouraging or assisting suicide);

(c) offences under section 4(1) (assisting offenders) or 5(1) (accepting or agreeing to accept consideration for not disclosing information about a relevant offence) of the Criminal Law Act 1967.

KEYNOTE

Most attempts at committing criminal offences will be governed by s. 1. Although some statutory exceptions apply, the sentence generally for such attempts will be:

- for murder—life imprisonment;
- for indictable offences—the same maximum penalty as the substantive offence;
- for either way offences—the same maximum penalty as the substantive offence when tried *summarily*.

If the attempted offence is triable summarily only, it cannot be an offence under s. 1. However, if the only reason the substantive offence is triable summarily is because of a statutory limit imposed in some cases (e.g. in cases of low-value shoplifting (**see chapter 1.13**) or criminal damage to property of a low value (**see chapter 1.15**)), the offence can be attempted.

If the offence attempted is triable only on indictment, the attempt will be triable only on indictment. Similarly, if the offence attempted is an 'either way' offence, so too will the attempt be triable either way (s. 4(1)).

Many other statutory offences contain references to 'attempts', including:

- Theft Act 1968, s. 9(1)(b) (burglary);
- Firearms Act 1968, s. 17 (using firearm to resist arrest).

Section 3 of the Criminal Attempts Act 1981 deals with such statutory provisions and they will generally be governed by the same principles as those set out here.

1.3.4.1 An Act which is More than Merely Preparatory

An attempt requires an act—an omission to act would not create liability for an attempt (e.g. a refusal to call an ambulance for a person who is gravely ill cannot amount to attempted murder).

A defendant's actions must be shown to have gone beyond mere preparation towards the commission of the substantive offence. Whether the defendant did or did not go beyond that point will be a question of fact for the jury/magistrate(s). There is no formula used by the courts in interpreting this requirement so it is useful to examine several cases where the courts have considered what this element of the offence means.

An example of where the defendant was held to have done no more than merely preparatory acts was *R* v *Campbell* [1991] Crim LR 268, where the appellant armed himself with an imitation gun, approached to within a yard of a post office which he intended to rob, but never drew his weapon; it was held that there was no evidence on which a jury could properly have concluded that his acts went beyond mere preparation. In *R* v *Bowles* [2004] EWCA Crim 1608, the defendant had been convicted of several offences involving dishonesty against an elderly neighbour. The neighbour's long-standing will left her estate to charity but, following his arrest, police officers searched the defendant's premises and found a new will, fully complete except for the signature. The defendant and his wife were named as the main beneficiaries and were to inherit the neighbour's house. Although the defendant's son was said to have been heard making reference to the fact that he was going to inherit the house, the 'new' will had been drafted over six months earlier and there was no evidence of any steps to have it executed, or any evidence of it being used. The Court of Appeal held that the making of the will was no more than merely preparatory and the defendant's conviction for attempting to make a false instrument was quashed.

In *R* v *Geddes* [1996] Crim LR 894, the defendant was found trespassing in the lavatory block of a school, armed with a knife, lengths of rope and tape. It appears he intended to kidnap a child; his conviction for attempted false imprisonment was quashed on appeal. Citing *Campbell* with approval, Lord Bingham CJ held that no jury could have concluded that the defendant's acts had gone beyond mere preparation. He may have equipped himself, and put himself in a position to commit the crime, but it could not be said that he had actually tried or started to commit it.

Courts have accepted an approach of questioning whether the defendant had 'embarked on the crime proper' (*R* v *Gullefer* [1990] 1 WLR 1063) but there is no requirement to have passed a point of no return leading to the commission of the substantive offence.

In *R* v *MS* [2021] EWCA Crim 600, the defendant, a teenage mother, forged the signature of her child's father on a form entitled 'Permission to Take a Child Abroad', booked a car ferry from Dover to Calais and two overnight hotel stops in France for herself, the child and her new boyfriend, helped load their car and set out for Dover, en route for North Africa. They were stopped by the police 85 miles from Dover, but the Court of Appeal held that it was still open to a jury to convict her of attempting to abduct her child by taking him out of the UK (contrary to the Child Abduction Act 1984, s. 1). Fulford LJ said:

> ... Child abduction by a person connected with the child is an entirely different offence to murder, assault and robbery. The action necessary for an attempted parental abduction, as in the instant case, may have been 'embarked upon' at a considerable distance from the port or airport. For child abduction, geographical proximity does not have the same relevance as other crimes ... when arrested, the defendant was in the position of attempting to commit the offence in question, rather than simply getting ready or putting herself in a position to do so, and we have no doubt she had 'embarked on the crime proper'.

1.3.4.2 *Mens Rea* for Attempt

To prove an 'attempt' you must show an *intention* on the part of the defendant to commit the substantive offence.

This requirement means a higher level or degree of *mens rea* may be required to prove an attempt than for the substantive offence. For instance, the *mens rea* required to prove an offence of murder is the intention to kill *or* cause grievous bodily harm, whereas the *mens rea* for attempted murder is nothing less than an *intent* to kill (*R* v *Whybrow* (1951) 35 Cr App R 141). In *R* v *Jones* [1990] 1 WLR 1057, the defendant was charged with attempted murder. He climbed into the car of the victim and drew a loaded gun with the intention of killing him, but was disarmed in a struggle that followed. The Court of Appeal held that it was open to a jury to regard this as attempted murder.

A defendant's intention may be *conditional*; that is, he/she may only intend to steal from a house if something worth stealing is later found inside. The conditional nature of this intention will not generally prevent the charge of attempt being brought and the defendant's intentions will, in accordance with s. 1(3), be judged *on the facts as he/she believed them to be*.

Although 'intent to commit' the offence is required under s. 1(1), there are occasions where a state of mind that falls short of such a precise intention may suffice. For instance, in cases of attempted rape (**see chapter 1.12**) the courts have accepted that recklessness as to whether the victim is consenting was (under the earlier sexual offences legislation) sufficient *mens rea* for attempted rape because it is sufficient for the substantive offence (*R* v *Khan* [1990] 1 WLR 813).

In proving an 'attempt' it is enough to show that defendants were in one of the states of mind required for the substantive offence and that they did their best, so far as they were able, to do what was necessary for the commission of the full offence (*Attorney-General's Reference (No. 3 of 1992)* [1994] 1 WLR 409).

1.3.5 Impossibility

Difficulties have arisen where, despite the efforts of the defendant, his/her ultimate intention has been impossible (such as trying to extract cocaine from a powder which is, unknown to the defendant, only talc). Impossibility is dealt with by s. 1(3) of the Criminal Attempts Act 1981 and its interpretation through the courts. It differs, however, in some incomplete offences.

EXAMPLE

If a person tries to handle goods which are not in fact stolen, the following rules would apply:

- A defendant could *not* be guilty of encouraging another or of common law conspiracy to defraud in these circumstances. The *physical* impossibility (the goods are not actually stolen) of what the defendant sought to do would preclude such a charge.
- A defendant *could* be guilty of a statutory conspiracy with another to handle 'stolen' goods and also of attempting to handle 'stolen' goods under these circumstances. The physical impossibility would not preclude such charges as a result of the Criminal Attempts Act 1981 and the House of Lords' decision in *R* v *Shivpuri* [1987] AC 1 (you can conspire and/or attempt to commit the impossible). The only form of impossibility which would preclude liability under the Criminal Attempts Act 1981 or for a statutory conspiracy would be the *legal* impossibility.

1.4 General Defences

1.4.1 Introduction

There are various defences available to a person charged with an offence. Some defences are specific to certain offences (e.g. criminal damage and murder), whereas others can be used to answer a wider range of charges and are often referred to as 'general defences'. This chapter examines several of these 'general defences'.

1.4.2 Inadvertence and Mistake

There are occasions where a defendant makes a mistake about some circumstance or consequence; however, claims that a defendant 'made a mistake' or did something 'inadvertently' will only be an effective defence if they negate the *mens rea* for that offence. Therefore, if someone wanders out of a shop with something that has not yet been paid for, that mistake or inadvertence might negate any *mens rea* of 'dishonesty'. As the requirement for the *mens rea* in such a case is *subjective*, then the defendant's mistake or inadvertence will be judged subjectively. The same will generally be true for offences requiring subjective recklessness. It does not matter whether the mistake was 'reasonable' (*DPP* v *Morgan* [1976] AC 182). The appropriate test is whether the defendant's mistaken belief was an honest and genuine one.

There are occasions where a genuine mistake on the part of the defendant may amount to a defence. In *R* v *Lee* [2001] 1 Cr App R 19, a case arising from an assault on two arresting police officers, the Court of Appeal reviewed the law in this area, reaffirming the following points:

- A genuine or honest mistake could provide a defence to many criminal offences requiring a particular state of mind, including assault with intent to resist arrest (*R* v *Brightling* [1991] Crim LR 364).
- A defence of mistake has to involve a mistake of fact not a mistake of law (see below).
- People under arrest are not entitled to form their own view as to the lawfulness of that arrest. They have a duty to comply with the police and hear the details of the charge against them (*R* v *Bentley* (1850) 4 Cox CC 406).
- Belief in one's own innocence, however genuine or honestly held, cannot afford a defence to a charge of assault with intent to resist arrest under s. 38 of the Offences Against the Person Act 1861 (as to which, **see chapter 1.10**).

A defendant attempted to argue that his honest and reasonable mistake as to the *facts* of his arrest (as opposed to the law), after he was lawfully arrested for a public order offence, was different from the decision in *Lee*. The Divisional Court did not agree (*Hewitt* v *DPP* [2002] EWHC 2801 (QB)).

Generally, it is no defence to claim a mistake as to the law because all people are presumed to know the law once it is made. With statutory instruments, a defendant can show that the instrument in question was not in force at the time of the offence or that the behaviour that it sought to control was beyond the powers (*ultra vires*) of that instrument.

There is one particular example, however, where a mistaken belief in the legal position is specifically provided for in a criminal offence. This is where a person appropriates property in the belief that he/she has a legal right to deprive another person of it under s. 2 of the Theft Act 1968 (**see chapter 1.14**).

In relation to offences involving negligence, inadvertence would clearly not amount to a defence and any 'mistake' would generally need to be shown to be a reasonable one.

1.4.3 Duress

Where a person is threatened with death or serious physical injury unless he/she carries out a criminal act, he/she may have a defence of duress (*R* v *Graham* [1982] 1 WLR 294). The threat of serious physical injury does not appear to include serious *psychological* injury (*R* v *Baker* [1997] Crim LR 497). Where relevant intent is an ingredient of the offence, defendants might claim that they only formed that intent as a result of duress. However, unless it is shown that the intent had or could have been formed *only* by reason of that duress (e.g. the duress was the only thing causing the defendant to form that intent), the defence will fail (*R* v *Fisher* [2004] EWCA Crim 1190).

It would seem that the threat need not be made solely to the person who goes on to commit the relevant offence; there are authorities to suggest that threats of death/serious harm to loved ones may allow a defence of duress.

KEYNOTE

The defence is not available in respect of an offence of murder (*R* v *Howe* [1987] AC 417) or attempted murder (*R* v *Gotts* [1992] 2 AC 412), as a principal or secondary offender. It is, however, *available in other offences even in offences of strict liability* (*Eden District Council* v *Braid* [1998] COD 259—taxi driver threatened and forced to carry excessive number of people in breach of his licensing conditions).

There are several key elements to this defence:

- the threat must have driven the defendant to commit the offence;
- the defendant must have acted as a sober and reasonable person sharing the defendant's characteristics would have done;
- the threatened death/injury must be anticipated at or near the time of the offence—not some time in the distant future.

Duress is not available as a defence if it is proved that the defendant failed to take advantage of an opportunity to neutralise the effects of the threat (perhaps by escaping from it), which a reasonable person of a similar sort to the defendant would have taken in the same position. An example of this approach is the case of *R* v *Heath* [2000] Crim LR 109, where the defendant alleged that he had been pressurised into transporting drugs. Because the defendant had more than one safe avenue of escape (going to the police, which he did not do because he was scared and because he was a drug addict, and going to his parents in Scotland, which he did not do because he did not want them to know about the position he was in) the defence failed. Whether a defendant could be expected to take such an opportunity of rendering the threat ineffective, e.g. by seeking police protection, will be a matter for the jury. Therefore, a defendant who is ordered to steal from a shop in 24 hours' time, or suffer a serious physical injury for failing to do so, might be unable to utilise the defence as a jury may consider that the defendant had ample opportunity to take evasive action and avoid the threat.

If defendants knowingly expose themselves to a risk of such a threat of death or serious physical injury, they cannot claim duress as a defence. So if a person joins a violent gang or an active terrorist organisation, he/she cannot claim duress as a defence to any crimes he/she may go on to commit under threat of death or serious injury from another member or rival of that organisation (*R* v *Sharp* [1987] QB 853). However, if the purpose of the organisation or gang is not predominantly violent or dangerous (e.g. a gang of shoplifters), the defence of duress *may* be available in relation to offences committed while under threat of death or serious physical injury from other gang members (*R* v *Shepherd* (1987) 86 Cr App R 47).

1.4.4 Duress of Circumstances

There may be times when circumstances leave the defendant no alternative but to commit an offence. In *R* v *Martin* [1989] 1 All ER 652, the defendant had driven whilst disqualified from driving. He claimed he did so because his wife had threatened to commit suicide if he did not drive their son to work. His wife had attempted suicide on previous occasions and the son was late for work and she feared he would lose his job if her husband did not get him to work. The Court of Appeal stated that, in these circumstances, the defence of duress of circumstances was *available* to the defendant. In such cases, the court will consider the reasonableness of the defendant's behaviour in the light of the prevailing circumstances. If the defendant commits a very serious offence in order to avoid very minor or trivial consequences, this defence is unlikely to be available.

This type of duress should be distinguished from that at **para. 1.4.3**. There the duress comes from a threat which compels a person to commit an OFFENCE: a 'gun to the head' type of situation where one person says to another '*Do this or else* ...'. With duress of circumstances, there is no such threat being made. Rather, there is a threatening situation or set of circumstances from which the defendant wishes to escape and, in so doing, feels impelled to commit an offence as the lesser of two present evils. Here the threat is 'situational' and the defendant feels '*If I don't do this, then the consequence will be death or serious physical injury* ...'.

This defence was examined by the Court of Appeal in a case where someone jumped onto the bonnet of the car that the appellant was driving. The appellant drove for some distance with the man on the bonnet of the car, braking after a short time to go over a speed ramp. The man fell from the bonnet and the appellant drove on, running the man over and causing him grievous bodily harm (as to which, **see chapter 1.10**). In determining whether or not the defence of 'duress of circumstances' was available, the court held that the jury must ask two questions in relation to the appellant:

- Was he (or might he have been) impelled to act as he did because, as a result of what he reasonably believed to be the situation, he had good cause to fear he would suffer death or serious injury if he did not do so?
- If so, would a sober person of reasonable firmness and sharing the same characteristics have responded to the situation in the way that he did?

If each question were answered 'yes', the defence would be made out (*R* v *Cairns* [1999] 2 Cr App R 137).

The important aspect to this defence, then, is that it will only be available to defendants as long as they are acting under compulsion of the prevailing circumstances when committing the offence. It appears that defendants need only hold an *honest* belief that those circumstances exist without necessarily having *reasonable grounds* for that belief (*DPP* v *Rogers* [1998] Crim LR 202) and there is no need for the threat to be 'real'. There is certainly no need for the threat (perceived threat) to amount to a criminal offence. The Court of Appeal has accepted the possibility of a 'duress of circumstances' defence being applicable where a defendant acted in fear of the consequences of war being declared on Iraq (*R* v *Jones (Margaret)* [2004] EWCA Crim 1981). However, the defendant's actions in order to avoid that perceived threatening situation must be reasonable and proportionate to the threat presented. Therefore defendants in situations like *Willer* and *Cairns* would not be able to claim duress of circumstances if they drove at their victims repeatedly until all had been injured to a point where they no longer posed a threat.

An attempt to extend the defence was made in *R* v *Altham* [2006] EWCA Crim 7, where the defendant had been charged with possessing a controlled drug (cannabis). The defendant appealed against his conviction, arguing that he needed to smoke cannabis to ease the pain he suffered from injuries received in a car accident. It was argued that the defence of duress of circumstances should be open to the defendant on the basis that he was suffering serious physical harm. The prosecution countered that pain can never amount to serious physical harm. The appeal was dismissed and the court stated that the defence could not be available in this type of circumstance because it would allow unlawful activity to be undertaken and would conflict with the purpose and effect of the intention of the Misuse of Drugs Act 1971.

The defence is not available in relation to offences of murder, attempted murder, treason and offences under the Misuse of Drugs Act 1971. The defence is available against any other charge.

1.4.5 Defence of Self, Others or Property

Where the common law defences of self-defence, defence of property or the Criminal Law Act 1967 defence of lawful arrest are raised in relation to taking someone's life, the provisions of Article 2 of the European Convention on Human Rights will apply. As Article 2 is relevant to such defences, it is appropriate to consider its provisions.

1.4.5.1 Human Rights—The Right to Life

Article 2 of the Convention states:

1. Everyone's right to life shall be protected by law. No one shall be deprived of his life intentionally save in the execution of a sentence of a court following his conviction of a crime for which this penalty is provided by law.
2. Deprivation of life shall not be regarded as inflicted in contravention of this Article when it results from the use of force which is no more than absolutely necessary:
   (a) in defence of any person from unlawful violence;
   (b) in order to effect a lawful arrest or to prevent the escape of a person lawfully detained;
   (c) in action lawfully taken for the purpose of quelling a riot or insurrection.

KEYNOTE

Taking Life

It can be seen that the Article allows for a number of limited exceptions when the taking of life by the State may not be a violation of this Convention right. All of the situations covered are generally concerned with protecting life, preventing crime and preserving order. The exceptions include actions taken in defending another person (*not property*) from unlawful violence and effecting a lawful arrest. Therefore the Convention acknowledges that there will be occasions when the State is compelled to take the life of an individual, such as where a police officer has to use lethal force to protect the life of another.

However, while limited in themselves, these exceptions will also be subject to very restrictive interpretation by the courts.

When a life is taken under any of the three situations set out at para. 2(a)–(c), the force used must be shown to have been *no more than absolutely necessary* (a more stringent test than the general test imposed in our domestic criminal law by s. 3 of the Criminal Law Act 1967 (as to which, **see para. 1.4.5.3**)). This test was examined by the European Commission on Human Rights in *Stewart* v *United Kingdom* (1985) 7 EHRR CD 453. There the Commission held that force will be absolutely necessary only if it is strictly proportionate to the legitimate purpose being pursued. In order to meet those criteria, regard must be had to:

- the nature of the aim being pursued;
- the inherent dangers to life and limb from the situation; and
- the degree of risk to life presented by the amount of force employed.

This test applies not only to cases where there has been an intentional taking of life, but also where there has been a permitted use of force that has led to the death of another. The test has been held to be a stricter one than even the general requirement of 'proportionality' that runs throughout the Convention (*McCann* v *United Kingdom* (1996) 21 EHRR 97).

This area is of importance because not only are the courts concerned with any individual actions that directly lead to the death of another, but also because they will take into account 'other factors' surrounding and leading up to the incident that caused the loss of life.

Such other factors are likely to include:

- the planning and control of the operation;
- the training given to the officers concerned; and
- the briefing/instructions that they received.

Protecting Life

A further area of importance lies in the second arm of Article 2—that of protecting the lives of others. This area was considered in the case of *Osman* v *United Kingdom* (2000) 29 EHRR 245. In *Osman*, the European Commission said that Article 2 must be interpreted as requiring preventive steps to be taken to protect life from '*known and avoidable dangers*' (emphasis added). The Commission went on to say that the extent of this obligation (which is clearly of the first importance to those tasked with investigating and preventing crime) will vary 'having regard to the source and degree of danger and the means available to combat it'. The European Court of Human Rights said in *Osman* that it will be enough for an applicant to show that the authorities did not do all that could reasonably be expected of them to avoid a '*real and immediate risk to life*' (emphasis added) of which they have or ought to have knowledge. As such, whether a police officer or police force has failed in this positive obligation to protect life will only be answerable in the light of all the circumstances of a particular case. This requirement is, therefore, very similar to the test for negligence in civil law in England and Wales.

1.4.5.2 Use of Force in Defence, Prevention of Crime and Lawful Arrest

Considered against the backdrop of Article 2 of the European Convention on Human Rights, there are circumstances where the use of force against a person or property will be permissible. This aspect of criminal law is dealt with by s. 76 of the Criminal Justice and Immigration Act 2008. Section 76 provides a gloss on the common law of self-defence and the defences provided by s. 3(1) of the Criminal Law Act 1967, which relate to the use of force in the prevention of crime or making an arrest. Section 76 aims to improve understanding of the practical application of these areas of law using elements of case law to illustrate how the defence operates. It does not change the current test that allows the use of reasonable force.

KEYNOTE

The law can be set out along the following lines:

A person may use such force as is reasonable in the circumstances as he/she believes them to be for the purpose of:

(a) self-defence; or
(b) defence of another; or
(c) defence of property; or
(d) prevention of crime; or
(e) lawful arrest.

1.4.5.3 Criminal Law Act 1967

A defendant charged with an offence may seek to rely on the common law defence of self-defence or the defence provided by s. 3(1) of the Criminal Law Act 1967.

The Criminal Law Act 1967, s. 3(1) states:

> A person may use such force as is reasonable in the circumstances in the prevention of crime or in effecting or assisting in the lawful arrest of offenders or suspected offenders or of persons unlawfully at large.

It is to these potential defences that s. 76 of the Criminal Justice and Immigration Act 2008 applies, particularly to the question of whether the degree of force used was reasonable in the circumstances. The 'degree of force' means the type and amount of force used. Section 76(10)(b) states that reasonable force in self-defence includes acting in the defence of another person.

The question whether the degree of force used by the defendant was reasonable in the circumstances is to be decided by reference to the circumstances *as the defendant believed them to be* (s. 76(3)). If the defendant claims to have held a particular belief as to the existence of any circumstances, the reasonableness or otherwise of that belief is relevant to the question whether the defendant genuinely held it. If it is determined that the defendant did genuinely hold the belief, then the defendant is entitled to rely on it even if the belief was mistaken or, if it was mistaken, the mistake was a reasonable one to have made.

EXAMPLE

X has a long and violent history and has been convicted of several wounding offences involving the use of a knife. In an unprovoked attack, X attacks Y in a pub by punching Y in the face. Y is aware of X's violent past and, after being punched, Y sees X's hand move towards the inside of his jacket. Y genuinely believes that X is going to stab him and so grabs hold of a chair and smashes it against X's arm, breaking X's arm in the process. X was not going to stab Y as he did not have a knife.

Y reacted to the circumstances as he believed them to be. The reasonableness of Y's belief is relevant in deciding whether or not Y actually held the belief. If the court accepted that Y held the belief, the fact that X did not have a knife and was not going to stab Y (a mistake by Y) will not affect Y's ability to utilise the defence.

The situation would be different if Y had been drunk and, simply seeing X walk into the pub, mistakenly thought X was going to stab him. This is because s. 76(5) would not enable Y to rely on any mistaken belief due to intoxication that was voluntarily induced.

Section 76(6) adds that the degree of force used by the defendant is not to be regarded as reasonable in the circumstances as the defendant believed them to be if it was disproportionate in those circumstances.

In deciding whether or not the degree of force used was reasonable in the circumstances, s. 76(7) requires certain considerations to be taken into account:

- that a person acting for a legitimate purpose (the purposes of the defences to which s. 76 applies) may not be able to weigh to a nicety the exact measure of any necessary action; and
- that evidence of a person having only done what the person honestly and instinctively thought was necessary for a legitimate purpose constitutes strong evidence that only reasonable action was taken by that person for that purpose.

This does not prevent other matters from being taken into account where they are relevant in deciding whether the degree of force used was reasonable in the circumstances.

KEYNOTE

Section 76 retains a single test for self-defence and the prevention of crime (or the making of an arrest). The law has been developed in line with case law regarding self-defence and the use of force, most notably *Palmer* v *The Queen* [1971] AC 814. The defence will be available if a person honestly believed it was necessary to use force and if the degree of force used was not disproportionate in the circumstances as he/she viewed them. The person who uses force is to be judged on the basis of the circumstances as he/she perceived them. In the heat of the moment, he/she will not be expected to have judged exactly what action was called for, and a degree of latitude may be given to a person who only did what he/she honestly and instinctively thought was necessary. Defendants are entitled to have their actions judged on the basis of their view of the facts as they honestly believed them to be.

1.4.5.4 'Householder' Cases

Section 43 of the Crime and Courts Act 2013 amends s. 76 of the Criminal Justice and Immigration Act 2008 so that the use of *disproportionate* force can be regarded as reasonable in the circumstances as the accused believed them to be when householders are acting to protect themselves or others from trespassers in their homes (self-defence). The use of *grossly* disproportionate force would still not be permitted. The provisions also extend to people who live and work in the same premises and armed forces personnel who may live and work in buildings such as barracks for periods of time. The provisions *will not* cover other scenarios where the use of force might be required, for example when people are defending themselves from attack on the street, preventing crime or protecting property; the current law on the use of reasonable force will apply in these situations.

1.4.5.5 Defence of Property

Section 76(2)(aa) of the Criminal Justice and Immigration Act 2008 makes it clear that the 'common law defence of defence of property' is governed by s. 76 (as well as self-defence, the prevention of crime and making an arrest).

In addition, s. 3(1) of the Criminal Law Act 1967 states that reasonable force may be used in the prevention of crime. Therefore, if a person is acting in order to prevent a crime against his/her property, it follows that force can be used to protect property.

Whether or not such force is reasonable will be subject to the requirements of s. 76 of the Criminal Justice and Immigration Act 2008. However, it might be somewhat problematic (if not impossible) to reconcile reasonable force to protect property with the taking of a person's life. It may be that such lethal force would fall foul of s. 76(6) which states that if the force used is disproportionate then it will not be regarded as being reasonable in the circumstances. Allied to this, is the fact that Article 2 of the European Convention on Human Rights does not support the taking of life in the defence of property and it can be seen that such a defence may well fail.

1.4.6 Police Officers

When using force against others, police officers will be criminally liable for any assaults they commit, in the same way as any other person.

However, just as the same offences and sentences will apply, similarly the same general defences will potentially be available to the officer. One specific issue that can often arise where force is used by a police officer is the technique employed by the officer in applying force or striking someone. This may consist of a particular technique that the officer has been trained to use—either with or without some form of weapon. The issue of whether a particular technique is a 'proper' or 'recognised' one, is not the same as the question of the *lawfulness* of any force used on that occasion. Clearly, the controlled use of a technique in which an officer has been trained may help a court in determining the issue of the lawfulness or otherwise of the use of force. So, too, will any training that the officer has (or has not) received in relation to the use of force and personal protection. However, there are times when using an 'authorised technique' will nevertheless be unlawful; conversely, there will be circumstances in which the use of an improvised strike or use of an object may be lawful. All will turn on the circumstances of the case.

1.4.7 Infancy

Children under the age of 10 are *irrebuttably* presumed to be incapable of criminal responsibility (*doli incapax*) by virtue of s. 50 of the Children and Young Persons Act 1933.

1.5 Homicide

1.5.1 Introduction

Homicide covers offences of murder, manslaughter and other occasions where a person causes, or is involved in, the death of another. The common law in relation to homicide is important, not only because of the gravity of the offences themselves, but also because the cases have defined a number of key issues in criminal law applicable to many other offences.

In all cases of homicide, the general criminal conduct (*actus reus*) is the same—the killing of another person.

1.5.2 Murder

OFFENCE: **Murder—*Common Law***

- Life imprisonment (mandatory)

Murder is committed when a person unlawfully kills another human being under the King's Peace, with malice aforethought.

KEYNOTE

A conviction for murder carries a mandatory sentence of life imprisonment (if the offence is committed by a person aged 18 but under 21, the sentence is 'custody for life' (also mandatory) and in the case of a defendant who is under 18, 'detention at His Majesty's pleasure': Powers of Criminal Courts (Sentencing) Act 2000, s. 90).

'Unlawful killing' means actively causing the death of another without justification. 'Unlawfully' can be taken to exclude killings for which the accused has a complete and valid justification, such as killing (reasonably) in self-defence. It also includes occasions where someone fails to act after creating a situation of danger (**see chapter 1.2**).

'Another human being' includes a baby who has been born alive and has an existence independent of its mother. 'Existence independent of its mother' means that the child is fully expelled from the womb; the umbilical cord need not be cut. If a defendant intended to kill or cause serious injury to the mother, that intention cannot support a charge of murder in respect of the baby if it goes on to die after being born alive. It may, however, support a charge of manslaughter (*Attorney-General's Reference (No. 3 of 1994)* [1998] AC 245). It would certainly be appropriate to charge a person with the murder of the child if he/she intended the child to die after having been born alive.

'Under the King's Peace' appears to exclude deaths caused during the legitimate prosecution of warfare (War Crimes Act 1991).

Under the provisions of the Offences Against the Person Act 1861 (s. 9), any British citizen who commits a murder anywhere in the world may be tried in England or Wales. It does not matter what nationality the victim was or where in the world the act took place—all that matters is that at the time the offence was committed, the defendant was a British citizen.

It should be noted that the only state of mind or *mens rea* that will support a charge of attempted murder is an *intention to kill*. Nothing less will suffice.

1.5.2.1 Malice Aforethought

The cases of *R* v *Moloney* [1985] AC 905 and *R* v *Hancock* [1986] AC 455 identify the *mens rea* required for murder as an intention:

- to kill; or
- to cause grievous bodily harm.

Murder is therefore a crime of 'specific intent'.

The term 'malice aforethought' is often associated with some form of premeditation; this is not required.

1.5.2.2 Year and a Day

Section 1 of the Law Reform (Year and a Day Rule) Act 1996 abolished the limitation that death had to occur within a year and a day of the infliction of injury.

However, by s. 2 of the Act, the consent of the Attorney-General is required before proceedings can be instituted for a 'fatal offence' where either:

(a) the injury alleged to have caused the death was sustained more than three years before death occurred; or
(b) the person has previously been convicted of an offence committed in circumstances alleged to be connected to the death.

1.5.3 Voluntary Manslaughter and 'Special Defences'

As a conviction for murder leaves a judge no discretion in sentencing a defendant, a number of 'special defences' have developed around the offence (diminished responsibility, loss of control and suicide pact). Rather than securing an acquittal, they allow for a conviction of 'voluntary manslaughter' instead of murder (hence, they are also termed 'partial' defences to murder). Consequently, voluntary manslaughter is more a finding by a court than an offence with which a person can be charged. It should be noted that these 'special defences' are only available to a defendant who is charged with an offence of murder—they cannot be used in answer to any other charge, e.g. attempted murder.

1.5.3.1 Diminished Responsibility

The Homicide Act 1957, s. 2 states:

> (1) A person ('D') who kills or is a party to a killing of another is not to be convicted of murder if D was suffering from an abnormality of mental functioning which—
> (a) arose from a recognised medical condition,
> (b) substantially impaired D's ability to do one or more of the things mentioned in subsection (1A), and
> (c) provides an explanation for D's acts and omissions in doing or being party to the killing.
>
> (1A) Those things are—
> (a) to understand the nature of D's conduct;
> (b) to form a rational judgment;
> (c) to exercise self-control.
>
> (1B) For the purposes of subsection (1)(c), an abnormality of mental functioning provides an explanation for D's conduct if it causes, or is a significant contributory factor in causing, D to carry out that conduct.
>
> (2) On a charge of murder, it shall be for the defence to prove that the person charged is by virtue of this section not liable to be convicted of murder.

(3) A person who but for this section would be liable, whether as principal or as accessory, to be convicted of murder shall be liable instead to be convicted of manslaughter.

(4) The fact that one party to a killing is by virtue of this section not liable to be convicted of murder shall not affect the question whether the killing amounted to murder in the case of any other party to it.

KEYNOTE

The definition requires that the abnormality *substantially* impaired the defendant's ability to do one (or more) of three things and also provides that the defendant's abnormality of mental functioning should be at least a significant contributory factor in causing the defendant's acts or omissions. Whether the 'impairment of mental responsibility' is 'substantial' or not will be a question of fact for the jury to decide. Minor lapses of lucidity will not be enough.

The abnormality must arise from a *recognised medical condition*. 'Abnormality of mind' has been held to be 'a state of mind so different from that of ordinary human beings that the reasonable man would term it abnormal' (*R* v *Byrne* [1960] 2 QB 396). This includes the mental inability to exert control over one's behaviour and to form a rational judgement.

There may be any number of causes of the 'abnormality' of the mind. Examples include post-natal depression and pre-menstrual symptoms (*R* v *Reynolds* [1988] Crim LR 679) and 'battered wives' syndrome' (*R* v *Hobson* [1998] 1 Cr App R 31). In *R* v *Dietschmann* [2003] UKHL 10, the House of Lords accepted that a mental abnormality caused by a grief reaction to the recent death of an aunt with whom the defendant had had a physical relationship could suffice. In that case, their lordships went on to hold that there is no requirement to show that the 'abnormality of mind' was the *sole* cause of the defendant's acts in committing the killing.

The burden of proving these features lies with the defence and the standard required is one of a balance of probabilities.

1.5.3.2 Loss of Control

The Coroners and Justice Act 2009, s. 54 states:

(1) Where a person ('D') kills or is a party to the killing of another ('V'), D is not to be convicted of murder if—
   (a) D's acts and omissions in doing or being a party to the killing resulted from D's loss of self-control,
   (b) the loss of self-control had a qualifying trigger, and
   (c) a person of D's sex and age, with a normal degree of tolerance and self-restraint and in the circumstances of D, might have reacted in the same or in a similar way to D.

(2) For the purposes of subsection (1)(a), it does not matter whether or not the loss of control was sudden.

(3) In subsection (1)(c) the reference to 'the circumstances of D' is a reference to all of D's circumstances other than those whose only relevance to D's conduct is that they bear on D's general capacity for tolerance or self-restraint.

(4) Subsection (1) does not apply if, in doing or being a party to the killing, D acted in a considered desire for revenge.

(5) On a charge of murder, if sufficient evidence is adduced to raise an issue with respect to the defence under subsection (1), the jury must assume that the defence is satisfied unless the prosecution proves beyond reasonable doubt that it is not.

(6) For the purposes of subsection (5), sufficient evidence is adduced to raise an issue with respect to the defence if evidence is adduced on which, in the opinion of the trial judge, a jury, properly directed, could reasonably conclude that the defence might apply.

(7) A person who, but for this section, would be liable to be convicted of murder is liable instead to be convicted of manslaughter.

(8) The fact that one party to a killing is by virtue of this section not liable to be convicted of murder does not affect the question whether the killing amounted to murder in the case of any other party to it.

KEYNOTE

In *R* v *Asmelash* [2013] EWCA Crim 157, the Court of Appeal confirmed that in considering the question under s. 54(1)(c) of whether 'a person of D's sex and age, with a normal degree of tolerance and self-restraint and in the circumstances of D, might have reacted in the same or similar way to D', the fact that the accused had voluntarily consumed alcohol was not to be included in D's circumstances.

The loss of control *need not be sudden* (s. 54(2)). Although subs. (2) in the partial defence states that *it is not a requirement* for the partial defence that the loss of self-control be sudden, it will remain open for the judge (in deciding whether to leave the defence to the jury) and the jury (in determining whether the killing did in fact result from a loss of self-control and whether the other aspects of the partial defence are satisfied) to take into account any delay between a relevant incident and the killing.

Section 54(3) supplements s. 54(1)(c) by clarifying that the reference to the defendant's circumstances in that subsection means all of those circumstances except those whose only relevance to the defendant's conduct is that they impact upon the defendant's general level of tolerance and self-restraint. Thus, a defendant's history of abuse at the hands of the victim could be taken into account in deciding whether an ordinary person might have acted as the defendant did, whereas the defendant's generally short temper could not. Consequently, when applying the test in s. 54(1)(c) the jury will consider whether a person of the defendant's sex and age with an ordinary level of tolerance and self-restraint and in the defendant's specific circumstances (in the sense described earlier in this paragraph) might have acted as the defendant did.

Those acting in a considered desire for revenge cannot rely on the partial defence, even if they lose self-control as a result of a qualifying trigger.

Qualifying Trigger

Section 55 of the Coroners and Justice Act 2009 explains the phrase 'qualifying trigger' mentioned in s. 54(1)(b). The loss of self-control must be attributable to:

- *The defendant's fear of serious violence from the victim against the defendant or another identified person.* This will be a subjective test and the defendant will need to show that he/she lost self-control because of a genuine fear of serious violence, whether or not the fear was in fact reasonable. The fear of serious violence needs to be in respect of violence against the defendant or against another identified person. For example, the fear of serious violence could be in respect of a child of the defendant, but it could not be a fear that the victim would in the future use serious violence against people generally.
- *To a thing or things done or said (or both) which constituted circumstances of an extremely grave character and caused the defendant to have a justifiable sense of being seriously wronged.* Whether a defendant's sense of being seriously wronged is justifiable will be an objective question for a jury to determine. This sets a high threshold for the circumstances in which a partial defence is available where a person loses self-control in response to words or actions. It effectively restricts the potential availability of a partial defence in cases where a loss of control is attributable to things done or said.
- *A combination of the above two factors.*

Section 55(6) states that in determining whether a loss of self-control had a qualifying trigger:

- the defendant's fear of serious violence is to be disregarded to the extent that it was caused by a thing which the defendant incited to be done or said for the purpose of providing an excuse to use violence;
- a sense of being seriously wronged by a thing done or said is not justifiable if the defendant incited the thing to be done or said for the purpose of providing an excuse to use violence;
- the fact that a thing done or said constituted sexual infidelity is to be disregarded.

1.5.3.3 Suicide Pact

The Homicide Act 1957, s. 4 states:

> (1) It shall be manslaughter, and shall not be murder, for a person acting in pursuance of a suicide pact between him and another to kill the other or be a party to the other being killed by a third person.

KEYNOTE

The burden of proof that the defendant was acting in the pursuance of a suicide pact is placed on the accused. He/she must show that:

- a suicide pact had been made; and
- he/she had the intention of dying at the time the killing took place.

'Suicide pact' is defined by the Homicide Act 1957, s. 4(3) as:

> a common agreement between two or more persons having for its object the death of all of them, whether or not each is to take his own life, but nothing done by a person who enters into a suicide pact shall be treated as done by him in pursuance of the pact unless it is done while he has the settled intention of dying in pursuance of the pact.

An example of a suicide pact can be seen in *R* v *Sweeney* (1986) 8 Cr App R (S) 419. The offender was prone to depression and had married the deceased when she was suffering from advanced muscular dystrophy. They decided to commit suicide together by taking tablets and then setting fire to their car while they were inside it. Once the fire started, both tried to escape, but the wife was killed. The offender suffered serious burns. He pleaded guilty to the manslaughter of his wife.

1.5.4 Involuntary Manslaughter

Involuntary manslaughter occurs where the defendant causes the death of another but is not shown to have had the required *mens rea* for murder.

OFFENCE: **Manslaughter—*Common Law***

• Triable on indictment • Life imprisonment

KEYNOTE

Manslaughter, like murder, is the unlawful killing of another human being; it does not require the intention to kill or to cause grievous bodily harm.

Involuntary manslaughter—that is, those cases which do not involve the 'special defences' under the Homicide Act 1957 or Coroners and Justice Act 2009—can be separated into occasions where a defendant:

- kills another by an *unlawful* act which was *likely to cause bodily harm*; or
- kills another by *gross negligence*.

1.5.4.1 Manslaughter by Unlawful Act

There are three elements to the offence of manslaughter by an unlawful act (also called constructive manslaughter). You must prove:

(1) an unlawful act;
(2) that the unlawful act is likely to cause bodily harm; and
(3) the defendant had the *mens rea* for the unlawful act.

An Unlawful Act

The accused's act must be inherently unlawful, in that it constitutes *a criminal offence in its own right*, irrespective of the fact that it ultimately results in someone's death. An act that only becomes unlawful by virtue of the way in which it is carried out will not be enough. For instance, 'driving' is clearly not an inherently unlawful act but becomes so if done dangerously or carelessly on a road or public place. If someone drives dangerously and thereby causes the death of another, the act of driving, albeit carried out in a way that attracts criminal liability, is *not* an 'unlawful act' for the purposes of unlawful act manslaughter (*Andrews* v *DPP* [1937] AC 576). Hence, the existence of statutory offences addressing most instances of death that are caused by poor standards of driving. If a defendant uses a motor vehicle as a means to commit an 'unlawful act' (e.g. an assault), he/she can be charged with manslaughter as long as the 'act' goes beyond poor driving. The CPS has published a policy document which sets out the way in which it will deal with cases of bad driving. Unlawful act manslaughter will be considered the most appropriate charge when there is evidence to prove that the vehicle was used as an instrument of attack (but where the necessary intent for murder was absent), or to cause fright, and death resulted. There are, however, reasons of policy (*R* v *Lawrence* [1982] AC 510) why, in all but the most deliberate of cases, the offences under the Road Traffic Act 1988 should be used (**see *General Police Duties*, chapter 3.21**). The inherently unlawful act need not be directed or aimed at anyone and can include acts committed against or towards property, such as criminal damage or arson (*R* v *Goodfellow* (1986) 83 Cr App R 23). Generally, if the actions of the victim break the chain of causation between the defendant's unlawful act and the cause of death, the defendant will not be responsible for the death of that victim (**see chapter 1.2**). This is why drug dealers who supply controlled drugs cannot generally be held liable for the ultimate deaths of their 'victims' unless they have done far more than just supply a drug (*R* v *Dalby* [1982] 1 WLR 425 and *R* v *Armstrong* [1989] Crim LR 149). This view was affirmed in the case of *R* v *Kennedy* [2007] UKHL 38. The circumstances were that the defendant had prepared a dose of heroin for the deceased and had given the syringe to the deceased before leaving the room they were both in. The deceased injected the drug and as a result died. The House of Lords ruled that a supplier of a drug is not guilty of manslaughter where the deceased freely and voluntarily self-administered the drug. An *omission* to do something will not suffice as manslaughter by unlawful act requires *an act*.

The Unlawful Act is Likely to Cause Bodily Harm

The unlawful act must involve a risk of some bodily harm (albeit not serious harm). That risk will be judged *objectively*; that is, would the risk of harm be foreseen by a reasonable and sober person watching the act (*R* v *Church* [1966] 1 QB 59)? Such acts might include dropping a paving stone off a bridge into the path of a train (*DPP* v *Newbury* [1977] AC 500), setting fire to your house (*Goodfellow*) or firing a gun at police officers and then holding someone else in front of you when the officers return fire (*R* v *Pagett* (1983) 76 Cr App R 279).

The 'harm' likely to result from the act must be physical; the risk of emotional or psychological harm does not appear to be enough (*R* v *Dawson* (1985) 81 Cr App R 150). In *R* v *Carey* [2006] EWCA Crim 17, the Court of Appeal observed that the law of unlawful act manslaughter required the commission of an unlawful act which was recognised, by a sober and reasonable person, as being *dangerous* and likely to subject the victim to the risk of some physical harm *which in turn* caused the victim's death.

The Defendant had the *Mens Rea* for the Unlawful Act

The defendant must possess the *mens rea* for the unlawful act which led to the death of a victim. If he/she did not have that *mens rea*, the offence of manslaughter by unlawful act will not be made out. For example, in *R* v *Lamb* [1967] 2 QB 981 the defendant pretended to fire a revolver at his friend. Although the defendant believed that the weapon would not fire, the chamber containing a bullet moved round to the firing pin and the defendant's friend was killed. Lamb was charged with manslaughter by unlawful act (the unlawful act being assault) but it could not be proved that Lamb had the *mens rea* required (an intent or recklessness to cause a person to apprehend immediate unlawful violence) for an assault (**see chapter 1.10**) and his conviction for manslaughter was quashed.

The accused cannot rely on his/her lack of *mens rea* induced by voluntary intoxication as manslaughter is a crime of basic intent (*R* v *Lipman* [1970] 1 QB 152). This was an extreme case in many ways, in which the accused killed his girlfriend while suffering LSD-induced hallucinations that he was at the centre of the earth being attacked by snakes. If the unlawful act alleged were to be a crime of specific intent, then the accused's intoxication should be relevant.

1.5.4.2 Manslaughter by Gross Negligence

Manslaughter is the only criminal offence at common law capable of being committed by negligence.

A charge of manslaughter may be brought where a person, by an instance of *gross negligence*, has brought about the death of another. The ingredients of this offence essentially consist of death resulting from a negligent breach of a duty of care owed by the defendant to the victim in circumstances so reprehensible as to amount to gross negligence (*R* v *Misra and Srivastava* [2004] EWCA Crim 2375). The most difficult task in defining the degree of negligence that will qualify as 'gross' falls to the trial judge when addressing the jury. Whether a defendant's conduct will amount to gross negligence is a question of fact for the jury to decide in the light of all the evidence (*R* v *Bateman* (1925) 19 Cr App R 8).

What is clear from the decided cases is that civil liability, although a starting point for establishing the breach of a duty of care, is not enough to amount to 'gross negligence' (*R* v *Adomako* [1995] 1 AC 171). The test in *Adomako* as summarised by Lord Mackay seems to provide the leading authority on the area—that test for the jury being: '... whether, having regard to the risk of death involved, the conduct of the defendant was so bad in all the circumstances as to amount in their judgment to a criminal act or omission'.

It is not possible to bring proceedings for gross negligence manslaughter against a company or other organisation to which the offence under the Corporate Manslaughter and Corporate Homicide Act 2007 applies (s. 20 of the Corporate Manslaughter and Corporate Homicide Act 2007).

1.5.5 Causing or Allowing a Child or Vulnerable Adult to Die or Suffer Serious Physical Harm

This offence deals with the situation where a child or other vulnerable person dies or suffers serious physical harm as a result of an unlawful act (or omission) of one of several people but it cannot be shown which of them actually caused the death or allowed it to occur.

OFFENCE: **Causing or Allowing a Child or Vulnerable Adult to Die or Suffer Serious Harm—*Domestic Violence, Crime and Victims Act 2004, s. 5***

• Triable on indictment • Where the child or vulnerable adult dies, life imprisonment or a fine or both • Where the child or vulnerable adult suffers serious physical harm, 14 years' imprisonment or a fine or both

The Domestic Violence, Crime and Victims Act 2004, s. 5 states:

(1) A person ('D') is guilty of an offence if—
- (a) a child or vulnerable adult ('V') dies or suffers serious physical harm as a result of the unlawful act of a person who—
  - (i) was a member of the same household as V, and
  - (ii) had frequent contact with him,
- (b) D was such a person at the time of that act,
- (c) at that time there was a significant risk of serious physical harm being caused to V by the unlawful act of such a person, and
- (d) either D was the person whose act caused the death or serious physical harm—
  - (i) D was, or ought to have been, aware of the risk mentioned in paragraph (c),
  - (ii) D failed to take such steps as he could reasonably have been expected to take to protect V from the risk, and
  - (iii) the act occurred in circumstances of the kind that D foresaw or ought to have foreseen.

KEYNOTE

'Child' means a person under the age of 16 and 'vulnerable adult' means a person aged 16 or over whose ability to protect him/herself from violence, abuse or neglect is significantly impaired through physical or mental disability or illness, through old age or otherwise (s. 5(6)).

It is necessary to prove that the victim died or suffered serious physical harm *as a result of the unlawful act* of a person who fits a number of criteria. For these purposes, 'act' includes 'omissions' and an act or omission will generally only be 'unlawful' if it would have amounted to an offence (s. 5(5) and (6)). It must be shown that the defendant was, *at the time of the act*, a member of the same household as the victim *and* had frequent contact with the victim. For these purposes, people will be a member of a particular household if they visit it so often and for such periods of time that it is reasonable to regard them as a member of it *even if they do not actually live there* (s. 5(4)(a)). Where, as often happens, the victim lived in different households at different times, the 'same household' criterion will mean the household in which the victim was living at the time of the act that caused the death or serious physical harm (s. 5(4)(b)).

Unless the defendant is the mother or father of the victim: (a) he/she cannot be charged with an offence under this section if aged under 16 at the time of the act; and (b) restrictions will be made on what steps would have been reasonable for a defendant to have taken while under that age (see s. 5(3)).

1.5.6 Encouraging or Assisting Suicide

There is no defence of 'mercy killing' or formal recognition of euthanasia under the current legal system. However, there is a specific offence of encouraging or assisting another to take their own life.

OFFENCE: **Encouraging or Assisting Suicide—*Suicide Act 1961, s. 2***

- Triable on indictment • 14 years' imprisonment

The Suicide Act 1961, s. 2 states:

(1) A person ('D') commits an offence if—
  (a) D does an act capable of encouraging or assisting the suicide or attempted suicide of another person, and
  (b) D's act was intended to encourage or assist suicide or an attempt at suicide.

(1A) The person referred to in subsection (1)(a) need not be a specific person (or class of persons) known to, or identified by, D.

(1B) D may commit an offence under this section whether or not a suicide, or an attempt at suicide, occurs.

KEYNOTE

This offence is an alternative verdict on a charge of murder/manslaughter (Suicide Act 1961, s. 2(2)). The person committing the offence need not know, or even be able to identify, the other person. For example, the author of a website promoting suicide who intends that one of more of its readers will commit suicide is guilty of an offence, even though the author may never know the identity of those who access the website. The offence applies whether or not a person commits or attempts suicide.

The consent of the DPP is required to initiate proceedings for this offence (s. 2(4) of the Suicide Act 1961).

1.5.6.1 Acts Capable of Encouraging or Assisting

The Suicide Act 1961, s. 2A states:

(1) If D arranges for a person ('D2') to do an act that is capable of encouraging or assisting the suicide or attempted suicide of another person and D2 does that act, D is also to be treated for the purposes of this Act as having done it.

(2) Where the facts are such that an act is not capable of encouraging or assisting suicide or attempted suicide, for the purposes of this Act it is to be treated as so capable if the act would have been so capable had the facts been as D believed them to be at the time of the act or had subsequent events happened in the manner D believed they would happen (or both).

(3) A reference in this Act to a person ('P') doing an act that is capable of encouraging the suicide or attempted suicide of another person includes a reference to P doing so by threatening another person or otherwise putting pressure on another person to commit or attempt suicide.

KEYNOTE

Section 2A(1) creates a liability when a defendant arranges for another to encourage or assist suicide so that responsibility cannot be avoided by using a third party as a conduit to commit the offence. Note that that third party must actually do the 'act', i.e. he/she must encourage or assist the suicide.

Section 2A(2) has the effect that an act can be capable of encouraging or assisting suicide even if the circumstances are such that it was impossible for the act actually to encourage or assist suicide. An act is therefore treated as capable of encouraging and assisting suicide if it would have been so capable had the facts been as the defendant believed them to be at the time of the act (e.g. if pills provided with the intention that they would assist a person to commit suicide are thought to be lethal but are in fact harmless) or had subsequent events happened as the defendant believed they would (e.g. if lethal pills which were sent to a person with the intention that the person would use them to commit or attempt to commit suicide are lost in the post), or both.

Section 2A(3) clarifies that references to doing an act capable of encouraging or assisting another to commit or attempt suicide include a reference to doing so by threatening another person or otherwise putting pressure on another person to commit or attempt suicide.

An 'act' will include a course of conduct.

Providers of information society services (any service normally provided for remuneration, at a distance, by electronic means and at the individual request of a recipient of services) which are established in England, Wales or Northern Ireland are covered by the offence of encouraging or assisting suicide even when they are operating in other European Economic Area States (sch. 12 to the Coroners and Justice Act 2009). The schedule provides exemptions for Internet Service Providers from the offence in limited circumstances, such as where they are acting as mere conduits for information that is capable, and provided with the intention, of encouraging or assisting suicide or are storing it as caches or hosts.

1.5.7 Solicitation of Murder

OFFENCE: **Encouraging Another to Murder—*Offences Against the Person Act 1861, s. 4***

- Triable on indictment • Life imprisonment

The Offences Against the Person Act 1861, s. 4 states:

Whosoever shall solicit, encourage, persuade or endeavour to persuade, or shall propose to any person, to murder any other person, whether he be a subject of Her Majesty or not, and whether he be within the Queen's dominions or not, shall be guilty of [an offence].

KEYNOTE

Examples of this offence include *R* v *El-Faisal* [2004] EWCA Crim 343, where the defendant, a minister of Islam, was convicted after creating audio tapes containing public speeches given by him encouraging the killing of non-believers. A further example is *R* v *Ahmad* [2012] EWCA Crim 959, where the offender published material on a website encouraging the murder of Members of Parliament and providing their personal details.

Although the soliciting must be done from within the jurisdiction, the phrase 'whether he be a subject of Her Majesty or not, and whether he be within the Queen's dominions or not' has been interpreted so that it applies not only to the person to be murdered but also to the person being solicited. Thus, in *R* v *Abu Hamza* [2007] QB 659, it was no defence that the persons being solicited were of various nationalities and the murders were to take place abroad and that it was not proved that any of those solicited to murder were British nationals.

The proposed victim may be outside the United Kingdom.

It does not matter whether or not the person is in fact encouraged to commit murder, but the offence is not complete until someone is in receipt of the solicitation, although the act of sending it can constitute an attempt (*R* v *Krause* (1902) 66 JP 121). Encouraging a pregnant woman to kill her child in the future, after it is born alive, is an offence within this section (*R* v *Shephard* (1919) 2 KB 125).

This offence may be appropriate in cases where a person is trying to arrange a 'contract killing'. In R v Kayani [1997] 2 Cr App R (S) 313, the defendant was sentenced to 12 years' imprisonment for soliciting the murder of his niece and her husband. He was arrested by an undercover police officer posing as a contract killer, to whom payment of £20,000 was tendered, partly in cash and partly in heroin. For this reason, this offence may be preferred in cases where the defendant has 'conspired' with one other person and that person is an undercover police officer.

1.6 Misuse of Drugs

1.6.1 Introduction

This chapter deals, in the main, with offences created by the Misuse of Drugs Act 1971. As some of the concepts associated with drug offences, e.g. 'possession' and 'supply', are important to assist in understanding the legislation, they are dealt with before any offences associated with them. A methodical approach is then taken by dealing with drug offences in the order of possession, supply and production, finishing with an examination of other drug-related offences and police powers.

1.6.2 Classification

Drugs that are subject to the provisions of the Misuse of Drugs Act 1971 are listed in parts I, II and III of sch. 2 to the Act.

The divisions are made largely on the basis of each substance's potential effects on both the person taking it and society in general. The list of controlled drugs is large, and for full details reference should be made to sch. 2 to the Misuse of Drugs Act 1971. Examples of some of the more commonly encountered drugs include:

- **Class A**—this class includes heroin (diamorphine), methadone, cocaine, LSD, 'Ecstasy' (MDMA) and 'crystal meth' (methylamphetamine). It also includes fungus (of any kind) which contains psilocin (such as 'magic mushrooms').
- **Class B**—this class includes cannabis, cannabis resin, codeine, ketamine and ritalin (methylphenidate).
- **Class C**—this class includes valium (diazepam), khat (the leaves, stems or shoots of the plant of the species *Catha edulis*) and GHB (gamma hydroxybutyrate).

If the charge alleges possession of one particular drug, then that drug must be identified.

Note that although a substance may appear in sch. 2 to the Act, there may be restrictions on the occasions where possession is treated as an offence (**see paras 1.6.2.1** and **1.6.3.7**).

It is not necessary, when prosecuting an offence, to distinguish between the various chemical forms in which a drug exists (i.e. as a salt, ester or other form) (*R* v *Greensmith* [1983] 1 WLR 1124).

A defendant's admission may, in some cases, be relied upon to prove his/her knowledge as to what a particular substance is (*R* v *Chatwood* [1980] 1 WLR 874).

1.6.2.1 Temporary Class Drug Orders

The Home Secretary has the power, under the Misuse of Drugs Act 1971, to make any drug subject to temporary control.

Temporary class drug orders can be made if the following two conditions are met:

(1) the drug is not already controlled under the Act as a Class A, B or C drug;
(2) the ACMD (Advisory Council on the Misuse of Drugs) has been consulted and determined that the order should be made, or the Home Secretary has received a

recommendation from the Advisory Council that the order should be made, on the basis that it appears to the Home Secretary that:

(a) the drug is being, or is likely to be, misused; and
(b) the misuse is having, or is capable of having, harmful effects.

The order will come into immediate effect and will last for up to 12 months, subject to Parliament agreeing to it within 40 sitting days of the order being made. The order enables the government to act to protect the public against harmful new psychoactive substances while expert advice is being prepared.

Such a drug will be referred to as a 'temporary class drug' and will be a 'controlled drug' for the purposes of the Misuse of Drugs Act 1971, and other legislation such as the Proceeds of Crime Act 2002, unless otherwise stated. With the *exception of the possession* offence, all the offences under the Misuse of Drugs Act will apply including possession in connection with an offence or prohibition, under ss. 3, 4 and 5(3) of the Act, i.e. possession with intent to supply. Offences committed under the Act in relation to a temporary class drug are subject to the following maximum penalties:

- 14 years' imprisonment and an unlimited fine on indictment; and
- six months' imprisonment and a £5,000 fine on summary conviction.

Simple possession of a temporary class drug is not an offence under the 1971 Act; however, law enforcement officers have been given the following powers to enable them to take action to prevent possible harm to the individual:

- Search and detain a person (or vehicle etc.) where there are reasonable grounds to suspect that the person is in possession of a temporary class drug.
- Seize, detain and dispose of a suspected temporary class drug.
- Arrest or charge a person who commits the offence of intentionally obstructing an enforcement officer in the exercise of their powers.

1.6.2.2 Cannabis

The Misuse of Drugs Act 1971, s. 37 states:

> 'cannabis' (except in the expression 'cannabis resin') means any plant of the genus *Cannabis* or any part of any such plant (by whatever name designated) except that it does not include cannabis resin or any of the following products after separation from the rest of the plant, namely—
> (a) mature stalk of any such plant,
> (b) fibre produced from mature stalk of any such plant, and
> (c) seed of any such plant,
> 'cannabis resin' means the separated resin, whether crude or purified, obtained from any plant of the genus *Cannabis*.

KEYNOTE

Cannabis is a Class B drug. Therefore cannabis, cannabis resin, cannabis oil, cannabinol and its derivatives, any preparations or other product containing these substances and any substance which is an ester or ether either of cannabinol or of a cannabinol derivative are also Class B drugs. As cannabis and cannabis resin are both in the same class for the purposes of the 1971 Act, there would be no duplicity if a person is charged with possessing either one or the other in the same charge (*R* v *Best* (1980) 70 Cr App R 21).

1.6.3 Possession

'Possession' is a neutral concept, not implying any kind of fault, blame or guilt. This is the key feature to recognise before considering specific offences under *any* legislation. There are two elements to possession; the physical element and the mental element (*R* v *Lambert* [2002] 2 AC 545).

1.6.3.1 Custody or Control

The physical element involves proof that the thing is in the custody of the defendant or subject to his/her control. For example, if X has a wrap of cocaine in his jacket pocket, X has control of the wrap of cocaine (although *mere custody* does not mean that X is in 'possession' at this stage).

This approach is enlarged by s. 37(3) of the Misuse of Drugs Act 1971 which states that: 'For the purposes of this Act the things which a person has in his possession shall be taken to include anything subject to his control which is in the custody of another'.

EXAMPLE

X buys a controlled drug via the internet, directing that it be sent by post to his home address. X is in possession of that drug from the time it arrives through his letterbox (*R* v *Peaston* (1979) 69 Cr App R 203).

1.6.3.2 Knowledge of Possession

The second element involves that the defendant knows that the thing in question is under his/her control. He/she need not know what its nature is, but as long as he/she knows that the thing, whatever it is, is under his/her control, it is in his/her possession.

EXAMPLE

X and Y are walking along a street. X is going through his pockets looking for his wallet and, as he is searching for the wallet, he hands Y several tablets of Ecstasy and asks him to hold onto them while he continues searching. Y has no idea that the tablets he takes hold of are a controlled drug.

- Y has control of the Ecstasy tablets (they are in his hand);
- Y has knowledge of the presence of the Ecstasy tablets in his hand;
- *therefore Y has possession of the Ecstasy tablets.*

Nobody is suggesting, at this stage, that Y is guilty of an offence. Of course, Y could rightly be arrested on *suspicion* of possessing a controlled drug but arresting on suspicion that a person has committed an offence and *proving* guilt in relation to it are two different things. Indeed, Y's lack of knowledge about what the tablets are may afford him a defence (**see para. 1.6.9**). But the fact remains that ignorance of, or mistake as to the quality of, the thing in question does not prevent the accused being in possession of it.

What if the thing is inside a container, e.g. a box, a bag or a cigarette packet, and the person claims not to have known the thing was inside the container? In such cases, the common law makes the same requirements; you need to show that the person had custody of the container together with a knowledge that it (the container) contained *something*.

EXAMPLE

X is given a packet of cigarettes by Y. X believes the packet contains cigarettes only. The packet does contain several cigarettes but also contains a wrap of cocaine. X does not know about the wrap of cocaine and puts the pack of cigarettes into his pocket.

- X has custody of the pack of cigarettes (they are in his pocket);
- X has knowledge of the presence of the pack of cigarettes (X put them there);
- X knows that the pack of cigarettes contains something;
- *therefore X has possession of the wrap of cocaine.*

Nobody is suggesting X is guilty of an offence but he is in 'possession' of the wrap of cocaine.

In *R* v *Forsyth* [2001] EWCA Crim 2926, the defendant argued that there was a distinction between a person carrying something *in* a container and a person carrying *something inside something else* in a container. In that particular case, the defendant was found in possession of a box which contained a safe; inside the safe was a significant quantity of a controlled drug. The defendant argued that this type of possession should be differentiated from the situation where someone simply had possession of a box with drugs in it. The Court of Appeal ruled that there was no difference and the issues of proof were the same.

A person does not possess something of which he/she is completely unaware as there would be no knowledge of possession. If a drug is put into someone's pocket without his/her knowledge, he/she is not in possession of it (*Warner* v *Metropolitan Police Commissioner* [1969] 2 AC 256).

1.6.3.3 Joint Possession

To show that two or more persons are in possession of a controlled drug requires more than a mere ability to control it (*R* v *Kousar* [2009] EWCA Crim 139). Mere knowledge of the presence of a drug in the hands of a confederate is not enough; joint possession must be established (*R* v *Searle* [1971] Crim LR 592). In *Searle*, it was stated that this could be established by asking the question 'do the drugs form part of a common pool from which all had the right to draw?' In *R* v *Strong* (1989) *The Times*, 26 January 1990, the prosecution put the case on the basis that there was joint possession; that is, each of the co-accused had control of one or more of the packages of cannabis. The Court of Appeal followed *Searle*, and said that what was being looked for was whether each person had the right to say what should be done with the cannabis. Mere presence in the same vehicle as the drugs, and knowing they were there, was not sufficient.

Further issues that can arise from this view of 'possession' were highlighted in *Adams* v *DPP* [2002] EWHC 438 (Admin), where a small quantity of controlled drugs were found in the defendant's home during the execution of a search warrant. There was no proof that the drugs were owned by the defendant or that she was specifically aware of their presence but she *did* know that her home was used by various people who were highly likely to bring controlled drugs into it. She was convicted of possession. In hearing her appeal, the Administrative Court held that where knowledge of possession of drugs was limited to the fact that a visitor had brought drugs into the defendant's home intending to take them, that was not sufficient evidence from which it was appropriate to infer that she had control over the drugs.

The court also held that giving consent (explicitly or impliedly) for the use of a controlled drug did not of itself constitute possession. Similarly, an inference that the defendant knew whose drugs had been found in her home did not amount to evidence of control over the drug itself even though she may well have been able to exercise control over what actually took place in her home.

1.6.3.4 Points to Prove

Once 'possession' has been proved, it is then necessary to prove that what the defendant possesses is, in fact, a controlled drug. If this is established, then the defendant has a case to answer in relation to the offence of possession of a controlled drug.

EXAMPLE

X is subject to a stop and search procedure under s. 23 of the Misuse of Drugs Act 1971 (**see para. 1.6.16.1**). During the search, several packets containing cannabis resin are found in X's coat pocket.

In order to prove 'possession' of the cannabis for the purpose of the possession of a controlled drug offence, you must show:

- that X possessed the cannabis (X has custody/control of it and he knows it is in his possession); and
- that the contents of the packets are a controlled drug.

1.6.3.5 Quality

In the above example, *you would not have to show that X knew what the resin was*. That is, you do not need to show that X knew the *quality* of what he possessed to prove that X 'possessed' it.

If the defendant admits to knowing that the cannabis resin was there but thought it was chocolate, he is in possession of it (*R* v *Marriott* [1971] 1 WLR 187).

Therefore, if a defendant had a packet of cigarettes with him and admitted to knowing that he had them, he would be in possession of a controlled drug if one cigarette was shown to have contained cannabis. The fact that the defendant thought they contained tobacco would be irrelevant to the 'possession' concept (*R* v *Searle* [1971] Crim LR 592) (although he may have a defence under s. 28: **see para. 1.6.9**).

1.6.3.6 Quantity

The *quantity* of a controlled drug, however, may be so small that the defendant could not possibly have known about it; therefore it could not be 'possessed'.

The House of Lords suggested that if something is 'visible, tangible and measurable' that may be sufficient (*R* v *Boyesen* [1982] AC 768). If the amount recovered is too small to support a charge of possession, it might be used to prove earlier possession of the drug (*R* v *Graham* [1970] 1 WLR 113 and *Hambleton* v *Callinan* [1968] 2 QB 427 where traces of a controlled drug in a urine sample were held to be possible evidence of earlier possession of that drug).

Quantity is not only relevant to the fact of possession, it is also relevant to the intention of the person in whose possession the drug is found. Larger quantities (particularly if they are also divided into smaller amounts) may indicate an intention to supply and may be proof of that intention in some circumstances.

1.6.3.7 Possession of a Controlled Drug

OFFENCE: **Possession of Controlled Drug—*Misuse of Drugs Act 1971, s. 5***

• Triable either way • Class A (seven years' imprisonment and/or a fine on indictment; six months' imprisonment and/or prescribed sum summarily) • Class B (five years' imprisonment and/or a fine on indictment; three months' imprisonment and/or a fine summarily) • Class C (two years' imprisonment and/or a fine on indictment; three months' imprisonment and/or a fine summarily) • See keynote for possession of cannabis or cannabis resin

The Misuse of Drugs Act 1971, s. 5 states:

(2) Subject to section 28 of this Act and to subsection (4) below, it is an offence for a person to have a controlled drug in his possession in contravention of subsection (1) ...

KEYNOTE

Where the controlled drug involved is a fungus containing psilocin (a Class A drug) or an ester of psilocin (commonly known as magic mushrooms), possession will not be unlawful in certain circumstances. In summary, those circumstances are generally where the fungus is growing *uncultivated* and it:

- is picked by a person already in *lawful possession* of it (e.g. the landowner on whose land the mushrooms are growing) for the purpose of delivering it (as soon as is reasonably practicable) into the custody of a person lawfully entitled to take custody of it and it remains in that person's possession for (and in accordance with) that purpose; or
- it is picked by anyone either for the purpose of delivering it (as soon as reasonably practicable) into the custody of a person lawfully entitled to take custody of it or destroying it (as soon as is reasonably practicable) and it is held for that purpose.

Possession of cannabis, cannabis resin or khat can be dealt with under the Penalty Notice for Disorder (PND) Scheme (PNDs cannot be issued for any other drug-related offences). PNDs may be issued to any adult found in possession of cannabis, cannabis resin or khat for personal use; they are not appropriate for offenders under the age of 18 and can only be given on one occasion.

Possession of a 'temporary class drug' (**see para. 1.6.2.1**) is not an offence under this section (s. 5(2A)).

1.6.3.8 Section 5—The Defence to Unlawful Possession

Section 5 provides a defence to an offence of unlawful possession:

(4) In any proceedings for an offence under subsection (2) above in which it is proved that the accused had a controlled drug in his possession, it shall be a defence for him to prove—

(a) that, knowing or suspecting it to be a controlled drug, he took possession of it for the purpose of preventing another from committing or continuing to commit an offence in connection with that drug and that as soon as possible after taking possession of it he took all such steps as were reasonably open to him to destroy the drug or to deliver it into the custody of a person lawfully entitled to take custody of it; or

(b) that, knowing or suspecting it to be a controlled drug, he took possession of it for the purpose of delivering it into the custody of a person lawfully entitled to take custody of it and that as soon as possible after taking possession of it he took all such steps as were reasonably open to him to deliver it into the custody of such a person.

KEYNOTE

Defence under s. 5(4)(a)

The purpose in taking possession of the controlled drug under s. 5(4)(a) must be to prevent *another* from committing (in the future) or continuing to commit an offence in connection with *that* drug.

This situation might arise where a parent finds a child in possession of something which appears to be a controlled drug. Provided that that person takes all reasonable steps to destroy the drug or to take it to someone lawfully entitled to possess it (like a police officer), *as soon as possible after taking possession of it*, he/she would be able to use the defence under s. 5(4)(a).

When the accused buried drugs (cannabis), it was not sufficient to satisfy the defence under s. 5(4)(a) that the forces of nature might or would destroy the drug eventually: rather, it was for the accused to show that he took all such reasonable steps as were reasonably open to him to destroy them and the acts of destruction must be his (*R* v *Murphy* [2002] EWCA Crim 1587).

Defence under s. 5(4)(b)

The second situation (under s. 5(4)(b)) may arise where a person finds what he/she believes to be a controlled drug and he/she takes possession *of it solely for the purpose of delivering it to a person lawfully entitled to take custody of it.* The defendant must prove that this was his/her intention at the time of taking possession (*R* v *Dempsey* (1986) 82 Cr App R 291).

Section 5(4) will not provide a defence to any other offence connected with the controlled drug (e.g. supplying or offering to supply).

Duress of circumstances is not a defence to this, or any other, offence under the Misuse of Drugs Act 1971 (see para. 1.4.4).

1.6.4 Supplying

In *R* v *Maginnis* [1987] AC 303, the House of Lords held that 'supply' involves more than a mere transfer of physical control of the item from one person to another but includes a further concept; namely, that of 'enabling the recipient to apply the thing handed over to purposes for which he desires or has a duty to apply it'. In other words, *the person to whom the drug is given must derive some benefit from being given the drug.*

Supplying Explained

So the key to working out if there has been a 'supply' is to ask 'Does being given the drug benefit the person to whom the drug has been given?' If the answer is 'yes', then the person *giving the drug* is 'supplying' it.

KEYNOTE

In *R* v *Dempsey* (1986) 82 Cr App R 291, a registered drug addict (A) was in lawful possession of a drug. A asked his partner (B) to hold on to some of that drug while he went to administer the remainder of it to himself in a gents' toilet. Both A and B were arrested, A being subsequently charged with 'supplying' B with the drug.

There is no 'supply' from A to B as when A gives the drug to B, B *does not benefit from* the action; B is simply holding on to the drug (although, of course, B would be in unlawful possession of the drug at that stage). If A had given the drug to B for B to use, there would be a 'supply' by A to B as B *is benefiting* from the action; B gets to use the drug. If B intends to give back the drug to A, then B would commit the offence of possession with intent to supply.

In *R* v *Maginnis* [1987] AC 303, a drug trafficker (A) temporarily left drugs with (B); B expected A to pick up the drugs the following day and was charged and convicted of possession with intent to supply. The same approach taken with *Dempsey* applies. In *Maginnis*, when A gives the drugs to B, B does not benefit from it and there is no 'supply' from A to B; if B returns the drugs to A, there is a 'supply' from B to A as A benefits from being given the drug (to sell or use). As B intends to return the drug to A, B is in possession with intent to supply.

If the drug trafficker in *Maginnis* had given the custodian of the drug £50 as a reward for holding the drug, then there would have been a 'supply' from A to B as B would benefit from holding the drug (he has been paid £50, benefiting financially from being given the drug).

The issue has been further explored in a case involving a person who claimed that he had been coerced into holding controlled drugs for unnamed dealers. When found in possession of the drugs, the defendant claimed the defence of duress (as to which, **see chapter 1.4**) and said that he had only been an 'involuntary custodian' of them, intending to return them at a later date. The Court of Appeal decided that it was irrelevant whether a person was a voluntary or involuntary custodian of the drugs and that an intention to return them to their depositor amounted to an 'intention to supply' (*R* v *Panton* [2001] EWCA Crim 611).

Dividing up controlled drugs which have been jointly purchased and then handing them out so that persons may use the drug will amount to 'supplying' (*R* v *Buckley* (1979) 69 Cr App R 371).

If a police informer provides a controlled drug to another in order that the other be arrested, there will still be a 'supplying' of the drug (*R* v *X* [1994] Crim LR 827).

Injecting Others

Injecting another with that person's own controlled drug has been held *not to amount* to 'supplying' in a case where the defendant assisted in pushing down the plunger of a syringe that the other person was already using (*R* v *Harris* [1968] 1 WLR 769). It may amount to an offence of 'poisoning' under s. 23 of the Offences Against the Person Act 1861 (**see chapter 1.10**). The problem with charging the supplier of drugs for self-injection by someone who then dies as a result lies in the issues of causation. The general view is that the supplier is unlikely to be held liable for *causing* death in such a case (*R* v *Dias* [2001] EWCA Crim 2986). Where the defendant *actually carries out* the injection, liability for causing the death of another in this way can be made out even if the drug injected is not a controlled drug (*R* v *Andrews* [2002] EWCA Crim 3021, involving an injection of insulin with consent).

1.6.4.1 Supplying a Controlled Drug

OFFENCE: **Supplying Controlled Drug—*Misuse of Drugs Act 1971, s. 4(3)***

• Triable either way • Class A (life imprisonment and/or a fine on indictment; six months' imprisonment and/or prescribed sum summarily) • Class B (14 years' imprisonment and/or a fine on indictment; six months' imprisonment and/or prescribed sum summarily) • Class C (14 years' imprisonment and/or a fine on indictment; three months' imprisonment and/or a fine summarily)

The Misuse of Drugs Act 1971, s. 4 states:

(3) Subject to section 28 of this Act, it is an offence for a person—
- (a) to supply or offer to supply a controlled drug to another in contravention of subsection (1) above; or
- (b) to be concerned in the supplying of such a drug to another in contravention of that subsection; or
- (c) to be concerned in the making to another in contravention of that subsection of an offer to supply such a drug.

KEYNOTE

The three ingredients of this offence were set out in *R* v *Hughes* (1985) 81 Cr App R 344:
- (a) the supply of a drug to another, or as the case may be, the making of an offer to supply the drug to another in contravention of s. 4(1) of the Misuse of Drugs Act 1971;
- (b) participation by the accused in an enterprise involving such supply or, as the case may be, such an offer to supply; and
- (c) knowledge by the accused of the nature of the enterprise, i.e. that it involved supply of a drug or, as the case may be, offering to supply a drug.

Proof of actual supply is a prerequisite for an offence charged under s. 4(3)(b).

'Supplying' includes distributing (s. 37(1)).

Offering to Supply

An offer may be by words or conduct. If by words, it must be ascertained whether an offer to supply a controlled drug was made. If words are used, the defence under s. 28 (**see para. 1.6.9**) does not appear to apply (*R* v *Mitchell* [1992] Crim LR 723).

Whether the accused had a controlled drug in his/her possession, had access to controlled drugs or whether the substance in his/her possession was a controlled drug at all is immaterial (*R* v *Goodward* [1992] Crim LR 588). The offence is committed whether or not the offer is genuine and once an offer is made the offence is complete; it cannot be withdrawn. If the offer is made to an undercover police officer, the offence is still committed and the defendant cannot claim that such an offer was not a 'real' offer (*R* v *Kray* [1998] EWCA Crim 3211).

If the object of a conspiracy (**see chapter 1.3**) is to supply a controlled drug to a co-conspirator, any subsequent charge must make that clear; stating that the defendants conspired to supply the drug to 'another' implies that the supply was to be made to someone *other than any of the conspirators* (*R* v *Jackson* [2000] 1 Cr App R 97).

1.6.4.2 Specific Situations

Section 4A of the Misuse of Drugs Act 1971 requires courts to treat certain conditions as 'aggravating' factors when considering the seriousness of the offence under s. 4(3) if committed by a person aged 18 or over.

The conditions are either:

(1) that the offence was committed on or in the vicinity of school premises at a relevant time. 'Vicinity' is not defined and will be left to each court relying on its local knowledge. Other buildings and premises (e.g. cafes and shopping centres) can fall within this description and courts may decide that a route used to get to or from a school or a place where schoolchildren gather (even if trespassing) may be in the 'vicinity'. School premises are land used for the purposes of a school but *excluding* any land occupied solely as a dwelling *by a person employed at the school* (s. 4A(8)). A 'relevant time' is any time when the school premises are in use by people under the age of 18 (and one hour before the start/after the end of any such time) (s. 4A(5)); or

(2) that in connection with the commission of the offence, the offender used a 'courier' who, at the time the offence was committed, was under the age of 18. A person uses a courier if he/she causes or permits another person (the courier):
   (a) to deliver a controlled drug to a third person, or
   (b) to deliver a 'drug related consideration' (basically any money, goods etc. obtained or intended to be used in connection with the supply of a controlled drug) to him/herself or a third person (s. 4A(6) and (7)).

1.6.5 Possession with Intent to Supply

This is an offence that brings the concepts of 'possession' and 'supply' together.

OFFENCE: **Possession with Intent to Supply—*Misuse of Drugs Act 1971, s. 5(3)***

• Triable either way • Class A (life imprisonment and/or a fine on indictment; six months' imprisonment and/or a prescribed sum summarily) • Class B (14 years' imprisonment and/or a fine on indictment; six months' imprisonment and/or prescribed sum summarily) • Class C (14 years' imprisonment and/or a fine on indictment; three months' imprisonment and/or a fine summarily)

The Misuse of Drugs Act 1971, s. 5 states:

(3) Subject to section 28 of this Act, it is an offence for a person to have a controlled drug in his possession, whether lawfully or not, with intent to supply it to another in contravention of section 4(1) of this Act.

KEYNOTE

The lawfulness or otherwise of the *possession* is irrelevant; what matters is the lawfulness of the intended supply. If a police officer is in lawful possession of a controlled drug but intends to supply it unlawfully to another, the offence is committed.

You must show that the intention was that the *person in possession of the controlled drug* (rather than some third party) would supply it at some point in the future (*R* v *Greenfield* [1984] 78 Cr App R 179).

If more than one person has possession of the relevant controlled drug, you must show an individual intention to supply it by each person charged; it is not enough to show a joint venture whereby one or more parties simply knew of another's intent (*R* v *Downes* [1984] Crim LR 552). Given the decision of the Court of Appeal in *R* v *Kray* [1998] EWCA Crim 3211, possession with intent to supply a controlled drug to a person who is in fact an undercover police officer would appear to amount to an offence under this section.

All that is necessary in proving the offence under s. 5(3) is to show that the defendant had a controlled drug in his/her possession and intended to supply that substance to another. If the substance in the defendant's possession is a Class A drug and he/she intended to supply it to another person, the fact that he/she thought the drug was some other type of drug does not matter (*R* v *Leeson* [2000] 1 Cr App R 233).

Possession of drugs paraphernalia (e.g. clingfilm, contact details etc.) will be relevant evidence to show that a defendant was an active dealer in drugs but it does not prove the intention to supply and the trial judge will give a jury careful directions as to the probative value of such items found in the defendant's possession (*R* v *Haye* [2002] EWCA Crim 2476).

Where a Rastafarian was prosecuted for possessing cannabis with intent to supply others as part of their religious worship, he claimed that his rights under Articles 8 and 9 of the European Convention on Human Rights had been unnecessarily and disproportionately interfered with. The Court of Appeal, while reducing the sentence, held that such a prosecution had been properly brought (*R* v *Taylor* [2001] EWCA Crim 2263).

In proving an intention to supply, you may be able to adduce evidence of the defendant's unexplained wealth (*R* v *Smith (Ivor)* [1995] Crim LR 940) or the presence of large sums of money with the drugs seized (*R* v *Wright* [1994] Crim LR 55).

For the purposes of this offence (and the offence under s. 4 (supplying a controlled drug)), the 'another' cannot be someone charged in the same count, but can be someone charged in other counts in the same indictment.

1.6.6 Supply of Articles

OFFENCE: **Supplying Articles for Administering or Preparing Controlled Drugs—*Misuse of Drugs Act 1971, s. 9A***

- Triable summarily • Six months' imprisonment and/or a fine

The Misuse of Drugs Act 1971, s. 9A states:

(1) A person who supplies or offers to supply any article which may be used or adapted to be used (whether by itself or in combination with another article or other articles) in the administration by any person of a controlled drug to himself or another, believing that the article (or the article as adapted) is to be so used in circumstances where the administration is unlawful, is guilty of an offence.

(2) It is not an offence under subsection (1) above to supply or offer to supply a hypodermic syringe, or any part of one.

(3) A person who supplies or offers to supply any article which may be used to prepare a controlled drug for administration by any person to himself or another believing that the article is to be so used in circumstances where the administration is unlawful is guilty of an offence.

KEYNOTE

This offence is designed to address the provision of drug 'kits'.

The administration for which the articles are intended must be 'unlawful'. Section 9A states:

(4) For the purposes of this section, any administration of a controlled drug is unlawful except—
  (a) the administration by any person of a controlled drug to another in circumstances where the administration of the drug is not unlawful under section 4(1) of this Act, or
  (b) the administration by any person of a controlled drug, other than a temporary class drug, to himself in circumstances where having the controlled drug in his possession is not unlawful under section 5(1) of this Act, or
  (c) the administration by any person of a temporary class drug to himself in circumstances where having the drug in his possession is to be treated as excepted possession for the purposes of this Act (see section 7A(2)(c)).

(5) In this section, references to administration by any person of a controlled drug to himself include a reference to his administering it to himself with the assistance of another.

For the law relating to temporary class drugs, see para. 1.6.2.1.

1.6.7 Production of a Controlled Drug

OFFENCE: **Producing Controlled Drug—*Misuse of Drugs Act 1971, s. 4(2)***

• Triable either way • Class A (life imprisonment and/or a fine on indictment; six months' imprisonment and/or prescribed sum summarily) • Class B (14 years' imprisonment and/or a fine on indictment; six months' imprisonment and/or prescribed sum summarily) • Class C (five years' imprisonment and/or a fine on indictment; three months' imprisonment and/or a fine summarily)

The Misuse of Drugs Act 1971, s. 4 states:

(2) Subject to section 28 of this Act, it is an offence for a person—
  (a) to produce a controlled drug in contravention of subsection (1) ... ; or
  (b) to be concerned in the production of such a drug in contravention of that subsection by another.

KEYNOTE

'Produce' means producing by manufacture, cultivation or any other method and 'production' has a corresponding meaning (Misuse of Drugs Act 1971, s. 37).

Converting one form of a Class A drug into another is 'producing' (*R* v *Russell* (1991) 94 Cr App R 351), as is harvesting, cutting and stripping a cannabis plant (*R* v *Harris* [1996] 1 Cr App R 369).

The addition of adulterants or bulking agents can amount to the production of a controlled drug (*R* v *Williams* [2011] EWCA Crim 232).

Being 'concerned in the production' requires evidence that the accused played an identifiable role in the production of the drug in question. This was not satisfied where the accused simply permitted two others who were producing drugs to use his kitchen (*R* v *Farr* [1982] Crim LR 745).

1.6.8 Cultivation of Cannabis

OFFENCE: **Cultivation of Cannabis—*Misuse of Drugs Act 1971, s. 6***

• Triable either way • 14 years' imprisonment and/or a fine on indictment
• Six months' imprisonment and/or prescribed sum summarily

The Misuse of Drugs Act 1971, s. 6 states:

(1) Subject to any regulations under section 7 of this Act for the time being in force, it shall not be lawful for a person to cultivate any plant of the genus *Cannabis*.
(2) Subject to section 28 of this Act, it is an offence to cultivate any such plant in contravention of subsection (1) above.

KEYNOTE

The definition of 'cannabis' provided by s. 37(1) of the Misuse of Drugs Act 1971 (see para. 1.6.2.2) does not apply to the use of the word 'cannabis' in s. 6 of the Act, since the context of the instant offence clearly requires that the plant itself be cultivated.

'Cultivate' is not defined but it appears that you need to show some element of attention (e.g. watering) to the plant by the defendant in order to prove this offence. This offence does not permit police officers to tend plants which have been seized as evidence in order to preserve them as exhibits for court.

You need only show that the plant is of the genus *Cannabis* and that the defendant cultivated it; you need not show that the defendant knew it to be a cannabis plant (*R* v *Champ* [1981] 73 Cr App R 367).

1.6.9 General Defence under Section 28

There is a general defence (available under s. 28 of the Misuse of Drugs Act 1971) to a defendant charged with certain drugs offences. Section 28 applies to offences of:

- unlawful production (s. 4(2));
- unlawful supply (s. 4(3));
- unlawful possession (s. 5(2));
- possession with intent to supply (s. 5(3));
- unlawful cultivation of cannabis (s. 6(2));
- offences connected with opium (s. 9) (not covered in the NPPF Step 2 Exam syllabus).

The defences under s. 28 are *not* available in cases of conspiracy as conspiracy is not an offence under the 1971 Act (*R* v *McGowan* [1990] Crim LR 399).

The Misuse of Drugs Act 1971, s. 28 states:

(2) Subject to subsection (3) below, in any proceedings for an offence to which this section applies it shall be a defence for the accused to prove that he neither knew of nor suspected nor had reason to suspect the existence of some fact alleged by the prosecution which it is necessary for the prosecution to prove if he is to be convicted of the offence charged.
(3) Where in any proceedings for an offence to which this section applies it is necessary, if the accused is to be convicted of the offence charged, for the prosecution to prove that some substance or product involved in the alleged offence was the controlled drug which the prosecution alleges it to have been, and it is proved that the substance or product in question was that controlled drug, the accused—
    (a) shall not be acquitted of the offence charged by reason only of proving that he neither knew nor suspected nor had reason to suspect that the substance or product in question was the particular controlled drug alleged; but
    (b) shall be acquitted thereof—
        (i) if he proves that he neither believed nor suspected nor had reason to suspect that the substance or product in question was a controlled drug; or
        (ii) if he proves that he believed the substance or product in question to be a controlled drug, or a controlled drug of a description, such that, if it had in fact been that controlled drug, or a controlled drug of that description, he would not at the material time have been committing any offence to which this section applies.

KEYNOTE

This defence envisages three distinct situations:

- a lack of knowledge by the defendant of some fact which is alleged by the prosecution;
- a general lack of knowledge by the defendant about the drug in question;
- a conditional belief held by the defendant about the drug in question.

1.6.9.1 Lack of Knowledge of Some Alleged Fact

Section 28(2) allows a defence where the defendant did not *know, suspect* or *have reason to suspect* the existence of some fact which is essential to proving the case.

EXAMPLE

X is stopped in the street by Y who asks him to drop off a letter in an envelope at a nearby address in exchange for £10. As X approaches the address, he is arrested for possessing a controlled drug (which is inside the envelope), with intent to supply.

X is in 'possession' of the drug as he has custody of it and knows that the envelope contains *something*; what s. 28(2) does is to allow X a defence. X can discharge the evidential burden by showing that he neither knew nor suspected that the envelope contained a controlled drug, and that he neither knew nor suspected that he was supplying it to another. Both of these elements would be facts which the prosecution would have to allege to prove the offence.

If X knew the person to be a local drug dealer, or the reward for his errand was disproportionately large, say £1,000, then he may not be able to discharge this evidential burden.

The test for 'reason to suspect' is an *objective* one (*R* v *Young* [1984] 1 WLR 654). Consequently, where a 'reason to suspect' was not apparent to a defendant because he/she was too intoxicated to see it, the defence will not apply.

1.6.9.2 General Lack of Knowledge about Drug in Question

The wording of s. 28(3)(a) prevents defendants from claiming a 'defence' when what they thought was one type of controlled drug was in fact another different controlled drug.

Section 28(3)(b), however, has two strands, one concerned with the defendant's general lack of knowledge about the drug in question and the other (**see para. 1.6.9.3**) concerning the defendant's conditional belief.

Section 28(3)(b)(i) will allow defendants to prove that they did not believe or suspect the substance in question to be a controlled drug and that they had no reason so to suspect.

This clearly overlaps with s. 28(2), and X in the above example would also be able to claim this lack of knowledge. However, if he believed the envelope to contain amphetamine when it turned out to contain heroin, this lack of knowledge would not be permitted as a defence under s. 28(3).

1.6.9.3 Conditional Belief about Drug in Question

In contrast to s. 28(3)(a), the second strand of s. 28(3)(b)(ii) allows defendants to discharge the evidential burden by showing that they *did* believe the drug in question to be a particular controlled drug. It is then open to defendants to claim that, had the drug in question actually been the drug which they believed it to be, then they would not have committed any offences in relation to that drug.

EXAMPLE

A registered heroin addict is prescribed methadone. She collects her prescription from a chemist but is mistakenly given pethidine instead. She may be able to discharge the evidential burden by showing that she *believed* the drug in question to be methadone and that, if it had been, she would not have committed an offence by possessing it.

1.6.10 Regulated Possession and Supply of Controlled Drugs

The statutory framework governing controlled drugs does not simply ban substances and their possession outright. People working at various levels within the system need to be able to access, analyse and prescribe substances that are controlled by the 1971 Act. To that end, the framework takes account of the differing legitimate activities that may be relevant to individual people or particular circumstances. The majority of the exceptions and conditions imposed on this lawful possession and use can be found in the Misuse of Drugs Regulations 2001 and also in the Misuse of Drugs and Misuse of Drugs (Safe Custody) (Amendment) Regulations 2007 (SI 2007/2154).

The importance of the 2001 Regulations lies in the fact that they exempt certain drugs and certain people (pharmacists, laboratory workers, police officers etc.) from the main offences of possession, supply and importation *as long as they are acting lawfully within the parameters set out by those regulations*. A person in such an occupation who possesses, supplies or imports a controlled drug outside the terms of the exemptions will commit an offence.

Among the key regulations (SI 2001/3998) are:

- Regulation 4—which sets out those controlled drugs which will be exempted from the main offences of importation/exportation when they are contained in medicinal products.
- Regulation 5—allowing people holding a licence issued by the Secretary of State to produce, supply, offer to supply or have in their possession a controlled drug.
- Regulation 6—this allows anyone who is *lawfully* in possession of a controlled drug to give the drug back to the person from whom he/she obtained it and would cover registered heroin addicts properly returning methadone to a chemist. Regulation 6 also allows others to possess and supply certain controlled drugs under strict conditions. Regulation 6 allows police constables to have any controlled drug in their possession, or to supply such a drug to anyone who is lawfully allowed to have it (reg. 6(5)–(7)). These exemptions only apply where constables are *acting in the course of their duty as such*.

Other people who are given the same protection are Customs and Excise officers, postal workers and people engaged in conveying the drug to someone who may lawfully possess it. This last category would include civilian support staff, exhibits officers and others who, although not police constables, are nevertheless properly engaged in conveying controlled drugs to others.

The Misuse of Drugs (Amendments) (Cannabis and Licence Fees) (England, Wales and Scotland) Regulations 2018 (SI 2018/1055), in force as of 1 November 2018, amend the Misuse of Drugs Regulations 2001 to allow the wider use of cannabis-based products for medicinal use in humans, essentially for medical purposes. Additional controls, beyond those generally provided for in relation to drugs specified in sch. 2 to the 2001 Regulations, are imposed for cannabis-based products for medicinal use in humans. The law does not limit the types of conditions that can be considered for treatment and doctors will no longer need to seek approval from an expert panel in order for patients to access the medicines. The decision to prescribe these unlicensed medicines must be made by a specialist doctor—not a GP. These doctors focus on one field of medicine, such as neurology or paediatrics, and are listed on the General Medical Council's specialist register. They must make decisions on prescribing cannabis-based products for medicinal use on a case-by-case basis, and only when the patient has an unmet special clinical need that cannot be met by licensed products.

1.6.11 Occupiers, etc.

OFFENCE: **Occupier or Manager of Premises Permitting Drug Misuse—*Misuse of Drugs Act 1971, s. 8***

• Triable either way • Class A or B (14 years' imprisonment and/or a fine on indictment; six months' imprisonment and/or prescribed sum summarily) • Class C (14 years' imprisonment and/or a fine on indictment; three months' imprisonment and/or a fine summarily)

The Misuse of Drugs Act 1971, s. 8 states:

> A person commits an offence if, being the occupier or concerned in the management of any premises, he knowingly permits or suffers any of the following activities to take place on those premises, that is to say—
> (a) producing or attempting to produce a controlled drug in contravention of section 4(1) of this Act;
> (b) supplying or attempting to supply a controlled drug to another in contravention of section 4(1) of this Act, or offering to supply a controlled drug to another in contravention of section 4(1);
> (c) preparing opium for smoking;
> (d) smoking cannabis, cannabis resin or prepared opium.

KEYNOTE

Occupier

A person does not have to be a tenant, or to have estate in land, in order to be an 'occupier'. The term 'occupier' should be given a 'common sense' interpretation (*R* v *Tao* [1977] QB 141). For the purposes of s. 8, a person is in occupation of premises, whatever his/her legal status, if the prosecution can show that the accused exercised control, or had the authority of another, to exclude persons from the premises or to prohibit any of the activities referred to in s. 8 (*R* v *Coid* [1998] Crim LR 199).

Concerned in the Management

To be a manager, the accused must run, organise and plan the use of the premises (*R* v *Josephs* (1977) 65 Cr App R 253) and so must be involved in more than menial or routine duties.

'Premises' is not defined.

The permitting or suffering of these activities requires a degree of *mens rea* (*Sweet* v *Parsley* [1970] AC 132) even if that degree is little more than wilful blindness (*R* v *Thomas* (1976) 63 Cr App R 65). For the purposes of s. 8(b), and therefore presumably s. 8(a), it is not necessary to show that the defendant knew exactly which drugs were being produced, supplied etc.; only that they were 'controlled drugs' (*R* v *Bett* [1999] 1 WLR 2109).

However, the precise activities that are described under s. 8 will need to be proved. So, for instance, if the offence charged is one of knowingly permitting the smoking of cannabis (under subs. (d)), it must be shown that this actually took place; it is not enough that the owner/occupier had given permission for this to happen (*R* v *Auguste* [2003] EWCA Crim 3929). This is also the case when the offence charged is one of supplying or attempting to supply a controlled drug to another (under s. 8(b)), i.e. it must be shown that the supply or attempted supply actually took place (*R* v *McGee* [2012] EWCA Crim 613).

An occupier who permits the growing of cannabis plants commits this offence (*Taylor* v *Chief Constable of Kent* [1981] 1 WLR 606).

1.6.12 Community Protection Notices

Community Protection Notices (under part 4 of the Anti-social Behaviour, Crime and Policing Act 2014) provide powers allowing the police to close premises where drugs offences (amongst other things) take place. This area of law is dealt with in ***General Police Duties*, chapter 3.7**.

1.6.13 Assisting or Inducing Offence Outside United Kingdom

OFFENCE: **Assisting or Inducing Misuse of Drugs Offence Outside UK—*Misuse of Drugs Act 1971, s. 20***

- Triable either way • 14 years' imprisonment and/or a fine on indictment
- Six months' imprisonment and/or a fine summarily

The Misuse of Drugs Act 1971, s. 20 states:

> A person commits an offence if in the United Kingdom he assists in or induces the commission in any place outside the United Kingdom of an offence punishable under the provisions of a corresponding law in force in that place.

KEYNOTE

In order to prove this offence, you must show that the offence outside the United Kingdom actually took place. This offence may overlap with the offences of importation/exportation.

'Assisting' includes taking containers to another country in the knowledge that they will later be filled with a controlled drug and sent on to a third country (*R* v *Evans* (1977) 64 Cr App R 237). For an offence to amount to one under 'corresponding law' for these purposes, a certificate relating to the domestic law concerned with the misuse of drugs must be obtained from the government of the relevant country (s. 36).

1.6.14 Incitement

OFFENCE: **Incitement—*Misuse of Drugs Act 1971, s. 19***

- Triable and punishable as for substantive offence incited

The Misuse of Drugs Act 1971, s. 19 states:

> It is an offence for a person to incite another to commit an offence under any other provision of this Act.

KEYNOTE

A person inciting an undercover police officer may commit an offence under s. 19, even though there was no possibility of the officer actually being induced to commit the offence (*DPP* v *Armstrong* [2000] Crim LR 379).

1.6.15 Travel Restriction Orders

The Criminal Justice and Police Act 2001 allows courts (in practice, the Crown Court) to impose travel restrictions on offenders convicted of drug trafficking offences. Travel restriction orders prohibit offenders from leaving the United Kingdom at any time during the period beginning from their release from custody (other than on bail or temporary release for a fixed period) and up to the end of the order. The minimum period for such an order is two years (s. 33(3)); there is no maximum period prescribed in the legislation.

Where a court:

- has convicted a person of a drug trafficking offence; and
- it has determined that a sentence of four years or more is appropriate;

it is under a *duty* to consider whether or not a travel restriction order would be appropriate (s. 33). If the court decides not to impose an order, it must give its reasons for not doing so.

A 'drug trafficking offence' is defined by s. 34 of the Act and includes the production of a controlled drug (s. 4(2)), the supply of a controlled drug (s. 4(3)) and the importation/exportation offences under s. 3 along with inciting a person to commit these offences under s. 19 of the Misuse of Drugs Act 1971. It also includes aiding, abetting, counselling or procuring these offences.

The sentence of four years or more must be a single sentence of over four years (not an aggregate) in order to impose a travel restriction order.

Offenders may also be required to surrender their UK passport as part of the order.

An offender may apply to the court that made a restriction order to have it revoked or suspended (s. 35) and the court must consider the strict criteria set out in s. 35 when considering any such suspension or revocation. If an order is suspended, the offender has a legal obligation to be back in the United Kingdom when the period of suspension ends (s. 35(5)(a)).

OFFENCE: **Contravening a Travel Restriction Order—*Criminal Justice and Police Act 2001, s. 36***

- Triable either way • Five years' imprisonment and/or a fine on indictment
- Six months' imprisonment and/or a fine summarily

The Criminal Justice and Police Act 2001, s. 36 states:

(1) A person who leaves the United Kingdom at a time when he is prohibited from leaving it by a travel restriction order is guilty of an offence ...

(2) A person who is not in the United Kingdom at the end of a period during which a prohibition imposed on him by a travel restriction order has been suspended shall be guilty of an offence ...

KEYNOTE

These offences do not require a particular state of mind.

The first offence requires proof of two things: (a) that there was an order in existence in respect of the offender; and (b) that he/she left the United Kingdom during the time it was in force. There is no requirement that the person leave the United Kingdom *voluntarily* in order to be guilty (although he/she would have a good argument if he/she were taken out of the jurisdiction against his/her will or without his/her knowledge).

Travel restriction orders do not prevent the proper exercise of any prescribed power to remove a person from the United Kingdom (s. 37). So if the Secretary of State deports someone who is under a travel restriction order, that person would not commit the above offence.

The second offence requires proof that there was a suspended order in existence in respect of the offender and that, at the end of the suspension period, the offender was not in the United Kingdom.

Failing to deliver up a passport when required by an order is a summary offence (six months' imprisonment and/or a fine (s. 36(3))).

1.6.16 Police Powers

The 1971 Act provides a number of specific enforcement powers.

1.6.16.1 Powers of Entry, Search and Seizure

The Misuse of Drugs Act 1971, s. 23 states:

(1) A constable or other person authorised in that behalf by a general or special order of the Secretary of State (or in Northern Ireland either of the Secretary of State or the Ministry of Home Affairs for Northern Ireland) shall, for the purposes of the execution of this Act, have power to enter the premises of a person carrying on business as a producer or supplier of any controlled drugs and to demand the production of, and to inspect, any books or documents relating to dealings in any such drugs and to inspect any stocks of any such drugs.

(2) If a constable has reasonable grounds to suspect that any person is in possession of a controlled drug in contravention of this Act or of any regulations or orders made thereunder, the constable may—

(a) search that person, and detain him for the purpose of searching him;

(b) search any vehicle or vessel in which the constable suspects that the drug may be found, and for that purpose require the person in control of the vehicle or vessel to stop it;

(c) seize and detain, for the purposes of proceedings under this Act, anything found in the course of the search which appears to the constable to be evidence of an offence under this Act.

In this subsection 'vessel' includes a hovercraft within the meaning of the Hovercraft Act 1968; and nothing in this subsection shall prejudice any power of search or any power to seize or detain property which is exercisable by a constable apart from this subsection.

(3) If a justice of the peace (or in Scotland a justice of the peace, a magistrate or a sheriff) is satisfied by information on oath that there is reasonable ground for suspecting—

(a) that any controlled drugs are, in contravention of this Act or of any regulations or orders made thereunder, in the possession of a person on any premises; or

(b) that a document directly or indirectly relating to, or connected with, a transaction or dealing which was, or an intended transaction or dealing which would if carried out be, an offence under this Act, or in the case of a transaction or dealing carried out or intended to be carried out in a place outside the United Kingdom, an offence against the provisions of a corresponding law in force in that place, is in the possession of a person on any premises,

he may grant a warrant authorising any constable at any time or times within one month from the date of the warrant, to enter, if need be by force, the premises named in the warrant, and to search the premises and any persons found therein and, if there is reasonable ground for suspecting that an offence under this Act has been committed in relation to any controlled drugs found on the premises or in the possession of any such persons, or that a document so found is such a document as is mentioned in paragraph (b) above, to seize and detain those drugs or that document, as the case may be.

KEYNOTE

If a warrant obtained under s. 23 authorises the search of premises only, that in itself will not give the officers authority to search people found on those premises unless the officer can point to some other power authorising the search (*Hepburn* v *Chief Constable of Thames Valley* [2002] EWCA Civ 1841).

However, where the warrant authorises the search of premises and people, the Divisional Court has held that it is reasonable to restrict the movement of people within the premises to allow the search to be conducted properly (*DPP* v *Meaden* [2003] EWHC 3005 (Admin)).

PACE Code A (see ***General Police Duties***) applies to the exercise of any power to search people for controlled drugs specifically included in a warrant issued under s. 23.

A warrant issued under s. 23 of the Act lasts for a period of one month from the date of issue.

1.6.16.2 Obstruction

OFFENCE: **Obstruction—*Misuse of Drugs Act 1971, s. 23(4)***

- Triable either way • Two years' imprisonment and/or a fine on indictment
- Six months' imprisonment and/or a fine summarily

The Misuse of Drugs Act 1971, s. 23 states:

(4) A person commits an offence if he—
  (a) intentionally obstructs a person in the exercise of his powers under this section; or
  (b) conceals from a person acting in the exercise of his powers under subsection (1) above any such books, documents, stocks or drugs as are mentioned in that subsection; or
  (c) without reasonable excuse (proof of which shall lie on him) fails to produce any such books or documents as are so mentioned where their production is demanded by a person in the exercise of his powers under that subsection.

KEYNOTE

The offence of obstructing a person in the exercise of his/her powers is only committed if the obstruction was intentional (*R* v *Forde* (1985) 81 Cr App R 19).

1.6.17 Psychoactive and Intoxicating Substances

The Psychoactive Substances Act 2016 creates a number of offences and powers in relation to 'psychoactive substances', including the offence of supplying, or offering to supply, a psychoactive substance.

OFFENCE: **Supplying, or Offering to Supply, a Psychoactive Substance—*Psychoactive Substances Act 2016, s. 5***

- Triable either way • Seven years' imprisonment and/or fine on indictment
- Six months' imprisonment and/or a fine

The Psychoactive Substances Act 2016, s. 5 states:

(1) A person commits an offence if—
  (a) the person intentionally supplies a substance to another person,
  (b) the substance is a psychoactive substance,
  (c) the person knows or suspects, or ought to know or suspect, that the substance is a psychoactive substance, and
  (d) the person knows, or is reckless as to whether, the psychoactive substance is likely to be consumed by the person to whom it is supplied, or by some other person, for its psychoactive effects.

(2) A person ('P') commits an offence if—
  (a) P offers to supply a psychoactive substance to another person ('R'), and
  (b) P knows or is reckless as to whether R, or some other person, would, if P supplied a substance to R in accordance with the offer, be likely to consume the substance for its psychoactive effects.

(3) For the purposes of subsection 2(b), the reference to a substance's psychoactive effects includes a reference to the psychoactive effects which the substance would have if it were the substance which P had offered to supply to R.

(4) ...

KEYNOTE

'Psychoactive Substance' and 'Psychoactive Effect'

Section 2 of the Act defines a 'psychoactive substance' as any substance which is capable of producing a psychoactive effect in a person who consumes it.

A substance produces a psychoactive effect in a person if, by stimulating or depressing the person's central nervous system, it affects the person's mental functioning or emotional state. The main effect of psychoactive substances is on a person's brain, the major part of the central nervous system. By speeding up or slowing down activity on the central nervous system, psychoactive substances cause an alteration in the individual's state of consciousness by producing a range of effects including, but not limited to: hallucinations; change in alertness, perception of time and space, mood or empathy with others; and drowsiness (s. 2(2)).

An individual consumes a substance if the individual causes or allows the substance, or fumes given off by the substance, to enter the individual's body in any way. For example, this includes injecting, eating or drinking, snorting, inhaling and smoking (s. 2(3)).

For the supply offence, the conduct element is satisfied if a person supplies a substance to another person and that substance is a psychoactive substance. By virtue of s. 59(2)(b), supplying for these purposes covers distribution. The transaction does not need to result in payment or reward and would include social supply between friends.

There are three mental elements of the supply offence.

- First, the prosecution must show that the supplying of the substance is intentional.
- Second, the defendant must have known or suspected, or ought to have known or suspected, that the substance is a psychoactive substance.
- Third, the defendant must know, or be reckless as to whether, the psychoactive substance is likely to be consumed by the person to whom it is supplied or another person for its psychoactive effects.

The recklessness test would prevent a *head* shop proprietor escaping liability by arguing that because the psychoactive substances sold in his/her shop were labelled as 'plant food', 'research chemicals' or 'not for human consumption', he/she did not know that the substances were likely to be consumed.

The conduct element of the offering to supply offence is that the defendant offers to supply a psychoactive substance to another person. Such an offer could take the form of an advertisement, including a catalogue of psychoactive substances on display on a website with the facility to purchase online.

There is one mental element to the offer to supply offence, namely that the defendant knows, or is reckless as to whether, the substance that is being offered is likely to be consumed by the person to whom it is supplied or by another person for its psychoactive effects. This element of the offence is constructed in such a way that it would capture circumstances where a person purports to offer to supply a psychoactive substance to another person but, in fact, either has no intention of fulfilling his/her side of the deal or intends to pass off some other substance as a psychoactive substance. Subsection (3) ensures that such conduct would still be caught by the offering to supply offence.

It is worth noting that this offence covers the supply/offer to supply of a psychoactive substance to a person of *any age*.

OFFENCE: **Supply of Butane Lighter Refill to Person under 18—*Cigarette Lighter Refill (Safety) Regulations 1999, reg. 2***

- Triable summarily • Six months' imprisonment and/or a fine

The Cigarette Lighter Refill (Safety) Regulations 1999 (SI 1999/1844), reg. 2 states:

> No person shall supply any cigarette lighter refill canister containing butane or a substance with butane as a constituent part to any person under the age of eighteen years.

KEYNOTE

There is no requirement that the person believed or even suspected the person to be under 18. The 1999 Regulations are made under the Consumer Protection Act 1987, s. 11.

1.7 Firearms and Gun Crime

1.7.1 Introduction

The key piece of legislation governing firearms is the Firearms Act 1968. The Act covers numerous activities involving firearms and also deals with serious offences involving the criminal use of firearms.

1.7.2 Definitions—Firearm, Ammunition and Imitation Firearm

Before examining any offences relating to firearms, it is useful to begin with some definitions.

1.7.2.1 Firearms

The Firearms Act 1968, s. 57 states:

(1) In this Act, the expression 'firearm' means—
- (a) a lethal barrelled weapon (see subsection (1B));
- (b) a prohibited weapon;
- (c) a relevant component part in relation to a lethal barrelled weapon or a prohibited weapon (see subsection (1D));
- (d) an accessory to a lethal barrelled weapon or a prohibited weapon where the accessory is designed or adapted to diminish the noise or flash caused by firing the weapon.

KEYNOTE

Lethal Barrelled Weapon

A 'lethal barrelled weapon' means a barrelled weapon of any description from which a shot, bullet or other missile, with kinetic energy of more than one joule at the muzzle of the weapon, can be discharged (s. 57(1B)).

An item which could only discharge a missile in combination with other tools extraneous to it would not be a lethal barrelled weapon. Section 57(1) refers to the capacity of an item and not to its capacity in combination with other equipment. Thus, an old and damaged starting pistol with a partially drilled barrel could not be regarded as a 'prohibited weapon', and thus a firearm within s. 57, merely because it could be made to discharge a pellet with the aid of a vice-clamp, a mallet and a metal punch (*R* v *Bewley* [2012] EWCA Crim 1457).

Air pistols (*R* v *Thorpe* [1987] 1 WLR 383) and imitation revolvers (*Cafferata* v *Wilson* [1936] 3 All ER 149) have been held to be lethal barrelled weapons. A signalling pistol which fired explosive magnesium and phosphorous flares capable of killing at short range has been held to be lethal (*Read* v *Donovan* [1947] KB 326). That is not to say, however, that they will always be so; each case must be determined in the light of the evidence available.

Prohibited Weapon

The effect of s. 57(1)(b) is to make a prohibited weapon a firearm whether it is lethal barrelled or not. It follows that *all prohibited weapons are firearms* although not all firearms will be prohibited weapons (prohibited weapons are discussed at **para. 1.7.4**).

Relevant Component Part

For the purpose of s. 57(1)(c), each of the following items is a relevant component part in relation to a lethal barrelled weapon or a prohibited weapon—

- the barrel, chamber or cylinder;
- frame, body or receiver;
- a breech, block, bolt or other mechanism for containing the pressure of discharge at the rear of the chamber, but only where the item is capable of being used as a part of a lethal barrelled weapon or a prohibited weapon (s. 57(1D)).

Magazines, sights and furniture are not considered 'component parts'.

Accessory

While silencers and flash eliminators are accessories, a silencer or a flash eliminator *on its own* is not a firearm. However, if a defendant is found in possession of a silencer or flash eliminator which has been manufactured for a weapon *that is also in the defendant's possession*, that will be enough to bring the silencer or flash eliminator under s. 57(1). If the silencer is made for a different weapon, it may still come under the s. 57 definition but the prosecution will have to show that it could be used with the defendant's weapon and that he/she had it for that purpose (*R* v *Buckfield* [1998] Crim LR 673). Section 57(1) does not include telescopic sights or magazines.

Exception for Airsoft Guns

Airsoft is a skirmishing game in which players shoot small spherical plastic missiles at opponents from imitation firearms using compressed air.

An 'airsoft gun' is not to be regarded as a firearm for the purposes of this Act (s. 57A).

Section 57A(2) states that an 'airsoft gun' is a barrelled weapon of any description which—

- is designed to discharge only a small plastic missile (whether or not it is also capable of discharging any other kind of missile); and
- is not capable of discharging a missile (of any kind) with kinetic energy at the muzzle of the weapon that exceeds the permitted level.

A 'small plastic missile' is a missile made wholly or partly from plastics, is spherical and does not exceed 8 millimetres in diameter (s. 57A(3)).

The exemption is not absolute—if the kinetic energy at the muzzle exceeds the permitted level, then it will be a firearm. The 'permitted kinetic energy level' is:

- in the case of a weapon which is capable of discharging two or more missiles successively without repeated pressure on the trigger (an automatic weapon), 1.3 joules;
- in any other case (a single shot variant), 2.5 joules.

1.7.2.2 Deactivation of Firearms

A weapon ceases to be a firearm if it is deactivated in line with the provisions of the Firearms (Amendment) Act 1988, s. 8 which states:

> For the purposes of the principal Act and this Act it shall be presumed, unless the contrary is shown, that a firearm has been rendered incapable of discharging any shot, bullet or other missile, and has consequently ceased to be a firearm within the meaning of those Acts, if—
>
> (a) it bears a mark which has been approved by the Secretary of State for denoting that fact and which has been made either by one of the two companies mentioned in section 58(1) of the principal Act or by such other person as may be approved by the Secretary of State for the purposes of this section; and
>
> (b) that company or person has certified in writing that work has been carried out on the firearm in a manner approved by the Secretary of State for rendering it incapable of discharging any shot, bullet or other missile.

KEYNOTE

A deactivated weapon must remain in its complete state. Where it is disassembled, the parts that are then made available are capable of being reassembled into a working weapon and are therefore component parts of a firearm (*R* v *Ashton* [2007] EWCA Crim 234).

The 'two companies' referred to in s. 8(a) are the Society of the Mystery of Gunmakers of the City of London and the Birmingham Proof House.

1.7.2.3 Ammunition

Ammunition is defined by s. 57 of the Firearms Act 1968 which states:

(2) In this Act, the expression 'ammunition' means any ammunition for any firearm and includes grenades, bombs and other like missiles, whether capable of use with a firearm or not, and also includes prohibited ammunition.

KEYNOTE

The definition of ammunition does not include ingredients and components of ammunition; it is only assembled ammunition that is controlled under the Act. Empty cartridge cases, for example, are not 'ammunition'. The exception to this is missiles for ammunition prohibited under s. 5 of the Act, for example expanding or armour-piercing bullets. Such missiles are themselves regarded as 'ammunition' and are subject to control accordingly (s. 5(1A)(g)).

1.7.2.4 Imitation Firearm

Some, though not all, offences which regulate the use of firearms will also apply to *imitation* firearms. Whether they do so can be found either in the specific wording of the offence or by virtue of the Firearms Act 1982.

There are two types of imitation firearms:

- general imitations—those which have the appearance of firearms (which are covered by s. 57 of the Firearms Act 1968); and
- imitations of section 1 firearms—those which both have the appearance of a section 1 firearm and which can be readily converted into such a firearm (which are covered by ss. 1 and 2 of the Firearms Act 1982).

KEYNOTE

The 'general imitation' firearm definition is the most commonly used in firearms legislation. That definition is 'anything which has the appearance of being a firearm ... whether or not it is capable of discharging any shot, bullet or other missile'.

For that reason, the definition of an imitation of a section 1 firearm will be considered separately and dealt with later in this chapter. Therefore, when imitation firearms are referred to in legislation or future Keynotes, think of it as a 'general imitation' unless otherwise stated.

It has been held that the definition in s. 57 requires the defendant to be carrying a 'thing' which is separate and distinct from the person and therefore capable of being possessed (*R* v *Bentham* [2005] UKHL 18). Holding your fingers under your coat and pretending that it is a firearm (*Bentham*) will not therefore amount to an imitation firearm for the relevant offences, as an unsevered hand or finger was part of oneself and therefore could not be 'possessed' in the way envisaged by the Act. The 'imitation' must have the appearance of a firearm and it is not necessary for any object to have been constructed, adapted or altered so as to resemble a firearm (*R* v *Williams* [2006] EWCA Crim 1650). In *K* v *DPP* [2006] EWHC 2183 (Admin), it was held that in some circumstances a realistic toy gun, in this case a plastic ball-bearing gun, could become an imitation firearm. This category does not include anything which resembles a prohibited weapon that is designed or adapted to discharge noxious liquid etc.

Whether or not something has the appearance of being a firearm will be a question of fact for the jury/magistrate(s) to decide in each case.

1.7.3 Categories of Firearms and Related Offences

The law regulating firearms classifies weapons into several categories, each of which is specifically defined. These definitions have associated offences dealing with activities such as their possession etc. Alongside these offences are exemptions which allow those activities to be lawful.

1.7.4 Section 1 Firearm

There is a group of firearms which, although not a category defined in the 1968 Act, is subject to a number of offences including s. 1 (see below). Firearms which fall into this group are often referred to as 'section 1 firearms' and include all firearms except shotguns and conventional air weapons. However, shotguns which have been 'sawn off' (i.e. had their barrels shortened) are section 1 firearms, as are air weapons declared to be 'specially dangerous'.

Section 1 ammunition includes any ammunition for a firearm except:

- cartridges containing five or more shot, none of which is bigger than 0.36 inches in diameter;
- ammunition for an airgun, air rifle or air pistol; and
- blank cartridges not more than one inch in diameter (s. 1(4)).

1.7.4.1 Conversion

Some weapons which began their life as section 1 firearms or prohibited weapons will remain so even after their conversion to a shotgun, air weapon or other type of firearm (s. 7 of the Firearms (Amendment) Act 1988).

1.7.4.2 Possessing etc. Firearm or Ammunition without Certificate

OFFENCE: **Possessing etc. Firearm or Ammunition without Certificate—*Firearms Act 1968, s. 1***

- Triable either way • Five years' imprisonment and/or a fine on indictment
- Six months' imprisonment and/or a fine summarily

The Firearms Act 1968, s. 1 states:

> (1) Subject to any exemption under this Act, it is an offence for a person—
> (a) to have in his possession, or to purchase or acquire, a firearm to which this section applies without holding a firearm certificate in force at the time, or otherwise than as authorised by such a certificate;
> (b) to have in his possession, or to purchase or acquire, any ammunition to which this section applies without holding a firearm certificate in force at the time, or otherwise than as authorised by such a certificate, or in quantities in excess of those so authorised.

KEYNOTE

This offence relates to those firearms described above (**see para. 1.7.4**) as section 1 firearms.

If the firearm involved is a sawn-off shotgun, the offence becomes 'aggravated' (under s. 4(4)) and attracts a maximum penalty of seven years' imprisonment.

The Firearms Act 1982 applies to this section and so the 'general definition' of an imitation firearm *does not* apply. For this offence, the definition of an imitation firearm is one 'that has the appearance of a section 1 firearm and which can be readily converted into such a firearm' (which is covered by ss. 1 and 2 of the Firearms Act 1982).

The certificate referred to is issued by the chief officer of police under s. 26A. Such certificates may carry significant restrictions on the types of firearms which the holder is allowed, together with the circumstances under which he/she may have them (s. 44(1) of the Firearms (Amendment) Act 1997).

The issue of whether a certificate covers a particular category of weapon is a matter of law for the judge to decide and cannot be affected by the intentions or misunderstanding of the defendant (*R* v *Paul (Benjamin)* [1999] Crim LR 79).

A person may hold a European firearms pass or similar document, in which case he/she will be governed by the provisions of ss. 32A to 32C of the Firearms Act 1968.

If a person has such a certificate which allows the possession etc. of the firearm in question and under the particular circumstances encountered, no offence is committed.

Acquire will include hiring, accepting as a gift and borrowing, and 'acquisition' is to be construed accordingly (s. 57(4) of the Firearms Act 1968).

1.7.4.3 Shortening Section 1 Firearm

OFFENCE: **Shortening Barrel of Smooth-bore Section 1 Firearm to Less Than 24 Inches—*Firearms (Amendment) Act 1988, s. 6(1)***

- Triable either way • Five years' imprisonment and/or a fine on indictment
- Six months' imprisonment and/or a fine summarily

The Firearms (Amendment) Act 1988, s. 6 states:

(1) Subject to subsection (2) below, it is an offence to shorten to a length less than 24 inches the barrel of any smooth-bore gun to which section 1 of the principal Act applies other than one which has a barrel with a bore exceeding 2 inches in diameter; ...

KEYNOTE

The 'principal Act' is the Firearms Act 1968.

Section 6(2) of the Firearms (Amendment) Act 1988 exempts registered firearms dealers from the offence provided the shortening is done *for the sole purpose* of replacing a defective part of the barrel *so as to produce a new barrel having an overall length of at least 24 inches.*

The length of the barrel of a weapon will be measured from its muzzle to the point at which the charge is exploded (s. 57(6)(a) of the 1968 Act).

Once the shortening has taken place, the nature of the firearm will have changed in which case the person will also commit the relevant possession offence unless he/she has the appropriate authorisation.

1.7.5 Restrictions on Transfer of Firearms

The Firearms (Amendment) Act 1997 created a number of offences concerned with the transfer, lending, hiring etc. of firearms and ammunition. It is an offence to fail to comply with these requirements (ss. 32 to 35). The mode of trial and punishment depends on whether the weapon is a section 1 firearm or a shotgun.

In brief, a person 'transferring' (i.e. selling, letting on hire, lending or giving) a section 1 firearm or ammunition to another must:

- produce a certificate or permit entitling him/her to do so (s. 32(2)(a));
- comply with all the conditions of that certificate or permit (s. 32(2)(b)); and
- must personally hand the firearm or ammunition over to the receiver (s. 32(2)(c)).

The 1997 Act also requires that any person who is the holder of a certificate or permit who is involved in such a transfer (which includes lending a shotgun for a period of more than 72 hours) shall within seven days of the transfer give notice to the chief officer of police who granted the certificate or permit (s. 33(2)).

Notice is also required of certificate or permit holders where a firearm is lost, deactivated or destroyed or where ammunition is lost, or where firearms are sold outside Great Britain (see ss. 34 and 35).

OFFENCE: **Trade Transactions by Person not Registered as Firearms Dealer—*Firearms Act 1968, s. 3(1)***

- Triable summarily • Six months' imprisonment and/or a fine

The Firearms Act 1968, s. 3 states:

(1) A person commits an offence if, by way of trade or business, he—
(a) manufactures, sells, transfers, repairs, tests or proves any firearm or ammunition to which section 1 of this Act applies, or a shot gun;
(b) exposes for sale or transfer, or has in his possession for sale, transfer, repair, test or proof any such firearm or ammunition, or a shot gun, or
(c) sells or transfers an air weapon, exposes such a weapon for sale or transfer or has such a weapon in his possession for sale or transfer,
without being registered under this Act as a firearms dealer.

KEYNOTE

A registered firearms dealer is a person who, by way of trade or business, manufactures, sells, transfers, repairs, tests or proves firearms or ammunition to which s. 1 of this Act applies, or shotguns, or sells or transfers air weapons.

If the person undertakes the repair, proofing etc. of a section 1 firearm or ammunition or a shotgun otherwise than as a trade or business, he/she commits an offence (which is triable either way and is punishable by five years' imprisonment and/or a fine on indictment or by six months' imprisonment and/or a fine summarily) under s. 3(3) unless he/she can point to some authorisation under the Act allowing him/her to do so.

Section 3 goes on to create further either way offences of selling or transferring a firearm or ammunition to someone other than a registered firearms dealer or someone otherwise authorised under the Act to buy or acquire them and of falsifying certificates with a view to acquiring firearms.

Registration is under s. 33 of the 1968 Act.

'Transferring' is also defined under s. 57(4) and includes letting on hire, giving, lending and parting with possession.

Section 9(2) of the 1968 Act exempts auctioneers from the restrictions on selling and possessing for the purposes of sale of firearms and ammunition where the auctioneer has a permit from the chief officer of police. There are further defences provided by s. 9 (for carriers and warehouse staff) and also under s. 8 (transfer to people authorised to possess firearms without a certificate).

1.7.6 Imitation Firearm Offences

OFFENCE: **Converting Imitation Firearm—*Firearms Act 1968, s. 4(3)***

- Triable either way • Five years' imprisonment and/or a fine on indictment
- Six months' imprisonment and/or a fine summarily

The Firearms Act 1968, s. 4 states:

(3) It is an offence for a person other than a registered firearms dealer to convert into a firearm anything which, though having the appearance of being a firearm, is so constructed as to be incapable of discharging any missile through its barrel.

KEYNOTE

This offence involves the conversion of anything which has the appearance of a firearm so that it can be fired. Once the conversion has taken place, the nature of the imitation firearm will have changed, in which case the person will also commit the relevant possession offences unless he/she has the appropriate authorisation.

OFFENCE: **Possession of Articles for Use in Connection with Conversion—*Firearms Act 1968, s. 4A***

- Triable either way • Five years' imprisonment and/or a fine on indictment
- Six months' imprisonment and/or a fine summarily

The Firearms Act 1968, s. 4A states:

(1) A person, other than a registered firearms dealer, commits an offence if—
 (a) the person has in his or her possession or under his or her control an article that is capable of being used (whether by itself or with other articles) to convert an imitation firearm into a firearm, and
 (b) the person intends to use the article (whether by itself or with other articles) to convert an imitation firearm into a firearm.

KEYNOTE

This is not simply about mere possession or control—that possession or control must be accompanied by the relevant mental intent (to use the article to convert an imitation firearm into a firearm).

1.7.6.1 Violent Crime Reduction Act 2006—Imitation Firearm Offences

Sections 36 to 41 of the Violent Crime Reduction Act 2006 created three specific summary offences to deal with the misuse of firearms:

Section 36 makes it an offence to manufacture, import, modify or sell *realistic imitation firearms* as defined in s. 38.

Section 39 makes it an offence to manufacture, modify or import an imitation firearm that does not conform to specifications set out in regulations to be made by the Secretary of State.

Section 40 inserted s. 24A into the 1968 Act and makes it an offence to sell an imitation firearm to a person under 18. It also makes it an offence for a person under 18 to purchase an imitation firearm.

KEYNOTE

For the purposes of the 2006 Act, an 'imitation firearm' is defined as that used in the Firearms Act 1968, i.e. in the 'general sense' (see para. 1.7.2.4). A 'realistic imitation firearm' is effectively a 'sub-category' of an imitation firearm in the general sense. A 'realistic imitation firearm' is defined as an imitation firearm which has an appearance that is so realistic as to make it indistinguishable, for all practical purposes, from a real firearm and is neither a deactivated firearm nor itself an antique (s. 38(1)).

An imitation firearm will be regarded as distinguishable if its size, shape or principal colour is unrealistic for a real firearm (s. 38(3)). The Violent Crime Reduction Act 2006 (Realistic Imitation Firearms) Regulations 2007 (SI 2007/2606) provide defences for an offence under s. 36, and make provision in connection with the definition of 'realistic imitation firearm' in s. 38, specifying the sizes and colours which are to be regarded as unrealistic for a real firearm.

1.7.7 Prohibited Weapon

A prohibited weapon is defined under the Firearms Act 1968, s. 5. The definition covers the more powerful or potentially destructive firearms and their ammunition (such as automatic weapons and specialist ammunition) and also small firearms.

The test as to whether a weapon is a 'prohibited' weapon is a purely objective one and is not affected by the intentions of the defendant. Therefore, where a firearm was capable of successively discharging two or more missiles without repeated pressure on the trigger, that weapon was 'prohibited' irrespective of the intentions of the firearms dealer who was in possession of it (*R* v *Law* [1999] Crim LR 837).

1.7.7.1 List of Prohibited Weapons and Ammunition

The full list of prohibited weapons and ammunition is contained in s. 5(1) and (1A) of the Firearms Act 1968. This list often (but not always) relates to weapons used in a military context and includes:

- automatic weapons;
- most self-loading or pump-action weapons;
- any firearm which either has a barrel less than 30 cm in length or is less than 60 cm in length overall, other than an air weapon, a muzzle-loading gun or a firearm designed as signalling apparatus;
- most smooth-bore revolvers;
- any weapon, of whatever description, designed or adapted for the discharge of any noxious liquid, gas or other thing;
- any air rifle, air gun or air pistol which uses, or is designed or adapted for use with, a self-contained gas cartridge system;
- any cartridge with a bullet designed to explode on or immediately before impact;
- if capable of being used with a firearm of any description, any grenade or bomb (or other like missile) or rocket or shell designed to explode on or immediately before impact.

KEYNOTE

In relation to weapons designed or adapted for the discharge of any noxious liquid, gas or other thing, taking an empty washing-up bottle and filling it with hydrochloric acid does not amount to adapting it, neither is such a thing a 'weapon' for the purposes of s. 5 (*R* v *Formosa*; *R* v *Upton* [1991] 2 QB 1). This is because to do so does not change the nature of the washing-up bottle itself as the bottle has not been adapted or altered and is therefore not a weapon 'designed or adapted' for the discharge of any noxious liquid etc. The same logic applies to a water pistol filled with ammonia (*R* v *Titus* [1971] Crim LR 279). Any other approach could be problematic to say the least. In the words of Lloyd LJ (in *Formosa*), '[this] would mean that a householder who filled a milk bottle with acid in order to destroy a wasps' nest would be in possession of a weapon adapted for the discharge of a noxious liquid and would therefore be guilty of the offence of possessing a prohibited weapon; until, of course, he had used the acid for the purpose in question when the milk bottle would revert to its pristine innocence. That could not be right.'

An electric 'stun gun' has been held to be a prohibited weapon as it discharges an electric current (*Flack* v *Baldry* [1988] 1 WLR 393) and it continues to be such even if it is not working (*Brown* v *DPP* (1992) *The Times*, 27 March).

1.7.7.2 Possessing or Purchasing Prohibited Weapons or Ammunition

OFFENCE: **Possessing or Purchasing Prohibited Weapons or Ammunition—*Firearms Act 1968, s. 5***

- Triable either way • 10 years' imprisonment and/or a fine on indictment
- Six months' imprisonment and/or a fine summarily

The Firearms Act 1968, s. 5 states:

> (1) A person commits an offence if, without the authority of the Secretary of State or the Scottish Ministers, he has in his possession, or purchases, or acquires [a prohibited weapon or ammunition] ...

KEYNOTE

A person may still be in possession of a prohibited weapon even when it is in parts and the accused is in possession of those parts (*R* v *Pannell* (1983) 76 Cr App R 53), or where the weapon is missing an essential part such as the trigger (*R* v *Clarke* [1986] 1 WLR 209).

1.7.7.3 Possession

As an offence contrary to s. 5 of the 1968 Act is a strict liability offence, there is no need to prove that the accused knew the nature of the thing he/she possessed (that it was a firearm or ammunition) in order to prove the offence—it is sufficient to establish that the accused was in possession of the article (*R* v *Deyemi* [2007] EWCA Crim 2060). For example, in *Price* v *DPP* [1996] CLY 1469 an accused was held to have been in possession of the contents of a rucksack (ammunition) notwithstanding that he had no idea of its contents, and was indeed mistaken as to whom it belonged, and as to its nature and quality. If an accused is carrying a rucksack and the rucksack contains ammunition for a section 1 firearm, the accused is in 'possession' of the ammunition irrespective of his/her knowledge or ignorance of its presence in the rucksack (*R* v *Waller* [1991] Crim LR 381; *R* v *Cremin* [2007] EWCA Crim 666).

'Possession' means the firearm or ammunition is in the custody or under the control of the defendant (in *Sullivan* v *Earl of Caithness* [1976] QB 966, it was held that a person can remain in possession of a firearm even if someone else has custody of it).

1.7.7.4 Prohibited Weapons—Exemptions

Section 5A of the Firearms Act 1968 provides for a number of occasions where the authority of the Secretary of State will not be required to possess or deal with certain weapons under certain conditions.

The main areas covered by s. 5A are:

- authorised collectors and firearms dealers possessing or being involved in transactions of weapons and ammunition;
- authorised people being involved in transactions of particular ammunition used for lawful shooting and slaughtering of animals, the management of an estate or the protection of other animals and humans.

Special exemptions

There are a number of special exemptions to the offences under s. 5 of the Firearms Act 1968 involving firearms (under s. 5(1)(aba)).

The exemptions include:

- **Slaughterers**—a slaughterer, if entitled under s. 10 of the 1968 Act, may possess a slaughtering instrument. In addition, persons authorised by certificate to possess, buy, acquire, sell or transfer slaughtering instruments are exempt from the provisions of s. 5 (s. 2 of the Firearms (Amendment) Act 1997).

- **Humane killing of animals**—this exemption allows a person authorised by certificate to possess, buy, acquire or transfer a firearm solely for use in connection with the humane killing of animals (s. 3 of the Firearms (Amendment) Act 1997). When determining whether a firearm falls within the meaning of a 'humane killer', the definition of a 'slaughtering instrument' under s. 57(4) may be referred to (*R* v *Paul (Benjamin)* [1999] Crim LR 79).
- **Shot pistols for vermin**—this exemption allows a person authorised by certificate to possess, buy, acquire or transfer a 'shot pistol' solely for the shooting of vermin (s. 4(1) of the Firearms (Amendment) Act 1997). A 'shot pistol' is a smooth-bored gun chambered for .410 cartridges or 9 mm rim-fire cartridges (s. 4(2)).
- **Treatment of animals**—this exemption allows a person authorised by certificate to possess, buy, acquire or transfer a firearm for use in connection with the treatment of animals or for the purpose of tranquillising or otherwise treating any animal (s. 8 of the Firearms (Amendment) Act 1997). This exemption also applies to offences involving firearms under s. 5(1)(b) and (c).
- **Races at athletic meetings**—a person may possess a firearm at an athletic meeting for the purpose of starting races at that meeting (s. 5(a) of the Firearms (Amendment) Act 1997). Similarly, a person authorised by certificate to possess, buy or acquire a firearm solely for the purposes of starting such races may possess, buy, acquire, sell or transfer a firearm for such a purpose (s. 5(b)). The use of this exemption is less commonplace as many sporting events use electronic starting systems rather than a starting pistol.
- **Trophies of war**—a person authorised by certificate to do so may possess a firearm which was acquired as a trophy before 1 January 1946 (s. 6 of the Firearms (Amendment) Act 1997).
- **Firearms of historic interest**—some firearms are felt to be of particular historical, aesthetic or technical interest. Section 7(4) of the Firearms (Amendment) Act 1997 makes detailed provision for the exemption of such firearms, exemptions which exist in addition to the general exemptions under s. 58 of the Firearms Act 1968 (**see para. 1.7.8**).
- **Air weapons**—in relation to air weapons with self-contained gas cartridges, owned before 20 January 2004, owners, if they applied for a firearms certificate before 1 April 2004, may retain their weapons.

1.7.8 General Exemptions

The general exemptions apply to the provisions of ss. 1 to 5 of the Firearms Act 1968. They include:

Police Permit Holders

Under s. 7(1) of the 1968 Act, the chief officer of police may grant a permit authorising the possession of firearms or ammunition under the conditions specified in the permit.

Clubs, Athletics and Sporting Purposes

Section 11 of the 1968 Act provides exemptions for a person:

- borrowing the firearm/ammunition from a certificate holder *for sporting purposes only* but where the person carrying the firearm/ammunition is under 18, this applies only if the other person is aged 18 or over (s. 11(1));
- of or over the age of 18 may possess a firearm at an athletic meeting for the purposes of starting races (s. 11(2)) (**see para. 1.7.7.4** for comments on the prevalence of starting pistols);

- in charge of a miniature rifle range buying, acquiring or possessing miniature rifles and ammunition, and using them at such a rifle range (s. 11(4));
- who is a member of an approved rifle club, miniature rifle club or pistol club to possess a firearm or ammunition *when engaged as a club member in target practice* (s. 15(1) of the Firearms (Amendment) Act 1988);
- using a shotgun at a time and place approved by the chief officer of police for shooting at artificial targets (s. 11(6)).

Authorised Lending and Possession of Firearms for Hunting etc.

Section 11A of the Firearms Act 1968 states:

> (1) A person ('the borrower') may, without holding a certificate under this Act, borrow a rifle or shot gun from another person on private premises ('the lender') and have the rifle or shot gun in his or her possession on those premises if—
> (a) the four conditions set out in subsections (2) to (5) are met, and
> (b) in the case of a rifle, the borrower is aged 17 or over.
>
> (2) The first condition is that the borrowing and possession of the rifle or shot gun are for either or both of the following purposes—
> (a) hunting animals or shooting game or vermin;
> (b) shooting at artificial targets.
>
> (3) The second condition is that the lender—
> (a) is aged 18 or over,
> (b) holds a certificate under this Act in respect of the rifle or shot gun, and
> (c) is either—
> (i) a person who has a right to allow others to enter the premises for the purposes of hunting animals or shooting game or vermin, or
> (ii) a person who is authorised in writing by a person mentioned in sub-paragraph (i) to lend the rifle or shot gun on the premises (whether generally or to persons specified in the authorisation who include the borrower).
>
> (4) The third condition is that the borrower's possession and use of the rifle or shot gun complies with any conditions as to those matters specified in the lender's certificate under this Act.
>
> (5) The fourth condition is that, during the period for which the rifle or shot gun is borrowed, the borrower is in the presence of the lender or—
> (a) where a rifle is borrowed, a person who, although not the lender, is aged 18 or over, holds a certificate under this Act in respect of that rifle and is a person described in subsection (3)(c)(i) or (ii);
> (b) where a shot gun is borrowed, a person who, although not the lender, is aged 18 or over, holds a certificate under this Act in respect of that shot gun or another shot gun and is a person described in subsection (3)(c)(i) or (ii).
>
> (6) Where a rifle is borrowed on any premises in reliance on subsection (1), the borrower may, without holding a firearm certificate, purchase or acquire ammunition on the premises, and have the ammunition in his or her possession on those premises for the period for which the firearm is borrowed, if—
> (a) the ammunition is for use with the firearm,
> (b) the lender's firearm certificate authorises the lender to have in his or her possession during that period ammunition of a quantity not less than that purchased or acquired by, and in the possession of, the borrower, and
> (c) the borrower's possession and use of the ammunition complies with any conditions as to those matters specified in the certificate

Visitors' Permits

Section 17 of the Firearms (Amendment) Act 1988 provides for the issuing of a visitor's permit by a chief officer of police and for the possession of firearms and ammunition by the holder of such a permit.

Antiques as Ornaments or Curiosities

Section 58(2) of the 1968 Act allows for the sale, buying, transfer, acquisition or possession of antique firearms *as curiosities or ornaments*. Whether a firearm is such an antique will be a question of fact to be determined by the court in each case. Mere belief in the fact that a firearm is an antique will not be enough (*R* v *Howells* [1977] QB 614).

Authorised firearms dealers

Section 8(1) of the 1968 Act provides for registered firearms dealers (or their employees) to possess, acquire or buy firearms or ammunition in the ordinary course of their business without a certificate. If the possession etc. is not in the ordinary course of their business, the exemption will not apply.

1.7.9 Criminal Use of Firearms

There is a series of firearms offences linked to criminal behaviour. The aggravating factor of the presence of a firearm is evidenced by the fact that the majority carry a life imprisonment sentence; those that do not, still carry 10 years' imprisonment.

1.7.9.1 Possession with Intent to Endanger Life

OFFENCE: **Possession with intent to Endanger Life—*Firearms Act 1968, s. 16***

- Triable on indictment • Life imprisonment and/or a fine

The Firearms Act 1968, s. 16 states:

> It is an offence for a person to have in his possession any firearm or ammunition with intent by means thereof to endanger life or to enable another person by means thereof to endanger life, whether any injury has been caused or not.

KEYNOTE

This offence cannot be committed by possessing an imitation firearm.

The offence involves 'possession' so there is no need for the firearm or ammunition to be produced/shown to another.

You will have to show an intention by the defendant to behave in a way that he/she knows will in fact endanger the life of another (*R* v *Brown and Ciarla* [1995] Crim LR 328); the intention is not to enable the defendant or another to *kill*. That intent does not have to be an immediate one and it may be conditional, e.g. an intent to shoot someone if they do not do as they are asked (*R* v *Bentham* [1973] QB 357).

The life endangered must be the life of 'another', not the defendant's (*R* v *Norton* [1977] Crim LR 478) so possession with intent to commit suicide would not be covered by the offence. The person whose life is endangered may be outside the United Kingdom (*R* v *El-Hakkaoui* [1975] 1 WLR 396).

The firearm or ammunition must provide the means by which life is endangered; it is not enough to have a firearm or ammunition at the time when life is endangered by some other means (e.g. by dangerous driving).

Self-defence can be raised in answer to a charge under s. 16 of the 1968 Act but such circumstances will be very unusual (*R* v *Georgiades* [1989] 1 WLR 759). This defence could potentially apply where the defendant is carrying a firearm for his/her own defence anticipating an imminent attack (*R* v *Salih* [2007] EWCA Crim 2750).

1.7.9.2 Possession with Intent to Cause Fear of Violence

OFFENCE: **Possession with Intent to Cause Fear of Violence—*Firearms Act 1968, s. 16A***

- Triable on indictment • 10 years' imprisonment and/or a fine

The Firearms Act 1968, s. 16A states:

> It is an offence for a person to have in his possession any firearm or imitation firearm with intent—
> (a) by means thereof to cause, or
> (b) to enable another person by means thereof to cause,
> any person to believe that unlawful violence will be used against him or another person.

KEYNOTE

Section 16A is committed by possession, accompanied by an intention to cause fear of violence at or immediately before the defendant's actions which are designed to cause such fear (*R* v *Goluchowski* [2006] EWCA Crim 1972). There is no need for a firearm/imitation firearm to be produced or shown to anyone, though it must provide the 'means' of the threat. Possession of a firearm/imitation firearm while making a general threat to someone who does not know of its presence is unlikely to fall within this section.

This offence includes imitation firearms in the general sense (**see para. 1.7.2.4**). In *K* v *DPP* [2006] EWHC 2183 (Admin), the appellant's submission that the knowledge of all those present, and in particular the complainant, that the gun was an imitation firearm was such as to make the commission of the offence impossible was rejected. K's purpose or intention was to make the complainant fear violence and it was not fatal to the conviction that the complainant was aware that it was an imitation firearm.

1.7.9.3 Using Firearm to Resist Arrest

OFFENCE: **Using Firearm to Resist Arrest—*Firearms Act 1968, s. 17(1)***

- Triable on indictment • Life imprisonment and/or a fine

The Firearms Act 1968, s. 17 states:

> (1) It is an offence for a person to make or attempt to make any use whatsoever of a firearm or imitation firearm with intent to resist or prevent the lawful arrest or detention of himself or another person.

KEYNOTE

The 'firearm' to which s. 17 refers is that defined at **para. 1.7.2.1**, except component parts and silencers/flash diminishers (s. 17(4)). For that reason, while the offence includes imitation firearms in the general sense (**see para. 1.7.2.4**), it does not include imitation component parts etc.

This offence requires proof, not of possession, but of evidence that the defendant made some *actual use* of the firearm and did so intending to resist/prevent the arrest of him/herself or someone else. Any arrest which the defendant intended to prevent/resist must have been 'lawful'.

1.7.9.4 Having Firearm with Intent to Commit Indictable Offence or Resist Arrest

OFFENCE: **Having Firearm with Intent to Commit an Indictable Offence or Resist Arrest—*Firearms Act 1968, s. 18(1)***

- Triable on indictment • Life imprisonment and/or a fine

The Firearms Act 1968, s. 18 states:

> (1) It is an offence for a person to have with him a firearm or imitation firearm with intent to commit an indictable offence, or to resist arrest or prevent the arrest of another, in either case while he has the firearm or imitation firearm with him.

KEYNOTE

This offence requires the defendant to 'have with him' a firearm. This is a more restrictive expression than 'possession' and requires that the firearm is 'readily accessible' to the defendant. In *R* v *Pawlicki* [1992] 1 WLR 827, the Court of Appeal decided that defendants in an auction room had firearms 'with them' which were in a car 50 yards away. Where a defendant left a firearm in his house which was a few miles from the scene of the relevant criminal offence, it was held that this was not enough to meet the requirement of 'having with him' (*R* v *Bradish* [2004] EWCA Crim 1340). Despite this narrower meaning, the defendant does not have to be shown to have been 'carrying' the firearm (*R* v *Kelt* [1977] 1 WLR 1365).

In *R* v *Stoddart* [1998] 2 Cr App R 25, the Court of Appeal made it clear that there are three elements to this offence:

(a) that the accused had with him a firearm or imitation firearm;
(b) that he intended to have it with him; and
(c) that at the same time he had the intention to commit an indictable offence or to resist or prevent arrest.

Proving (b) and (c) is made easier by s. 18(2) of the Act (below).

Intention

In proving the intent for this offence, s. 18 states:

(2) In proceedings for an offence under this section proof that the accused had a firearm or imitation firearm with him and intended to commit an offence, or to resist or prevent arrest, is evidence that he intended to have it with him while doing so.

It is not necessary to show that the defendant intended to use the firearm to commit the indictable offence or to prevent/resist the arrest (*Stoddart*).

The mental element is an essential part of this offence, so if the defendant only formed the intent as a result of duress (as to which, **see chapter 1.4**), this ingredient will not have been established (*R* v *Fisher* [2004] EWCA Crim 1190).

Section 18 does not appear to require that any arrest be 'lawful'.

This offence includes imitation firearms in the general sense **(see para. 1.7.2.4)**.

The power of entry and search under s. 47 of the 1968 Act applies to this offence **(see para. 1.7.11)**.

1.7.9.5 Possessing Firearm while Committing a Schedule 1 Offence

OFFENCE: **Possessing Firearm while Committing or Being Arrested for sch. 1 Offence—*Firearms Act 1968, s. 17(2)***

- Triable on indictment • Life imprisonment and/or a fine

The Firearms Act 1968, s. 17 states:

(2) If a person, at the time of his committing or being arrested for an offence specified in schedule 1 to this Act, has in his possession a firearm or imitation firearm, he shall be guilty of an offence under this subsection unless he shows that he had it in his possession for a lawful object.

KEYNOTE

This offence may be committed in two ways; either by being in possession of the weapon *at the time of committing* the sch. 1 offence or by being in possession of it *at the time of being arrested* for such an offence. In the second case, there may be some time between actually committing the sch. 1 offence and being arrested for it. Nevertheless, if the defendant is in possession of the firearm at the time of his/her arrest, the offence is committed (unless he/she can show that it was for a lawful purpose).

There is no need for the defendant to be subsequently *convicted* of the sch. 1 offence, or even to prove that it has been committed; all that is needed is to show that the defendant, at the time of the commission of the sch. 1 offence and/or of his/her arrest for a sch. 1 offence, had a firearm/imitation firearm in his/her possession (*R* v *Nelson* [2001] QB 55).

It is for the defendant to prove that the firearm was in his/her possession for a lawful purpose.

This offence includes imitation firearms in the general sense (**see para. 1.7.2.4**).

Schedule 1 Offences

There are a number of offences contained in sch. 1 but the *main* offences may be remembered by using the mnemonic ACTOR:

- Abduction—part I of the Child Abduction Act 1984 (child abduction).
- Criminal damage—s. 1 of the Criminal Damage Act 1971.
- Theft, robbery, burglary, blackmail and taking a conveyance—Theft Act 1968.
- Offences against the person—assaults and woundings (ss. 20 and 47 of the Offences Against the Person Act 1861), assault on police (s. 89 of the Police Act 1996) and civilian custody officers (s. 90(1) of the Criminal Justice Act 1991 and s. 13(1) of the Criminal Justice and Public Order Act 1994).
- Rape and other sexual/abduction offences—the following offences under the Sexual Offences Act 2003: s. 1 (rape), s. 2 (assault by penetration), s. 4 (causing a person to engage in sexual activity without consent), where the activity caused involved penetration within subs. (4)(a)–(d) of that section, s. 5 and s. 6 (rape and assault of a child under 13), s. 8 (causing or inciting a child under 13 to engage in sexual activity), where an activity involving penetration within subs. (2)(a)–(d) of that section was caused, s. 30 and s. 31 (sexual activity with/causing or inciting a person with a mental disorder impeding choice), where the touching involved or activity caused penetration within subs. (3)(a)–(d) of that section. Also offences under part I of the Child Abduction Act 1984.

Although covering several types of assault, sch. 1 does not extend to wounding/causing grievous bodily harm with intent (s. 18 of the Offences Against the Person Act 1861). Schedule 1 also covers the aiding, abetting or attempting to commit such offences.

1.7.9.6 Using Someone to Mind a Weapon

OFFENCE: **Using Someone to Mind a Weapon—*Violent Crime Reduction Act 2006, s. 28(1)***

- Triable on indictment • 10 years' imprisonment and/or a fine (firearms etc.)
- Four years' imprisonment and/or a fine (offensive weapons etc.)

The Violent Crime Reduction Act 2006, s. 28 states:

(1) A person is guilty of an offence if—
  (a) he uses another to look after, hide or transport a dangerous weapon for him; and
  (b) he does so under arrangements or in circumstances that facilitate, or are intended to facilitate, the weapon's being available to him for an unlawful purpose.

(2) For the purposes of this section the cases in which a dangerous weapon is to be regarded as available to a person for an unlawful purpose include any case where—
  (a) the weapon is available for him to take possession of it at a time and place; and
  (b) his possession of the weapon at that time and place would constitute, or be likely to involve or to lead to, the commission by him of an offence.

KEYNOTE

The offence was designed to close a perceived loophole in the law where people escaped prosecution by entrusting their weapon to another person, in particular to a child. Using children in this way may risk injury to them and draw them into gun/knife crime as a result of their early association with weapons. Using a minor to mind a firearm is an aggravating factor attracting harsher sentences (s. 29(13) and (14)(a)).

A 'dangerous weapon' means a firearm *other than* an air weapon or a component part of, or accessory to, an air weapon; or a weapon to which s. 141 or 141A of the Criminal Justice Act 1988 applies (specified offensive weapons, knives and bladed weapons—**see chapter 1.8**) (s. 28(3)).

1.7.10 Further Firearms Offences

Alongside offences associated with the criminal use of firearms are several offences dealing with an offender 'having with him' a firearm in a public place and whilst trespassing.

1.7.10.1 Having Firearm or Imitation Firearm in Public Place

OFFENCE: **Having Firearm/Imitation Firearm in Public Place—*Firearms Act 1968, s. 19***

• Triable either way • Seven years' imprisonment and/or a fine on indictment (if the weapon is an imitation firearm, 12 months' imprisonment and/or a fine)

• If the weapon is an air weapon, six months' imprisonment and/or a fine

The Firearms Act 1968, s. 19 states:

> A person commits an offence if, without lawful authority or reasonable excuse (the proof whereof lies on him), he has with him in a public place—
> (a) a loaded shot gun,
> (b) an air weapon (whether loaded or not),
> (c) any other firearm (whether loaded or not) together with ammunition suitable for use in that firearm, or
> (d) an imitation firearm.

KEYNOTE

The offence is triable only summarily when the firearm is an air weapon. The s. 19 offence may be committed whether the air weapon is lethal barrelled or not (*Street* v *DPP* [2003] EWHC 86 (Admin)).

A 'public place' includes any highway and any other premises or place to which, at the material time, the public have or are permitted to have access whether on payment or otherwise (s. 57(4) of the Act).

If the weapon is a shotgun, it must be loaded. 'Loaded' means there is ammunition in the chamber or barrel (or in any magazine or other device) whereby the ammunition can be fed into the chamber or barrel by the manual or automatic operation of some part of the weapon (see s. 57(6)(b)). If the weapon is an imitation firearm (**see para. 1.7.2.4**) or an air weapon, the offence is committed by the defendant having it with him/her. In the case of other firearms, the offence is committed by the defendant having the firearm with him/her together with ammunition suitable for use in it.

For the meaning of 'has with him', **see para. 1.7.19.4**.

This offence is one of strict liability. If you can show that the defendant knew that he/she had something with him/her and that the 'something' was a loaded shotgun, an air weapon, an imitation firearm or another firearm with ammunition, the offence is complete (*R* v *Vann and Davis* [1996] Crim LR 52). It is for the defendant to show lawful authority or reasonable excuse; possession of a valid certificate does not of itself provide lawful authority for having the firearm/ammunition in a public place (*Ross* v *Collins* [1982] Crim LR 368).

1.7.10.2 Trespassing with Firearms

OFFENCE: **Trespassing with Firearm in Building—*Firearms Act 1968, s. 20(1)***

• Triable either way (unless imitation firearm or air weapon) • Seven years' imprisonment and/or a fine on indictment • Six months' imprisonment and/or a fine summarily

The Firearms Act 1968, s. 20 states:

(1) A person commits an offence if, while he has a firearm or imitation firearm with him, he enters or is in any building or part of a building as a trespasser and without reasonable excuse (the proof whereof lies on him).

KEYNOTE

If the relevant firearm is an imitation or an air weapon, the offence is triable summarily.

It is immaterial whether the firearm is loaded or whether the accused has any ammunition with them.

This offence is committed either by entering a building/part of a building or simply by *being* in such a place, in each case as a trespasser while having the firearm. As there is no need for the defendant to have 'entered' the building as a trespasser in every case, the offence might be committed after the occupier has withdrawn any permission for the defendant to be there.

For the interpretation of 'has with him', see **para. 1.7.9.4**.

It will be for defendants to prove that they had reasonable excuse (on the balance of probabilities).

This offence includes imitation firearms in the general sense (**see para. 1.7.2.4**).

The power of entry and search under s. 47 of the 1968 Act applies to this offence (**see para. 1.7.11**).

OFFENCE: **Trespassing with Firearm on Land—*Firearms Act 1968, s. 20(2)***

• Triable summarily • Three months' imprisonment and/or a fine

The Firearms Act 1968, s. 20 states:

(2) A person commits an offence if, while he has a firearm or imitation firearm with him, he enters or is on any land as a trespasser and without reasonable excuse (the proof whereof lies on him).

KEYNOTE

The elements of this offence are generally the same as those for the s. 20(1) offence (**see para. 1.7.9.2**).

There is no requirement that the defendant had the firearm/imitation firearm with him/her when entering onto the land.

'Land' for these purposes will include land covered by water (s. 20(3)).

This offence includes imitation firearms in the general sense (**see para. 1.7.2.4**).

The power of entry and search under s. 47 of the 1968 Act applies to this offence (**see para. 1.7.11**).

1.7.11 Police Powers

The Firearms Act 1968, s. 47 states:

(1) A constable may require any person whom he has reasonable cause to suspect—
 (a) of having a firearm, with or without ammunition, with him in a public place; or
 (b) to be committing or about to commit, elsewhere than in a public place, an offence relevant for the purposes of this section,

 to hand over the firearm or any ammunition for examination by the constable.

KEYNOTE

An 'offence relevant to this section' is:

- an offence of having a firearm with intent to commit an indictable offence or resist arrest (contrary to s. 18(1) and (2) of the 1968 Act); or
- an offence of trespassing with a firearm (contrary to s. 20).

It is a summary offence to fail to hand over a firearm or ammunition when required under this section (s. 47(2)). In order to exercise this power, a police officer may search the person and may detain him/her for that purpose (s. 47(3)). The officer may also enter *any place* (s. 47(5)). If the officer has reasonable cause to suspect that:

- there is a firearm in a vehicle in a public place; or
- a vehicle is being/about to be used in connection with the commission of an 'offence relevant to this section' (see above);

he/she may search the vehicle and, for that purpose, may require the person driving or in control of the vehicle to stop the vehicle (s. 47(4)).

The provisions of the PACE Codes of Practice, Code A, will apply to the exercise of these powers of stop and search (see *General Police Duties*, chapter 3.1).

1.7.11.1 Power to Demand Documentation

The Firearms Act 1968, s. 48 states:

(1) A constable may demand, from any person whom he believes to be in possession of a firearm or ammunition to which section 1 of this Act applies, or of a shot gun, the production of his firearm certificate or, as the case may be, his shot gun certificate.

KEYNOTE

The demand for the relevant documentation may be made where the police officer 'believes' that a person is in possession of a section 1 firearm or ammunition or a shotgun. There is no requirement that the officer's belief is reasonable.

Failing to produce any of the required documents or to let the officer read them, or failing to show an entitlement to possess the firearm or ammunition, initiates the power of seizure under s. 48(2). It also gives the officer the power to demand the person's name and address.

If the person refuses to give his/her name or address or gives a false name and address, he/she commits a summary offence (s. 48(3)).

1.7.12 Possession or Acquisition of Firearms by Convicted Persons

Section 21 of the Firearms Act 1968 places restrictions on convicted persons in respect of their possession of firearms and/or ammunition.

Any person who has been sentenced to:

- custody for *life*; or
- to preventive detention, imprisonment, corrective training, youth custody or detention in a young offender institution for *three years or more*;

must not, *at any time*, have a firearm or ammunition in his/her possession, i.e. a lifetime ban.

Section 21 goes on to provide that any person who has been sentenced to imprisonment, youth custody, detention in a young offender institution or a secure training order for *three months or more, but less than three years*, must not have a firearm or ammunition in his/her possession at any time before the end of a five-year period beginning on the date of his/her release.

Date of release means, for a sentence partly served and partly suspended, the date on which the offender completes the part to be served and, in the case of a person subject to a secure training order, the date on which he/she is released from detention (under the various relevant statutes) or the date halfway through the total specified by the court making the order, whichever is the latest (s. 21(2A)).

Section 110 of the Anti-social Behaviour, Crime and Policing Act 2014 extends the definition of a prohibited person to include persons with suspended sentences of three months or more. The period of five years will begin on the second day after the date on which sentence was passed. A suspended sentence can only be for a maximum of two years so the permanent prohibition will not apply.

A person holding a licence under the Children and Young Persons Act 1933 or a person subject to a recognizance to keep the peace or be of good behaviour with a condition relating to the possession of firearms, must not, *at any time during the licence or the recognizance*, have a firearm or ammunition in his/her possession (s. 21(3)).

Where sentences or court orders are mentioned, their Scottish equivalents will also apply and a person prohibited in Northern Ireland from possessing a firearm/ammunition will also be prohibited in Great Britain (s. 21(3A)).

Section 21 *does not apply to imitation firearms* as there is no express reference to them in the section and because the reference in the Firearms Act 1982 does not apply.

Section 21(6) provides that a person prohibited under this section from having in his/her possession a firearm or ammunition may apply to the Crown Court for a removal of the prohibition and, if the application is granted, that prohibition shall not then apply to him/her.

1.7.12.1 Supplying Firearm to Person Prohibited by s. 21

OFFENCE: **Selling or Transferring Firearm to Person Prohibited by s. 21—*Firearms Act 1968, s. 21(5)***

- Triable either way • Five years' imprisonment and/or a fine on indictment
- Six months' imprisonment and/or a fine summarily

The Firearms Act 1968, s. 21 states:

> (5) It is an offence for a person to sell or transfer a firearm or ammunition to, or to repair, test or prove a firearm or ammunition for, a person whom he knows or has reasonable ground for believing to be prohibited by this section from having a firearm or ammunition in his possession.

KEYNOTE

Given that all people are presumed to know the law once it is published, it would seem that the knowledge or belief by the defendant would apply to the *convictions* of the other person, not the fact that possession by that person was an offence.

1.8 Weapons

This chapter is only tested in the Sergeants' examination—Inspectors' examination candidates SHOULD NOT study this material.

1.8.1 Introduction

Offences involving weapons are an important consideration for police officers who will be well acquainted with the consequences that the possession and use of such weapons can have. This chapter examines some of the legislation designed to deal with such behaviour.

1.8.2 Having Offensive Weapon in Public Place

OFFENCE: **Having Offensive Weapon in Public Place—*Prevention of Crime Act 1953, s. 1(1)***

- Triable either way • Four years' imprisonment and/or a fine on indictment
- Six months' imprisonment and/or a fine summarily

The Prevention of Crime Act 1953, s. 1 states:

> (1) Any person who without lawful authority or reasonable excuse, the proof whereof shall lie on him, has with him in any public place any offensive weapon shall be guilty of an offence.

1.8.2.1 Lawful Authority

'Lawful authority' means those occasions where people from time to time are required to carry weapons as a matter of duty, such as police officers or members of the armed forces (*Bryan* v *Mott* (1976) 62 Cr App R 71). Security guards carrying truncheons, even if required to do so by their contracts of employment, *are not covered* (*R* v *Spanner* [1973] Crim LR 704). If someone does not fall into this—very limited—group, he/she may still have a 'reasonable excuse' for having the weapon with him/her.

1.8.2.2 Reasonable Excuse

'Reasonable excuse' may arise from a number of circumstances. The courts retain a wide degree of discretion in what they accept as a 'reasonable excuse' and the cases below do *not* mean that this discretion is fettered and that the courts must follow this reasoning in every case (*DPP* v *Patterson* [2004] EWHC 2744 (Admin)).

A 'reasonable excuse'

- People having tools with them in the course of their trade (e.g. craft knives for fitting carpets or hammers for carpentry) may have a 'reasonable excuse' (*Ohlson* v *Hylton* [1975] 1 WLR 724).
- If a person passing the scene of a recent disturbance sees a weapon lying on the ground and he/she picks it up and puts it in his/her car intending to take it to the nearest

police station, those circumstances would amount to a reasonable excuse for having the weapon with him/her.

- A defendant in possession of a butterfly knife in a shopping centre because 'he needed it for feeding and stabling horses' and had meant to deposit it in a safe place that day but had not had the chance to do so, had a 'reasonable excuse' (*DPP* v *Patterson* (above)).
- Where the defendant was in 'fancy dress' costume as a police officer and had a truncheon with him as part of the costume, this was held to amount to 'reasonable excuse' (*Houghton* v *Chief Constable of Greater Manchester Police* (1987) 84 Cr App R 319).
- It may be reasonable to have a weapon if you have good grounds to anticipate an unprovoked or unlawful attack (e.g. for a person guarding cash transits (*Malnik* v *DPP* [1989] Crim LR 451)) but see the following section (general precaution).

Not a 'reasonable excuse'

- It is not reasonable to have a weapon with you as a general precaution in case you are attacked (*Evans* v *Hughes* [1972] 1 WLR 1452) nor is carrying a knife on the off-chance of being attacked (*R* v *Peacock* [1973] Crim LR 639).
- Not being aware that you have an offensive weapon with you is *not* a reasonable excuse in itself (*R* v *Densu* [1998] 1 Cr App R 400).
- Forgetting that you have a weapon with you is not a 'reasonable excuse' (*R* v *Lorimer* [2003] EWCA Crim 721) nor is forgetting that there is one in the car you are driving (*R* v *McCalla* (1988) 87 Cr App R 372).

The defendant's state of mind when deciding whether the defence of 'good reason' was made out, for example whether they had an angry and/or intoxicated and/or traumatised state of mind, is a matter that should be left to a jury (*R* v *Clancy* [2012] EWCA Crim 8).

The burden of proving the reasonable excuse or lawful authority rests with the defendant, but only when the prosecution has established that the defendant had an offensive weapon with him/her at the time. That burden of proof will be judged against the balance of probabilities.

1.8.2.3 Has With Him

The offence contrary to s. 1(1) of the 1953 Act is concerned with the carrying of any offensive weapon and not with its use—the use of an article as an offensive weapon can be dealt with by charging appropriate offences against the person (*R* v *Veasey* [1999] Crim LR 158). In *Ohlson* v *Hylton* [1975] 1 WLR 724, a workman was held not to be guilty of the offence when, during an argument and ensuing struggle, he took a hammer from his workbag and struck a fellow traveller at an Underground station. The hammer was properly in his possession. The comments of Lord Widgery CJ are helpful:

> . . . I would hold that an offence under section 1 is not committed where a person arms himself with a weapon for *instant* attack on his victim. It seems to me that the section is concerned only with a man who, possessed of a weapon, forms the necessary intent before an occasion to use actual violence has arisen. In other words, it is not the actual use of the weapon with which the section is concerned, but the carrying of a weapon with intent to use it if the occasion arises ...
>
> I accept that it is unnecessary for the prosecution to prove that the relevant intent was formed from the moment when the defendant set out on his expedition. An innocent carrying of say, a hammer can be converted into the unlawful carrying when the defendant forms the guilty intent, provided, in my view, that intent is formed before the actual occasion to use violence has arisen.

So having an article innocently will be converted into having the article guiltily but only if an intent to use the article offensively is formed before the actual occasion to use violence has arisen.

1.8.2.4 **Public Place**

The Prevention of Crime Act 1953, s. 1 states:

> (4) In this section 'public place' includes any highway and any other premises or place to which at the material time the public have or are permitted to have access, whether on payment or otherwise.

KEYNOTE

What is a public place is a question of fact, but whether it is capable of being a public place is a question of law (*R* v *Hanrahan* [2004] EWCA Crim 2943).

1.8.2.5 **Offensive Weapon**

The Prevention of Crime Act 1953, s. 1(4) also states:

> 'offensive weapon' means any article made or adapted for use for causing injury to the person, or intended by the person having it with him for such use by him or by some other person.

KEYNOTE

Offensive weapons fall into three categories for the purposes of this offence; namely, articles:

- made for causing injury (offensive weapons per se);
- adapted for causing injury; and
- intended by the person who has them for causing injury.

Made

Offensive weapons *per se* are those which have been manufactured for use for causing injury and include truncheons, PR-24 batons and bayonets. A swordstick has been held to be such a weapon (*R* v *Butler* [1988] Crim LR 695) as have flick-knives (*R* v *Simpson* [1983] 1 WLR 1494), butterfly knives (*DPP* v *Hynde* [1998] 1 WLR 1222) and petrol bombs (*R* v *Akhtar* [2015] EWCA Crim 176). In *Hynde*, the court took notice of the fact that butterfly knives were outlawed under the Criminal Justice Act 1988, deciding that such knives were clearly 'made' for causing injury. A flick-knife that also operates as a lighter remains an offensive weapon per se despite its alternative function (*R* v *Vasili* [2011] EWCA Crim 615).

Adapted

In *R* v *R* [2007] EWCA Crim 3312, the Court of Appeal held that a pair of combat gloves containing powdered lead/sand in the knuckle area were designed or adapted as an offensive weapon.

Weapons *adapted* for causing injury can include virtually anything. Whether something has in fact been so adapted is a question of fact for the court/jury to decide in each case. Bottles or glasses which have been broken in order to create a jagged edge have been held to be 'adapted' (*R* v *Simpson* [1983] 1 WLR 1494); so, too, has a potato with razor blades protruding from it (*R* v *Williamson* (1978) 67 Cr App R 35). If the article itself has not been altered in any physical way (such as by putting ammonia in a 'Jif' lemon to squirt in people's eyes—*R* v *Formosa* [1991] 2 QB 1), it has not been adapted.

It is still unclear whether the adaptation has to be to cause injury to *another* person or whether its capacity for self-inflicted injury (as in a suicide attempt) is enough. It is submitted that as it is the *adaptation* of the article which is relevant, and not the intention of the person carrying it, the ultimate 'victim' is irrelevant (*Bryan* v *Mott* (1976) 62 Cr App R 71).

Intended

Weapons *intended* to be used for causing injury can also include virtually anything. Here the intention of the person carrying it is *relevant* and you must prove an intention to cause injury. An intention to cause shock can be enough to satisfy this condition (*R* v *Rapier* (1980) 70 Cr App R 17 and also *R* v *Ali* [2012] EWCA Crim 934) but simply using the article to scare potential attackers away will not (*R* v *Snooks* [1997] Crim LR

230). To an extent, this overlaps with the issues of 'reasonable excuse' and 'has with him' discussed above. In *C* v *DPP* [2001] EWHC Admin 1093, the court held that it was necessary to examine how closely the adoption of the relevant object and the intention to use it occurred, along with the circumstances in which the offence took place. There is an important distinction between an article (not an offensive weapon *per se*) that is introduced into a public place with an intent to injure, and an article (already possessed lawfully and for good reason) that is used offensively to cause injury. Each case depends on its facts (*R* v *Tucker* [2016] EWCA Crim 13).

No Proof of Intention to Use Required

Once it has been shown that the article in question was in fact an offensive weapon, there is no need for the prosecution to show any intention to use it for causing injury (*Davis* v *Alexander* (1970) 54 Cr App R 398).

1.8.3 Threatening with Offensive Weapon in Public

OFFENCE: **Threatening with Offensive Weapon in Public—*Prevention of Crime Act 1953, s. 1A***

- Triable either way • Four years' imprisonment and/or a fine on indictment
- Six months' imprisonment and/or a fine summarily

The Prevention of Crime Act 1953, s. 1A states:

(1) A person is guilty of an offence if that person—
  (a) has an offensive weapon with him or her in a public place,
  (b) unlawfully and intentionally threatens another person ('A') with the weapon, and
  (c) does so in such a way that a reasonable person ('B') who was exposed to the same threat as A would think that there was an immediate risk of physical harm to B.

KEYNOTE

This section creates an offence relating to the aggravated use of an offensive weapon in a public place.

A's use of the weapon must be unlawful, allowing A to raise relevant defences to the use—such as self-defence, defence of others or property—and the prevention of crime.

1.8.4 Having Bladed or Pointed Article in Public Place

OFFENCE: **Having Bladed or Sharply Pointed Article in Public Place—*Criminal Justice Act 1988, s. 139(1)***

- Triable either way • Four years' imprisonment and/or a fine on indictment
- Six months' imprisonment and/or a fine summarily

The Criminal Justice Act 1988, s. 139 states:

(1) Subject to subsections (4) and (5) below, any person who has an article to which this section applies with him in a public place shall be guilty of an offence.

KEYNOTE

This offence applies to any sharply pointed article or article having a blade. Folding pocket knives are excluded unless the cutting edge of the blade exceeds three inches (7.62 cm). If the knife is a lock-knife, it will be covered by this offence irrespective of whether the blade is actually locked open at the time (*Harris* v *DPP* [1993] 1 WLR 82).

Whether an article falls within the parameters of s. 139 is a question of law for the judge/magistrate(s) to determine (*R* v *Deegan* [1998] 2 Cr App R 121—a case that concerned the carrying of a folding pocket-knife that was locked open). In *R* v *Davis* [1998] Crim LR 564, the Court of Appeal reiterated that the question of whether an article was 'bladed' or not was a matter of law for the judge to decide. In that case, the defendant had been carrying a screwdriver which, the prosecution contended, was a 'bladed' article capable of causing injury. The court decided that the test to be applied in such cases was not whether the 'bladed' article was capable of causing injury, but whether it had a cutting edge. Deciding whether or not an article was caught by the provisions of s. 139 was not a matter of interpreting the ordinary English word 'blade', but required the straightforward construction of the statute. This decision does not mean that a screwdriver can *never* fall within the type of article outlawed under s. 139, and if the screwdriver is pointed or it has been sharpened, it may still be caught by the above offence. There is no requirement for the item to be sharp as long as it has a blade. In *Brooker* v *DPP* [2005] EWHC 1132 (Admin), a blunt butter knife was held to fall within s. 139.

The fact that an article prohibited under s. 139 is part of something that has other innocuous features (e.g. a utility tool or 'Swiss army knife'), does not save it from falling under this offence if the other ingredients are present (*R* v *Giles* [2003] EWCA Crim 1287).

'Has with him' is discussed at **para. 1.8.2.3**. In *R* v *Henderson* [2016] EWCA Crim 965, where an article with a blade was found in the defendant's car when he was not in the car but in a second-floor flat some distance away, it was held that the defendant did not in law have the knife 'with him'. The need to prove that the defendant was aware that he/she had the weapon with him/her for this offence was reaffirmed by the Court of Appeal in *R* v *Daubney* (2000) 164 JP 519. If a person had with him a bladed article for even a very short time, that proved the *actus reus* of the offence, and the burden of showing that he had good reason or lawful authority fell upon him (*R* v *Szewczyk* [2019] EWCA Crim 1811).

'Public place' is similar to that under the Prevention of Crime Act 1953. The front garden of a house has been held *not* to be a public place for the purposes of this offence even where that garden is very narrow and the defendant would be able to inflict injuries on passers-by from within it (*R* v *Roberts* [2003] EWCA Crim 2753). It must also be determined whether public access was implied or tolerated (*Harriot* v *DPP* [2005] EWHC 965 (Admin)).

In *R* v *Monteiro* [2014] EWCA Crim 747, it was commented that cautions should be issued in accordance with the NPCC guidelines on Knife Crime Offences (2009) that indicates an expectation that 16- and 17-year olds should be charged with carrying a knife unless there were exceptional circumstances.

1.8.4.1 Defences

The Criminal Justice Act 1988, s. 139 states:

(4) It shall be a defence for a person charged with an offence under this section to prove that he had good reason or lawful authority for having the article with him in a public place.

(5) Without prejudice to the generality of subsection (4) above, it shall be a defence for a person charged with an offence under this section to prove that he had the article with him—
- (a) for use at work;
- (b) for religious reasons; or
- (c) as part of any national costume.

KEYNOTE

In relation to s. 139(4), 'good reason' is similar to 'lawful authority' (**para. 1.8.2.1**) and 'reasonable excuse' (**para. 1.8.2.2**). 'Good reason' can include self-defence (*R* v *Emmanuel* [1988] Crim LR 347). In *R* v *McAuley* [2010] EWCA Crim 2130, it was held that carrying a knife for one's own protection could amount to 'good reason' where it could be shown, on the balance of probabilities, that the person was in fear of imminent attack. It is for the defence to prove lawful authority or good reason and forgetting you have the article with you is not a general defence (*DPP* v *Gregson* (1993) 96 Cr App R 240; *R (On the Application of Hilton)* v *Canterbury Crown Court* [2009] EWHC 2867 (Admin)).

Under the legislation there is a 'strong public interest' in bladed articles not being carried in public without good reason and the requirement on the defendant to prove good reason for having the relevant article (in this instance, a lock-knife) was not an infringement of human rights legislation (*Lynch* v *DPP* [2001] EWHC 882 (Admin)). In *R* v *Matthews* [2003] EWCA Crim 813, it was held that the provisions of s. 139(4) and (5) imposed a persuasive burden on the accused and not merely an evidential burden.

While it is clear that forgetfulness alone cannot be a 'good reason', from a policing perspective the main thing is to gather any evidence that the defendant had the article with him/her in a public place and to record any explanation given. Whether the defendant had a 'good reason' (which might include forgetfulness combined with other circumstances) is then a matter for the court (*R* v *Jolie* [2003] EWCA Crim 1543). In *R* v *Chahal* [2010] EWHC 439 (Admin), quashing a conviction under this section, the court held that relevant consideration should have been given where the defendant, who undertook casual work at a relative's factory, forgot about a knife he was carrying.

1.8.5 Offences and Powers Relating to School Premises

The Criminal Justice Act 1988 provides a number of offences and powers dealing with weapons on school premises. The offence under s. 139AA (below) also applies to 'public places'.

1.8.5.1 Threatening with Article with Blade or Point or Offensive Weapon

OFFENCE: **Threatening with Article with Blade or Point or Offensive Weapon—*Criminal Justice Act 1988, s. 139AA***

- Triable either way • Four years' imprisonment and/or a fine on indictment
- 6 months' imprisonment and/or a fine summarily

The Criminal Justice Act 1988, s. 139AA states:

(1) A person is guilty of an offence if that person—
  (a) has an article to which this section applies with him or her in a public place or on school premises,
  (b) unlawfully and intentionally threatens another person ('A') with the article, and
  (c) does so in such a way that a reasonable person ('B') who was exposed to the same threat as A would think that there was an immediate risk of physical harm to B.

(1A) A person is guilty of an offence if that person—
  (a) has an article to which this section applies with them on further education premises,
  (b) unlawfully and intentionally threatens another person ('A') with the article, and
  (c) does so in such a way that a reasonable person ('B') who was exposed to the same threat as A would think that there was an immediate risk of physical harm to B.

KEYNOTE

This offence is similar to that in s. 1A of the Prevention of Crime Act 1953 but extends the threats to those made on school premises and includes articles with a blade or point (both on school premises and in a public place).

'School', under s. 4 of the Education Act 1996, means:

(1) ... an educational institution which is outside the further education sector and the higher education sector and is an institution for providing—
  (a) primary education;
  (b) secondary education, or
  (c) both primary and secondary education,
whether or not the institution also provides further education.

'School premises' means land used for the purposes of a school *excluding any land occupied solely as a dwelling by a person employed at the school.* This means that the provisions would not apply to someone found in the garden of a caretaker's house if that house was occupied solely as a dwelling by the school caretaker. 'Further education premises' means land used solely for the purposes of an institution within the further education sector (within the meaning of s. 91 of the Further and Higher Education Act 1992) or a 16 to 19 Academy (within the meaning of s. 1B of the Academies Act 2010) (s. 139AA(5)).

'Public place' has the same meaning as in s. 139.

1.8.5.2 Having Article with Blade or Point on School Premises

OFFENCE: **Having Bladed or Sharply Pointed Article on School Premises—*Criminal Justice Act 1988, s. 139A(1)***

- Triable either way • Four years' imprisonment and/or a fine on indictment
- Six months' imprisonment and/or a fine summarily

The Criminal Justice Act 1988, s. 139A states:

(1) Any person who has an article to which section 139 of this Act applies with him on school premises or further education premises shall be guilty of an offence.

KEYNOTE

This offence applies to the same articles as those covered under s. 139(1), see para. 1.8.4.

1.8.5.3 Having Offensive Weapon on School Premises

OFFENCE: **Having Offensive Weapon on School Premises—*Criminal Justice Act 1988, s. 139A(2)***

- Triable either way • Four years' imprisonment and/or a fine on indictment
- Six months' imprisonment and/or a fine summarily

The Criminal Justice Act 1988, s. 139A states:

(2) Any person who has an offensive weapon within the meaning of section 1 of the Prevention of Crime Act 1953 with him on school premises or further education premises shall be guilty of an offence.

KEYNOTE

For the purposes of this offence, 'offensive weapons' fall into the three categories discussed at para. 1.8.2.5.

1.8.5.4 Defences

The defences are the same as for s. 139(1) (**see para. 1.8.4.1**), although in relation to ss. 139A(1) and 139A(2) it is a defence for the person charged to prove that he/she had the article or weapon in question for educational purposes (s. 139A(4)(b)).

1.8.5.5 Power of Entry

The Criminal Justice Act 1988, s. 139B states:

(1) A constable may enter school premises or further education premises and search those premises and any person on those premises for—

(a) any article to which section 139 of this Act applies, or

(b) any offensive weapon within the meaning of section 1 of the Prevention of Crime Act 1953,

if he has reasonable grounds for suspecting that an offence under section 139A or 139AA of this Act is being, or has been, committed.

(2) If in the course of a search under this section a constable discovers an article or weapon which he has reasonable grounds for suspecting to be an article or weapon of a kind described in subsection (1) above, he may seize and retain it.

(3) The constable may use reasonable force, if necessary, in the exercise of the power of entry conferred by this section.

KEYNOTE

The PACE Code of Practice for the Exercise by Police Officers of Statutory Powers of Stop and Search (Code A) (2014) applies to searches under s. 139B of the Criminal Justice Act 1988, i.e. searches of persons for offensive weapons, bladed or sharply pointed articles on school premises.

1.8.5.6 Power of Members of Staff to Search Pupils for Prohibited Items

The Education Act 1996, s. 550ZA, provides that where a member of staff of a school in England has reasonable grounds for suspecting that a pupil at the school may have a prohibited item with him/her or in his/her possession, the pupil or their possessions may be searched for the item (subss. (1) and (2)). A 'member of staff', in relation to a school, means any teacher who works at the school and any other person who, with the authority of the headteacher, has lawful control or charge of pupils for whom education is being provided at the school. A prohibited item includes an article to which s. 139 of the Criminal Justice Act 1988 applies (knives and blades etc.) or an offensive weapon within the meaning of the Prevention of Crime Act 1953 (subs. (3)).

The same power for staff to search pupils in Wales is provided by s. 550AA of the 1996 Act.

The Higher Education Act 1992 provides similar powers to search students within the further education sector (s. 85AA (England) and s. 85B (Wales)).

In relation to these powers, a person who seizes anything as a result of a search must generally deliver it to a constable as soon as reasonably practicable (s. 550ZC).

1.8.6 Trespassing with Weapon of Offence

OFFENCE: **Trespassing with Weapon of Offence—*Criminal Law Act 1977, s. 8(1)***

• Triable summarily • Three months' imprisonment and/or a fine

The Criminal Law Act 1977, s. 8 states:

(1) A person who is on any premises as a trespasser, after having entered as such, is guilty of an offence if, without lawful authority or reasonable excuse, he has with him on the premises any weapon of offence.

KEYNOTE

'Premises' for this purpose means:

- any building; or
- any part of a building under separate occupation;
- any land adjacent to and used/intended for use in connection with a building;
- the site comprising any building(s) together with ancillary land;
- any fixed structure;
- any movable structure, vehicle or vessel designed or adapted for residential purposes (s. 12 of the 1977 Act).

This offence is restricted to a person who has entered the relevant premises as a trespasser. It does not, therefore, extend to a person who, having entered lawfully, then becomes a trespasser for whatever reason (e.g. because the occupier has told him/her to leave).

The definition of 'weapon of offence' is the same as that for aggravated burglary; namely, any article made or adapted for use for causing injury to or incapacitating a person, or intended by the person having it with him/her for that use (s. 8(2)).

1.8.7 Manufacture and Sale of Weapons

The legislation restricting the sale, manufacture, hire and buying of some weapons is aimed at restricting the supply of such weapons and their availability in England and Wales.

OFFENCE: **Manufacture, Sale or Hire of Weapons—*Restriction of Offensive Weapons Act 1959, s. 1(1)***

- Triable summarily • Six months' imprisonment and/or a fine

The Restriction of Offensive Weapons Act 1959, s. 1 states:

(1) Any person who manufactures, sells or hires or offers for sale or hire or exposes or has in his possession for the purpose of sale or hire, or lends or gives to any other person—
  (a) any knife which has a blade which opens automatically—
    (i) from the closed position to the fully opened position, or
    (ii) from a partially opened position to the fully opened position, by manual pressure applied to a button, spring or other device in or attached to the knife, and which is sometimes known as a 'flick knife' or 'flick gun'; or
  (b) any knife which has a blade which is released from the handle or sheath thereof by the force of gravity or the application of centrifugal force and which, when released, is locked in place by means of a button, spring, lever, or other device, sometimes known as a 'gravity knife',

shall be guilty of an offence.

OFFENCE: **Manufacture, Sale and Hire of Offensive Weapons—*Criminal Justice Act 1988, s. 141(1)***

- Triable summarily • 51 weeks' imprisonment and/or a fine

The Criminal Justice Act 1988, s. 141 states:

(1) Any person who manufactures, sells or hires or offers for sale or hire, exposes or has in his possession for the purpose of sale or hire, or lends or gives to any other person, a weapon to which this section applies shall be guilty of an offence ...

KEYNOTE

The importation of the weapons described in these offences is also prohibited (s. 141(4)).

1.8.7.1 Weapons Covered by s. 141

The weapons to which the 1988 Act applies are set out in the schedule to the Criminal Justice Act 1988 (Offensive Weapons) Order 1988 (SI 1988/2019). The weapons listed include knuckle-dusters, swordsticks, some telescopic truncheons, butterfly knives, a zombie knife, zombie killer knife or zombie slayer knife, samurai swords and a whole range of martial arts weapons.

KEYNOTE

The courts take notice of the fact that a weapon has been outlawed under this legislation in deciding whether or not it is 'made' for causing injury under the Prevention of Crime Act 1953.

There are a number of defences provided that include Crown servants and visiting forces (s. 141(5)–(7)), transactions made by or to museums and galleries (s. 141(8)–(11)), theatrical performances/rehearsals and the production of films or television programmes (s. 141(11A) and (11B)). For the purpose of these defences, the onus is on the defendant to provide sufficient evidence and the contrary is not proved beyond reasonable doubt (s. 141(11C)).

1.8.8 Possession of Offensive Weapons in Private

Section 141 of the Criminal Justice Act 1988 was amended by the Offensive Weapons Act 2019 to create an offence of possession of an offensive weapon in private.

OFFENCE: **Possession of an Offensive Weapon in Private—*Criminal Justice Act 1988, s. 141(1A)***

- Triable summarily • 51 weeks' imprisonment and/or a fine

The Criminal Justice Act 1988, s. 141 states:

(1A) Any person who possesses a weapon to which this section applies in private is guilty of an offence.

KEYNOTE

The weapons to which the 1988 Act applies are as per **para 1.8.7.1**.

Section 141(1C) states that a person possesses a weapon to which this section applies 'in private' if the person possesses the weapon in a place other than:

(a) a public place,
(b) school premises,
(c) further education premises, or
(d) a prison.

A 'public place' includes any place to which, at the time in question, the public have or are permitted access, whether on payment or otherwise.

'School premises' means land used for the purposes of a school, excluding any land occupied solely as a dwelling by a person employed at the school; and 'school' has the meaning given by s. 4 of the Education Act 1996.

'Further education premises' means land used solely for the purposes of an institution within the further education sector (within the meaning of s. 91 of the Further and Higher Education Act 1992) or a 16 to 19 Academy (within the meaning of s. 1B of the Academies Act 2010), excluding any land occupied solely as a dwelling by a person employed at the institution or the 16 to 19 Academy.

A 'prison' includes a young offender institution, a secure training centre and a secure college.

There are a number of defences to the offence under s. 1A that follow those available to the offence under s. 141(1) (Crown servants and visiting forces (s. 141(5) to (7)). Other defences include:

- It is a defence for a person charged with an offence under subs. (1A) to show that the weapon in question is one of historical importance (s. 141(7A)).
- It is a defence for a person charged with an offence under subs. (1A) to show that they possessed the weapon in question only in their capacity as the operator of, or as a person acting on behalf of, a museum or gallery (s. 141(8A)).
- It is a defence for a person charged with an offence under subs. (1A) to show that they possessed the weapon in question for educational purposes only.

1.8.9 Knives

Although some knives will fall into the categories of offence covered above, there are further restrictions which apply to knives specifically:

1.8.9.1 Sale of Knives etc. to Persons under 18

OFFENCE: **Selling Knives and Articles to under 18s—*Criminal Justice Act 1988, s. 141A***

- Triable summarily • 51 weeks' imprisonment and/or a fine

The Criminal Justice Act 1988, s. 141A states:

(1) Any person who sells to a person under the age of eighteen years an article to which this section applies shall be guilty of an offence ...
(2) Subject to subsection (3) below, this section applies to—
 (a) any knife, knife blade or razor blade,
 (b) any axe, and
 (c) any other article which has a blade or which is sharply pointed and which is made or adapted for use for causing injury to the person.
(3) This section does not apply to any article described in—
 (a) section 1 of the Restriction of Offensive Weapons Act 1959, or
 (b) ...
 (c) an order made by the Secretary of State under this section.

KEYNOTE

This offence does not apply to folding pocket knives with a cutting edge not exceeding three inches (7.62 cm), nor does it apply to razor blades permanently enclosed in a cartridge or housing where less than 2 mm of any blade is exposed (Criminal Justice Act 1988 (Offensive Weapons) (Exemption) Order 1996 (SI 1996/3064)).

Similar to the absurdity of a butter knife falling within the definition of an offence under s. 139 of the 1998 Act, in *R (On the Application of the Royal Borough of Windsor and Maidenhead)* v *East Berkshire Justices* [2010] EWHC 3020 (Admin), it was held that a grapefruit knife is not just a gadget but a knife within the meaning of s. 141A(2)(a).

It is a defence for a person charged under subs. (1) to prove that he/she took all reasonable precautions and exercised all due diligence to avoid the commission of the offence (s. 141A(4)).

1.8.9.2 Unlawful Marketing of Knives

OFFENCE: **Unlawful Marketing of Knives—*Knives Act 1997, s. 1***

- Triable either way • Two years' imprisonment and/or a fine on indictment
- Six months' imprisonment and/or a fine summarily

The Knives Act 1997, s. 1 states:

(1) A person is guilty of an offence if he markets a knife in a way which—
 (a) indicates, or suggests, that it is suitable for combat; or
 (b) is otherwise likely to stimulate or encourage violent behaviour involving the use of the knife as a weapon.

KEYNOTE

'Knife' for this purpose means any instrument which has a blade *or* which is sharply pointed (s. 10 of the 1997 Act).

Marketing will include selling, hiring, offering or exposing for sale or hire and possessing it for those purposes (s. 1(4)).

'Indicates or suggests' is a very loose concept requiring no *mens rea* on the part of the defendant (however, see defences at para. 1.8.9.3).

'Suitable for combat' means suitable for use as a weapon for inflicting injury to anyone *or causing them to fear injury*, and 'violent behaviour' means an unlawful act inflicting injury *or causing a person to fear injury* (s. 10). The elements in italics (author's emphasis) show that the legislation is intended to address the fear of the use of knives as well as their actual use.

The suggestion that knives are suitable for combat may be express or it may be implied by the name given to a product (e.g. 'commando') or by the packaging or advertisement relating to it (s. 1(3)). Therefore such packaging or advertising material, together with any surrounding advertisements, can be produced in evidence.

1.8.9.3 **Defences**

The Knives Act 1997, ss. 3 and 4 state:

3.—(1) It is a defence for a person charged with an offence under section 1 to prove that—
(a) the knife was marketed—
(i) for use by the armed forces of any country;
(ii) as an antique or curio; or
(iii) as falling within such other category (if any) as may be prescribed;
(b) it was reasonable for the knife to be marketed in that way; and
(c) there were no reasonable grounds for suspecting that a person into whose possession the knife might come in consequence of the way in which it was marketed would use it for an unlawful purpose.

...

4.—(1) It is a defence for a person charged with an offence under section 1 to prove that he did not know or suspect, and had no reasonable grounds for suspecting, that the way in which the knife was marketed—
(a) amounted to an indication or suggestion that the knife was suitable for combat; or
(b) was likely to stimulate or encourage violent behaviour involving the use of the knife as a weapon ...

KEYNOTE

There is also the general defence under s. 4(3) for the person to show that he/she took *all* reasonable precautions and exercised *all* due diligence to avoid committing the offence.

Section 5 allows a court to issue a warrant for the entry onto premises and for the search, seizure and removal of knives (or materials where an offence under s. 2 is involved). Any knives or publications which have been seized and removed by a constable under a warrant issued under this section may be retained until the conclusion of proceedings against the suspect (s. 5(4)).

1.8.9.4 **Publications Relating to Knives**

OFFENCE: **Publications Relating to Knives—*Knives Act 1997, s. 2(1)***

- Triable either way • Two years' imprisonment and/or a fine on indictment
- Six months' imprisonment and/or a fine summarily

The Knives Act 1997, s. 2 states:

(1) A person is guilty of an offence if he publishes any written, pictorial or other material in connection with the marketing of any knife and that material—
(a) indicates, or suggests, that the knife is suitable for combat; or
(b) is otherwise likely to stimulate or encourage violent behaviour involving the use of the knife as a weapon.

KEYNOTE

The offence under s. 2(1) is aimed at the publishers of advertisements rather than those who are involved in the sale and marketing of knives. A search warrant may be issued for relevant publications (s. 5).

The defences to an offence under s. 2(1) are exactly the same as those provided for in relation to an offence under s. 1(1) (**see para. 1.8.9.3**) (ss. 3(2) and 4(2)).

1.9 Racially and Religiously Aggravated Offences

1.9.1 Introduction

The Crime and Disorder Act 1998 sets out circumstances in which certain existing offences become racially or religiously aggravated. The 'aggravated' form of the offence carries a higher maximum penalty than the ordinary form of the offence. Those offences are dealt with in the relevant chapters of the Manuals—the first group is assaults and follows this chapter.

1.9.2 Offences Covered by the Legislation

The offences that can become racially or religiously aggravated can be grouped in four categories:

- Assaults:
  - wounding or grievous bodily harm—Offences Against the Person Act 1861, s. 20;
  - causing actual bodily harm—Offences Against the Person Act 1861, s. 47;
  - common assault—Criminal Justice Act 1988, s. 39 (**see chapter 1.10**).
- Criminal damage:
  - 'simple' criminal damage—Criminal Damage Act 1971, s. 1(1) (**see chapter 1.16**).
- Public order:
  - causing fear or provocation of violence—Public Order Act 1986, s. 4;
  - intentional harassment, alarm or distress—Public Order Act 1986, s. 4A;
  - causing harassment, alarm or distress—Public Order Act 1986, s. 5 (**see *General Police Duties,* chapter 3.9**).
- Harassment:
  - harassment—Protection from Harassment Act 1997, s. 2;
  - stalking—Protection from Harassment Act 1997, s. 2A;
  - putting people in fear of violence—Protection from Harassment Act 1997, s. 4;
  - stalking involving fear of violence or serious alarm or distress—Protection from Harassment Act 1997, s. 4A (**see *General Police Duties,* para. 3.12.6**).

KEYNOTE

The basic offence must have been committed. Only when that is accomplished should consideration then be given as to whether the offence is aggravated within the meaning of s. 28 of the Act (**see para. 1.9.3**). While the definition of a 'racist' incident is of critical importance to police officers, that definition ('a racist incident is any incident which is perceived to be racist by the victim or any other person') must not be confused with the definition of a 'racially or religiously aggravated' offence under s. 28 of the Act. A 'racist' incident does not automatically become a racially or religiously aggravated offence.

1.9.3 'Racially or Religiously Aggravated'

Section 28 of the Crime and Disorder Act 1998 states:

(1) An offence is racially or religiously aggravated for the purposes of sections 29 to 32 ... if—
   (a) at the time of committing the offence, or immediately before or after doing so, the offender demonstrates towards the victim of the offence hostility based on the victim's membership (or presumed membership) of a racial or religious group; or
   (b) the offence is motivated (wholly or partly) by hostility towards members of a racial or religious group based on their membership of that group.

(2) In subsection (1)(a) above—
   'membership', in relation to a racial or religious group, includes association with members of that group;
   'presumed' means presumed by the offender.

(3) It is immaterial for the purposes of paragraph (a) or (b) of subsection (1) above whether or not the offender's hostility is also based, to any extent, on any other factor not mentioned in that paragraph.

(4) In this section 'racial group' means a group of persons defined by reference to race, colour, nationality (including citizenship) or ethnic or national origins.

(5) In this section 'religious group' means a group of persons defined by reference to religious belief or lack of religious belief.

1.9.3.1 Timing of the Hostility

A racial insult uttered moments before an assault on a doorman was enough to make the offence racially aggravated for the purposes of s. 29 of the Crime and Disorder Act 1998 (*DPP* v *Woods* [2002] EWHC 85 (Admin)). In *DPP* v *McFarlane* [2002] EWHC 485 (Admin), it was decided that, where the expressions 'jungle bunny', 'black bastard' and 'wog' were used, the offence was made out as the words were used immediately before and at the time of the commission of the offence (contrary to s. 4 of the Public Order Act 1986).

The word 'immediately' in s. 28(1)(a) not only means immediately before but also *immediately after* the commission of the offence.

The need for any such hostility to be demonstrated *immediately* means that it must be shown to have taken place in the immediate context of the basic offence. In *Parry* v *DPP* [2004] EWHC 3112 (Admin), the defendant had caused damage to a neighbour's door by throwing nail polish over it. The police attended 20 minutes after the damage had occurred and spoke to the defendant who was, by that time, sitting in his own house. The defendant made comments demonstrating hostility based on the victim's membership of a racial group. The defendant was convicted of racially aggravated criminal damage but appealed and the conviction was quashed. The court held that the wording of the statute meant that any hostility had to be demonstrated *immediately* before or *immediately* after the substantive offence and that the courts below (magistrates') had not been entitled to consider the retrospective effect of the comments made later by the defendant.

1.9.3.2 Demonstration of Hostility

Section 28(1)(a) requires that the defendant demonstrate hostility immediately before, during or after committing the offence. This is not to establish the accused's state of mind, but what he/she *did* or *said* so as to demonstrate hostility towards the victim. The demonstration will often be by way of words, shouting, holding up a banner etc. or by adherence to a group that is demonstrating racial hostility.

In the context of criminal damage, the Divisional Court has confirmed that the relevant hostility can be demonstrated even if the victim is no longer present or is not present (*Parry*). However, the need for any such hostility to be demonstrated *immediately* means that it must be shown to have taken place in the immediate context of the offence.

1.9.3.3 Hostility

Common to both factors under s. 28(1)(a) and (b) is the notion of 'hostility' which is not defined by the Act. The *Oxford English Dictionary* defines 'hostile' as 'of the nature or disposition of an enemy; unfriendly, antagonistic'. It would seem relatively straightforward to show that someone's behaviour in committing the relevant offences was 'unfriendly or antagonistic'.

1.9.3.4 Victim

The demonstration of hostility will be towards the *victim* based on the *victim's* membership or presumed membership of a racial or religious group (under s. 28(1)(a)). This causes no difficulty where the offence is one of assault, public order or harassment where the victim is a person or where the offence is a criminal damage matter and the property is owned by a person (s. 30(3) of the Act provides that the person to whom the property belongs or is treated as belonging, will be treated as the victim). However, there are problems where the victim of criminal damage is a corporate body, e.g. where a bus shelter belonging to a transport company is damaged by racist graffiti. Of course, the transport company may have a legal personality but it is impossible for it to have a race or a religion. Therefore it cannot be possible to prove the offence under s. 28(1)(a) as it must be based on the victim's membership or presumed membership of a racial or religious group. In these circumstances, the most suitable charge will be under s. 28(1)(b) of the Act (motivation).

Police officers can be victims of these offences and are entitled to the same protection under the legislation as anyone else (*R* v *Jacobs* [2001] 2 Cr App R (S) 38).

> **KEYNOTE**
>
> The victim's perception of the incident (whatever it is) is totally irrelevant.

1.9.3.5 Motivation by Hostility

Section 28(1)(b) is concerned with the accused's motivation, which does concern his/her subjective state of mind. It will often be the case that the kind of demonstration referred to in **para. 1.9.3.2** would be evidence of such motivation. In *Taylor* v *DPP* [2006] EWHC 1202 (Admin), it was decided that use of phrases such as 'fucking nigger' and 'fucking coon bitch', patently not used in a jesting manner, must, in the circumstance of the case, have led any judge to find that the offence (in this case, the Public Order Act 1986, s. 5(1)(a)) was motivated, at least in part, by racial hostility as described in s. 28(1)(b). The fact that the offence is motivated only in part by such hostility would not alter the fact that the offence has been committed (motivated wholly or *partly* by such hostility).

1.9.3.6 Racial Groups

Section 28(4) of the Crime and Disorder Act 1998 states that a 'racial group' means a group of persons defined by reference to race, colour, nationality (including citizenship) or ethnic or national origins.

In determining whether or not a group is defined by *ethnic origins*, the courts will have regard to the judgment in the House of Lords in *Mandla* v *Dowell Lee* [1983] 2 AC 548. In that case, their lordships decided that Sikhs were such a group after considering whether they as a group had:

- a long shared *history*;
- a *cultural tradition* of their own, including family and social customs and manners, often, but not necessarily, associated with religious observance;

- either a *common geographical origin* or descent from a small number of *common ancestors*;
- a *common language*, not necessarily peculiar to that group;
- a *common literature* peculiar to that group;
- a *common religion* different from that of neighbouring groups or the general community surrounding the group; and
- the characteristic of being a *minority* or an *oppressed* or a *dominant* group within a larger community.

Lord Fraser's dictum in *Mandla* suggests that the first two characteristics above are essential in defining an 'ethnic group', while the others are at least relevant. His lordship also approved a decision from New Zealand to the effect that Jews are a group with common ethnic origins (*King-Ansell* v *Police* [1979] 2 NZLR 531).

KEYNOTE

When considering whether an offence was racially motivated under s. 28, hostility demonstrated to people who were foreign nationals simply because they were 'foreign' can be just as objectionable as hostility based on some more limited racial characteristic. In *DPP* v *M* [2004] EWHC 1453 (Admin), a juvenile used the words 'bloody foreigners' immediately before smashing the window of a kebab shop. The Divisional Court held that this was capable of amounting to an expression of hostility based on a person's membership or presumed membership of a racial group for the purposes of s. 28(1)(a) of the Crime and Disorder Act 1998. Although the statutory wording used the expression 'a racial group', the court held that a specific and inclusive definition of such a group had to be used by the defendant (e.g. the defendant did not have to single out a specific nationality) and the size of group referred to by a defendant (such as all 'foreigners') was irrelevant. In *R* v *Rogers* [2005] EWCA Crim 2863, the defendant had called three Spanish women 'bloody foreigners' and told them to 'go back to your own country'. The prosecution case was that the defendant had demonstrated hostility based on the women's membership of a racial group. The court's decision clarifies the position that for an offence to be aggravated under s. 28, the defendant has first to form a view that the victim is a member of a racial group (within the definition in s. 28(4)) and then has to say (or do) something that demonstrates hostility towards the victim based on membership of that group. However, the Court of Appeal noted that the very wide meaning of racial group under s. 28(4) gives rise to a danger of aggravated offences being charged where mere 'vulgar abuse' had included racial descriptions that did not truly indicate hostility to the race in question. Consequently, s. 28 should not be used unless the prosecuting authority is satisfied that the facts truly suggest that the offence was aggravated (rather than simply accompanied) by racism.

The Divisional Court has held that the words 'white man's arse licker' and 'brown Englishman' when used to accompany an assault on an Asian victim did not necessarily make the assault 'racially aggravated' and that the prosecution had not done enough to show that the assailants' behaviour fell under the definition set out in s. 28 of the 1998 Act (*DPP* v *Pal* [2000] Crim LR 756), a case that is hard to reconcile with s. 28(2).

Traditional Romany gypsies are capable of being a racial group on the basis of ethnic origin (*Commission for Racial Equality* v *Dutton* [1989] QB 783). The term 'Travellers' would not be covered, although in *O'Leary* v *Allied Domecq* (2000) 29 August, unreported (Case No. 950275-79) it was held that 'Irish Travellers' were a distinct group for the purposes of the Race Relations Act 1976. However, it should be noted that this decision is only 'persuasive' (as it was a county court decision) and our courts have yet to decide firmly whether 'Irish Travellers' are a 'racial group' for the purposes of the Crime and Disorder Act 1998. It is likely that the 'Irish' element would be covered anyway as English and Scottish people have been held to constitute groups defined by reference to national origins and thus as members of 'racial groups' in the broad sense as defined and protected from discrimination under the Race Relations Act 1976 (now the Equality Act 2010) (*Northern Joint Police Board* v *Power* [1997] IRLR 610). This decision ought logically to extend to Irish and Welsh people. This does not mean that 'travellers' are entirely excluded from the protection the Act offers as, for example, if a 'New-Age' traveller were subject to a trigger offence accompanied by a demonstration of hostility based on his/her skin colour or religion as opposed to being simply a 'New-Age' traveller, the offence would be committed.

In *Attorney-General's Reference (No. 4 of 2004), sub nom Attorney-General* v *D* [2005] EWCA Crim 889, the use of the word 'immigrant', in its simple implication that a person was 'non-British', was specific enough to denote membership of a 'racial group' within its meaning in s. 28(4) of the Crime and Disorder Act 1998.

1.9.3.7 **Religious Groups**

A 'religious group' may, for the purposes of the Act, include a group defined by its lack of religious beliefs. If, for example, D assaults V and at the time of the assault D demonstrates hostility towards V because V is an atheist or humanist who rejects religious beliefs, D must be guilty of a religiously aggravated offence. The same could be said of an assault on an agnostic.

A purely religious group such as Rastafarians (who have been held not to be members of an ethnic group *per se* (*Dawkins* v *Crown Suppliers (Property Services Agency)* [1993] ICR 517) are covered by the aggravated forms of offences as they are a religious group. In reality, a number of racial groups will overlap with religious groups in any event; Rastafarians would be a good example. An attack on a Rastafarian might be a racially aggravated offence under s. 28 because it was based on the defendant's hostility towards a *racial group* (e.g. African-Caribbeans) into which many Rastafarians fall. Alternatively, an attack might be made on a white Rastafarian based on the victim's religious beliefs (or lack of religious beliefs), i.e. his/her 'membership of a religious group'. Muslims have also been held not to be a racial group (*JH Walker* v *Hussain* [1996] ICR 291) but Muslims are clearly members of a religious group and, as such, are covered by the Act.

KEYNOTE

To be guilty of an offence that is racially or religiously aggravated, it is not necessary that the accused be of a different racial, national or ethnic (or religious) group from the victim (*R* v *White* [2001] EWCA Crim 216).

1.9.3.8 **Membership**

An important extension of 'racial or religious groups' is the inclusion of people who associate with members of that group. 'Membership' *for the purposes of s. 28(1)(a)* will include *association* with members of that group (s. 28(2)). This means that a white man who has a black female partner would potentially fall within the category of a 'member' of her racial group and vice versa. Moreover, people who work within certain racial or religious groups within the community could also be regarded as members of those groups for these purposes.

For the purposes of s. 28(1)(a), 'membership' will also include anyone *presumed by the defendant* to be a member of a racial or religious group. Therefore, if a defendant wrongly presumed that a person was a member of a racial or religious group, say a Pakistani Muslim, and assaulted that person as a result, the defendant's *presumption* would be enough to make his/her behaviour 'racially or religiously aggravated', even though the victim was in fact an Indian Hindu.

Such a presumption would not extend to the aggravating factors under s. 28(1)(b). The only apparent reason for this would seem to be that the s. 28(1)(a) offence requires hostility to be demonstrated towards a particular person ('the victim'), while the offence under s. 28(1)(b) envisages hostility towards members of a racial or religious group generally and does not require a specific victim.

1.9.3.9 Other Factors

Section 28(3) goes on to provide that it is immaterial whether the defendant's hostility (in either case under s. 28(1)) is also based to any extent on *any other factor*. This concession in s. 28(3) only prevents the defendant pointing to another *factor* in order to explain his/her behaviour in committing the relevant offence (assault, criminal damage etc.). Although it removes the opportunity for a defendant to argue that his/her behaviour was as a result of other factors (e.g. arising out of a domestic dispute), the subsection does not remove the burden on the prosecution to show that the defendant either demonstrated racial or religious hostility or was motivated by it.

1.10 Non-fatal Offences Against the Person

1.10.1 Introduction

Non-fatal offences against the person are common, so officers need to be able to consider what type of assault they are dealing with. This chapter begins by explaining some of the basic areas of assault law before moving on to deal with more serious assault crimes.

1.10.2 Assault

An assault is any act which intentionally or recklessly causes another to apprehend immediate unlawful violence (*Fagan* v *Metropolitan Police Commissioner* [1969] 1 QB 439). The mental elements involved, i.e. the intention or recklessness on the part of the defendant and the 'apprehension' on the part of the victim, means that *no physical contact* between the offender and victim is required. If X shouts at Y *'I'm going to kick your head in!'*, intending Y to believe the threat and Y does believe it, an assault has been committed by X against Y. Assault can only be committed by carrying out an act; it cannot be committed by an omission.

1.10.2.1 Mental Elements of Assault

On the part of the defendant, the *mens rea* needed to prove assault is either:

- the intention to cause apprehension of immediate unlawful violence; or
- subjective recklessness as to that consequence.

The victim must 'apprehend' (believe) that he/she is going to be subjected to immediate unlawful violence, so the state of mind of the *victim* in an assault is relevant. If X threatened to shoot Y with an imitation pistol, then X could be charged with assault provided Y believed that the pistol was real and that he/she was going to be shot (apprehending unlawful violence). The fact that the pistol was an imitation and could never actually physically harm Y is not important as X has caused Y to apprehend immediate violence being used (*Logdon* v *DPP* [1976] Crim LR 121). If Y knew that the pistol was an imitation and that it could not be fired to hurt him, then Y would not believe the threat and would not 'apprehend' immediate unlawful violence and there would be no assault committed by X. Likewise, if X threw a stone at Y, who has his back to X when the stone is thrown, and the stone sails past Y's head without Y noticing it, there would be no assault as Y did not 'apprehend' unlawful violence.

'Apprehension' does not mean 'fear' so there is no need to show that the victim was actually in fear. So if V is threatened with violence by D and V does apprehend the threat of immediate violence, it does not matter whether he/she is frightened by it. He/she may relish the opportunity to teach D a lesson, and yet still be regarded as the victim of D's assault. The violence apprehended by the victim does not have to be a 'certainty'. Causing a fear of some possible violence can be enough (*R* v *Ireland* [1998] AC 147) provided that the violence feared is about to happen in the *immediate* future (*R* v *Constanza* [1997] 2 Cr App R 492).

1.10.2.2 What is 'Immediate'?

Although the force threatened must be immediate, that immediacy is somewhat elastic. Courts have accepted that where a person makes a threat from outside a victim's house to the victim inside, an assault is committed even though there will be some time lapse before the defendant can carry out the threat.

In *Ireland*, the House of Lords suggested that a threat to cause violence 'in a minute or two' might be enough to qualify as an assault; a threat to provoke some apprehension of violence in the more distant future would not suffice.

The victim must be shown to have feared the use of *force*; it will not be enough to show that a person threatened by words (or silence) feared more words or silence.

1.10.2.3 Words

Words (and silence) can amount to an assault provided they are accompanied by the required *mens rea*. In *Ireland*, it was held that telephone calls to a victim, followed by silences (which led the victims to fear that unlawful force would be used against them), could fulfil the requirements for the *actus reus* of assault if it brought about the desired consequences (e.g. fear of the immediate use of unlawful force). It was accepted that 'a thing said is also a thing done' and the view that words can never amount to an assault was rejected.

Where the words threatening immediate unlawful force come in the form of letters, it has been held that an assault may have been committed (*Constanza* at **para. 1.10.2.1**). It is natural to assume that *any form of communication* can be used as a method for an assault. Thus, it would be possible to assault someone via an email or a text message.

1.10.2.4 Conditional Threats

Words can *negate* an assault if they make a conditional threat, e.g. where you attend an incident and one person says to another '*If these officers weren't here, I'd chin you!*'. In this situation the defendant is making a *hypothetical* threat and is really saying 'if it weren't for the existence of certain circumstances, I would assault you' (*Tuberville* v *Savage* (1669) 1 Mod Rep 3). This should be contrasted with occasions where the defendant makes an immediate threat conditional upon some real circumstance, e.g. '*If you don't cross the road, I'll break your neck*'. Such threats have been held, in a civil case, to amount to an assault (*Read* v *Coker* (1853) 138 ER 1437).

1.10.3 Battery

A battery is committed when a person intentionally or recklessly (subjectively) inflicts unlawful force on another (*Fagan* v *Metropolitan Police Commissioner* [1969] 1 QB 439). Battery *requires physical contact* with the victim, so the offence could not be carried out via the phone (causing psychiatric injury (*R* v *Ireland* [1998] AC 147)). It is sufficient to constitute battery that the defendant attacks the clothing which another is wearing (*R* v *Day* (1845) 1 Cox CC 207).

Battery need not be preceded by an assault. A blow may, for example, be struck from behind, without warning.

A very small degree of physical contact will be enough, not, as many think, an act involving serious violence.

That force can be applied directly or indirectly. For example, where a defendant punched a woman causing her to drop and injure a child she was holding, he was convicted of the offence against that child (*Haystead* v *Chief Constable of Derbyshire* [2000] 3 All ER 890). In *DPP* v *Santana-Bermudez* [2003] EWHC 2908 (Admin), the defendant was held to have committed a battery against a police officer when he falsely assured her that he had no 'sharps' in his possession, and thus caused her to stab herself on a hypodermic needle as she searched him.

1.10.4 Assault or Battery?

Although the terms 'assault' and 'battery' have distinct legal meanings, they are often referred to as simply 'assaults' or 'common assault'. It is, however, important to separate the two expressions when charging or laying an information against a defendant, as to include both may be bad for duplicity (*DPP* v *Taylor* [1992] QB 645). In *Taylor*, the Divisional Court held that all common assaults and batteries are now offences contrary to s. 39 of the Criminal Justice Act 1988 (**see para. 1.10.6.1**), and that the information must include a reference to that section.

1.10.5 Consent

A key element in proving an assault is the *unlawfulness* of the force used or threatened. Although the courts have accepted consent as a feature which negates any offence, they have been reluctant to accept this feature in a number of cases. The two principal questions that may arise in this context are:

- did the alleged victim in fact consent (expressly or by implication) to what was done; and
- if so, do public policy considerations invalidate that consent?

1.10.5.1 Legitimate Consent to Risk of Injury

One of the more straightforward policy considerations would include the implied consent to contact with others during the course of everyday activities. We are all 'deemed' to consent to various harmless and unavoidable contact, such as brushing against another on a crowded train. In such a case, it will be a matter of fact to decide whether the behaviour complained of went beyond what was acceptable in those particular circumstances.

There are times when a person may consent to even serious harm, such as during properly conducted sporting events (*Attorney-General's Reference (No. 6 of 1980)* [1981] QB 715), tattooing and medical operations. Participants in contact sports such as football are deemed to consent to the risk of clumsy or mistimed tackles or challenges; but this does not include tackles that are deliberately late or intended to cause harm (e.g. in an off-the-ball incident (*R* v *Lloyd* (1989) 11 Cr App R (S) 36)). Injuries caused in an unauthorised prize fight could not be consented to as this would not be a properly conducted sporting event. In *R* v *Barnes* [2004] EWCA Crim 3246, the defendant appealed against his conviction for inflicting grievous bodily harm after he caused a serious leg injury by way of a tackle during a football match. The tackle took place after the victim had kicked the ball into the goal but, while accepting that the tackle was hard, the defendant maintained that it had been a fair challenge and that the injury caused was accidental. The Court of Appeal held that where injuries were sustained in the course of contact sports, public policy limited the availability of the defence of consent to situations where there had been implicit consent to what had occurred. Whether conduct reached the required threshold to be treated as 'criminal' would depend on all the circumstances. The fact that the actions of the defendant had been within the rules and practice of the game would be a firm indication that what had occurred was not criminal, although in highly competitive sports even conduct *outside the rules* could be expected to occur in the heat of the moment, and such conduct still might not reach the threshold level required for it to be criminal. The court held that the threshold level was an objective one to be determined by the type of sport, the level at which it was played, the nature of the 'act', the degree of force used, the extent of the risk of injury and the state of mind of the defendant.

Teachers who are employed at schools for children with special needs, including behavioural problems, do not impliedly consent to the use of violence against them by pupils (*H* v *CPS* [2010] EWHC 1374 (Admin)).

What of the situation where the consent of the victim has been obtained by fraud? In *R* v *Richardson* [1999] QB 444, a dentist (Diane Richardson) who had been suspended by the General Dental Council continued practising dentistry. The circumstances came to light and charges of assault were brought. Although initially convicted, the Court of Appeal quashed the conviction on the basis that fraud will only negate consent if it relates to the identity of the person or to the nature and quality of the act. Richardson did not lie about her identity (she did not lie about her name) or about the nature and quality of the act (the dentistry carried out). While her behaviour was reprehensible, it did not amount to an offence. This does not mean that persons without appropriate qualifications sneaking into a surgery and putting on a white coat and calling themselves 'Doctor' followed by their true name could avoid liability if they then made physical contact with another in the guise of providing treatment. While there is no fraud as to identity, any treatment carried out would be caught by a fraud in respect of the quality of the act. Consent would also be negated if a genuine doctor indecently touched his patients on the basis that this was part of a routine medical examination when its true purpose was for sexual gratification (*R* v *Tabassum* [2000] 2 Cr App R 328).

1.10.5.2 Consent to Sado-masochistic Injuries

Where actual bodily harm (or worse) is deliberately inflicted, consent to it will ordinarily be deemed invalid on the grounds of public policy even if 'victims' know exactly what they are consenting to.

An example of this approach can be seen in the case of *R* v *Brown* [1994] 1 AC 212. That case involved members of a sado-masochist group who inflicted varying degrees of injuries on one another (under ss. 20 and 47 of the Offences Against the Person Act 1861) for their own gratification. The group claimed that they had consented to the injuries and therefore no assault or battery had taken place. Their lordships followed an earlier policy that *all assaults which result in more than transient harm will be unlawful unless there is good reason for allowing the plea of 'consent'*. Good reason will be determined in the light of a number of considerations:

- the practical consequences of the behaviour;
- the dangerousness of the behaviour;
- the vulnerability of the 'consenting' person.

Sado-masochistic injury may justifiably be made the subject of criminal law on grounds of the 'protection of health'. It was for this reason that the European Court of Human Rights held that there had been no violation of the defendants' right to respect for private and family life (under Article 8) in *Brown*.

Further issues in clarifying what will amount to 'true' or effective consent were added by the decision of the Court of Appeal in *R* v *Wilson* [1997] QB 47. In that case, the court accepted that a husband might lawfully brand his initials on his wife's buttocks with a hot knife provided she consented (as she appeared to have done). The reasoning behind the judgment seems to be based on the fact that the branding was similar to a form of tattooing, but also on the policy grounds that consensual activity between husband and wife is not a matter for criminal investigation. Therefore, if a situation arose where a husband and wife took part in mutual branding in the privacy of their home, their criminal liability would arguably depend on whether they caused the harm for purposes of sado-masochistic pleasure or out of some affectionate wish to be permanently adorned with the mark of their loved one.

1.10.5.3 Consent to Serious Harm for Sexual Gratification

Section 71(2) of the Domestic Abuse Act 2021 states that it is *not a defence* that the victim of a 'relevant offence' consented to the infliction of the serious harm for the purposes of obtaining sexual gratification.

KEYNOTE

'Relevant Offence'

A 'relevant offence' means an offence under s. 18, 20 or 47 of the Offences Against the Person Act 1861. 'Serious harm' means:

- grievous bodily harm, within the meaning of s. 18 of the 1861 Act;
- wounding, within the meaning of that section; or
- actual bodily harm, within the meaning of s. 47 of the 1861 Act.

Section 71(2) does not apply in the case of an offence under s. 20 or s. 47 of the 1861 Act where:

- the serious harm consists of, or is as a result of, the infection of the victim with a sexually transmitted infection in the course of sexual activity; and
- the victim consented to the activity in the knowledge or belief that the defendant had the sexually transmitted infection.

It does not matter whether the harm was inflicted for the purposes of obtaining sexual gratification for the defendant, for the victim or for some other person (s. 71(5)).

1.10.6 Assault Offences

Having considered the key common elements in this area, the specific offences are set out below.

1.10.6.1 Common Assault and Battery

OFFENCE: **Common Assault/Battery—*Criminal Justice Act 1988, s. 39***

- Triable summarily • Six months' imprisonment

OFFENCE: **Racially or Religiously Aggravated—*Crime and Disorder Act 1998, s. 29(1)(c)***

- Triable either way • Two years' imprisonment and/or a fine on indictment
- Six months' imprisonment and/or a fine summarily

KEYNOTE

The racially or religiously aggravated offence can be tried on indictment without having to be included alongside another indictable offence as is the case with common assaults generally (Criminal Justice Act 1988, s. 40).

CPS Charging Standards state that a charge under s. 39 of the Act is appropriate where *no injury or injuries which are not serious occur.* In *R* v *Misalati* [2017] EWCA Crim 2226, the appellant spat towards the complainant. The appeal court confirmed that although there was no actual violence, spitting is an assault whether it makes contact with the victim or causes fear of immediate unlawful physical contact.

The injury sustained by the victim should always be considered first, and in most cases the degree of injury will determine the appropriate charge. The appropriate charge will usually be contrary to s. 39 where injuries amount to *no more* than the following:

- grazes;
- scratches;
- abrasions;
- minor bruising;
- swellings;
- reddening of the skin;
- superficial cuts.

1.10.6.2 Assaults on Emergency Workers

The Assaults on Emergency Workers (Offences) Act 2018 states that a common assault or battery committed against an emergency worker acting in the exercise of functions as such a worker is punishable:

- on summary conviction, to imprisonment for a term not exceeding six months, or to a fine, or to both;
- on conviction on indictment, to imprisonment for a term not exceeding two years, or to a fine, or to both.

KEYNOTE

When Does it Apply?

The circumstances in which an offence is to be taken as committed against a person acting in the exercise of functions as an emergency worker include circumstances where the offence takes place at a time when the person is not at work but is carrying out functions which, if done in work time, would have been in the exercise of functions as an emergency worker.

Increased Sentence

The fact that the victim of the offence is an emergency worker is an aggravating factor when considering other offences under the Offences Against the Person Act 1861. This is the case for a number of offences, such as s. 20 (malicious wounding/GBH), s. 18 (wounding/GBH with intent) and s. 47 (assault occasioning actual bodily harm) (s. 2(3)). Where this is the case, the court must treat the fact that the offence was committed on an emergency worker as an aggravating factor (that is to say, a factor that increases the seriousness of the offence) and must state in open court that the offence is so aggravated (s. 2(2)).

'Emergency Worker'

An 'emergency worker' means:

- a constable;
- a person (other than a constable) who has the powers of a constable or is otherwise employed for police purposes or is engaged to provide services for police purposes;
- a National Crime Agency officer;
- a prison officer;
- a person (other than a prison officer) employed or engaged to carry out functions in a custodial institution of a corresponding kind to those carried out by a prison officer;
- a prisoner custody officer, so far as relating to the exercise of escort functions;
- a custody officer, so far as relating to the exercise of escort functions;
- a person employed for the purposes of providing, or engaged to provide, fire services or fire and rescue services;

- a person employed for the purposes of providing, or engaged to provide, search services or rescue services (or both);
- a person employed for the purposes of providing, or engaged to provide:
  - NHS health services; or
  - services in the support of the provision of NHS health services;

  and whose general activities in doing so involve face-to-face interaction with individuals receiving the service or with other members of the public.

It is immaterial whether the employment or engagement is paid or unpaid (s. 3(2)).

Custodial Institution

A 'custodial institution' includes a prison, a young offender institution, a secure training centre, secure college or remand centre. It also includes a removal centre, a short-term holding facility or pre-departure accommodation (as defined by s. 147 of the Immigration and Asylum Act 1999) (s. 3(3)).

Custody Officer

This is not to be confused with the term 'custody officer' at a designated police station. A 'custody officer' means a person in respect of whom a certificate is for the time being in force certifying that he/she has been approved by the Secretary of State for the purpose of performing escort duties and/or custodial duties at secure training centres.

Escort Functions

'Escort functions', in the case of a prisoner custody officer, means the functions specified in s. 80(1) of the Criminal Justice Act 1991. In the case of a custody officer, it means the functions specified in para. 1 of sch. 1 to the Criminal Justice and Public Order Act 1994.

NHS Health Services

'NHS health services' means any kind of health services provided as part of the health service continued under s . 1(1) of the National Health Services Act 2006 and under s. 1(1) of the National Health Service (Wales) Act 2006.

1.10.6.3 Assault Occasioning Actual Bodily Harm

OFFENCE: **Assault Occasioning Actual Bodily Harm—*Offences Against the Person Act 1861, s. 47***

- Triable either way • Five years' imprisonment on indictment
- Six months' imprisonment and/or a fine summarily

OFFENCE: **Racially or Religiously Aggravated—*Crime and Disorder Act 1998, s. 29(1)(b)***

- Triable either way • Seven years' imprisonment and/or a fine on indictment
- Six months' imprisonment and/or a fine summarily

The Offences Against the Person Act 1861, s. 47 states:

> Whosoever shall be convicted ... of any assault occasioning actual bodily harm shall be liable ... to be kept in penal servitude ...

KEYNOTE

The only difference between an assault committed under s. 39 of the Criminal Justice Act 1988 and an assault under s. 47 of the Offences Against the Person Act 1861 is the degree of harm suffered by the victim and the sentence available. The *mens rea* and *actus reus* of the offence under s. 39 of the Criminal Justice Act 1988 and the offence under s. 47 of the Offences Against the Person Act 1861 are exactly the same.

It must be shown that 'actual bodily harm' was a consequence, directly or indirectly, of the defendant's actions.

So what is 'actual bodily harm'? In *DPP* v *Smith* [1961] AC 290, it was noted that the expression needed 'no explanation' and, in *R* v *Chan-Fook* ([1994] 1 WLR 689), the court advised that the phrase consisted of 'three words of the English language which require no elaboration and in the ordinary course should not receive any'. While the phrase 'bodily harm' has its ordinary meaning, it has been said to include any hurt calculated to interfere with the health or comfort of the victim: such hurt need not be permanent, but must be more than transient and trifling (*R* v *Miller* [1954] 2 QB 282).

CPS Charging Standards state that a charge under s. 47 would be appropriate where the injuries are serious. Whilst CPS charging standards may be considered persuasive and/or influential regarding the appropriate charge, the fact remains that they do not represent the law—consequently, it is useful to consider specific case law decisions where the courts stated that the injuries amounted to a s. 47 offence for more authoritative direction.

Psychological harm that involves more than mere emotions such as fear, distress or panic can amount to a s. 47 offence. This may amount to shock (*Miller*) and mental 'injury' (*Chan-Fook*). Where psychiatric injury is relied upon as the basis for an allegation of assault occasioning actual bodily harm, and the matter is not admitted by the defence, then expert evidence must be called by the prosecution (*Chan-Fook*).

The Administrative Court has accepted that a momentary loss of consciousness caused by a kick but without any physical injury can be 'actual harm' because it involved an injurious impairment of the victim's sensory abilities which did not fall within the 'trifling' category described in *R* v *Miller* (*T* v *DPP* [2003] EWHC 266 (Admin)).

It was held in *DPP* v *Smith (Ross Michael)* [2006] EWHC 94 (Admin) that the substantial cutting of a person's hair against his/her will could amount to actual bodily harm even though no pain or other injury may be involved. In *Smith*, the defendant cut off his ex-partner's ponytail, deliberately and without her permission. Even though medically and scientifically speaking, the hair above the surface of the scalp is no more than dead tissue, it remains part of the body and is attached to it. While it is so attached, it falls within the meaning of 'bodily' in the phrase 'actual bodily harm' as it is concerned with the body of the individual victim. Therefore the same would be true of fingernails.

CPS Charging Standards state that ABH should generally be charged where injuries and overall circumstances indicate that the offence clearly merits more than six months' imprisonment and where the prosecution intends to represent that the case is not suitable for summary trial. Examples may include cases where there is a need for a number of stitches (but not superficial application of steri-strips) or a hospital procedure under anaesthetic.

1.10.6.4 Wounding or Inflicting Grievous Bodily Harm

OFFENCE: **Wounding or Inflicting Grievous Bodily Harm—*Offences Against the Person Act 1861, s. 20***

- Triable either way • Five years' imprisonment on indictment
- Six months' imprisonment and/or a fine summarily

OFFENCE: **Racially or Religiously Aggravated—*Crime and Disorder Act 1998, s. 29(1)(a)***

- Triable either way • Seven years' imprisonment and/or a fine on indictment
- Six months' imprisonment and/or a fine summarily

The Offences Against the Person Act 1861, s. 20 states:

> Whosoever shall unlawfully and maliciously wound or inflict any grievous bodily harm upon any other person, either with or without any weapon or instrument, shall be guilty of a misdemeanor ...

KEYNOTE

Maliciously

Although the word maliciously suggests some form of evil premeditation, 'malice' here amounts to *subjective recklessness*. It means that the defendant must realise that there is a risk of *some harm* being caused to the victim but took the risk anyway. The defendant does not need to foresee the degree of harm which is eventually caused, only that his/her behaviour may bring about some harm to the victim.

Wound

Wounding requires the breaking of the continuity of the whole of the skin (dermis and epidermis) or the breaking of the inner skin within the cheek, lip or urethra. A cut which breaks all the layers of a person's skin, whether caused externally (e.g. a knife wound) or internally (e.g. a punch causing a tooth to puncture the cheek), will amount to a wound. It does not include the rupturing of internal blood vessels (bruising).

The definition of wounding may encompass injuries that are relatively minor in nature, e.g. a small cut. CPS Charging Standards state that an assault contrary to s. 20 should be reserved for the type of wounds considered to be *really serious* (thus equating the offence with the infliction of grievous, or serious, bodily harm). For example, a cut on the back of a person's hand requiring two stitches and not resulting in 'really serious harm' is likely to be considered as a s. 39 or perhaps a s. 47 assault. If the same injury were across the surface of the eye causing loss of sight in the eye and thereby resulting in 'really serious harm', a charge of s. 20 or s. 18 assault may be appropriate.

Inflict

In *R* v *Ireland* [1998] AC 147, it was stated that no 'assault' is needed for this offence and that harm could be 'inflicted' indirectly (in this case, by menacing telephone calls inflicting psychiatric harm). Therefore there is now little, if any, difference between inflicting harm and 'causing' harm. It should be enough to show that the defendant's behaviour brought about the resulting harm to the victim.

Grievous Bodily Harm

CPS Charging Standards are, once again, helpful but it should be noted that there is no definitive list of the kind of injuries that may be considered to be 'really serious'.

A case involving a visible disfigurement is *R* v *Marsh* [2011] EWCA Crim 3190, where the female offenders became involved in a fight with a 16-year-old girl. One held the girl's arms behind her back while the second cut the girl's face with a key, causing a 4 cm laceration which would leave a permanent scar; the offenders were convicted of a s. 20 offence.

In *R* v *Birmingham* [2002] EWCA Crim 2608, it was held that a large number of minor wounds were capable of amounting to grievous bodily harm on a charge of aggravated burglary

Sexually Transmitted Infections (STIs)

The courts have recognised that person-to-person transmission of a sexual infection that will have serious consequences for the infected person's health can amount to grievous bodily harm under the Offences Against the Person Act 1861 (in *R* v *Dica* [2004] EWCA Crim 1103, there was an acceptance that the deliberate infection of another with the HIV virus could amount to grievous bodily harm). This issue was explored further in *R* v *Konzani* [2005] EWCA Crim 706. In that case, the defendant appealed against convictions for inflicting grievous bodily harm on three women contrary to s. 20. The defendant had unprotected consensual sexual intercourse with the women, but without having disclosed that he was HIV-positive. The women subsequently contracted the HIV virus. The Court of Appeal held that there was a critical distinction between taking a risk as to the various potentially adverse (and possibly problematic) consequences of unprotected consensual intercourse, and the giving of informed consent *to the risk of infection with a fatal disease*. Before consent to the risk of contracting HIV could provide a defence, that consent had to be an *informed* consent in this latter sense (*Dica*). Therefore, simply having an honestly held belief that the other person was consenting would only help if that consent would itself have provided a defence to the passing of the infection (see para. 1.10.5.3).

The case of *R* v *Golding* [2014] EWCA Crim 889 raised the issue of whether genital herpes could be described as 'really serious harm' so as to come within s. 20 of the Act. The defendant did not disclose his diagnosis of genital herpes to the victim which he passed on to her. The court found that Golding understood both that he had the infection and how it is transmitted, and by not preventing transmission—or disclosing his condition thereby allowing the complainant to make an informed decision whether or not she wanted to risk acquiring herpes—he was guilty of reckless grievous bodily harm under s. 20 of the Act.

CPS Charging Standards state that 'informed consent' does not necessarily mean that the suspect must disclose his/her condition to the complainant. A complainant may be regarded as being informed for the purposes of giving consent where a third party informs the complainant of the suspect's condition, and the complainant then engages in unprotected sexual activity with the suspect. Similarly, a complainant may be regarded as being informed if he/she becomes aware of certain circumstances that indicate that the suspect is suffering from a sexually transmitted infection, such as visiting the suspect while he/she is undergoing treatment for the infection in hospital, or the appearance of sores on the suspect's genitalia.

1.10.6.5 Wounding or Causing Grievous Bodily Harm with Intent

OFFENCE: **Wounding or Causing Grievous Bodily Harm with Intent—*Offences Against the Person Act 1861, s. 18***

- Triable on indictment only • Life imprisonment

The Offences Against the Person Act 1861, s. 18 states:

> Whosoever shall unlawfully and maliciously by any means whatsoever wound or cause any grievous bodily harm to any person with intent to do some grievous bodily harm to any person, or with intent to resist or prevent the lawful apprehension or detainer of any person, shall be guilty of felony …

KEYNOTE

An offence under s. 18 may take one of four different forms, namely:

(a) wounding with intent to do grievous bodily harm;
(b) causing grievous bodily harm with intent to do so;
(c) maliciously wounding with intent to resist or prevent the lawful apprehension etc. of any person; or
(d) maliciously causing grievous bodily harm with intent to resist or prevent the lawful apprehension etc. of any person.

Although there are similarities with the offence under s. 20 (**see para. 1.10.6.4**), you must show the appropriate *intent* (e.g. to do grievous bodily harm to *anyone* or to resist/prevent the lawful apprehension/detention of *anyone*). Factors that may indicate such a specific intent include:

- a repeated or planned attack;
- deliberate selection of a weapon or adaptation of an article to cause injury, such as breaking a glass before an attack;
- making prior threats;
- using an offensive weapon against, or kicking a victim's head.

In form (a) or (b), where the intent was to cause grievous bodily harm, the issue of 'malice' will not arise. However, where the intent was to resist or prevent the *lawful* arrest of someone (in form (c) or (d)), the element of maliciousness (subjective recklessness) as set out above (**see para. 1.10.6.4**) will need to be proved. In addition, where it is alleged that D acted with the intent to avoid or resist the lawful apprehension of any person, it may be his/her own arrest or that of another he/she resisted, but the lawfulness of that arrest or detention must in either event be proved by the prosecution. It does not follow that D must be proved to have known the arrest etc. was lawful, but in a case such as *Kenlin* v *Gardiner* [1967] 2 QB 510, where D mistook the arresting officers for kidnappers, mistaken self-defence may be raised by the defence.

The word 'cause', together with the expression 'by any means whatsoever', seems to give this offence a wider meaning than s. 20. However, the increasingly broad interpretation of the s. 20 offence means that there is little difference in the *actus reus* needed for either offence.

The intentional infliction of a sexually transmitted infection can amount to an offence under s. 18 of the Act. CPS guidance states that for such a prosecution to proceed, there must be scientific and/or medical and factual evidence which proves the contention that the defendant intentionally and actually transmitted the infection to the complainant. The consent of the complainant to sexual activity in the knowledge that the defendant is infectious does not amount to a defence in cases of intentional infection (*R* v *Donovan* [1934] 2 KB 498; *Attorney-General's Reference (No. 6 of 1980)* [1981] QB 715, CA).

In relation to injuries brought about by driving motor vehicles, the Court of Appeal has held that there is nothing wrong in principle in charging a driver with causing grievous bodily harm as well as dangerous driving in appropriate circumstances (*R* v *Bain* [2005] EWCA Crim 7). It follows that bringing about other forms of significant or lasting injury with a motor vehicle could be dealt with under the offences in this part of the chapter. However, in *Bain* it was held that where a driver was charged with both offences (causing grievous bodily harm and dangerous driving), a court could not impose consecutive terms of imprisonment for both offences arising out of the same incident. The specific offence of causing serious injury by dangerous driving (under s. 143 of the Legal Aid, Sentencing and Punishment of Offenders Act 2012) may be a far more appropriate charge when the offence has been brought about by driving a mechanically propelled vehicle (see *General Police Duties*, para. 3.21.3).

The provisions of ss. 28 and 29 of the Crime and Disorder Act 1998 in relation to racially or religiously aggravated assaults do not apply to this offence. However, the courts must still take notice of any element of racial or religious aggravation when determining sentence (Criminal Justice Act 2003, s. 145—increase in sentences for racial or religious aggravation).

1.10.7 Other Assault Offences

1.10.7.1 Assault with Intent to Resist Arrest

OFFENCE: **Assault with Intent to Resist Arrest—*Offences Against the Person Act 1861, s. 38***

- Triable either way • Two years' imprisonment on indictment
- Six months' imprisonment and/or fine summarily

The Offences Against the Person Act 1861, s. 38 states:

> Whosoever … shall assault any person with intent to resist or prevent the lawful apprehension or detainer of himself or of any other person for any offence, shall be guilty of a misdemeanor …

KEYNOTE

It must be shown that the defendant intended to resist or prevent the lawful arrest or detention of a person (his/her own arrest/detention or that of another) and that the arrest was lawful (*R* v *Self* [1992] 1 WLR 657). Provided they were acting within their powers, this offence can apply to arrests made not only by police officers but also by any person who has a power of arrest, i.e. members of the public.

Once the lawfulness of the arrest is established, the state of mind necessary for the above offence is that required for a common assault coupled with an intention to resist/prevent that arrest/detention. It is irrelevant whether or not the person being arrested/detained had actually committed an offence. These principles were set out by the Court of Appeal in a case where the defendant mistakenly believed that the arresting officers had no lawful power to do so. The court held that such a mistaken belief does not provide a defendant with the defence of 'mistake'. Similarly, a belief in one's own innocence, however genuine or honestly held, cannot afford a defence to a charge under s. 38.

1.10.7.2 Assault on Constables

There is an offence which deals specifically with assaults on police officers and those assisting them.

OFFENCE: **Assaults on Constable—*Police Act 1996, s. 89***

- Triable summarily • Six months' imprisonment and/or a fine

The Police Act 1996, s. 89 states:

> (1) Any person who assaults a constable in the execution of his duty, or a person assisting a constable in the execution of his duty, shall be guilty of an offence ...

KEYNOTE

This offence requires that the officer was acting in the execution of his/her duty when assaulted. If this is not proved, then part of the *actus reus* will be missing. Even a minor, technical and inadvertent act of unlawfulness on the part of the officer will mean that he/she cannot have been acting in the lawful execution of his/her duty. While the precise limits of a constable's duty remain undefined, it is clear that a police officer may be acting in the course of his/her duty even when doing more than the minimum the law requires (*R* v *Waterfield* [1964] 1 QB 164). It is also clear that any action amounting to assault, battery, unlawful arrest or trespass to property takes the officer outside the course of his/her duty (*Davis* v *Lisle* [1936] 2 KB 434).

A court may infer from all the circumstances that an officer was in fact acting in the execution of his/her duty (*Plowden* v *DPP* [1991] Crim LR 850).

Where the assault is made in reaction to some form of physical act by the officer, it must be shown that the officer's act was not in itself unlawful.

Other than the powers of arrest and detention, police officers have no general power to take hold of people in order to question them or keep them at a particular place while background inquiries are made about them. Therefore, if an officer does hold someone by the arm for questioning without arrest, there may well be a 'battery' by that officer (*Collins* v *Wilcock* [1984] 1 WLR 1172). The courts have accepted, however, that there may be occasions where a police officer is justified in taking hold of a person to attract his/her attention or to calm him/her down (*Mepstead* v *DPP* [1996] COD 13).

Where a prisoner is arrested and brought before a custody officer, that officer is entitled to assume that the arrest has been lawful. Therefore, if the prisoner goes on to assault the custody officer, that assault will be an offence under s. 89(1) even if the original arrest turns out to have been unlawful (*DPP* v *L* [1999] Crim LR 752).

There is no need to show that the defendant knew, or suspected, that the person was in fact a police officer or that the police officer was acting in the lawful execution of his/her duty (*Blackburn* v *Bowering* [1994] 1 WLR 1324). However, if the defendant claims to have been acting in self-defence under the mistaken and honestly held belief that he/she was being attacked, there may not be sufficient *mens rea* for a charge of assault.

These offences are simply a form of common assault upon someone carrying out a lawful function.

1.10.7.3 Obstructing a Police Officer

OFFENCE: **Obstruct Police—*Police Act 1996, s. 89***

- Triable summarily • One month's imprisonment and/or a fine

The Police Act 1996, s. 89 states:

> (2) Any person who resists or wilfully obstructs a constable in the execution of his duty, or a person assisting a constable in the execution of his duty, shall be guilty of an offence ...

KEYNOTE

No offence under s. 89(2) can be committed unless the officer was acting in the lawful execution of his/her duty.

Resistance suggests some form of physical opposition; obstruction does not and may take many forms, e.g. warning other drivers of a speed check operation (*R (DPP)* v *Glendinning* (2005) EWHC 2333 (Admin)—note that the persons warned about the speed check must be actually committing or about to commit the speeding offence), deliberately providing misleading information (*Ledger* v *DPP* [1991] Crim LR 439), deliberately drinking alcohol before providing a breath specimen (*Ingleton* v *Dibble* [1972] 1 QB 480) or 'tipping off' people who were about to commit an offence (*Green* v *Moore* [1982] QB 1044). Obstruction has been interpreted as making it more difficult for a constable to carry out his/her duty (*Hinchcliffe* v *Sheldon* [1955] 1 WLR 1207). Refusing to answer an officer's questions is not obstruction (*Rice* v *Connolly* [1966] 2 QB 414), neither is advising a person not to answer questions (*Green* v *DPP* (1991) 155 JP 816) unless perhaps the defendant was under some duty to provide information. Any obstruction must be *wilful*, that is the defendant must intend to do it. The obstruction will not be 'wilful' if the defendant was simply trying to help the police, even if that help turned out to be more of a hindrance (*Willmot* v *Atack* [1977] QB 498).

Obstruction can be caused by omission but only where the defendant was already under some duty towards the police or the officer. There is also a common law offence of refusing to go to the aid of a constable when asked to do so in order to prevent or diminish a breach of the peace (*R* v *Waugh* (1986) *The Times*, 1 October).

1.10.8 Threats to Kill

OFFENCE: **Making a Threat to Kill—*Offences Against the Person Act 1861, s. 16***

- Triable either way • 10 years' imprisonment on indictment
- Six months' imprisonment and/or a fine summarily

The Offences Against the Person Act 1861, s. 16 (amended by the Criminal Law Act 1977, s. 65, sch. 12) states:

> A person who without lawful excuse makes to another a threat, intending that that other would fear it would be carried out, to kill that other or a third person shall be guilty of an offence …

KEYNOTE

The proviso that the threat must be made 'without lawful excuse' means that a person acting in self-defence or in the course of his/her duty in protecting life (e.g. an armed police officer) would not commit this offence (provided that his/her behaviour was 'lawful').

A threat can be communicated in any way. In *R* v *Martin* (1993) 14 Cr App R (S) 645, the offender sent two anonymous notes stained with blood to the victim and in *R* v *Patel* [2012] EWCA Crim 2172 the offender threatened his former partner that he would kill their young son and then sent a text message to her that he had done so.

You must show that the threat was made (or implied (*R* v *Solanke* [1970] 1 WLR 1)) with the intention that the person receiving it would fear that it would be carried out. It is the *intention* of the person who makes the threat which is important in this offence. It does not matter whether the person to whom the threat is made does fear that the threat will be carried out.

The threat may be to kill another person at some time in the future or it may be an immediate threat, but the threatened action must be directly linked with the defendant. Simply passing on a threat on behalf of a third person *without the necessary intent* would be insufficient for this offence.

A threat to a pregnant woman in respect of her unborn child is not sufficient if the threat is to kill it before its birth (the unborn child is not a 'person'). But if it is a threat to kill the child after its birth, this would appear to be an offence within this section (*R* v *Tait* [1990] 1 QB 290).

1.10.9 Strangulation or Suffocation

OFFENCE: **Strangulation or Suffocation—*Serious Crime Act 2015, s. 75A***

- Triable either way • Five years' imprisonment and/or fine on indictment
- Six months' imprisonment and/or a fine summarily

The Serious Crime Act 2015, s. 75A states:

(1) A person ('A') commits an offence if—
  (a) A intentionally strangles another person ('B'), or
  (b) A does any other act to B that—
    (i) affects B's ability to breathe, and
    (ii) constitutes battery of B.
(2) It is a defence to an offence under this section for A to show that B consented to the strangulation or other act.
(3) But subsection (2) does not apply if—
  (a) B suffers serious harm as a result of the strangulation or other act, and
  (b) A either—
    (i) intended to cause B serious harm, or
    (ii) was reckless as to whether B would suffer serious harm.
(4) A is to be taken to have shown the fact mentioned in subsection (2) if—
  (a) sufficient evidence of the fact is adduced to raise an issue with respect to it, and
  (b) the contrary is not proved beyond reasonable doubt.
(5) ...
(6) In this section 'serious harm' means—
  (a) grievous bodily harm, within the meaning of section 18 of the Offences Against the Person Act 1861,
  (b) wounding, within the meaning of that section, or
  (c) actual bodily harm, within the meaning of section 47 of that Act.

Offences under section 75A committed outside the United Kingdom

The Serious Crime Act 2015, s. 75B states:

(1) If—
  (a) a person does an act in a country outside the United Kingdom,
  (b) the act, if done in England and Wales, would constitute an offence under section 75A, and
  (c) the person is a United Kingdom national or is habitually resident in England and Wales, the person is guilty in England and Wales of that offence.
(2) In this section—
  'country' includes territory;
  'United Kingdom national' means an individual who is—
  (a) a British citizen, a British overseas territories citizen, a British National (Overseas) or a British Overseas citizen,
  (b) a person who under the British Nationality Act 1981 is a British subject, or
  (c) a British protected person within the meaning of that Act.

KEYNOTE

'Strangulation' or 'strangles' are not specifically defined and have their ordinary meaning.

Battery in this section is a reference to the common law offence of battery. An act that affects the ability of the other person to breathe and constitutes a battery can include, but is not limited to, suffocation.

Section 75A(2) makes clear that it is a defence for a person accused of the offence to show that the other person consented to the strangulation or other act that affected their ability to breathe. This reflects the current law as set out in the case of *R* v *Brown* [1993] 2 WLR 556 (see para. **1.10.5.2**) and subsequent cases, that where a person consents to an act that amounts to no more than a battery, consent of the victim is a valid defence for the person who committed the battery. This subsection has, however, to be read in conjunction with s. 75A(3) which provides that the defence will not apply when the person suffers 'serious harm' as a result of the strangulation or other act that affects their ability to breathe. Section 75A(3) further reflects the law as set out in *R* v *Brown* and subsequent cases, which means that where a person consents to an act that causes serious harm, by which is meant injury that constitutes actual bodily harm or more serious injury, the consent does not give rise to a valid defence. In short, a person cannot validly consent to having serious harm inflicted upon them.

Section 75A(3)(b) clarifies that serious harm must be intended by the perpetrator, or that the perpetrator is reckless as to the other person suffering serious harm. This means that where a person intends to inflict harm that amounts only to a battery and the other person consents to that act, but where serious harm occurs, a valid defence of consent would only be available where the prosecution cannot prove that he/she intended to cause serious harm or were reckless as to serious harm being caused.

1.11 Offences Involving the Deprivation of Liberty

1.11.1 Introduction

In addition to the offences examined in the previous chapter, there are further offences against the person that, while not as prevalent, are nevertheless important. This chapter also examines offences and powers contained in the Modern Slavery Act 2015.

1.11.2 False Imprisonment

OFFENCE: **False Imprisonment—*Common Law***

- Triable on indictment • Unlimited maximum penalty

It is an offence at common law falsely to imprison another person.

KEYNOTE

The elements required for this offence are the unlawful and intentional/reckless restraint of a person's freedom of movement (*R* v *Rahman* (1985) 81 Cr App R 349). Locking someone in a vehicle or keeping him/her in a particular place for however short a time may amount to false imprisonment if done unlawfully. An unlawful arrest may amount to such an offence and it is not uncommon for such an allegation to be levelled at police officers against whom a public complaint has been made. On the other hand, making a *lawful* arrest will mean that the person was lawfully detained and no offence would be committed in such circumstances.

In *R* v *Shwan Faraj* [2007] EWCA Crim 1033, the court stated that there was no reason why a householder should not be entitled to detain someone in his house whom he genuinely believed to be a burglar; he would be acting in defence of his property in doing so (a lawful detention of the person). However, a householder would have to honestly believe he needed to detain the suspect and would have to do so in a way that was reasonable.

1.11.3 Kidnapping

OFFENCE: **Kidnapping—*Common Law***

- Triable on indictment • Unlimited maximum penalty

It is an offence at common law to take or carry away another person without the consent of that person and without lawful excuse.

KEYNOTE

The required elements of this offence are the unlawful taking or carrying away of one person by another by force or fraud (*R* v *D* [1984] AC 778). Force includes the threat of force (*R* v *Archer* [2011] EWCA Crim 2252). These requirements go beyond those of mere restraint needed for false imprisonment. Parents may be acting without lawful excuse, for instance if they are acting in breach of a court order in respect of their children (**see chapter 1.13**). The 'taking or carrying away' need not involve great distances as a short distance (just a few yards/metres) will suffice (*R* v *Wellard* [1978] 1 WLR 921).

The taking or carrying away of the victim must be without the consent of the victim. If the victim consents to an initial taking but later withdraws that consent, the offence would be complete. If the consent is obtained by fraud, the defendant cannot rely on that consent and the offence will be made out (*R* v *Cort* [2003] EWCA Crim 2149). In *R* v *Hendy-Freegard* [2007] EWCA Crim 1236, the defendant was a confidence trickster who pretended to be an undercover agent working for MI5 or Scotland Yard. He told his victims that he was investigating the activities of the IRA and that his investigations had revealed that they were in danger. This allowed him to take control of their lives for years and, in doing so, to direct them to move about the country from location to location. The defendant was eventually arrested and convicted of kidnapping on the basis that the offence of kidnapping had occurred as his victims had made journeys around the country which they had been induced to make as a result of the defendant's false story. The defendant successfully appealed against the kidnapping conviction, with the court stating that causing a person to move from place to place when unaccompanied by the *defendant* could not itself constitute either taking or carrying away or deprivation of liberty, which were necessary elements of the offence.

The state of mind required for this offence is the same as that for false imprisonment, indeed the only thing separating the two offences seems to be *actus reus* (*R* v *Hutchins* [1988] Crim LR 379).

1.11.4 Slavery, Servitude and Forced or Compulsory Labour

The Modern Slavery Act 2015 consists of seven parts. Part 1 provides for offences of slavery and human trafficking. Modern slavery includes sexual exploitation, forced criminality and begging, labour exploitation, domestic servitude and organ or tissue harvesting. Victims can be of any age, culture, background or gender. Part 2 of the Act provides for two civil preventative orders, the Slavery and Trafficking Prevention Order and the Slavery and Trafficking Risk Order.

1.11.4.1 Offence of Slavery, Servitude and Forced or Compulsory Labour

OFFENCE: **Slavery, Servitude and Forced or Compulsory Labour—*Modern Slavery Act 2015, s. 1***

• Triable either way • Life imprisonment on indictment • 12 months' imprisonment and/or a fine summarily

The Modern Slavery Act 2015, s. 1 states:

(1) A person commits an offence if—
- (a) the person holds another person in slavery or servitude and the circumstances are such that the person knows or ought to know that the other person is held in slavery or servitude, or
- (b) the person requires another person to perform forced or compulsory labour and the circumstances are such that the person knows or ought to know that the other person is being required to perform forced or compulsory labour.

KEYNOTE

In s. 1(1), the references to holding a person in slavery or servitude or requiring a person to perform forced or compulsory labour are to be construed in accordance with Article 4 of the European Convention on Human Rights (s. 1(2)).

Article 4 of the European Convention on Human Rights states:

1. No one shall be held in slavery or servitude.
2. No one shall be required to perform forced or compulsory labour.
3. For the purpose of this Article the term 'forced or compulsory labour' shall not include:
   (a) any work required to be done in the ordinary course of detention imposed according to the provisions of Article 5 of this Convention or during conditional release from such detention;

(b) any service of a military character or, in case of conscientious objectors in countries where they are recognised, service exacted instead of compulsory military service;
(c) any service exacted in case of an emergency or calamity threatening the life or well-being of the community;
(d) any work or service which forms part of normal civic obligations.

In determining whether a person is being held in slavery or servitude or required to perform forced or compulsory labour, regard may be had to all the circumstances (s. 1(3)). The list of particular vulnerabilities which may be considered is non-exhaustive but explicitly includes regard being made to any of the person's personal circumstances (such as the person being a child under the age of 18, the person's family relationships and any mental or physical illness) which may make the person more vulnerable than other persons. Regard may also be had to any work or services provided by the person, including work or services provided in circumstances which constitute exploitation within s. 3(3)–(6) (**see para. 1.11.4.2, Keynote** for the meaning of 'exploitation'). This makes it clear that the forced and compulsory labour offence can cover a broad range of types of work and services including, for example begging or pick-pocketing, which could amount to exploitation under s. 3(5) or (6).

Section 1(5) states that the consent of a person (whether an adult or a child) to any of the acts alleged to constitute holding the person in slavery or servitude, or requiring the person to perform forced or compulsory labour, does not preclude a determination that the person is being held in slavery or servitude, or required to perform forced or compulsory labour.

1.11.4.2 Offence of Human Trafficking

OFFENCE: **Human Trafficking—*Modern Slavery Act 2015, s. 2***

• Triable either way • Life imprisonment on indictment • 12 months' imprisonment and/or a fine summarily

The Modern Slavery Act 2015, s. 2 states:

(1) A person commits an offence if the person arranges or facilitates the travel of another person ('V') with a view to V being exploited.
(2) It is irrelevant whether V consents to the travel (whether V is an adult or a child).
(3) A person may in particular arrange or facilitate V's travel by recruiting V, transporting or transferring V, harbouring or receiving V, or transferring or exchanging control over V.
(4) A person arranges or facilitates V's travel with a view to V being exploited only if—
(a) the person intends to exploit V (in any part of the world) during or after the travel, or
(b) the person knows or ought to know that another person is likely to exploit V (in any part of the world) during or after the travel.
(5) 'Travel' means—
(a) arriving in, or entering, any country,
(b) departing from any country,
(c) travelling within any country.
(6) A person who is a UK national commits an offence under this section regardless of—
(a) where the arranging or facilitating takes place, or
(b) where the travel takes place.
(7) A person who is not a UK national commits an offence under this section if—
(a) any part of the arranging or facilitating takes place in the United Kingdom, or
(b) the travel consists of arrival in or entry into, departure from, or travel within, the United Kingdom.

KEYNOTE

Meaning of Exploitation

The s. 2 trafficking offence is committed by arranging or facilitating travel with a view to the victim's exploitation. Section 3 of the Modern Slavery Act 2015 sets out the meaning of exploitation for the purposes of s. 2.

Exploitation includes slavery, servitude and forced or compulsory labour by reference to the offence under s. 1. Equivalent conduct outside England and Wales also comes within this definition (s. 3(2)).

Section 3(3) sets out that exploitation includes sexual exploitation by reference to conduct which would constitute the commission of an offence of taking, or permitting to take, indecent photographs of children or any of the sexual offences provided for in part 1 of the Sexual Offences Act 2003 (these include offences relating to rape, sexual assault, prostitution and child pornography). Section 3(3)(b) ensures that equivalent conduct committed outside England and Wales also comes within the definition even though for jurisdictional reasons it would not be an offence under English law.

Exploitation includes exploitation in the context of trafficking for organ removal or for the sale of human tissue by reference to offences in the Human Tissue Act 2004. Again, equivalent conduct outside England and Wales is within the definition (s. 3(4)).

Section 3(5) states that exploitation also includes all other types of exploitation where a person is subject to force, threats or deception which is designed to induce him/her:

(a) to provide services of any kind;
(b) to provide a person with benefits of any kind; or
(c) to enable another person to acquire benefits of any kind.

The above would include forcing a person to engage in activities such as begging or shop theft. It is not necessary for this conduct to be a criminal offence. Section 3(6) broadens the type of exploitation described in s. 3(5) so that it includes where a person is used (or there is an attempt to use the person) to do something for such a purpose, having been chosen on the grounds that he/she is a child, is ill, disabled or related to a person, in circumstances where a person without the illness, disability or family relationship would be likely to refuse.

Committing an Offence with Intent to Commit an Offence under Section 2

A person commits an offence under s. 4 of the Modern Slavery Act 2015 if the person commits any offence with the intention of committing an offence under s. 2 (including an offence committed by aiding, abetting, counselling or procuring an offence under that section).

A person guilty of an offence under s. 4 is liable, on indictment, to imprisonment for a term not exceeding 10 years and, on summary conviction, to imprisonment for a term of six months or a fine or both (s. 5(2)).

Where the offence under s. 4 is committed by kidnap or false imprisonment, a person guilty of that offence is liable, on conviction on indictment, to imprisonment for life (s. 5(3)).

UK National

'UK national' means:

(a) a British citizen,
(b) a person who is a British subject by virtue of Part 4 of the British Nationality Act 1981 and who has a right of abode in the United Kingdom, or
(c) a person who is a British overseas territories citizen by virtue of a connection with Gibraltar.

Detention of Land Vehicle, Ship or Aircraft

The Modern Slavery Act 2015, s. 12 states:

(1) If a person ('P') has been arrested for an offence under section 2, a constable or senior immigration officer may detain a relevant land vehicle, ship or aircraft.
(2) A land vehicle, ship or aircraft is relevant if the constable or officer has reasonable grounds to believe that an order for its forfeiture could be made under section 11 if P were convicted of the offence.
(3) The land vehicle, ship or aircraft may be detained—
  (a) until a decision is taken as to whether or not to charge P with the offence,
  (b) if P has been charged, until P is acquitted, the charge against P is dismissed or the proceedings are discontinued, or
  (c) if P has been charged and convicted, until the court decides whether or not to order forfeiture of the vehicle, ship or aircraft.
(4) A person (other than P) may apply to the court for the release of the land vehicle, ship or aircraft on the grounds that the person—
  (a) owns the vehicle, ship or aircraft,

(b) was, immediately before the detention of the vehicle, ship or aircraft, in possession of it under a hire-purchase agreement, or

(c) is a charterer of the ship or aircraft.

(5) The court to which an application is made under subsection (4) may, if satisfactory security or surety is tendered, release the land vehicle, ship or aircraft on condition that it is made available to the court if—

(a) P is convicted, and

(b) an order for its forfeiture is made under section 11.

(6) In this section, 'the court' means—

(a) if P has not been charged, or P has been charged but proceedings for the offence have not begun to be heard, a magistrates' court;

(b) if P has been charged and proceedings for the offence have begun to be heard, the court hearing the proceedings.

(7) In this section, 'senior immigration officer' means an immigration officer not below the rank of chief immigration officer.

A reference to being an owner of a vehicle, ship or aircraft includes a reference to being any of a number of persons who jointly own it.

1.12 Sexual Offences

1.12.1 Introduction

The majority of offences in this chapter are dealt with under the Sexual Offences Act 2003. The Act provides measures such as the presumptions about consent that will be made by a court under certain circumstances. Apart from the offence of rape (under ss. 1 and 5 of the Act), the offences are 'gender neutral', i.e. they can be committed by a male or a female.

It is important to note that there is an overlap between many of the offences, for example a mentally disordered person could be raped under s. 1 (because of his/her lack of ability to give true consent) or subjected to sexual activity contrary to s. 30 (due to an inability to refuse). In all circumstances, it is essential that the most appropriate option is chosen.

1.12.2 Anonymity

The Sexual Offences (Amendment) Act 1992, s. 1 states:

(1) Where an allegation has been made that an offence to which this Act applies has been committed against a person, no matter relating to that person shall during that person's lifetime be included in any publication, if it is likely to lead members of the public to identify that person as the person against whom the offence is alleged to have been committed.

(2) Where a person is accused of an offence to which this Act applies, no matter likely to lead members of the public to identify a person as the person against whom the offence is alleged to have been committed ('the complainant') shall during the complainant's lifetime, be included in any publication.

(3) ...

(3A) The matters relating to a person in relation to which the restrictions imposed by subsection (1) or (2) apply (if their inclusion in any publication is likely to have the result mentioned in that subsection) include in particular
- (a) the person's name,
- (b) the person's address,
- (c) the identity of any school or other educational establishment attended by the person,
- (d) the identity of any place of work, and
- (e) any still or moving picture of the person.

KEYNOTE

Offences Covered

The Sexual Offences (Amendment) Act 1992 provides anonymity to a victim/complainant of most sexual offences. It applies to almost all sexual offences under part 1 of the Sexual Offences Act 2003 (such as rape, assault by penetration, sexual assault by touching etc.) as well as attempts and conspiracy to commit such acts. It also applies to aiding, abetting, counselling or procuring any of these offences. It *does not* apply to the offences dealing with sex with an adult relative (ss. 64 and 65) and sexual activity in a public lavatory (s. 71).

Publication

Includes any speech, writing, relevant programme or other communication in whatever form, which is addressed to the public at large or any section of the public (and for this purpose every relevant programme shall be taken to be so addressed), but does not include an indictment or other document prepared for use in particular legal proceedings (s. 6(1)).

Lifetime Anonymity

The alleged victim/complainant is entitled to anonymity *throughout their lifetime*. Once an allegation of one of the offences in question has been made, nothing may be published which is likely to lead members of the public to identify the alleged victim/complainant. The protection under s. 1(2) applies from the time someone is accused for that person's lifetime even if proceedings are later abandoned.

Lifting Restrictions

Under s. 3 of the Act, the prohibition on publicity may be lifted by order of the court if either:

- publicity is required by the accused so that witnesses will come forward and the conduct of the defence is likely to be seriously prejudiced if the direction is not given; or
- the trial judge is satisfied that imposition of the prohibition imposes a substantial and unreasonable restriction on the reporting of the proceedings and it is in the public interest to relax the restriction.

1.12.3 Rape

OFFENCE: **Rape—*Sexual Offences Act 2003, s. 1***

• Triable on indictment • Life imprisonment

The Sexual Offences Act 2003, s. 1 states:

(1) A person (A) commits an offence if—
  (a) he intentionally penetrates the vagina, anus or mouth of another person (B) with his penis,
  (b) B does not consent to the penetration, and
  (c) A does not reasonably believe that B consents.
(2) Whether a belief is reasonable is to be determined having regard to all the circumstances, including any steps A has taken to ascertain whether B consents.

KEYNOTE

Rape is an offence that can *only* be committed via the use of the penis. Therefore rape (as a principal offender) can only be committed by a man, although a woman who encourages or assists a man to penetrate another person with his penis, not reasonably believing the other person is consenting, may be convicted of aiding and abetting rape (*R* v *Cogan* [1976] QB 217). It can be committed if the defendant penetrates the vagina, anus or mouth of the victim with the penis. 'Vagina' is taken to include the vulva (s. 79(9)). In respect of penetration of the vagina, it is not necessary to show that the hymen was ruptured.

You must show that the victim did not in fact consent at the time and that the defendant did not reasonably believe that he/she consented. The wording is supported by the further provision that whether or not the defendant's belief is reasonable will be determined having regard to all the circumstances (s. 1(2)). Section 1(2) does not positively require an accused to have taken steps to ascertain whether the complainant consents. However, this is something a jury will consider when considering the reasonableness of his belief. More steps are likely to be expected where there is no established relationship.

1.12.3.1 Criminal Conduct

To prove rape, you must show that the defendant intentionally penetrated the vagina, mouth or anus of the victim with his penis. Penetration is a continuing act from entry to withdrawal (s. 79(2)). The 'continuing' nature of this act is of importance when considering the issue of consent and the statutory presumptions under ss. 75 and 76. While it is not necessary to prove ejaculation (indeed, it is entirely irrelevant to the offence), the presence of semen or sperm may be important in proving the elements of a sexual offence. References to a part of the body (for example, penis, vagina) will include references to a body part which has been surgically constructed, particularly if it is through gender reassignment (s. 79(3)). The offence thus protects transsexuals. It also means, however, that a person who has a surgically constructed penis can commit the offence of rape.

1.12.3.2 Consent

The Sexual Offences Act 2003, s. 74 states:

> For the purpose of this Part, a person consents if he agrees by choice, and has the freedom and capacity to make that choice.

The issue of consent is a question of fact although legislation has included some specific situations which allow presumptions and conclusions to be made regarding a lack of consent.

Any consent given must be 'true' consent, not simply a *submission* induced by fear or fraud. Therefore, if the person does not have any real choice in the matter, or the choice is not a genuine exercise of free will, then he/she has not 'consented'.

An example of how 'true' consent operates is the case involving PC Stephen Mitchell who committed a number of sexual offences against vulnerable women over a period of years. On one occasion, Mitchell drove one of his victims to a dirt track and told her that if she did not do as he said, he would ensure her children were taken away from her for good, and then raped her. Any 'consent' given by the victim could not be 'true' because her choice to participate in the act of sexual intercourse would not be by the genuine exercise of free will (a 'gun to the head'-type scenario).

'Capacity' is an integral part of the definition of consent. A valid consent can only be given by a person who has the capacity to give it. The Sexual Offences Act 2003 does not define 'capacity'. Common law principles that developed under the old law suggest that complainants will not have had the capacity to agree by choice where their understanding and knowledge were so limited that they were not in a position to decide whether or not to agree (*R* v *Howard* (1965) 1 WLR 13). Some people are not capable of giving the required consent—these are addressed in further sections of this chapter.

Even if freely given, consent may still be withdrawn at any time. Once the 'passive' party to sexual penetration withdraws consent, any continued activity (for example, penetration in rape: *R* v *Cooper* [1994] Crim LR 531) can amount to a sexual offence provided all the other ingredients are present.

In *R* v *B* [2006] EWCA Crim 2945, the Court of Appeal stated that whether an individual had a sexual disease or condition, such as being HIV-positive, was not an issue as far as consent was concerned. The case related to a man who was alleged to have raped a woman after they had met outside a nightclub. When arrested, the man informed the custody officer that he was HIV-positive, a fact he had not disclosed to the victim prior to sexual intercourse. At the original trial, the judge directed that this non-disclosure was relevant to the issue of consent. On appeal, the court stated that this was not the case and that the consent issue for a jury to consider was whether or not the victim consented to sexual intercourse, not whether she consented to sexual intercourse with a person suffering from a sexually transmitted disease. However, in *R* v *McNally* [2013] EWCA Crim 1051 (**see para. 1.12.3.3**), the Court of Appeal observed that *B* was not an authority that HIV status *could not* vitiate consent. *B* left the issue open and HIV status *could* vitiate consent if, for example, the complainant had been positively assured that the accused was not HIV-positive.

> **KEYNOTE**
>
> So the situation with a person who is *HIV-positive* and *is aware* of his condition, is as follows:
>
> - if the accused makes no mention of his condition, this will not be rape (*R* v *B*). However, it may constitute an offence under the Offences Against the Person Act 1861 (s. 20 or s. 18) (*R* v *Dica* and *R* v *Konzani*, at para. 1.10.6.4);
> - if the accused positively assures the complainant that he is not HIV-positive, this could constitute rape (*R* v *McNally*).

1.12.3.3 Conditional Consent

Section 74 has been considered by the High Court and the Court of Appeal in a series of cases where apparent consent in relation to sexual offences was considered *not to be true consent*, either because a condition upon which consent was given was not complied with or because of a material deception (other than one which falls within s. 76 of the Sexual Offences Act 2003 (**see para. 1.12.3.5**)). The judgments identified three sets of circumstances in which the consent to sexual activity might be vitiated where the condition was breached.

In *Assange* v *Sweden* [2011] EWHC 2489 (Admin), the Divisional Court considered the situation in which A knew B (the complainant) would only consent to sexual intercourse if he used a condom. The court rejected the view that the conclusive presumption in s. 76 of the Sexual Offences Act 2003 would apply and concluded that the issue of consent could be determined under s. 74 rather than s. 76, and stated that it would be open to a jury to hold that if B had made it clear that she would only consent to sexual intercourse if A used a condom, then there would be no consent if, without B's consent, A did not use a condom or removed or tore the condom. A's conduct in having sexual intercourse without a condom in circumstances where B had made it clear that she would only have sexual intercourse if A did use a condom, would therefore amount to an offence.

In *R (F)* v *DPP* [2013] EWHC 945 (Admin), the High Court examined an application for judicial review of the refusal of the DPP to initiate a prosecution for rape and/or sexual assault on B by A (her former partner). 'Choice' and the 'freedom' to make any particular choice must, the court said, be approached in 'a broad common-sense way'. Against what the court described as the 'essential background' of A's 'sexual dominance' of B and B's 'unenthusiastic acquiescence to his demands', the court considered a specific incident when B consented to sexual intercourse only on the clear understanding that A *would not* ejaculate inside her vagina. B believed that A intended and agreed to withdraw before ejaculation, and A knew and understood that this was the *only basis* on which B was prepared to have sexual intercourse with him. When he deliberately ejaculated inside B, the result, the court said, was B being deprived of choice relating to the crucial feature on which her original consent to sexual intercourse was based and, accordingly, her consent was negated. Contrary to B's wishes, and knowing that she would not have consented and did not consent to penetration or the continuation of penetration, if B had an inkling of A's intention, A deliberately ejaculated within her vagina. This combination of circumstances falls within the statutory definition of rape.

The third case, *McNally* v *R* [2013] EWCA Crim 1051, differs from the other two cases. Unlike *Assange* and *F*, both of which turned on an express condition, *McNally* was concerned with the material deception of B by A. The unusual facts considered by the court involved the relationship between two girls which, over three years, developed from an internet relationship to an 'exclusive romantic relationship' that involved their meeting and engaging in sexual activity. From the start, A presented herself to B as a boy, a deception she maintained throughout their relationship. Examining the nature of 'choice' and 'freedom', the court determined that 'deception as to gender can vitiate consent'. The court's reasoning is that while, in a physical sense, the acts of assault by penetration of the vagina are the same whether perpetrated by a male or a female, the sexual nature of the acts is, on any common-sense view, different where the complainant is deliberately deceived by a defendant into believing the latter is male. Assuming the facts to be proved as alleged, B chose to have sexual encounters with a boy and her preference (her freedom to choose whether or not to have a sexual encounter with a girl) was removed by A's deception. Demonstrating that the circumstances in which consent may be vitiated are not limitless, the court explained that, in reality, some deceptions (such as in relation to wealth) will *obviously not be sufficient* to vitiate consent.

In *R* v *Lawrence* [2020] EWCA Crim 971, the Court of Appeal considered whether a lie about fertility could negate consent. Lawrence had been convicted on two counts of rape on the basis that his false representation to the complainant that he had had a vasectomy vitiated her consent in that she had only agreed to unprotected sex as a result of the representation. Otherwise she would have insisted on him wearing a condom. The appeal was allowed—the court stated that a lie about fertility was different from a lie about whether a condom was being worn during sex, different from engaging in intercourse not intending to withdraw having promised to do so and different from engaging in sexual activity having misrepresented one's gender. The complainant agreed to sexual intercourse with Lawrence without imposing any physical restrictions. She agreed both to penetration of her vagina and to ejaculation without the protection of a condom. In so doing, she was deceived about the nature or quality of the ejaculate and therefore of the risks and possible consequences of unprotected intercourse. The deception was one which related not to the physical performance of the sexual act but to risks or consequences associated with it. It made no difference to the issue of consent whether there was an express deception or a failure to disclose. The issue was whether Lawrence's lie was sufficiently closely connected to the performance of the sexual act, rather than the broad circumstances surrounding it and, in this case, it was not. Lawrence's lie about his fertility was not capable in law of negating consent.

1.12.3.4 Sections 75 and 76—Applicability

Sections 75 and 76 of the Sexual Offences Act 2003 allow presumptions to be made in relation to the absence of consent. They apply to offences under:

- s. 1 (rape);
- s. 2 (assault by penetration);
- s. 3 (sexual assault);
- s. 4 (causing sexual activity without consent).

1.12.3.5 Section 75—Evidential Presumptions about Consent

The Sexual Offences Act 2003, s. 75 states:

> (1) If in proceedings for an offence to which this section applies it is proved—
> (a) that the defendant did the relevant act,
> (b) that any of the circumstances specified in subsection (2) existed, and
> (c) that the defendant knew that those circumstances existed,
> the complainant is to be taken not to have consented to the relevant act unless sufficient evidence is adduced to raise an issue as to whether he consented, and the defendant is to be taken not to have reasonably believed that the complainant consented unless sufficient evidence is adduced to raise an issue as to whether he reasonably believed it.

KEYNOTE

This means that if the prosecution can show that the defendant carried out the relevant act in relation to certain specified sexual offences (for example, penetration in rape) and that any of the circumstances below existed and the defendant knew they existed, it will be presumed that the victim did not consent. Then the defendant will have to satisfy the court, by reference to evidence, that this presumption should not be made.

Section 75(2) sets out the circumstances in which evidential presumptions may apply. They are that:

(a) *any person* was, at the time of the relevant act (or immediately before it began), using violence against *the complainant* or causing *the complainant* to fear that immediate violence would be used against him/her;
(b) *any person* was, at the time of the relevant act or immediately before it began, causing *the complainant* to fear that violence was being used, or that immediate violence would be used, against *another person*;
(c) *the complainant* was, and the defendant was not, unlawfully detained at the time of the relevant act;
(d) *the complainant* was asleep or otherwise unconscious at the time of the relevant act;
(e) because of *the complainant's* physical disability, the complainant would not have been able at the time of the relevant act to communicate to the defendant whether the complainant consented;
(f) *any person* had administered to or caused to be taken by the complainant, without the complainant's consent, a substance which, having regard to when it was administered or taken, was capable of causing or enabling the complainant to be stupefied or overpowered at the time of the relevant act.

The 'relevant act' for each offence covered by s. 75 will generally be obvious but is set out specifically at s. 77.

It is important to note that the circumstances set out in s. 75(2) are not exhaustive in terms of deciding when consent will be absent. There may be circumstances that fall outside the situations described in s. 75(2) where consent does not exist. For example, the case of PC Stephen Mitchell (**see para. 1.12.3.2**) did not involve any of the circumstances set out in s. 75(2) and yet he was still guilty of rape as his victim's consent was not *true* consent; it was obtained by a threat to take her children away (submission). The fact that this situation does not appear in the sets of circumstances listed in s. 75(2) merely means that a presumption in relation to consent cannot be made in such a case—*it does not mean that the victim consented to the activity.*

1.12.3.6 Conclusive Presumptions about Consent

Section 76 of the Sexual Offences Act 2003 states:

(1) If in proceedings for an offence to which this section applies it is proved that the defendant did the relevant act and that any of the circumstances specified in subsection (2) existed, it is to be conclusively presumed—
    (a) that the complainant did not consent to the relevant act, and
    (b) that the defendant did not believe that the complainant consented to the relevant act.
(2) The circumstances are that—
    (a) the defendant intentionally deceived the complainant as to the nature or purpose of the relevant act;
    (b) the defendant intentionally induced the complainant to consent to the relevant act by impersonating a person known personally to the complainant.

These provisions deal with situations where the defendant either misrepresents the nature or purpose of what he/she is doing (for example, pretending that inserting a finger into the victim's vagina is for medical reasons) or impersonates the victim's partner. Section 76 requires that a misunderstanding was created by the defendant and that it was done deliberately. Once it is proved, beyond a reasonable doubt, that these circumstances existed then it is conclusive and the defendant cannot argue against them.

In *R* v *Bingham* [2013] 2 Cr App R 307 (seven counts of causing his girlfriend to engage in sexual activity without consent under s. 4 of the Sexual Offences Act 2003 (**see para. 1.12.5**)), B, using pseudonyms, established an online Facebook relationship with his girlfriend so as to persuade and then blackmail her into providing him with photographs of her engaging in sexual activity. The Court of Appeal held that the reliance at trial upon s. 76 was misplaced. The motive behind the conduct was sexual gratification, and there was no deception as to that (i.e. there was no deception as to the purpose of the act). The prosecution would have had forceful arguments under s. 74 on the basis that the victim only complied because she was being blackmailed. In the light of s. 76(2), it would appear that deception as to the identity of the recipient would not be sufficient as it was impersonation of a person unknown to the complainant. This case can be contrasted with *R* v *Devonald* [2008] EWCA Crim 527 (another s. 4 offence). In this case, the court held that s. 76 did apply; it was open to the jury to conclude that the complainant was deceived into believing he was masturbating for the gratification of a 20-year-old girl via a webcam when in fact he was doing it for the father of a former girlfriend who was teaching him a lesson. Here, 'purpose' has been given a wide meaning in that the deception was not as to sexual gratification, rather it was to the purpose of the masturbation (to teach the victim a lesson).

It is important to emphasise the fact that s. 76 deals with situations where the defendant:

- deceives the victim regarding the nature and purpose of the act; or
- induces the victim to consent to the relevant act by impersonating a person known personally to the complainant.

If the deception/inducement *does not* relate to either of these aims, then s. 76 has no application. For example, in *R* v *Jheeta* [2007] EWCA Crim 1699, the defendant deceived the complainant into having sex more frequently than she would have done otherwise. In these circumstances, the conclusive presumptions under the Sexual Offences Act 2003 had no relevance as the complainant had not been deceived as to the nature or purpose of the sexual intercourse. Likewise, a false promise to marry made by A to B to encourage B to have sexual intercourse would not be covered, nor would a false promise to pay B in exchange for sexual intercourse.

1.12.4 Assault

There are several specific offences dealing with types of sexual assault: these are discussed below.

1.12.4.1 Assault by Penetration

OFFENCE: **Assault by Penetration—*Sexual Offences Act 2003, s. 2***

- Triable on indictment • Life imprisonment

The Sexual Offences Act 2003, s. 2 states:

(1) A person (A) commits an offence if—
  (a) he intentionally penetrates the vagina or anus of another person (B) with a part of his body or anything else,
  (b) the penetration is sexual,
  (c) B does not consent to the penetration, and
  (d) A does not reasonably believe that B consents.

KEYNOTE

This offence involves penetration by any part of the body or anything else whatsoever. It is therefore a broad offence covering insertion into the vagina or anus (though not the mouth) of *anything* (such as a dildo or even an animal), provided that the penetration is 'sexual'. Whether a belief is reasonable is to be determined having regard to all the circumstances, including any steps the defendant has taken to ascertain whether the victim consents (s. 2(2)).

1.12.4.2 The Definition of the Term 'Sexual'

Section 78 of the Act defines the term 'sexual' and provides that penetration, touching or any other activity will be sexual if a reasonable person would consider that:

(a) whatever its circumstances or any person's purpose in relation to it, it is sexual by its very nature; or
(b) because of its nature, it *may* be sexual and, because of its circumstances or the purpose of any person in relation to it, it is sexual.

Therefore, activity under (a) covers things that a reasonable person would always consider to be sexual (for example, masturbation), while activity under (b) covers things that may or may not be considered sexual by a reasonable person depending on the circumstances or the intentions of the person carrying it out (or both). For instance, a doctor inserting his/her finger into the vagina of a patient might be considered sexual by its nature, but if done for a purely medical purpose in a hospital (the circumstances and genuine medical purpose of the doctor in examining the patient), it would not be sexual.

If the activity would not appear to a reasonable person to be sexual, then it will not meet either criterion and, irrespective of any sexual gratification the person might derive from it, the activity will not be 'sexual'. Therefore weird or exotic fetishes that no ordinary person would regard as being sexual or potentially sexual will not be covered. This pretty well follows the common law developments in this area (*R* v *Court* [1989] AC 28 and *R* v *Tabassum* [2000] 2 Cr App R 328).

KEYNOTE

The offence of assault by penetration contains the first reference to the term 'sexual'. The term is exceptionally important for a variety of offences contained in the Sexual Offences Act 2003. What has been said above in relation to how this term is interpreted will apply to *all* offences contained in the Sexual Offences Act 2003 where the term 'sexual' is used, apart from the offence under s. 15A (sexual communication with a child) and s. 71 (sexual activity in a public lavatory).

1.12.4.3 Sexual Assault

OFFENCE: **Sexual Assault—*Sexual Offences Act 2003, s. 3***

- Triable either way • 10 years' imprisonment on indictment
- Six months' imprisonment and/or fine summarily

The Sexual Offences Act 2003, s. 3 states:

(1) A person (A) commits an offence if—
 (a) he intentionally touches another person (B),
 (b) the touching is sexual,
 (c) B does not consent to the touching, and
 (d) A does not reasonably believe that B consents.

KEYNOTE

Touching for the purposes of the above offence includes touching a person's clothing while they are wearing it. Therefore, where a man approached a woman and asked *'Do you fancy a shag?'*, grabbing at a pocket on her tracksuit bottoms as she tried to walk away, he was properly convicted of the s. 3 offence even though he did not touch her person (*R* v *H* [2005] EWCA Crim 732).

The conduct must be intentional (rather than reckless or accidental).

Whether a belief is reasonable is to be determined having regard to all the circumstances, including any steps the defendant has taken to ascertain whether the victim consents (s. 3(2)).

The statutory ingredients of the offence under s. 3 *do not* contain the requirement that the defendant intended the touching to be sexual. In *Attorney-General's Reference (No. 1 of 2020)* [2020] EWCA Crim 1665, the defendant, while travelling on a train, had kissed the victim, a fellow passenger, on the lips without her consent. At trial, the defendant stated that the kiss had not been sexual. Rather, it had been a friendly reassuring gesture. The trial judge accepted submissions that it was a necessary ingredient of the offence for the prosecution to prove that the defendant intended the touching to be sexual—the Court of Appeal disagreed. The scheme of the Act is that wherever an offence is committed against the victim by sexual touching, proof of sexual intention as part of the *mens rea* is not required.

1.12.4.4 The Definition of the Term 'Touching'

Section 79(8) states that touching includes touching:

- with any part of the body;
- with anything else;
- through anything;

and in particular, touching amounting to penetration (this could include kissing).

The part of the body touched does not have to be a sexual organ or orifice. There is no requirement for force or violence so the lightest touching will suffice. 'Touching' for the purposes of an offence under s. 3 includes the touching of a victim's clothing while they are wearing it even though the person of the victim is not touched through the clothing (*R* v *H* [2005] EWCA Crim 732). In *H*, it was held that it was not Parliament's intention to preclude the touching of a victim's clothing from amounting to a sexual 'assault'. Where touching was not automatically by its nature 'sexual', the test under s. 78(b) applies (**see para. 1.12.4.2**). In a case where that section applies, it will be appropriate for a trial judge to ask the jury to determine whether touching was 'sexual' by answering two questions. First, would the jury, as 12 reasonable people, consider that the touching could be sexual and, if so, whether in all the circumstances of the case, they would consider that the purpose of the touching *had in fact been* sexual.

The victim need not be aware of the touching. For example, in the case of *R* v *Bounekhla* [2006] EWCA Crim 1217 the accused surreptitiously took his penis out of his trousers and ejaculated onto a woman's clothing when pressed up against her dancing at a nightclub.

If touching does not occur, the offence is not completed, although the circumstances may amount to an attempt. Nevertheless, it remains arguable that ejaculation onto a victim's clothing without contact with any part of the accused's body still constitutes a touching.

KEYNOTE

The offence of sexual assault contains the first reference to the term 'touching'. The term is exceptionally important for a variety of offences contained in the Sexual Offences Act 2003. What has been said above in relation to how this term is interpreted will apply to all offences contained in the Sexual Offences Act 2003 where the term 'touching' is used.

1.12.5 Causing Sexual Activity without Consent

OFFENCE: **Causing a Person to Engage in Sexual Activity without Consent—*Sexual Offences Act 2003, s. 4***

- If it involves penetration: of the victim's anus or vagina, of victim's mouth with penis, of any other person's anus or vagina with a part of victim's body or by the victim, or of any person's mouth by victim's penis—triable on indictment; life imprisonment
- Otherwise triable either way; 10 years' imprisonment on indictment; six months' imprisonment and/or a fine summarily

The Sexual Offences Act 2003, s. 4 states:

(1) A person (A) commits an offence if—
  (a) he intentionally causes another person (B) to engage in an activity,
  (b) the activity is sexual,
  (c) B does not consent to engaging in the activity, and
  (d) A does not reasonably believe that B consents.

KEYNOTE

The offence is committed when A causes B to engage in sexual activity without B's consent, whether or not A also engages in it and whether or not A is present.

The offence can involve a number of permutations, for example a woman making a man penetrate her, a man forcing someone else to masturbate him, a woman making another woman masturbate a third person or even an animal. The shocking circumstances of *R* v *H* [2008] EWCA Crim 1202 are an example of where an animal was used in the commission of the offence where the visibly mentally disabled victim was forced, among other things, to be penetrated in the anus by a dog. It would include causing a person to act as a prostitute. Apart from the defendant and the victim, there may be others involved who also consent—they may be liable for aiding and abetting under the right circumstances.

The term 'activity' is not defined and is capable of being given a wide interpretation, although it must have actually taken place. The activity engaged in must be 'sexual' in accordance with s. 78. It can include engaging someone in a conversation of a sexual nature (*R* v *Grout* [2011] EWCA Crim 299).

This offence overlaps partly with rape in that it deals with vaginal, anal and oral penetration. The offence is wider than rape, in that rape can only be committed by a man, as a principal, and does not involve penetration with an object. The offence can be committed by and against persons of either sex and includes cases of 'female rape', i.e. where A causes B to penetrate her vagina with his penis. Furthermore, the offence makes A criminally liable for causing B to engage in sexual activity where B cannot himself be convicted of any offence because he has a defence such as duress or is under the age of criminal responsibility (**see chapter 1.4**).

Whether a belief is reasonable is to be determined having regard to all the circumstances, including any steps the defendant has taken to ascertain whether the victim consents (s. 4(2)).

1.12.6 Rape and Other Offences Against Children Under 13

Offences under ss. 1 to 4 of the Sexual Offences Act 2003 are 'mirrored' by ss. 5 to 8 of the Act. The common features of the offences under ss. 5 to 8 are that the victim is a child under the age of 13 and that, once the *actus reus* of the offence is proved, no issue of 'consent' to the activity arises—a child under 13 cannot 'consent' to such activity.

OFFENCE		OFFENCE—VICTIM U13		MODE OF TRIAL/SENTENCE
Section 1 Rape	→	Section 5 Rape	→	Triable on Indictment—life imprisonment
Section 2 Assault by Penetration	→	Section 6 Assault by Penetration	→	
Section 3 Sexual Touching	→	Section 7 Sexual Touching	→	Triable Either Way Indictment—14 years' imprisonment Summary—six months' imprisonment and/or fine
Section 4 Causing Sexual Activity	→	Section 8 Causing or Inciting Activity	→	

In *R* v *Walker* [2006] EWCA Crim 1907, the Court of Appeal held that s. 8 of the Act created two offences: (a) intentionally causing; and (b) intentionally inciting a child under 13 to engage in sexual activity. The offence is centred on the concept of incitement and the acts had to be intentional or deliberate, but it was not a necessary ingredient for incitement of sexual activity that the defendant had intended the sexual activity to take place. An individual can commit an offence of incitement even if the activity he/she is encouraging etc. does not take place.

1.12.7 Child Sex Offences

The Sexual Offences Act 2003 contains specific offences relating to sexual activity involving or directed towards children.

The Act makes special exceptions to some offences of aiding, abetting or counselling some offences involving children (an example is provided in **para. 1.12.7.4** but the full list of offences is set out in s. 73(2); basically, it covers specific offences against children under 13 and offences involving sexual activity with a child under 16).

1.12.7.1 Sexual Activity with a Child

OFFENCE: **Sexual Activity with a Child—*Sexual Offences Act 2003, s. 9***

- If involves penetration of victim's anus or vagina by a part of defendant's body or anything else, of victim's mouth with defendant's penis, of defendant's anus or vagina by a part of victim's body or of defendant's mouth by victim's penis—triable on indictment; 14 years' imprisonment • Otherwise triable either way; 14 years' imprisonment on indictment; six months' imprisonment summarily

The Sexual Offences Act 2003, s. 9 states:

(1) A person aged 18 or over (A) commits an offence if—
 (a) he intentionally touches another person (B),
 (b) the touching is sexual, and
 (c) either—
  (i) B is under 16 and A does not reasonably believe that B is 16 or over, or
  (ii) B is under 13.

KEYNOTE

You must show that the defendant intentionally touched the victim sexually and either that the victim was under 13 (in which case the offence is complete) or that the victim was under 16 and that the defendant did not reasonably believe he/she was 16 or over. In either case, consent is irrelevant.

The sexual activity caused or envisaged may be with the defendant or with a third person. In the case of incitement, there is no need for the sexual activity itself to take place.

1.12.7.2 Causing or Inciting a Child to Engage in Sexual Activity

OFFENCE: **Causing or Inciting a Child to Engage in Sexual Activity—*Sexual Offences Act 2003, s. 10***

• If it involves penetration of the victim's anus or vagina, of victim's mouth with penis, of any other person's anus or vagina with a part of victim's body or by victim, or of any person's mouth by victim's penis—triable on indictment; 14 years' imprisonment • Otherwise triable either way; 14 years' imprisonment on indictment; six months' imprisonment and/or fine summarily

The Sexual Offences Act 2003, s. 10 states:

(1) A person aged 18 or over (A) commits an offence if—
 (a) he intentionally causes or incites another person (B) to engage in an activity,
 (b) the activity is sexual, and
 (c) either—
  (i) B is under 16 and A does not reasonably believe that B is 16 or over, or
  (ii) B is under 13.

KEYNOTE

Where the child is aged 13 or over, but under 16, the prosecution must prove that A did not reasonably believe that he/she was 16 or over. The sexual activity which is caused or incited may be activity with A (e.g. where A causes or incites the child to have sexual intercourse with him), on the child him/herself (e.g. where A causes or incites the child to strip for A's sexual gratification) or with a third person (e.g. where A causes or incites the child to have sexual intercourse with A's friend). The incitement constitutes an offence whether or not the activity incited actually takes place. Whether or not the child consented to the activity caused or incited, or to the incitement, is irrelevant.

1.12.7.3 Sexual Activity in Presence of a Child

OFFENCE: **Engaging in Sexual Activity in the Presence of a Child—*Sexual Offences Act 2003, s. 11***

• Triable either way • 10 years' imprisonment on indictment • Six months' imprisonment summarily

The Sexual Offences Act 2003, s. 11 states:

(1) A person aged 18 or over (A) commits an offence if—
 (a) he intentionally engages in an activity,
 (b) the activity is sexual,
 (c) for the purpose of obtaining sexual gratification, he engages in it—
  (i) when another person (B) is present or is in a place from which A can be observed, and
  (ii) knowing or believing that B is aware, or intending that B should be aware, that he is engaging in it, and
 (d) either—
  (i) B is under 16 and A does not reasonably believe that B is 16 or over, or
  (ii) B is under 13.

KEYNOTE

The activity in which the offender is engaged must be 'sexual' and intentional and must be in order to obtain sexual gratification (for the defendant).

A person under 16 must be present or in a place from which the defendant can be observed and the defendant must know, believe or intend that the child was aware that he/she was engaging in that activity. Therefore, it is not necessary to show that the child was in fact aware of the activity in every case. Because of the wording in s. 79(7), 'observation' includes direct observation or by looking at any image.

In relation to the child, you must show that either the child was under 13 (in which case the offence is complete) or that he/she was under 16 and that the defendant did not reasonably believe him/her to be 16 or over.

This offence is aimed at, for example, people masturbating in front of children or performing sexual acts with others where they know they can be seen (or they want to be seen) by children directly or via a camera/video phone etc.

1.12.7.4 Causing a Child to Watch a Sex Act

OFFENCE: **Causing a Child to Watch a Sexual Act—*Sexual Offences Act 2003, s. 12***

• Triable either way • 10 years' imprisonment on indictment • Six months' imprisonment summarily

The Sexual Offences Act 2003, s. 12 states:

(1) A person aged 18 or over (A) commits an offence if—
   (a) for the purpose of obtaining sexual gratification, he intentionally causes another person (B) to watch a third person engaging in an activity, or to look at an image of any person engaging in an activity,
   (b) the activity is sexual, and
   (c) either—
      (i) B is under 16 and A does not reasonably believe that B is 16 or over, or
      (ii) B is under 13.

KEYNOTE

This offence is concerned with intentionally causing a child to watch a third person engaging in sexual activity or to look at an image of a person *engaging in sexual activity*. 'Image' includes a moving or still image and includes an image produced by any means and, where the context permits, a three-dimensional image (s. 79(4)); it also includes images of an imaginary person (s. 79(5)).

The display of sexual images or sexual activity might, in certain circumstances, be appropriate, for example for medical or educational reasons, hence the requirement that the offence depended on the corrupt purpose of 'sexual gratification'. The offence under s. 12 of the Act does not require that such gratification has to be taken immediately; i.e. the section does not require that the offence can only be committed if the proposed sexual gratification and the viewed sexual act, or display of images, were simultaneous, contemporaneous or synchronised. For example, the defendant may cause a child to watch a sexual act to put the child in a frame of mind for future sexual abuse, as well as where the defendant does so to obtain enjoyment from seeing the child watch the sexual act (*R* v *Abdullahi* [2006] EWCA Crim 2060). The approach to 'sexual gratification' taken in *Abdullahi* is equally applicable to other offences where this phrase appears (the offences under ss. 11 and 15A of the Act, for example).

You must show that either the child was under 13 (in which case the offence is complete) or that he/she was under 16 and that the defendant did not reasonably believe him/her to be 16 or over.

1.12.7.5 Child Sex Offences Committed by Children or Young Persons

The offences under ss. 9 to 12 can only be committed by a person aged 18 or over. So what happens if the offender is under 18? This situation is catered for by s. 13(1) of the Sexual Offences Act 2003 which states that a person under 18 commits an offence under this section (s. 13) if he/she does anything which would be an offence under any of ss. 9 to 12 if he/she were aged 18. A person guilty of an offence under s. 13 is liable:

- on conviction on indictment, to imprisonment for a term not exceeding five years; or
- on summary conviction, to imprisonment for a term not exceeding six months and/or a fine.

1.12.7.6 **Arranging or Facilitating the Commission of a Child Sex Offence**

OFFENCE: **Arranging or Facilitating Commission of Child Sex Offence—*Sexual Offences Act 2003, s. 14***

The Sexual Offences Act 2003, s. 14 states:

(1) A person commits an offence if—
(a) he intentionally arranges or facilitates something that he intends to do, intends another person to do, or believes that another person will do, in any part of the world, and
(b) doing it will involve the commission of an offence under any of sections 5 to 13.

KEYNOTE

The relevant offences are those set out in ss. 5 to 13 of the Act described in the earlier paragraphs of this chapter. The mode of trial and sentence will be the same as the respective offences under ss. 5 to 13.

The offence applies to activities by which the defendant intends to commit one of those relevant child sex offences him/herself, or by which the defendant intends or believes another person will do so, in either case in any part of the world. The offence is complete whether or not the sexual activity actually takes place. Examples of the offence would include a defendant approaching a third person to procure a child to take part in sexual activity with him or where the defendant makes travel arrangements for another in the belief that the other person will commit a relevant child sex offence.

This part of the Act specifically excludes the actions of those acting for the child's protection who arrange or facilitate something that they believe another person will do, but that they do not intend to do or intend another person to do. Acting for the child's protection must fall within one of the following:

- protecting the child from sexually transmitted infection;
- protecting the physical safety of the child;
- preventing the child from becoming pregnant; or
- promoting the child's emotional well-being by the giving of advice, and not for obtaining sexual gratification or for causing or encouraging the activity constituting the relevant child sex offence or the child's participation in it. This statutory exception (contained in s. 14(2) and (3)) covers activities such as health workers supplying condoms to people under 16 who are intent on having sex in any event and need protection from infection.

1.12.7.7 **Meeting a Child Following Sexual Grooming**

OFFENCE: **Meeting a Child Following Sexual Grooming—*Sexual Offences Act 2003, s. 15***

• Triable either way • 10 years' imprisonment on indictment • Six months' imprisonment summarily

The Sexual Offences Act 2003, s. 15 states:

(1) A person aged 18 or over (A) commits an offence if—
(a) A has met or communicated with another person (B) on one or more occasions and subsequently—
(i) A intentionally meets B,
(ii) A travels with the intention of meeting B in any part of the world or arranges to meet B in any part of the world, or
(iii) B travels with the intention of meeting A in any part of the world,
(b) A intends to do anything to or in respect of B, during or after the meeting mentioned in paragraph (a)(i) to (iii) and in any part of the world, which if done will involve the commission by A of a relevant offence,
(c) B is under 16, and
(d) A does not reasonably believe that B is 16 or over.

KEYNOTE

The initial action of the defendant involves either a meeting or a communication with the victim (who must be under 16) on at least *one previous occasion*. Such meetings or communications can be innocuous, such as family occasions or during the course of youth activities and so on. The only requirement prior to an intentional meeting during which an offender intends to do anything to a complainant which, if carried out, would involve the commission by the offender of a relevant offence is a meeting or communication 'on one or more occasions'. There is no requirement that either communication be sexual in nature (*R* v *G* [2010] EWCA Crim 1693).

The communication can include text messaging or interactions in internet 'chat rooms'. Such contact can have taken place in any part of the world.

Once the earlier meeting or communication has taken place, the offence is triggered by:

- an intentional meeting with the victim;
- a defendant travelling with the intention of meeting the victim;
- a defendant arranging to meet the victim;
- the victim travelling to meet the defendant in any part of the world.

The activity at s. 15(1)(a)(iii) means that an offence will be committed by an adult where a child under 16 travels to meet the adult or the adult arranges to meet the child.

At the time of any of the above activities, the defendant must intend to do anything to or in respect of the victim, during or even after the meeting, that would amount to a relevant offence. A relevant offence here is generally any offence under part I of the Act (all the Sexual Offences Act 2003 offences covered in this chapter). Note that the intended offence *does not* have to take place.

You must show that the victim was under 16 and that the defendant did not reasonably believe that he/she was 16 or over.

1.12.7.8 Sexual Communication with a Child

OFFENCE: **Sexual Communication with a Child—*Sexual Offences Act 2003, s. 15A***

• Triable either way • Two years' imprisonment on indictment • 12 months' imprisonment summarily

The Sexual Offences Act 2003, s. 15A states:

(1) A person aged 18 or over (A) commits an offence if—
  (a) for the purpose of obtaining sexual gratification, A intentionally communicates with another person (B),
  (b) the communication is sexual or is intended to encourage B to make (whether to A or another) a communication that is sexual, and,
  (c) B is under 16, and A does not reasonably believe that B is 16 or over.

KEYNOTE

'Sexual'

The definition of the term 'sexual' under s. 78 of the Act does not apply to this offence.

For the purposes of this section, a communication is sexual if—

- any part of it relates to 'sexual activity'; or
- a reasonable person would, in all the circumstances but regardless of any person's purpose, consider any part of the communication to be sexual.

'Sexual activity' means any activity that a reasonable person would, in all the circumstances but regardless of any person's purpose, consider to be sexual (s. 15A(2)).

The offence criminalises conduct where an adult intentionally communicates (for example, by email, text message, written note or orally) with a child under 16 (whom the adult does not reasonably believe to be aged 16 or over) for the purpose of obtaining sexual gratification if the communication is sexual or intended to encourage the child to make a communication that is sexual. The offence may be committed, for example, by talking sexually to a child via an internet chat room or sending sexually explicit text messages to a child as well as inviting a child to communicate sexually (irrespective of whether the invitation is itself sexual).

The offence is designed to ensure that it does not criminalise, for example, ordinary social or educational interactions between children and adults or communications between young people themselves as the communication must be for the corrupt purpose of obtaining '*sexual gratification*'.

The interpretation of the term 'sexual gratification' is the same as that taken in ss. 11 and 12 of the Act so it would not matter if the defendant made a relevant communication in order to obtain immediate sexual gratification or the obtaining of such gratification was part of a longer term plan, or both.

1.12.8 Abuse of Position of Trust

The prohibited behaviour under ss. 16 to 19 is along the same lines as that prohibited by the child sex offences in ss. 9, 10, 11 and 12 (**see paras 1.12.7.1 to 1.12.7.4**), except that they are committed by a person in 'a position of trust' (POT) and can be committed against a 'child' who is 'under 18' (so the victim can be 16 or 17 years old).

The following table illustrates the relationship between the offences:

OFFENCE		OFFENCE OFFENDER IN POT POT VICTIM IS A 'CHILD' = UNDER 18 YEARS	MODE OF TRIAL/ SENTENCE
Section 9 Sexual Activity with a Child	→	Section 16 Sexual Activity with a Child	Triable Either Way Indictment—five years' imprisonment Summary—six months' imprisonment and/or fine
Section 10 Causing/Inciting a Child to Engage in Sexual Activity	→	Section 17 Causing/Inciting a Child to Engage in Sexual Activity	
Section 11 Sexual Activity in the Presence of a Child	→	Section 18 Sexual Activity in the Presence of a Child	
Section 12 Causing a Child to Watch a Sexual Act	→	Section 19 Causing a Child to Watch Sexual Act	

KEYNOTE

Position of Trust

A person commits an offence under ss. 16 to 19 when they are aged 18 or over and are in a 'position of trust' in relation to the victim. A 'position of trust' is defined under s. 21 of the Act which is a lengthy, wide-ranging and detailed provision that is beyond the scope of this Manual; however, several examples are provided below:

- where the child is detained following conviction for a criminal offence, for example in a secure training centre or a young offenders institution (s. 21(2);
- in a wide range of settings in which young people are accommodated, including foster care, residential care (local authority, private or voluntary, including secure accommodation) and semi-independent accommodation (s. 21(3);
- where young people with medical conditions, physical or learning disabilities, mental illness or behavioural problems might be accommodated and includes NHS, private and voluntary accommodation (s. 21(4);
- where the child is receiving education in an educational institution (and the offender is not receiving education at that institution) (s. 21(5));

- where, on a regular basis, the child is coached, taught, trained, supervised or instructed in a sport or a religion (s. 22A(1)).

If the position of trust held by the defendant falls within any of the above four categories, it will be presumed that the defendant knew (or could reasonably have been expected to know) that there was a position of trust between him/her and the victim unless he/she can point to some evidence to the contrary.

An exception to the offences under ss. 16 to 19 is where the defendant and the victim were lawfully married to each other at the time (s. 23) and where a lawful sexual relationship existed between the defendant and the victim before the position of trust arose (s. 24).

1.12.9 Familial Child Sex Offences

Sections 25 and 26 of the Sexual Offences Act 2003 deal with offences where there is a familial relationship between the offender and the victim.

1.12.9.1 Sexual Activity with a Child Family Member

OFFENCE: **Sexual Activity with Child Family Member—*Sexual Offences Act 2003, s. 25***

• Where defendant is 18 or over at the time of the offence and if involves penetration of victim's anus or vagina by a part of defendant's body or anything else, of victim's mouth with defendant's penis, of defendant's anus or vagina by a part of victim's body or of defendant's mouth by victim's penis—triable on indictment: 14 years' imprisonment • Otherwise triable either way; 14 years' imprisonment on indictment; six months' imprisonment and/or a fine summarily • Or, where defendant is under 18 at the time of the offence; five years' imprisonment on indictment; six months' imprisonment and/or a fine summarily

The Sexual Offences Act 2003, s. 25 states:

(1) A person (A) commits an offence if—
  (a) he intentionally touches another person (B),
  (b) the touching is sexual,
  (c) the relation of A to B is within section 27,
  (d) A knows or could reasonably be expected to know that his relation to B is of a description falling within that section, and
  (e) either—
    (i) B is under 18 and A does not reasonably believe that B is 18 or over, or
    (ii) B is under 13.

KEYNOTE

For the relevant definitions of touching and sexual, **see paras 1.12.4.4** and **1.12.4.2**.

The further elements that must be proved are the existence of the relevant family relationship between the defendant and the victim, and the age of the victim.

Where the relevant family relationship is proved, it will be presumed that the defendant knew or could reasonably have been expected to know that he/she was related to the victim in that way. Similarly, where it is proved that the victim was under 18, there will be a presumption that the defendant did not reasonably believe that the victim was 18 or over. In respect of both the relationship and the age of the defendant under these circumstances, the defendant will have an evidential burden to discharge in that regard (s. 25(2) and (3)).

The relevant family relationships are set out in s. 27. These cover all close family relationships along with adoptive relationships. They are where:

- the defendant or the victim is the other's parent, grandparent, brother, sister, half-brother, half-sister, aunt or uncle; or
- the defendant is or has been the victim's foster parent.

Additional categories are where the defendant and victim live or have lived in the same household, or the defendant is or has been regularly involved in caring for, training, supervising or being in sole charge of the victim and:

- one of them is or has been the other's step-parent;
- they are cousins;
- one of them is or has been the other's stepbrother or stepsister; or
- they have the same parent or foster parent.

There are exceptions for situations where the defendant and the victim are lawfully married at the time or where (under certain circumstances) the sexual relationship pre-dates the family one. For example, where two divorcees each have a child of 17 who are engaged in a sexual relationship before their respective parents marry and move all four of them into the same household.

1.12.9.2 Inciting a Child Family Member to Engage in Sexual Activity

OFFENCE: **Inciting Sexual Activity with a Child Family Member—*Sexual Offences Act 2003, s. 26***

• Where defendant is 18 or over at the time of the offence and if involves incitement to penetration: of victim's anus or vagina by a part of defendant's body or anything else, of victim's mouth with defendant's penis, of defendant's anus or vagina by a part of victim's body or of defendant's mouth by victim's penis—triable on indictment: 14 years' imprisonment • Otherwise triable either way; 14 years' imprisonment on indictment; six months' imprisonment and/or a fine summarily • Or, where defendant is under 18 at the time of the offence, five years' imprisonment on indictment; six months' imprisonment and/or a fine summarily

The Sexual Offences Act 2003, s. 26 states:

(1) A person (A) commits an offence if—
  (a) he intentionally incites another person (B) to touch, or allow himself to be touched by, A,
  (b) the touching is sexual,
  (c) the relation of A to B is within section 27,
  (d) A knows or could reasonably be expected to know that his relation to B is of a description falling within that section, and
  (e) either—
    (i) B is under 18 and A does not reasonably believe that B is 18 or over, or
    (ii) B is under 13.

KEYNOTE

An example of this offence would be where A encourages B to masturbate A or cajoles B into agreeing to have sex with him. The offence is committed whether or not the sexual touching takes place. So where in the above example A has encouraged B to masturbate him, but the masturbation does not take place because another person enters the room, the offence is nevertheless complete.

The further elements that must be proved are the existence of the relevant family relationship between the defendant and the victim, and the age of the victim.

Where the relevant family relationship is proved, it will be presumed that the defendant knew or could reasonably have been expected to know that he/she was related to the victim in that way. Similarly, where it is proved that the victim was under 18, there will be a presumption that the defendant did not reasonably believe that the victim was 18 or over. In respect of both the relationship and the age of the defendant under these circumstances, the defendant will have an evidential burden to discharge in that regard (s. 26(2) and (3)).

Whether or not the child consented to the incitement or the activity being incited is irrelevant.

1.12.10 Offences Involving Photographs and Images of Children

There are various offences dealing with prohibited and/or pornographic photographs and images.

1.12.10.1 Indecent Photographs

The Protection of Children Act 1978 and the Criminal Justice Act 1988 detail offences relating to the taking, possession of and distribution of indecent photographs of children. The term 'photograph' is common to both offences and covers far more than the traditional image of what a 'photograph' might be considered to be.

1.12.10.2 What is a Photograph?

Section 7 of the Protection of Children Act 1978 provides a definition of a photograph for the purposes of the Act (the same definition applies to the offence under s. 160 of the Criminal Justice Act 1988) and states:

> (1) The following subsections apply for the interpretation of this Act.
> (2) References to an indecent photograph include an indecent film, a copy of an indecent film, and an indecent photograph comprised in a film.
> (3) Photographs (including those comprised in a film) shall, if they show children and are indecent, be treated for all purposes of this Act as indecent photographs of children and so as respects of pseudo-photographs.
> (4) References to a photograph include—
> (a) the negative as well as the positive version; and
> (b) data stored on a computer disc or by other electronic means which is capable of conversion into a photograph.
> (4A) References to a photograph also include—
> (a) a tracing or other image, whether made by electronic or other means (of whatever nature)—
> (i) which is not itself a photograph or pseudo-photograph, but
> (ii) which is derived from the whole or part of a photograph or pseudo-photograph (or a combination of either or both); and
> (b) data stored on a computer disc or by other electronic means which is capable of conversion into an image within paragraph (a);
> and subsection (8) applies in relation to such an image as it applies in relation to a pseudo-photograph.
> (5) 'Film' includes any form of video-recording.
> (6) 'Child', subject to subsection (8), means a person under the age of 18.
> (7) 'Pseudo-photograph' means an image, whether made by computer graphics or otherwise howsoever, which appears to be a photograph.
> (8) If the impression conveyed by a pseudo-photograph is that the person shown is a child, the pseudo-photograph shall be treated for all purposes of this Act as showing a child and so shall a pseudo-photograph where the predominant impression conveyed is that the person shown is a child notwithstanding that some of the physical characteristics shown are those of an adult.
> (9) References to an indecent pseudo-photograph include—
> (a) a copy of an indecent pseudo-photograph; and
> (b) data stored on a computer disc or by other electronic means which is capable of conversion into an indecent pseudo-photograph.

KEYNOTE

'Pseudo-photographs' include computer images and the above offences will cover the situation where part of the photograph is made up of an adult form. The use of the internet to facilitate such offences has led to a great deal of case law on the subject and what follows is a summary of several key decisions by the courts on these issues:

- Downloading images from the internet will amount to 'making' a photograph for the purposes of s. 1(1)(a) of the 1978 Act (*R* v *Bowden* [2001] QB 88).

- 'Making' pseudo-photographs includes voluntary browsing through indecent images of children on and from the internet. Once an image is downloaded, the length of time it remains on the screen is irrelevant (*R* v *Smith and Jayson* [2002] EWCA Crim 683).
- In the same case, the Court of Appeal held that a person receiving an unsolicited email attachment containing an indecent image of a child would not commit the offence under s. 1(1)(a) by opening it if he/she was unaware that it contained or was likely to contain an indecent image. This was because s. 1(1)(a) does not create an absolute offence.
- Copying onto a hard drive and storing 'pop-ups' containing indecent images of children amounts to possessing those images (*R* v *Harrison* [2007] EWCA Crim 2976).
- If images have been deleted from a computer so that their retrieval is impossible and, at the material time, a person cannot gain access to them and the images are beyond a person's control, that person cannot be in possession of them (*R* v *Porter* [2006] EWCA Crim 560).
- Evidence indicating an interest in paedophile material generally along with evidence to show how a computer had been used to access paedophile news groups, chat lines etc. can be relevant to show it was more likely than not that a file containing an indecent image of a child had been created deliberately (*R* v *Toomer* [2001] 2 Cr App R (S) 8).
- An image consisting of two parts of two different photographs taped together (the naked body of a woman taped to the head of a child) is not a 'pseudo-photograph'. If such an image were to be photocopied, it could be (*Atkins* v *DPP* [2000] 1 WLR 1427).
- Where a defendant had knowledge that images were likely to be accessed by others, any images would be downloaded 'with a view to distribute' (*R* v *Dooley* [2005] EWCA Crim 3093).

1.12.10.3 Protection of Children Act 1978

OFFENCE: **Indecent Photographs—*Protection of Children Act 1978, ss. 1, 1A and 1B***

- Triable either way • 10 years' imprisonment on indictment • Six months' imprisonment and/or a fine summarily

The Protection of Children Act 1978, s. 1 states:

1 Indecent photographs of children

(1) Subject to sections 1A and 1B, it is an offence for a person—

(a) to take, or permit to be taken or to make, any indecent photograph or pseudo-photograph of a child; or

(b) to distribute or show such indecent photographs or pseudo-photographs; or

(c) to have in his possession such indecent photographs or pseudo-photographs, with a view to their being distributed or shown by himself or others; or

(d) to publish or cause to be published any advertisement likely to be understood as conveying that the advertiser distributes or shows such indecent photographs or pseudo-photographs, or intends to do so.

(2) For purposes of this Act, a person is to be regarded as distributing an indecent photograph or pseudo-photograph if he parts with possession of it to, or exposes or offers it for acquisition by, another person.

(3) ...

(4) Where a person is charged with an offence under subsection (1)(b) or (c), it shall be a defence for him to prove—

(a) that he had a legitimate reason for distributing or showing the photographs or pseudo-photographs or (as the case may be) having them in his possession; or

(b) that he had not himself seen the photographs or pseudo-photographs and did not know, nor had any cause to suspect, them to be indecent.

(5) References in the Children and Young Persons Act 1933 (except in sections 15 and 99) to the offences mentioned in Schedule 1 to that Act shall include an offence under subsection (1)(a) above.

KEYNOTE

A person will be a 'child' for the purposes of the Act if it appears from the evidence as a whole that he/she was, at the material time, under the age of 18 (Protection of Children Act 1978, s. 2(3)).

Once the defendant realises, or should realise, that material is indecent, any distribution, showing or retention of the material with a view to its being distributed will result in an offence being committed under the 1978 Act if the person depicted turns out to be a child (*R* v *Land* [1999] QB 65).

If the impression conveyed by a pseudo-photograph is that the person shown is a child or where the predominant impression is that the person is a child, that pseudo-photograph will be treated for these purposes as a photograph of a child, notwithstanding that some of the physical characteristics shown are those of an adult (s. 7(8) of the 1978 Act).

'Distributing' will include lending or offering to another.

Although the offences include video recordings, possession of exposed but undeveloped film (i.e. film in the form in which it is taken out of a camera) does not appear to be covered. The offence at s. 1(1)(b) and (c) of the 1978 Act can only be proved if the defendant showed/distributed the photograph etc. or intended to show or distribute the photograph etc. to someone else (*R* v *Fellows* [1997] 1 Cr App R 244 and *R* v *T* [1999] 163 JP 349). If no such intention can be proved, or if the defendant only had the photographs etc. for his/her own use, the appropriate charge would be under s. 160 of the Criminal Justice Act 1988.

Sections 1 and 2 of the Criminal Evidence (Amendment) Act 1997 apply to an offence under s. 1 of the Protection of Children Act 1978 (and to conspiracies, attempts or incitements in the circumstances set out in the 1997 Act).

A legitimate purpose for possessing such material might be where someone has the material as an exhibits officer or as a training aid for police officers or social workers.

The consent of the DPP is needed before prosecuting an offence under the Protection of Children Act 1978.

The Protection of Children Act 1978, s. 1A states:

1A Marriage and other relationships

(1) This section applies where, in proceedings for an offence under section 1(1)(a) of taking or making an indecent photograph or pseudo-photograph of a child, or for an offence under section 1(1)(b) or (c) relating to an indecent photograph or pseudo-photograph of a child, the defendant proves that the photograph was of the child aged 16 or over, and that at the time of the offence charged the child and he—
   (a) were married, or civil partners of each other or
   (b) lived together as partners in an enduring family relationship.

(2) Subsections (5) and (6) also apply where, in proceedings for an offence under section 1(1)(b) or (c) relating to an indecent photograph or pseudo-photograph of a child, the defendant proves that the photograph was of the child aged 16 or over, and that at the time when he obtained it the child and he—
   (a) were married, or civil partners of each other or
   (b) lived together as partners in an enduring family relationship.

(3) This section applies whether the photograph or pseudo-photograph showed the child alone or with the defendant, but not if it showed any other person.

(4) In the case of an offence under section 1(1)(a), if sufficient evidence is adduced to raise an issue as to whether the child consented to the photograph or pseudo-photograph being taken or made, or as to whether the defendant reasonably believed that the child so consented, the defendant is not guilty of the offence unless it is proved that the child did not so consent and that the defendant did not reasonably believe that the child so consented.

(5) In the case of an offence under section 1(1)(b), the defendant is not guilty of the offence unless it is proved that the showing or distributing was to a person other than the child.

KEYNOTE

There is a specific defence to offences under s. 1(1)(a), (b) and (c) of the Protection of Children Act 1978 (making, distributing or possessing with a view to distributing) where the defendant can prove that the photograph was of a child aged 16 or over, the photograph only showed the defendant and the child and that, at the time of the offence, they were married, in a civil partnership or lived together as partners in an enduring family relationship (s. 1A). If the defendant can show these elements, then the following further conditions of the defence will apply:

- In the case of an offence under s. 1(1)(a) (taking or permitting to be taken etc.), the defendant will have an evidential burden of showing that the child consented or that the defendant reasonably believed that the child consented to the making of the photograph (s. 1A(4)).
- In the case of an offence under s. 1(1)(b) (distributing or showing), you must prove that the distributing or showing was to a person other than the child in the photograph (s. 1A(5)).
- In the case of an offence under s. 1(1)(c) (possession with a view to distribution or showing etc.), the defendant will have an evidential burden of demonstrating that the image was to be shown/distributed to no person other than the child and that the child consented to the defendant's possession of the photograph (s. 1A(6)).

The Protection of Children Act 1978, s. 1B states:

1B Exception for criminal proceedings, investigations etc.

(1) In proceedings for an offence under section 1(1)(a) of making an indecent photograph or pseudo-photograph of a child, the defendant is not guilty of the offence if he proves that—

(a) it was necessary for him to make the photograph or pseudo-photograph for the purposes of the prevention, detection or investigation of crime, or for the purposes of criminal proceedings, in any part of the world,

(b) at the time of the offence charged he was a member of the Security Service or the Secret Intelligence Service, and it was necessary for him to make the photograph or pseudo-photograph for the exercise of any of the functions of that Service, or

(c) at the time of the offence charged he was a member of GCHQ, and it was necessary for him to make the photograph or pseudo-photograph for the exercise of any of the functions of GCHQ.

KEYNOTE

There is a limited defence in relation to the making of an indecent photograph or pseudo-photograph contrary to s. 1(1)(a) of the Protection of Children Act 1978 where the defendant proves that:

- it was necessary for the defendant to make the photograph or pseudo-photograph for the purposes of the prevention, detection or investigation of crime or for criminal proceedings in any part of the world; or
- at the time the defendant was a member of the Security Service, Secret Intelligence Service or GCHQ (Government Communications Headquarters) and it was necessary for the exercise of any of the functions of that Service/GCHQ (s. 1B).

In order to assist police officers and prosecutors, NPCC and the CPS have published a Memorandum of Understanding. It sets out factors that will be taken into account in deciding whether the intention of someone accused of an offence under s. 1(1)(a) attracted criminal liability when 'making' a photograph etc. As the Memorandum points out:

> This reverse burden is intended to allow those people who need to be able to identify and act to deal with such images to do so. It also presents a significant obstacle to would-be abusers and those who exploit the potential of technology to gain access to paedophilic material for unprofessional (or personal) reasons.

The purpose of the Memorandum is to reassure those whose duties properly involve the prevention, detection or investigation of this type of crime and also as a warning to others who might claim this defence having taken it upon themselves to investigate such offences. In summary, the following criteria will be considered:

- How soon after its discovery the image was reported and to whom.
- The circumstances in which it was discovered.
- The way in which the image was stored and dealt with, and whether it was copied.
- Whether the person's actions were reasonable, proportionate and necessary.

1.12.10.4 Criminal Justice Act 1988

OFFENCE: **Indecent Photographs—*Criminal Justice Act 1988, s. 160***

• Triable either way • Five years' imprisonment on indictment • Six months' imprisonment and/or a fine

The Criminal Justice Act 1988, ss. 160 and 160A state:

160 Possession of indecent photograph of child

(1) Subject to section 160A, it is an offence for a person to have any indecent photograph or pseudo-photograph of a child in his possession.

(2) Where a person is charged with an offence under subsection (1) above, it shall be a defence for him to prove—

(a) that he had a legitimate reason for having the photograph or pseudo-photograph in his possession; or

(b) that he had not himself seen the photograph or pseudo-photograph and did not know, nor had any cause to suspect, it to be indecent; or

(c) that the photograph or pseudo-photograph was sent to him without any prior request made by him or on his behalf and that he did not keep it for an unreasonable time.

160A Marriage and other relationships

(1) This section applies where, in proceedings for an offence under section 160 relating to an indecent photograph or pseudo-photograph of a child, the defendant proves that the photograph or pseudo-photograph was of the child aged 16 or over, and that at the time of the offence charged the child and he—

(a) were married, or civil partners of each other or

(b) lived together as partners in an enduring family relationship.

(2) This section also applies where, in proceedings for an offence under section 160 relating to an indecent photograph or pseudo-photograph of a child, the defendant proves that the photograph or pseudo-photograph was of the child aged 16 or over, and that at the time when he obtained it the child and he—

(a) were married, or civil partners of each other or

(b) lived together as partners in an enduring family relationship.

(3) This section applies whether the photograph or pseudo-photograph showed the child alone or with the defendant, but not if it showed any other person.

(4) If sufficient evidence is adduced to raise an issue as to whether the child consented to the photograph or pseudo-photograph being in the defendant's possession, or as to whether the defendant reasonably believed that the child so consented, the defendant is not guilty of the offence unless it is proved that the child did not so consent and that the defendant did not reasonably believe that the child so consented.

KEYNOTE

For the meaning of 'photograph' and 'pseudo-photograph', **see para. 1.12.10.2, Keynote.**

A person will be a 'child' for the purposes of the Act if it appears from the evidence as a whole that he/she was, at the material time, under the age of 18 (Criminal Justice Act 1988, s. 160(4)).

The statutory defence under s. 160(2)(b) of the 1988 Act requires that the defendant (1) has not seen the material and (2) did not know or have any cause to suspect it was indecent. The defendant will be acquitted of the offence under s. 160 if he/she proves that (1) he/she had not seen the material and (2) did not know (and had no cause to suspect) that it was an indecent photograph of a child. This was confirmed in *R* v *Collier* [2004] EWCA Crim 1411 and arose from an argument where the material relating to children had been among other adult material that the defendant did know was indecent—he just did not know that it was an indecent photograph of a child.

1.12.10.5 Coroners and Justice Act 2009

OFFENCE: **Possession of Prohibited Images of Children—*Coroners and Justice Act 2009, s. 62***

• Triable either way • Three years' imprisonment on indictment and/or a fine • 12 months' imprisonment and/or a fine

The Coroners and Justice Act 2009, s. 62 states:

(1) It is an offence for a person to be in possession of a prohibited image of a child.
(2) A prohibited image is an image which—
  (a) is pornographic,
  (b) falls within subsection (6), and
  (c) is grossly offensive, disgusting or otherwise of an obscene character.

KEYNOTE

An image is 'pornographic' if it is of such a nature that it must reasonably be assumed to have been produced solely or principally for the purpose of sexual arousal.

An image falls within subs. (6) if it is an image which focuses solely or principally on a child's genitals or anal region, or portrays any of the acts mentioned below. Those acts are:

- the performance by a person of an act of intercourse or oral sex with or in the presence of a child;
- an act of masturbation by, of, involving or in the presence of a child;
- an act which involves penetration of the vagina or anus of a child with a part of a person's body or with anything else;
- an act of penetration, in the presence of a child, of the vagina or anus of a person with a part of a person's body or with anything else;
- the performance by a child of an act of intercourse or oral sex with an animal (whether dead or alive or imaginary);
- the performance by a person of an act of intercourse or oral sex with an animal (whether dead or alive or imaginary) in the presence of a child.

Penetration is a continuing act from entry to withdrawal.

Section 62(4) of the offence states that where (as found in a person's possession) an individual image forms part of a series of images, the question of whether it is pornographic must be determined by reference both to the image itself and the context in which it appears in the series of images. Where an image is integral to a narrative (for example, a mainstream film) which when it is taken as a whole could not reasonably be assumed to be pornographic, the image itself may not be pornographic, even though if considered in isolation the contrary conclusion might have been reached (s. 62(5)). This is related to the exclusion from the scope of the offence of certain excluded images under s. 63 of the Act.

Proceedings for an offence under s. 62(1) may not be instituted in England and Wales except by or with the consent of the DPP.

Meaning of 'Image' and 'Child'

Section 65 states that an 'image' includes a moving or still image (produced by any means) such as a photograph or film, or data (stored by any means) which is capable of conversion into a movable or still image, such as data stored electronically (as on a computer disk), which is capable of conversion into an image. This covers material available on computers, mobile phones or any other electronic device. It should be noted that the term 'image' *does not* include an indecent photograph, or indecent pseudo-photograph, of a child as these are subject to other controls (see s. 160 of the Criminal Justice Act 1988 at **para. 1.12.10.4**).

A 'child' means a person under the age of 18 (s. 65(5)). Where an image shows a person, the image is to be treated as an image of a child if the impression conveyed by the image is that the person shown is a child, or the predominant impression conveyed is that the person shown is a child despite the fact that some of the physical characteristics shown are not those of a child (s. 65(6)).

References to an image of a person include references to an image of an imaginary person. References to an image of a child include references to an image of an imaginary child.

Defence

The Coroners and Justice Act 2009, s. 64 states:

> (1) Where a person is charged with an offence under section 62(1), it is a defence for the person to prove any of the following matters—
> (a) that the person had a legitimate reason for being in possession of the image concerned;
> (b) that the person had not seen the image concerned and did not know, nor had any cause to suspect, it to be a prohibited image of a child;
> (c) that the person—
> (i) was sent the image concerned without any prior request having been made by or on behalf of the person, and
> (ii) did not keep it for an unreasonable time.

This section sets out a series of defences to the s. 62 offence of possession of prohibited images of children.

1.12.11 Sexual Exploitation of Children

Offences under ss. 47 to 50 of the Act deal with the sexual exploitation of children

1.12.11.1 Paying for the Sexual Services of a Child

OFFENCE: **Paying for Sexual Services of a Child—*Sexual Offences Act 2003, s. 47***

• If victim is child under 13: triable on indictment; life imprisonment • Where victim is under 16 at the time of the offence and if involves penetration of victim's anus or vagina by a part of defendant's body or anything else, of victim's mouth with defendant's penis, of defendant's anus or vagina by a part of victim's body or by victim with anything else—triable on indictment: 14 years' imprisonment • Otherwise triable either way: seven years' imprisonment on indictment; six months' imprisonment and/or a fine summarily

The Sexual Offences Act 2003, s. 47 states:

> (1) A person (A) commits an offence if—
> (a) he intentionally obtains for himself the sexual services of another person (B),
> (b) before obtaining those services, he has made or promised payment for those services to B or a third person, or knows that another person has made or promised such a payment, and
> (c) either—
> (i) B is under 18, and A does not reasonably believe that B is 18 or over, or
> (ii) B is under 13

KEYNOTE

Payment means any financial advantage, including the discharge of an obligation to pay or the provision of goods or services (including sexual services) gratuitously or at a discount (s. 47(2)). This would include situations where the child victim is given drugs or other goods/services at a cheaper rate in exchange for sexual services from the child.

1.12.11.2 Causing, Inciting, Arranging or Facilitating the Sexual Exploitation of Children

OFFENCE: **Causing, Inciting, Controlling, Arranging or Facilitating the Sexual Exploitation of Children—*Sexual Offences Act 2003, ss. 48 to 50***

• Triable either way • 14 years' imprisonment on indictment • Six months' imprisonment and/or a fine summarily

The Sexual Offences Act 2003, s. 48 states:

(1) A person (A) commits an offence if—
  (a) he intentionally causes or incites another person (B) to be sexually exploited, in any part of the world, and
  (b) either—
    (i) B is under 18, and A does not reasonably believe that B is 18 or over, or
    (ii) B is under 13.

The Sexual Offences Act 2003, s. 49 states:

(1) A person (A) commits an offence if—
  (a) he intentionally controls any of the activities of another person (B) relating to B's sexual exploitation in any part of the world, and
  (b) either—
    (i) B is under 18, and A does not reasonably believe that B is 18 or over, or
    (ii) B is under 13.

The Sexual Offences Act 2003, s. 50 states:

(1) A person (A) commits an offence if—
  (a) he intentionally arranges or facilitates the sexual exploitation in any part of the world of another person (B), and
  (b) either—
    (i) B is under 18, and A does not reasonably believe that B is 18 or over, or
    (ii) B is under 13.

KEYNOTE

These offences are aimed at those who seek to recruit children for prostitution or to take part in pornography, or otherwise control these activities and arrangements anywhere in the world. For the accused to be guilty of the incitement offence, it is not necessary that B actually becomes a prostitute or involves him/herself in pornography.

If the child is under 13, the offences are complete once the relevant conduct of the defendant has been proved and any belief the defendant may have had as to the child's age is irrelevant to guilt. If the child is under 18, you must prove that the defendant did not reasonably believe that the child was 18 or over (see subs. (1)(b) of each).

For the purposes of ss. 48 to 50, a person (B) is sexually exploited if:

- on at least one occasion and whether or not compelled to do so, B offers or provides sexual services to another person in return for payment or a promise of payment to B or a third person; or
- an indecent image of B is recorded and sexual exploitation is to be interpreted accordingly (s. 51(2)).

Payment means any financial advantage, including the discharge of an obligation to pay or the provision of goods or services (including sexual services) gratuitously or at a discount (s. 51(3)).

These offences would be committed if the child is recruited on a one-off basis, as well as on those occasions where the child is habitually involved. Unlike the general offence of controlling prostitution (**see para. 1.12.15.2**), there is no need to show that the causing or inciting was done for gain. The expressions used in the sections are deliberately wide and will, in places, overlap. Controlling the activities of the child would include, for example, setting the relevant price or specifying which room or equipment is to be used. Arranging will include taking an active part in the transport or travel arrangements or organising relevant facilities (such as hotel rooms etc.).

1.12.11.3 Information About Guests at Hotels

Section 116 of the Anti-social Behaviour, Crime and Policing Act 2014 confers a power on a police officer, of at least the rank of inspector, to serve a notice on the owner, operator or manager of a hotel that the officer reasonably believes has been or will be used for the purposes of child sexual exploitation or conduct preparatory to or connected with it.

For the purposes of s. 116, 'child sexual exploitation' is defined at s. 116(8) to include offences under any of the following sections of the Sexual Offences Act 2003:

- ss. 1 to 13 (rape, assault and causing sexual activity without consent, rape and other offences against children under 13 and child sex offences);
- ss. 16 to 19 (abuse of position of trust);
- ss. 25 and 26 (familial child sex offences);
- ss. 30 to 41 (persons with a mental disorder impeding choice, inducements etc. to persons with a mental disorder, and care workers for persons with a mental disorder);
- ss. 47 to 50 (abuse of children through sexual exploitation);
- s. 61 (administering a substance with intent);
- ss. 66 and 67 (exposure and voyeurism).

An offence under s. 1 of the Protection of Children Act 1978 (indecent photographs of children) is also included under s. 116.

The notice must be in writing and specify the hotel to which it relates, the date on which it comes into effect and the date on which it expires. It must also explain the information that a constable may require the person issued with a notice to provide, avenues of appeal against the notice and the consequences of failure to comply. The notice must also specify the period for which it has effect which, under s. 116(3), must be no more than six months.

The Anti-social Behaviour, Crime and Policing Act 2014, s. 116 states:

> (4) A constable may require a person issued with a notice under this section to provide the constable with information about guests at the hotel.
> (5) The only information that a constable may require under subsection (4) is—
> (a) guests' names and addresses;
> (b) other information about guests that—
> (i) is specified in regulations made by the Secretary of State, and
> (ii) can be readily obtained from one or more of the guests themselves.
> (6) A requirement under subsection (4)—
> (a) must be in writing;
> (b) must specify the period to which the requirement relates;
> (c) must specify the date or dates on or by which the required information is to be provided.

The period specified under paragraph (b) must begin no earlier than the time when the requirement is imposed and must end no later than the expiry of the notice under this section.

KEYNOTE

'Guest' means a person who, for a charge payable by that person or another, has the use of a guest room at the hotel in question.

'Hotel' includes any guest house or other establishment of a similar kind at which accommodation is provided for a charge.

Section 118(1) states that an offence is committed by a person who fails without reasonable excuse to comply with a requirement imposed on the person under s. 116(4).

Section 118(2) states that an offence is committed by a person who, in response to a requirement imposed on the person under s. 116(4), provides incorrect information which the person:

(a) did not take reasonable steps to verify or to have verified; or
(b) knows to be incorrect.

A person does not commit an offence under s. 118(2)(a) if there were no steps that the person could reasonably have taken to verify the information or to have it verified.

These offences are punishable by a fine.

1.12.12 Possession of a Paedophile Manual

OFFENCE: **Possession of a Paedophile Manual—*Serious Crime Act 2015, s. 69***

• Triable either way • Three years' imprisonment and/or fine • 12 months' imprisonment and/or fine

The Serious Crime Act 2015, s. 69 states:

(1) It is an offence to be in possession of any item that contains advice or guidance about abusing children sexually.
(2) It is a defence for a person (D) charged with an offence under this section—
 (a) to prove that (D) had a legitimate reason for being in possession of the item, and
 (b) to prove that—
  (i) D had not read, viewed or (as appropriate) listened to the item, and
  (ii) D did not know, and had no reason to suspect, that it contained advice or guidance about abusing children sexually; or
 (c) to prove that—
  (i) the item was sent to D without any request made by D or on D's behalf, and
  (ii) D did not keep it for an unreasonable time.

KEYNOTE

This section creates an offence of possession of a paedophile manual; that is, any item containing advice or guidance about abusing children sexually. There are a number of criminal offences that seek to prevent the possession, creation and distribution of indecent images of children and the dissemination of obscene material. In particular:

- s. 1 of the Protection of Children Act 1978 makes it an offence for a person to take, permit to be taken, make, distribute or show, or have in his/her possession with a view to showing or distributing any indecent photograph or pseudo-photograph of a child;
- s. 160 of the Criminal Justice Act 1988 makes it an offence to possess an indecent photograph or pseudo-photograph of a child;
- s. 63 of the Criminal Justice and Immigration Act 2008 makes it an offence to possess extreme pornographic images; and
- s. 62 of the Coroners and Justice Act 2009 makes it an offence to possess a prohibited image of a child.

These offences *do not* criminalise mere possession of material containing advice and guidance about grooming and abusing a child sexually. This offence plugs this gap in the law.

'Abusing children sexually' means doing anything that constitutes an offence under part 1 of the Sexual Offences Act 2003 against a person under 16 or doing anything that constitutes an offence under s. 1 of the Protection of Children Act 1978 involving indecent photographs (but not pseudo-photographs) (s. 69(8)).

The term 'item' has a wide meaning and includes both physical and electronic documents (e.g. emails or information downloaded to a computer) (s. 69(8)).

Section 69(2) sets out a series of defences to the offence of possession of a paedophile manual. They are the same as for other comparable offences, for example the possession of indecent images of children under s. 160(2) of the Criminal Justice Act 1988. They are:

- that the person had a legitimate reason for being in possession of the item; this would be a question of fact for the jury to decide on the individual circumstances of a case. It could cover, for example, those who can demonstrate that they have a legitimate work reason for possessing the item;

- that the person had not seen (or listened to) the item in his/her possession and therefore neither knew, nor had cause to suspect, that it contained advice or guidance about abusing children sexually; and
- that the person had not asked for the item—it having been sent without request—and that he/she had not kept it for an unreasonable period of time; this will cover those who are sent unsolicited material and who act quickly to delete it or otherwise get rid of it.

The standard of proof in making out the defence is the balance of probabilities.

Proceedings for an offence under s. 69(1) may not be instituted in England and Wales except by or with the consent of the DPP.

1.12.13 Offences Outside the United Kingdom

Section 72 of and sch. 2 to the Sexual Offences Act 2003 allow for the prosecution of British citizens and UK residents for sexual offences against children committed abroad. Section 72(1) makes it an offence for a UK national to commit an act outside the United Kingdom which would constitute a relevant sexual offence if done in England and Wales. This has the effect of removing the requirement that the act committed must have been illegal in the country where it took place, in respect of the prosecution of UK nationals.

Section 72 applies to:

- an offence under any of ss. 5 to 19, 25, 26 and 47 to 50;
- an offence under any of ss. 1 to 4, 30 to 41 and 61 where the victim of the offence was under 18 at the time of the offence;
- an offence under s. 62 or 63 where the intended offence was an offence against a person under 18;
- an offence under:
  - (i) s. 1 of the Protection of Children Act 1978 (indecent photographs of children); or
  - (ii) s. 160 of the Criminal Justice Act 1988 (possession of indecent photograph of a child).

1.12.14 Sexual Offences Against People with a Mental Disorder

The Sexual Offences Act 2003 is centred largely upon the fact that certain mental disorders deprive the sufferer of the ability to refuse involvement in sexual activity. This is different from, and wider than, a lack of consent at the time and focuses on the victim's inability to refuse.

1.12.14.1 Definition of 'Mental Disorder'

The relevant definition of a 'mental disorder' is that of s. 1(2) of the Mental Health Act 1983 which defines mental disorder as meaning any disorder or disability of the mind, so a person with learning difficulties finds protection in the Act.

1.12.14.2 Sexual Activity with Mentally Disordered Person

OFFENCE: **Sexual Activity with a Person with a Mental Disorder—*Sexual Offences Act 2003, s. 30***

• If involves penetration of victim's anus or vagina, of victim's mouth with defendant's penis, or of defendant's mouth by victim's penis—triable on indictment; life imprisonment • Otherwise triable either way; 14 years' imprisonment on indictment; six months' imprisonment and/or a fine summarily

The Sexual Offences Act 2003, s. 30 states:

(1) A person (A) commits an offence if—
  (a) he intentionally touches another person (B),
  (b) the touching is sexual,
  (c) B is unable to refuse because of or for a reason related to a mental disorder, and
  (d) A knows or could reasonably be expected to know that B has a mental disorder and that because of it or for a reason related to it B is likely to be unable to refuse.

KEYNOTE

A person is unable to refuse if:

- he/she lacks the capacity to choose whether to agree to the touching (whether because of a lack of sufficient understanding of the nature or reasonably foreseeable consequences of what is being done, or for any other reason); or
- he/she is unable to communicate such a choice to the defendant (s. 30(2)).

You must show that the defendant knew or could reasonably have been expected to know both that the victim had a mental disorder *and* that because of it (or for a reason related to it) he/she was likely to be unable to refuse. In *Hulme* v *DPP* [2006] EWHC 1347 (Admin), the Divisional Court examined a decision reached by a magistrates' court in relation to a complainant who was a cerebral palsy sufferer with a low IQ (aged 27). The magistrates' court had decided that the complainant was unable to refuse to be touched sexually; the Divisional Court agreed and the conviction against the defendant (who was 73) was upheld.

If the defendant obtains the victim's agreement to sexual touching by means of any inducement (offered or given), or a threat or deception for that purpose, the defendant commits a specific (and similarly punishable) offence under s. 34. An example would be where the defendant promises to give the victim some reward in exchange for allowing sexual touching. If the defendant uses an inducement, threat or deception to cause the victim to engage in or agree to engage in sexual activity, there is a further specific offence (similarly punishable) under s. 35.

In these specific cases of inducements, threats or deception, there is still the need to prove that the defendant knew (or could reasonably have been expected to know) of the victim's mental disorder but *no need to prove that the victim was unable to refuse.*

1.12.14.3 Causing or Inciting a Person with a Mental Disorder to Engage in Sexual Activity

OFFENCE: **Causing or Inciting a Person with a Mental Disorder to Engage in Sexual Activity—*Sexual Offences Act 2003, s. 31***

• If the activity involves causing or inciting penetration of victim's anus or vagina, of victim's mouth with defendant's penis, or of defendant's mouth by victim's penis—triable on indictment; life imprisonment • Otherwise triable either way; 14 years' imprisonment on indictment; six months' imprisonment and/or a fine summarily

The Sexual Offences Act 2003, s. 31 states:

(1) A person (A) commits an offence if—
  (a) he intentionally causes or incites another person (B) to engage in an activity,
  (b) the activity is sexual,
  (c) B is unable to refuse because of or for a reason related to a mental disorder, and
  (d) A knows or could reasonably be expected to know that B has a mental disorder and that because of it or for a reason related to it B is likely to be unable to refuse.

KEYNOTE

Section 31 covers the situation where A causes or incites B to engage in sexual activity, for example where A causes B to have sexual intercourse with A's friend or incites him/her to do so, even if the incitement does not result in B engaging in sexual activity. As that is an 'incomplete' or unfinished offence (as to which, **see chapter 1.3**), it is not necessary to prove that the sexual activity took place.

1.12.14.4 Sexual Activity in Presence of Mentally Disordered Person

OFFENCE: **Sexual Activity in Presence of a Person with a Mental Disorder—*Sexual Offences Act 2003, s. 32***

• Triable either way • 10 years' imprisonment on indictment • Six months' imprisonment and/or a fine summarily

The Sexual Offences Act 2003, s. 32 states:

(1) A person (A) commits an offence if—
  (a) he intentionally engages in an activity,
  (b) the activity is sexual,
  (c) for the purpose of obtaining sexual gratification, he engages in it—
    (i) when another person (B) is present or is in a place from which A can be observed, and
    (ii) knowing or believing that B is aware, or intending that B should be aware, that he is engaging in it,
  (d) B is unable to refuse because of or for a reason related to a mental disorder, and
  (e) A knows or could reasonably be expected to know that B has a mental disorder and that because of it or for a reason related to it B is likely to be unable to refuse.

KEYNOTE

For the requirements in proving the victim's inability to refuse, see the previous offence under s. 30.

'Observation' includes direct observation or by looking at any image (s. 79(7)).

If the victim agrees to be present or in the place referred to in s. 32(1)(c)(i) because of any inducement (offered or given), or a threat or deception practised by the defendant for that purpose, the defendant commits a specific (and similarly punishable) offence under s. 36. For instance, where the defendant pays the mentally disordered person to stay in a particular place while the activity occurs. In these specific cases of inducements, threats or deception, there is still the need to prove that the defendant knew (or could reasonably have been expected to know) of the victim's mental disorder but *no need to prove that the victim was unable to refuse.*

1.12.14.5 Causing Person with Mental Disorder to Watch Sexual Act

OFFENCE: **Causing a Person with a Mental Disorder to Watch a Sexual Act—*Sexual Offences Act 2003, s. 33***

• Triable either way • 10 years' imprisonment on indictment • Six months' imprisonment summarily

The Sexual Offences Act 2003, s. 33 states:

(1) A person (A) commits an offence if—
  (a) for the purpose of obtaining sexual gratification, he intentionally causes another person (B) to watch a third person engaging in an activity, or to look at an image of any person engaging in an activity,
  (b) the activity is sexual, and
  (c) B is unable to refuse because of or for a reason related to a mental disorder, and
  (d) A knows or could reasonably be expected to know that B has a mental disorder and that because of it or for a reason related to it B is likely to be unable to refuse.

KEYNOTE

The above offence is concerned with intentionally causing a person with a mental disorder to watch a third person engaging in such activity *or* to look at an image of a person engaging in such activity. 'Image' includes a moving or still image and includes an image produced by any means and, where the context permits, a three-dimensional image (s. 79(4); it also includes images of an imaginary person (s. 79(5))).

If the victim agrees to watch or look because of any inducement (offered or given), or a threat or deception practised by the defendant for that purpose, the defendant commits a specific (and similarly punishable) offence under s. 37. For example, where the defendant (with the appropriate motive) deceives the mentally disordered person into watching a film which is actually a live video feed of sexual activity. In these specific cases of inducements, threats or deception, there is still the need to prove that the defendant knew (or could reasonably have been expected to know) of the victim's mental disorder but *no need to prove that the victim was unable to refuse.*

1.12.15 Offences Relating to Prostitution

There are numerous offences connected with prostitution. This section begins with the definition of a prostitute before examining some of those offences.

1.12.15.1 Definition of a Prostitute

The Sexual Offences Act 2003 defines prostitution and provides that a prostitute is a person (A) who:

- on at least one occasion; and
- whether or not compelled to do so;
- offers or provides sexual services to another person;
- in return for payment or a promise of payment to A or a third person (s. 51(2)).

This definition applies to both men and women.

1.12.15.2 Offence of Causing, Inciting or Controlling Prostitution

OFFENCE: **Causing, Inciting or Controlling Prostitution—*Sexual Offences Act 2003, s. 52***

• Triable either way • Seven years' imprisonment on indictment • Six months' imprisonment and/or a fine summarily

The Sexual Offences Act 2003, s. 52 states:

(1) A person commits an offence if—
  (a) he intentionally causes or incites another person to become a prostitute in any part of the world, and
  (b) he does so for or in the expectation of gain for himself or a third person.

The Sexual Offences Act 2003, s. 53 states:

(1) A person commits an offence if—
  (a) he intentionally controls any of the activities of another person relating to that person's prostitution in any part of the world, and
  (b) he does so for or in the expectation of gain for himself or a third person.

KEYNOTE

Where the victim is under 18, the specific offence under s. 48 should be considered (see para. 1.12.11.1).

The first offence above is concerned with intentional causing or inciting, the latter being an incomplete offence (see chapter 1.3).

The second offence above addresses those who intentionally control the activities of prostitutes (pimps).

Unlike the offence involving persons under 18, you must show the defendant acted for, or in the expectation of, gain for him/herself or another. Gain means any financial advantage, including the discharge of an obligation to pay or the provision of goods or services (including sexual services) gratuitously or at a discount or the goodwill of any person which is or appears likely, in time, to bring financial advantage (s. 54). This definition covers the actions of someone who hopes to build up a relationship with, say, a drug dealer who will eventually give the defendant cheaper drugs as a result of his/her activities. Although you do not need to show that money, goods or financial advantage actually passed to the defendant, you must show that he/she wanted or at least expected that someone would benefit from the conduct.

1.12.15.3 Paying for Sexual Services of a Prostitute Subjected to Force

OFFENCE: **Paying for Sexual Services of a Prostitute Subjected to Force—*Sexual Offences Act 2003, s. 53A***

- Triable summarily • Fine

The Sexual Offences Act 2003, s. 53A states:

(1) A person (A) commits an offence if—
  (a) A makes or promises payment for the sexual services of a prostitute (B),
  (b) a third person (C) has engaged in exploitative conduct of a kind likely to induce or encourage B to provide the sexual services for which A has made or promised payment, and
  (c) C engaged in that conduct for or in the expectation of gain for C or another person (apart from A or B).
(2) The following are irrelevant—
  (a) where in the world the sexual services are to be provided and whether those services are provided,
  (b) whether A is, or ought to be, aware that C has engaged in exploitative conduct.
(3) C engages in exploitative conduct if—
  (a) C uses force, threats (whether or not relating to violence) or any other form of coercion, or
  (b) C practises any form of deception.

KEYNOTE

This offence is committed if someone pays or promises payment for the sexual services of a prostitute who has been subject to exploitative conduct of a kind likely to induce or encourage the provision of sexual services for which the payer has made or promised payment. The person responsible for the exploitative conduct must have been acting for or in the expectation of gain for him/herself or another person, other than the payer or the prostitute.

It does not matter where in the world the sexual services are to be provided. An offence is committed regardless of whether the person paying or promising payment for sexual services knows or ought to know or be aware that the prostitute has been subject to exploitative conduct. In other words, the offence is one of *strict liability* and *no mental element* is required in respect of the offender's knowledge that the prostitute was forced, threatened, coerced or deceived.

1.12.15.4 Brothels and Keeping a Disorderly House

There are several summary offences aimed at landlords, tenants and occupiers of premises used as brothels (ss. 34 to 36 of the Sexual Offences Act 1956) as well as the offence under s. 33A of the Act (below) and the common law offence of keeping a disorderly house.

OFFENCE: **Keeping a Brothel Used for Prostitution—*Sexual Offences Act 1956, s. 33A***

- Triable either way • Seven years' imprisonment on indictment • Six months' imprisonment and/or a fine summarily

The Sexual Offences Act 1956, s. 33A states:

(1) It is an offence for a person to keep, or to manage, or act or assist in the management of, a brothel to which people resort for practices involving prostitution (whether or not also for other practices).

KEYNOTE

A brothel is a place to which people resort for the purposes of unlawful sexual intercourse with more than one prostitute; it is not necessary that full sexual intercourse takes place or is even offered. Homosexual activity is as capable as heterosexual activity of founding the existence of a brothel. A massage parlour where other acts of lewdness or indecency for sexual gratification are offered may be a brothel.

Prostitution means offering or providing sexual services, whether under compulsion or not, to another in return for payment or a promise of payment to the prostitute or a third person (s. 51(2)).

OFFENCE: **Keeping a Disorderly House—*Common Law***

• Triable on indictment • Unlimited sentence

It is an offence at common law to keep a disorderly house.

KEYNOTE

To prove this offence, you must show that the house is 'open' (i.e. to customers), that it is unregulated by the restraints of morality and that it is run in a way that violates law and good order (*R* v *Tan* [1983] QB 1053).

There must be 'knowledge' on the part of the defendant that a house is being so used (*Moores* v *DPP* [1992] QB 125).

The offence also requires some persistence and will not cover a single instance, for example of an indecent performance.

1.12.15.5 Soliciting

OFFENCE: **Soliciting by Persons—*Street Offences Act 1959, s. 1***

• Triable summarily • Fine

The Street Offences Act 1959, s. 1 states:

(1) It shall be an offence for a person aged 18 or over whether male or female persistently to loiter or solicit in a street or public place for the purpose of prostitution.

(2) ...

(3) [Repealed]

(4) For the purposes of this section—

(a) conduct is persistent if it takes place on two or more occasions in any period of three months;

(b) any reference to a person loitering or soliciting for the purposes of prostitution is a reference to a person loitering or soliciting for the purposes of offering services as a prostitute.

KEYNOTE

This offence is committed *only by those offering services as a prostitute*, not by those receiving such services (those receiving services may, however, be committing 'soliciting' offences as below).

Instead of a fine, the court may make a rehabilitative order against a person convicted of the soliciting by persons offence (s. 1(2A) of the Street Offences Act 1959, as amended).

A 'street' includes any bridge, road, lane, footway, subway, square, court, alley or passage, whether a thoroughfare or not, which is for the time being open to the public; and the doorways and entrances of premises abutting on a street and any ground adjoining and open to a street.

A prostitute soliciting from the balcony or window of a house adjoining a street or public place is taken to be in the street or public place if the person being solicited is in the street or public place (*Smith* v *Hughes* [1960] 2 All ER 859). The physical presence of the prostitute is necessary (the placing of notices in windows offering the services of a prostitute has been held not to be soliciting (*Weisz* v *Monahan* [1962] 1 All ER 664)).

'Public place' is not defined.

The person 'soliciting' need not be in a public place (provided the solicitation extends into the public place) nor is there any requirement that the soliciting must involve any active form of approach. It has been held that a prostitute sitting on a stool in a window under a light is soliciting (*Behrendt* v *Burridge* [1976] 3 All ER 285).

'Loitering' is simply lingering with no intent to move on either on foot or in a vehicle.

OFFENCE: **Soliciting by 'Kerb-crawling'—*Sexual Offences Act 2003, s. 51A***

• Triable summarily • Fine

The Sexual Offences Act 2003, s. 51A (as amended) states:

(1) It is an offence for a person in a street or public place to solicit another (B) for the purpose of obtaining B's sexual services as a prostitute.

(2) The reference to a person in a street or public place includes a person in a vehicle in a street or public place.

KEYNOTE

Kerb-crawling or soliciting is punishable on the *first occasion* the activity takes place. In the case of kerb-crawling, there is no requirement for the soliciting to be shown to be likely to cause nuisance or annoyance to others.

The term 'street' is as per the definition given in the Keynote above. 'Public place' is not defined.

1.12.16 Preparatory Offences

There are specific provisions to prevent substantive offences from happening.

1.12.16.1 Administering Substance with Intent

OFFENCE: **Administering Substance with Intent—*Sexual Offences Act 2003, s. 61***

• Triable either way • 10 years' imprisonment on indictment • Six months' imprisonment and/or a fine summarily

The Sexual Offences Act 2003, s. 61 states:

(1) A person commits an offence if he intentionally administers a substance to, or causes a substance to be taken by, another person (B)—

(a) knowing that B does not consent, and

(b) with the intention of stupefying or overpowering B, so as to enable any person to engage in a sexual activity that involves B.

KEYNOTE

This offence is aimed at the use of 'date rape' drugs administered without the victim's knowledge or consent but would also cover the use of any other substance with the relevant intention. It would cover A spiking B's soft drink with alcohol where B did not know he/she was consuming alcohol, but it would not cover A encouraging B to get drunk so that A could have sex with B, where B knew he/she was consuming alcohol.

The substance could be injected or applied by covering the victim's face with a cloth impregnated with the substance.

This offence applies both when A him/herself administers the substance to B, and where A causes the substance to be taken by B, for example when A persuades a friend (C) to administer a substance to B, so that A can have sex with B, because C knows B socially and can more easily slip the substance into B's drink than A.

However, the intended sexual activity need not involve A. In the example given above, it could be intended that C or any other person would have sex with B.

The term 'sexual' used in this section in the phrase 'sexual activity' is defined in s. 78 of the Act (**see para. 1.12.4.2**).

The sexual activity in this offence could involve A having sexual intercourse with or masturbating B, could involve A causing B to commit a sexual act upon him/herself (e.g. masturbation) or could involve B and a third party engaging in sexual activity together, regardless of whether the third party has administered the substance. This is an offence of intent rather than consequence so there is no need for the victim to be stupefied or overpowered or for the sexual activity to take place, for example because a friend of B saw what was happening and intervened to protect B.

1.12.16.2 Committing Criminal Offence with Intent to Commit a Sexual Offence

OFFENCE: **Committing Criminal Offence with Intent to Commit a Sexual Offence—*Sexual Offences Act 2003, s. 62***

• Where the offence committed is kidnapping or false imprisonment—triable on indictment only: life imprisonment • Otherwise triable either way: 10 years' imprisonment on indictment; six months' imprisonment and/or a fine summarily

The Sexual Offences Act 2003, s. 62 states:

(1) A person commits an offence under this section if he commits any offence with the intention of committing a relevant sexual offence.

KEYNOTE

'Relevant sexual offence' means an offence under part I of the Act (virtually all regularly occurring sexual offences) including aiding, abetting, counselling or procuring such an offence (s. 62(2)). It *does not extend* to other sexual offences under the Protection of Children Act 1978.

It is designed to deal with the commission of any criminal offence where the defendant's intention is to commit a relevant sexual offence. This would cover an array of possible circumstances where the defendant's ulterior motive in committing the first offence is to carry out the relevant sexual offence. It would apply, for example, where A kidnaps B so that A can rape B but is caught by the police before committing the rape. It would also apply where A detained B in his/her flat with this intention, or assaulted B to subdue him/her so that A could more easily rape B.

There is no express requirement for there to be any immediate link in time between the two offences. It could cover any situation from the theft of drugs or equipment to be used in the course of the sexual offence and going equipped for burglary, to the taking of a vehicle or even dangerous driving with the intention in each case of committing the further relevant sexual offence.

If A does commit the intended offence, he/she could be charged with the substantive sexual offence in addition to this offence.

1.12.16.3 Trespass with Intent to Commit Sexual Offence

OFFENCE: **Trespass with Intent to Commit a Relevant Sexual Offence—*Sexual Offences Act 2003, s. 63***

• Triable either way • 10 years' imprisonment on indictment • Six months' imprisonment and/or a fine summarily

The Sexual Offences Act 2003, s. 63 states:

(1) A person commits an offence if—
  (a) he is a trespasser on any premises,
  (b) he intends to commit a relevant sexual offence on the premises, and
  (c) he knows that, or is reckless as to whether, he is a trespasser.

KEYNOTE

For 'relevant sexual offence', see para. 1.12.16.2.

A person is a trespasser if they are on the premises without the owner's or occupier's consent, whether express or implied, or they are there without a power at law to be there. Generally, defendants ought to know whether they are trespassing or not and recklessness will be enough in that regard.

Premises here will include a structure or part of a structure (including a tent, vehicle or vessel or other temporary or movable structure (s. 63(2)).

This offence is intended to capture, for example, the situation where A enters a building owned by B, or goes into B's garden or garage without B's consent, and A intends to commit a relevant sexual offence against the occupier or other person on the premises.

The offence applies regardless of whether or not the substantive sexual offence is committed.

A will commit the offence if he/she has the intent to commit a relevant sexual offence at any time while he/she is a trespasser. The intent is likely to be inferred from what the defendant says or does to the intended victim (if there is one) or from items in the possession of the defendant at the time he/she commits the trespass (e.g. condoms, pornographic images, rope etc.).

A separate offence is needed to cover trespass (as opposed to relying on s. 62) because trespass is a civil tort and not a criminal offence.

The defendant must intend to commit the relevant offence *on the premises.*

1.12.17 Sex with an Adult Relative

OFFENCE: **Sex with an Adult Relative: Penetration—*Sexual Offences Act 2003, s. 64***

• Triable either way • Two years' imprisonment on indictment • Six months' imprisonment and/or a fine summarily

The Sexual Offences Act 2003, s. 64 states:

(1) A person aged 16 or over (A) (subject to subsection (3A)) commits an offence if
  (a) he intentionally penetrates another person's vagina or anus with a part of his body or anything else, or penetrates another person's mouth with his penis,
  (b) the penetration is sexual,
  (c) the other person (B) is aged 18 or over,
  (d) A is related to B in a way mentioned in subsection (2), and
  (e) A knows or could reasonably be expected to know that he is related to B in that way.

OFFENCE: **Sex with an Adult Relative: Consenting to Penetration—*Sexual Offences Act 2003, s. 65***

• Triable either way • Two years' imprisonment on indictment • Six months' imprisonment and/or a fine summarily

The Sexual Offences Act 2003, s. 65 states:

(1) A person aged 16 or over (A) (subject to subsection 3A)) commits an offence if—
  (a) another person (B) penetrates A's vagina or anus with a part of B's body or anything else, or penetrates A's mouth with B's penis,
  (b) A consents to the penetration,
  (c) the penetration is sexual,
  (d) B is aged 18 or over,
  (e) A is related to B in a way mentioned in subsection (2), and
  (f) A knows or could reasonably be expected to know that he is related to B in that way.

KEYNOTE

For either offence to be committed, the penetration must be 'sexual'. This requirement ensures that a penetration for some other purpose, for example where one sibling helps another to insert a pessary for medical reasons, is not caught by this offence.

A 'relative' for ss. 64 and 65 is a parent, grandparent, child, grandchild, brother, sister, half-brother, half-sister, uncle, aunt, nephew or niece.

The Criminal Justice and Immigration Act 2008 amended ss. 64 and 65 so that the offences of sex with an adult relative are committed where an adoptive parent has consensual sex with their adopted child when he/she is aged 18 or over.

The adopted person does not commit this offence unless he/she is aged 18 or over.

In both offences, where the relevant relationship is proved, it will be taken that the defendant knew or could reasonably have been expected to know that he/she was related in that way unless sufficient evidence is adduced to raise an issue as to whether he/she knew or could reasonably have been expected to know that he/she was so related.

1.12.18 Other Sexual Offences

There are several offences that involve sexual 'displays' of some description and of voyeurism.

1.12.18.1 Exposure

OFFENCE: **Exposure—*Sexual Offences Act 2003, s. 66***

• Triable either way • Two years' imprisonment on indictment • Six months' imprisonment summarily

The Sexual Offences Act 2003, s. 66 states:

(1) A person commits an offence if—
 (a) he intentionally exposes his genitals, and
 (b) he intends that someone will see them and be caused alarm or distress.

KEYNOTE

There is no requirement that the defendant acted for sexual gratification and simply exposing the genitals out of loutish behaviour will suffice if the other ingredients are present.

The offence is not restricted to public places and there is no need to show that anyone saw the genitals or was alarmed or distressed. The offence only applies to the genitals, not the buttocks, so the act of 'mooning' will not be covered. A woman who exposes her breasts will not be guilty of an offence under s. 66.

An offence that is connected to exposure is the common law offence of outraging public decency which criminalises behaviour or displays which are lewd, obscene or disgusting and take place in a public place.

OFFENCE: **Outraging Public Decency—*Common Law***

• Triable either way • Unlimited powers of sentence on indictment • Six months' imprisonment and/or a fine summarily

It is an offence at common law to commit an act of a lewd, obscene or disgusting nature and outrage public decency.

KEYNOTE

This offence is committed by the deliberate commission of an act that is, *per se*, lewd, obscene or disgusting (*R* v *Rowley* [1991] 1 WLR 1020). If an act is not lewd, obscene etc., the motives or intentions of the defendant cannot make it so. Therefore, where the defendant's acts involved leaving messages in public toilets that were not in themselves obscene, his motives (to induce young boys to engage in gross indecency with him) did not bring his actions under this offence (*Rowley*). In *Knuller (Publishing, Printing and Promotions) Ltd* v *DPP* [1973] AC 435, Lord Simon said that 'outraging public decency' goes considerably beyond offending the sensibilities of, or even shocking, reasonable people and that the recognised minimum standards of decency were likely to vary from time to time.

The offence can be committed by exposing the penis or engaging in simulated sexual acts (*R* v *Mayling* [1963] 2 QB 717); it is not restricted to offences committed by men.

The act must be committed where it might be seen by the public generally and it must be shown that more than one person could have seen the act take place (*R* v *Walker* [1996] 1 Cr App R 111).

It is not necessary to prove that someone was in fact annoyed or insulted (*R* v *May* (1990) 91 Cr App R 157).

1.12.18.2 Voyeurism

OFFENCE: **Voyeurism—*Sexual Offences Act 2003, s. 67***

• Triable either way • Two years' imprisonment on indictment • 12 months' imprisonment summarily

The Sexual Offences Act 2003, s. 67 states:

(1) A person commits an offence if—
  (a) for the purpose of obtaining sexual gratification, he observes another person doing a private act, and
  (b) he knows that the other person does not consent to being observed for his sexual gratification.
(2) A person commits an offence if—
  (a) he operates equipment with the intention of enabling another person to observe, for the purpose of obtaining sexual gratification, a third person (B) doing a private act, and
  (b) he knows that B does not consent to his operating equipment with that intention.
(3) A person commits an offence if—
  (a) he records another person (B) doing a private act,
  (b) he does so with the intention that he or a third person will, for the purpose of obtaining sexual gratification, look at an image of B doing the act, and
  (c) he knows that B does not consent to his recording the act with that intention.

KEYNOTE

A person is doing a private act if he/she is in a place which, in the circumstances, would reasonably be expected to provide privacy and:

- his/her genitals, buttocks or breasts are exposed or covered only with underwear;
- he/she is using a lavatory; or
- he/she is doing a sexual act that is not of a kind ordinarily done in public (s. 68).

The word 'breasts' does not extend to the exposed male chest (*R* v *Bassett* [2008] EWCA Crim 1174).

The three activities described above require proof that the victim does not consent to the observing, recording or operating of the relevant equipment *for the purpose of the defendant's or another's sexual gratification* (i.e. the victim might have consented to being observed, recorded etc. for other reasons).

The first offence involves a defendant observing another doing a private act (which will include looking at an image: s. 79(5)) with the relevant motive of gaining sexual gratification.

The second offence deals with people operating equipment such as hoteliers using webcams to enable others to view live footage of the residents for the sexual gratification of those others. There is no need to show that defendants intended to gain sexual gratification themselves.

The third offence deals with the recording of the private act with the intention that the person doing the recording or another will look at the image and thereby obtain sexual gratification. It does not matter that those who eventually look at the recording know that the victim did not consent, though all elements of the offence would be corroborated by the accompanying material (e.g. the descriptions of the pages on an internet website). In *R* v *Turner* [2006] EWCA Crim 63, the defendant (the manager of a gym) had recorded images of women showering and using the sun beds. The court regarded this as an abuse of the defendant's position of trust which took him 'over the custodial threshold' and he was sentenced (following an appeal) to nine months' imprisonment.

There is also a specific offence under s. 67(4) of installing equipment or adapting structures (e.g. drilling peepholes) with the intention of committing the first offence themselves or enabling others to do so. Structures will include tents, vehicles or vessels or other temporary or movable structures.

The restricted wording of s. 67(4) appears not to cover the situation where the defendant installs equipment to *record* the private act (under s. 67(2)) rather than observing it live.

These offences do not extend to activities such as covertly filming up women's skirts as they go about the public act of shopping.

1.12.18.3 Voyeurism—Additional Offences

OFFENCE: **Voyeurism—*Sexual Offences Act 2003, s. 67A***

- Triable either way • Two years' imprisonment on indictment • 12 months' imprisonment summarily

The Sexual Offences Act 2003, s. 67A states:

(1) A person (A) commits an offence if—
  (a) A operates equipment beneath the clothing of another person (B),
  (b) A does so with the intention of enabling A or another person (C), for the purpose mentioned in subsection (3), to observe—
    (i) B's genitals or buttocks (whether exposed or covered with underwear), or
    (ii) the underwear covering B's genitals or buttocks,
  in circumstances where the genitals, buttocks or underwear would not otherwise be visible, and
  (c) A does so—
    (i) without B's consent, and
    (ii) without reasonably believing that B consents.

(2) A person (A) commits an offence if—
  (a) A records an image beneath the clothing of another person (B),
  (b) the image is of—
    (i) B's genitals or buttocks (whether exposed or covered with underwear), or
    (ii) the underwear covering B's genitals or buttocks,
  in circumstances where the genitals, buttocks or underwear would not otherwise be visible,
  (c) A does so with the intention that A or another person (C) will look at the image for a purpose mentioned in subsection (3), and
  (d) A does so—
    (i) without B's consent, and
    (ii) without reasonably believing that B consents.

(2A) A person (A) commits an offence if—
  (a) A operates equipment,
  (b) A does so with the intention of enabling A or another person (C), for a purpose mentioned in subsection (3), to observe another (B) while B is breast-feeding a child, and
  (c) A does so—
    (i) without B's consent, and
    (ii) without reasonably believing that B consents.

(2B) A person (A) commits an offence if—
  (a) A records an image of another (B) while B is breast-feeding a child,
  (b) A does so with the intention that A or another person (C) will look at the image for a purpose mentioned in subsection (3), and

(c) A does so—
   (i) without B's consent, and
   (ii) without reasonably believing that B consents.
(3) The purposes referred to in subsections (1) to (2B) are—
   (a) obtaining sexual gratification (whether for A or C);
   (b) humiliating, alarming or distressing B.

KEYNOTE

The offences under s. 67A(1) and (2) are referred to as 'upskirting' and causes humiliation, distress or harm to other persons. Section 67A also covers where the offence has been committed to obtain sexual gratification.

The offence can be committed against any gender and in any location (regardless whether it is a public or private place). The offences under s. 67A(2A) and (2B) were introduced by the Police, Crime, Sentencing and Courts Act 2022. Breast-feeding a child includes B rearranging their clothes in the course of preparing to breast-feed the child or having just finished breast-feeding the child (s. 67A(3A)). It is irrelevant for the purposes of the offences under subss. (2A) and (2B) whether or not B is in a public place while breast-feeding the child, whether or not B's breasts are exposed while B is breast-feeding the child and what part of B's body is, or is intended by A to be, visible in the recorded image or is intended by A to be observed.

1.12.18.4 Sexual Activity in a Public Lavatory

OFFENCE: **Sexual Activity in a Public Lavatory—*Sexual Offences Act 2003, s. 71***

• Triable summarily • Six months' imprisonment and/or a fine

The Sexual Offences Act 2003, s. 71 states:

(1) A person commits an offence if—
   (a) he is in a lavatory to which the public or a section of the public has or is permitted to have access, whether on payment or otherwise,
   (b) he intentionally engages in an activity, and,
   (c) the activity is sexual.

KEYNOTE

This offence will apply to any lavatory to which the public or a section of it has access. For the purposes of this offence only, an activity is sexual if a reasonable person would, in all the circumstances but regardless of any person's purpose, consider it to be sexual.

1.12.19 Possession of Extreme Pornographic Images

This offence covers a more limited range of material than the Obscene Publications Act. It creates a possession offence in respect of a sub-text of extreme pornographic material which is defined in s. 63 of the Criminal Justice and Immigration Act 2008.

OFFENCE: **Possession of Extreme Pornographic Images—*Criminal Justice and Immigration Act 2008, s. 63***

• Triable either way • Three years' imprisonment on indictment and/or a fine (where the images contain life-threatening acts or serious injury) • Two years' imprisonment on indictment and/or a fine (where the images contain acts of necrophilia or bestiality) • Six months' imprisonment and/or a fine summarily

The Criminal Justice and Immigration Act 2008, s. 63 states:

(1) It is an offence for a person to be in possession of an extreme pornographic image.

KEYNOTE

There are three elements to the offence. An image must come within the terms of *all three elements* before it will fall foul of the offence. Those elements are:

- that the image is pornographic;
- that the image is grossly offensive, disgusting or otherwise of an obscene character; and
- that the image portrays in an explicit and realistic way, one of the following extreme acts:
  - an act which threatens a person's life (this could include depictions of hanging, suffocation or sexual assault involving a threat with a weapon);
  - an act which results in or is likely to result in serious injury to a person's anus, breasts or genitals (this could include the insertion of sharp objects or the mutilation of the breasts or genitals);
  - an act involving sexual interference with a human corpse (necrophilia);
  - a person performing an act of intercourse or oral sex with an animal (whether dead or alive) (bestiality);
  - an act which involves the non-consensual penetration of a person's vagina, anus or mouth by another with the other person's penis;
  - an act which involves the non-consensual sexual penetration of a person's vagina or anus by another with a part of the other person's body or anything else;
  - and a reasonable person looking at the image would think that the people and animals portrayed were real.

An 'extreme pornographic image' is an image which is both pornographic and an extreme image. An image is 'pornographic' if it is of such a nature that it must reasonably be assumed to have been produced solely or principally for the purpose of sexual arousal. Section 63(4) and (5) provides that where an image is integral to a narrative (e.g. a documentary film) which taken as a whole could not reasonably be assumed to be pornographic, the image itself may be taken not to be pornographic even though if considered in isolation the contrary conclusion would have been reached.

An 'image' means either still images (such as photographs) or moving images (such as those in a film). The term also incorporates any type of data, including that stored electronically (as on a computer disk), which is capable of conversion into an image. This covers material available on computers, mobile phones or any other electronic device. The scope of the definition of image is also affected by the requirement that the persons or animals portrayed in an image must appear to be real. Therefore animated characters, sketches, paintings and the like are excluded (s. 63(8)). References to parts of the body include body parts that have been surgically constructed (s. 63(9)). Section 64 of the Act provides an exclusion from the scope of the offence under s. 63 for classified films (by the British Board of Film Classification). Proceedings cannot be instituted without the consent of the DPP.

General Defences

Several defences to the offence are set out in s. 65 of the Act. They are:

- that the person had a legitimate reason for being in possession of the image; this will cover those who can demonstrate that their legitimate business means that they have a reason for possessing the image;
- that the person had not seen the image and therefore neither knew, nor had cause to suspect, that the images held were extreme pornographic images; this will cover those who are in possession of offending images but are unaware of the nature of the images; and
- that the person had not asked for the image—it having been sent without request—and that he/she had not kept it for an unreasonable period of time; this will cover those

who are sent unsolicited material and who act quickly to delete it or otherwise get rid of it.

Defence: Participation in Consensual Acts

Section 66 of the Act provides an additional defence for those who participate in the creation of extreme pornographic images. The defence is limited and will not cover images relating to bestiality and necrophilia images that depict a real corpse.

To use the defence, a defendant must prove (on the balance of probabilities) that he/she directly participated in the act or acts portrayed in the image and that the act(s) did not involve the infliction of non-consensual harm on any person. Where the image depicts necrophilia, the defendant must also prove that the human corpse portrayed was not in fact a corpse. Non-consensual harm is harm which is of such a nature that, in law, a person cannot consent to it being inflicted on him/herself, or harm to which a person can consent but did not in fact consent.

1.12.20 Disclosing or Threatening to Disclose Private Sexual Photographs/Films

More commonly known as 'revenge porn', this offence is designed to deal with the sharing of private, sexual materials, either photographs or videos, of another person without their consent and with the purpose of causing embarrassment or distress. The images are sometimes accompanied by personal information about the subject, including their full name, address and links to their social media profiles.

It is dealt with by s. 33 of the Criminal Justice and Courts Act 2015 which applies both online and offline and to images which are shared electronically or in a more traditional way so includes the uploading of images on the internet, sharing by text and email or showing someone a physical or electronic image.

1.12.20.1 Offence of Disclosing or Threatening to Disclose Private Sexual Photographs

OFFENCE: **Disclosing or Threatening to Disclose Private Sexual Photographs and Films with Intent to Cause Distress—*Criminal Justice and Courts Act 2015, s. 33***

- Triable either way • Two years' imprisonment on indictment and/or fine
- 12 months' imprisonment and/or a fine summarily

The Criminal Justice and Courts Act 2015, s. 33 states:

(1) A person commits an offence if—
  (a) the person discloses, or threatens to disclose, a private sexual photograph or film in which another individual ("the relevant individual") appears,
  (b) by so doing, the person intends to cause distress to that individual, and
  (c) the disclosure is, or would be, made without the consent of that individual.

(2) But it is not an offence under this section for the person to disclose or threaten to disclose the photograph or film to the relevant individual.

(2A) Where a person is charged with an offence under this section of threatening to disclose a private sexual photograph or film, it is not necessary for the prosecution to prove—
  (a) that the photograph or film referred to in the threat exists, or
  (b) if it does exist, that it is in fact a private sexual photograph or film.

KEYNOTE

The essence of the offence is that the disclosure is done without the consent of the individual appearing in the photograph or film and with intent to cause distress to that individual. An offence would be committed if a photograph or film was disclosed to someone appearing in it with intent to cause distress to someone else who appears in it. Section 33(2A) ensures that the prosecution will not have to prove the private sexual photograph or film referred to in the threat exists so long as the individual is said to feature in it.

Disclose

A disclosure takes place where a defendant, by any means, gives or shows the photograph or film to another person or makes it available to another person irrespective of whether the material in question had previously been disclosed to that person and whether or not the disclosure was for reward. Disclosure therefore includes electronic disclosure of a photograph or film, for example by posting it on a website or emailing it to someone. It also includes the disclosure of a physical document, for example by giving a printed photograph to another person or displaying it in a place where other people would see it.

Private

Section 35(2) states that a photograph or film is 'private' if it shows something that is not of a kind ordinarily seen in public. This means that a photograph or film of something sexual (such as people kissing) would not fall within the ambit of the offence if what was shown was the kind of thing that might ordinarily take place in public.

Sexual

Section 35(3) states that a photograph or film is 'sexual' if:

(a) it shows all or part of an individual's exposed genitals or pubic area,
(b) it shows something that a reasonable person would consider to be sexual because of its nature, or
(c) its content, taken as a whole, is such that a reasonable person would consider it to be sexual.

Where what is shown is not by its nature sexual, s. 35(3)(c) provides that a photograph or film is nevertheless to be considered sexual where a reasonable person would regard the content of the photograph or film when taken as a whole as sexual. For example, a photograph of someone wearing their underwear is not necessarily sexual, but a reasonable person might consider it to be so if the content of the picture, including for example what else was (or was not) shown or the manner in which the person was posing, would lead a reasonable person to consider it as such.

Photograph or Film

A photographed or filmed image is a still or moving image (or part of an image) originally captured by photography or by the making of a film recording. The offence applies only to material which appears to be, or to contain, a photographed or filmed image. Section 34(4) and (5) provide for altered or combined images and effectively only bring those within the offence where it is the original image of the individual which is private and sexual as opposed to the way it has been altered or combined.

The offence would not apply if the disclosed material looks like a photograph but does not in fact contain any photographic element (e.g. because it had been generated entirely by computer).

An image is still considered to be a photograph or film for the purpose of the offence even if the original photograph or film recording has been altered in any way (e.g. by being digitally enhanced).

References to a photograph or film include a negative version of a still or moving image that is a photograph or film and stored data that can be converted into such a still or moving image—for instance, data stored on a hard drive or disc.

1.12.20.2 Defences

The Criminal Justice and Courts Act 2015, s. 33 states:

(3) It is a defence for a person charged with an offence under this section to prove that he or she reasonably believed that the disclosure was necessary for the purposes of preventing, detecting or investigating crime.

(4) It is a defence for a person charged with an offence under this section to show that—
   (a) the disclosure or threat to disclose was made in the course of, or with a view to, the publication of journalistic material, and
   (b) he or she reasonably believed that, in the particular circumstances, the publication of the journalistic material was, or would be, in the public interest.

(5) It is a defence for a person charged with an offence under this section to show that—
   (a) he or she reasonably believed that the photograph or film had previously been disclosed for reward, whether by the relevant individual or another person, and
   (b) he or she had no reason to believe that the previous disclosure for reward was made without the consent of the relevant individual.

(6) A person is taken to have shown the matters mentioned in subsection (4) or (5) if—
   (a) sufficient evidence of the matters is adduced to raise an issue with respect to it, and
   (b) the contrary is not proved beyond reasonable doubt.

1.13 Child Protection

1.13.1 Introduction

The application of the law and the use of measures to protect children, particularly those relating to 'police protection', are among some of the most contentious issues that any police officer may be involved in.

1.13.2 Child Abduction

There are two offences of abducting children; the first applies to people 'connected with the child', the second to others 'not connected with the child'.

1.13.2.1 Person Connected with Child

OFFENCE: **Child Abduction—Person Connected with Child—*Child Abduction Act 1984, s. 1***

• Triable either way • Seven years' imprisonment on indictment • Six months' imprisonment and/or a fine summarily

The Child Abduction Act 1984, s. 1 states:

(1) Subject to subsections (5) and (8) below, a person connected with a child under the age of 16 commits an offence if he takes or sends the child out of the United Kingdom without the appropriate consent.

'Connected with a Child'

The Child Abduction Act 1984, s. 1 states:

(2) A person is connected with the child for the purposes of this section if—
- (a) he is a parent of the child; or
- (b) in the case of a child whose parents were not married to, or civil partners of, each other at the time of his birth, there are reasonable grounds for believing that he is the father of the child; or
- (c) he is a guardian of the child; or
- (ca) he is a special guardian of the child; or
- (d) he is a person named in a child arrangements order as a person with whom the child is to live; or
- (e) he has custody of the child.

KEYNOTE

Special Guardian

A 'special guardian' is created by a Special Guardian Order (SGO). A SGO fundamentally secures the child's long-term placement and is an order made by the court appointing one or more individuals to be the child's 'special guardian'. It is a private law order made under the Children Act 1989 and is intended for those children who cannot live with their birth parents and who would benefit from a legally secure placement. The order can enable a child to remain in his/her family as, unlike adoption, it does not end the legal relationship between a child and his/her parents.

A SGO usually lasts until the child is 18.

A parent of a child may not be appointed as a child's special guardian.

Child Arrangements Order

Section 8(1) of the Children Act 1989 states that a child arrangements order means an order regulating arrangements relating to any of the following:

(a) with whom a child is to live, spend time or otherwise have contact; and

(b) when a child is to live, spend time or otherwise have contact with any person.

'Appropriate Consent'

The Child Abduction Act 1984, s. 1 states:

(3) In this section 'the appropriate consent' in relation to a child, means—
- (a) the consent of each of the following—
  - (i) the child's mother;
  - (ii) the child's father, if he has parental responsibility for him;
  - (iii) any guardian of the child;
  - (iiia) any special guardian of the child;
  - (iv) any person named in a child arrangements order as a person with whom the child is to live;
  - (v) any person who has custody of the child; or
- (b) the leave of the court granted under or by virtue of any provision of Part II of the Children Act 1989; or
- (c) if any person has custody of the child, the leave of the court which awarded custody to him.

KEYNOTE

This offence can only be committed by those people listed in s. 1(2). Such a person must either take, or be responsible for sending, the child out of the United Kingdom him/herself. This offence is not committed by holding a child within the United Kingdom or by failing to return a child who has previously been taken abroad (*R (On the Application of Nicolaou)* v *Redbridge Magistrates' Court* [2012] EWHC 1647 (Admin)). The taking or sending must be shown to have been done without the consent of *each* of those persons listed in s. 1(3)(a) or, if there is a custody order in force, the court's permission must be sought. Alternatively, the leave of the court under part II of the Children Act 1989 will suffice.

The consent of the DPP is needed before a charge of child abduction is brought under this section (s. 4(2)); there are also restrictions on charging kidnapping (as to which, **see chapter 1.10**) where the offence involves an offence under s. 1 by a person connected with the child (s. 5).

For 'attempted' child abduction by a person connected with the child, see the case of *MS* (**chapter 1.3**).

1.13.2.2 'Defence' for Person Connected with a Child

The Child Abduction Act 1984, s. 1 states:

(4) A person does not commit an offence under this section by taking or sending a child out of the United Kingdom without obtaining the appropriate consent if—
- (a) he is a person named in a child arrangements order as a person with whom the child is to live, and he takes or sends the child out of the United Kingdom for a period of less than one month; or
- (b) he is a special guardian of the child and he takes or sends the child out of the United Kingdom for a period of less than three months.

(4A) Subsection (4) above does not apply if the person taking or sending the child out of the United Kingdom does so in breach of an order under Part II of the Children Act 1989.

(5) A person does not commit an offence under this section by doing anything without the consent of another person whose consent is required under the foregoing provisions if—
   (a) he does it in the belief that the other person—
      (i) has consented; or
      (ii) would consent if he was aware of all the relevant circumstances; or
   (b) he has taken all reasonable steps to communicate with the other person but has been unable to communicate with him; or
   (c) the other person has unreasonably refused to consent.

KEYNOTE

A further provision (s. 1(5A)) states that the 'defence' at s. 1(5)(c) will not apply if the person who refused to consent is a person:

- named in a child arrangements order as a person with whom the child is to live; or
- who has custody of the child; or
- who is a special guardian of the child; or
- is, by taking or sending the child out of the United Kingdom, acting in breach of a court order in the United Kingdom.

1.13.2.3 Person Not Connected with Child

OFFENCE: **Child Abduction—*Person Not Connected with Child—Child Abduction Act 1984, s. 2***

• Triable either way • Seven years' imprisonment on indictment • Six months' imprisonment and/or a fine summarily

The Child Abduction Act 1984, s. 2 states:

(1) Subject to subsection (3) below, a person other than one mentioned in subsection (2) below, commits an offence if, without lawful authority or reasonable excuse, he takes or detains a child under the age of 16—
   (a) so as to remove him from the lawful control of any person having lawful control of the child: or
   (b) so as to keep him out of the lawful control of any person entitled to lawful control of the child.

(2) The persons are—
   (a) where the father and mother of the child in question were married to, or civil partners of, each other at the time of his birth, the child's father and mother;
   (b) where the father and mother of the child in question were not married to each other at the time of his birth, the child's mother; and
   (c) any other person mentioned in section 1(2)(c) to (e) above.

KEYNOTE

This offence will include keeping a child in the place where he/she is found and inducing the child to remain with the defendant or another person.

The consent of the victim is irrelevant.

The word 'remove' for the purpose of s. 2(1)(a) effectively means a substitution of authority by a defendant for that of the person lawfully having it and physical removal from a particular place is not required (*Foster* v *DPP* [2004] EWHC 2955 (Admin)).

Section 2(1)(a) requires the child *there and then* to be in the lawful control of someone entitled to it when he/she is taken or detained, whereas s. 2(1)(b) requires only that the child be kept out of the lawful control of someone entitled to it when taken or detained. Whether or not a person is under the lawful control of another is a question of fact (*R* v *Leather* [1993] Crim LR 516). A child can be removed from lawful control without necessarily being taken to another place. It may suffice if the child is deflected into some unauthorised activity induced by the defendant.

1.13.2.4 Defence for Person Not Connected with a Child

The Child Abduction Act 1984, s. 2 states:

(3) ... it shall be a defence for [the defendant] to prove—

(a) where the father and mother of the child in question were not married to, or civil partners of, each other at the time of his birth—

(i) that he is the child's father; or

(ii) that, at the time of the alleged offence, he believed, on reasonable grounds, that he was the child's father; or

(b) that, at the time of the alleged offence, he believed that the child had attained the age of 16.

KEYNOTE

The defence under s. 2(3)(a) of the Child Abduction Act 1984 will not apply where D mistakenly takes the wrong child from a nursery, thinking it to be his daughter, although it is just possible that D may, in such circumstances, be able to advance a defence of reasonable excuse under s. 2(1) (*R* v *Berry* [1996] 2 Cr App R 226).

1.13.3 Child Cruelty

OFFENCE: **Child Cruelty—*Children and Young Persons Act 1933, s. 1***

• Triable either way • 14 years' imprisonment on indictment • Six months' imprisonment and/or a fine summarily

The Children and Young Persons Act 1933, s. 1 states:

(1) If any person who has attained the age of 16 years and has responsibility for any child or young person under that age, wilfully assaults, ill-treats (whether physically or otherwise), neglects, abandons, or exposes him, or causes or procures him to be assaulted, ill-treated (whether physically or otherwise), neglected, abandoned, or exposed, in a manner likely to cause him unnecessary suffering or injury to health (whether the suffering or injury is of a physical or a psychological nature), that person shall be guilty of an offence ...

KEYNOTE

This offence may be considered to fall into two broad categories:

- instances of violent assault;
- cases of cruelty and neglect.

Instances of violent assault may be more appropriately dealt with by charging with assault offences.

To be convicted of the offence, D must be over 16 at the time of the offence and have 'responsibility' for the child. Responsibility for a child or young person can be shared and whether a person had such responsibility in each case will be a matter of both fact and law (*Liverpool Society for the Prevention of Cruelty to Children* v *Jones* [1914] 3 KB 813). Anyone having parental responsibility or any other legal liability to maintain a child or young person will be presumed to have responsibility for that child and that responsibility does not cease simply because the person ceases to have care of the child. Others such as babysitters may also have 'responsibility' for the child while in their care (see generally s. 17).

The Act makes provisions and presumptions in relation to issues of causation. So, for example, if a parent or other person legally liable to maintain the child or young person, or a guardian, has failed to provide adequate food, clothing, medical aid or lodging for the child or young person, he/she will be deemed to have neglected the child or young person for the above purposes (s. 1(2)).

Similarly, a person will be presumed to have neglected the child where it is proved that the child was an infant under three years old who died as a result of suffocation (other than by disease or blockage of the airways by an object) while in bed with someone of 16 years or over who was under the influence of drink or a prohibited drug when he/she went to bed or at any later time before the suffocation (s. 1(2)(b)).

The reference in s. 1(2)(b) to the infant being 'in bed' with another ('the adult') includes a reference to the infant lying next to the adult in or on any kind of furniture or surface being used by the adult for the purpose of sleeping (and the reference to the time when the adult 'went to bed' is to be read accordingly) (s. 1(2A)). A drug is a prohibited drug for the purpose of s. 1(2)(b) in relation to a person if the person's possession of the drug immediately before taking it constituted an offence under s. 5(2) of the Misuse of Drugs Act 1971.

A defendant may be charged with the above offence even where the child has died (s. 1(3)(b)).

Section 1 creates only one single offence, albeit one that can be committed in many different ways, by both positive acts (assault, ill-treatment, abandonment or exposure) and omission (neglect) (*R* v *Hayles* [1969] 1 QB 364). Although any aspect of neglect must be shown to have occurred in a manner likely to cause unnecessary suffering or injury to health, there is no need to show that any such suffering or injury actually came about.

1.13.4 Police Powers under the Children Act 1989

The police have specific statutory powers to deal with the threat of significant harm posed to children and these are set out below.

Section 46 of the Children Act 1989 states:

(1) Where a constable has reasonable cause to believe that a child would otherwise be likely to suffer significant harm, he may—
 (a) remove the child to suitable accommodation and keep him there; or
 (b) take such steps as are reasonable to ensure the child's removal from any hospital, or other place, in which he is then being accommodated is prevented.

(2) For the purposes of this Act, a child with respect to whom a constable has exercised his powers under this section is referred to as having been taken into police protection.

KEYNOTE

For most purposes of the 1989 Act, someone who is under 18 years old is a 'child' (s. 105).

The wording of s. 46(1) means that an officer may use the powers at s. 46(1)(a) and (b) if he/she has reasonable cause to believe that, if the powers are not used, a child is likely to suffer significant harm. The issues arising from similar wording in relation to powers of arrest have been considered by the courts on a number of occasions. Generally, tests of reasonableness impose an element of objectivity and the courts will consider whether, in the circumstances, a reasonable and sober person might have formed a similar view to that of the officer.

'Harm' is defined under s. 31(9). It covers all forms of ill-treatment including sexual abuse and forms of ill-treatment that are not physical. It also covers the impairment of health (physical or mental) and also physical, intellectual, emotional, social or behavioural development. The definition also extends to impairment suffered from seeing or hearing the ill-treatment *of any other person.*

When determining whether harm to a child's health or development is 'significant', the child's development will be compared with that which could reasonably be expected of a similar child (s. 31(10)).

The power under s. 46 is split into two parts:

- a power to *remove* a child to suitable accommodation and keep him/her there; and
- a power to take reasonable steps to *prevent* the child's removal from a hospital or other place.

The longest a child can spend in police protection is 72 hours (s. 46(6)). It should be remembered that this is the *maximum* time that a child can be kept in police protection, not the norm.

As soon as is reasonably practicable after using the powers under the Act, the 'Initiating Officer' (the officer who takes the child into police protection and undertakes the initial inquiries) must do a number of things as set out above. These include:

- telling the local authority within whose area the child was found what steps have been, and are proposed to be, taken and why. This aspect of communicating with the local authority is a critical part of the protective powers;

- giving details to the local authority within whose area the child is ordinarily resident of the place at which the child is being kept;
- telling the child (if he/she appears capable of understanding) of what steps have been taken and why, and what further steps may be taken;
- taking such steps as are reasonably practicable to discover the wishes and feelings of the child;
- making sure that the case is inquired into by a 'designated officer' (see para. 1.13.4.1);
- taking such steps as are reasonably practicable to inform:
  - the child's parents;
  - every person who is not the child's parent but who has parental responsibility for the child; and
  - any other person with whom the child was living immediately before being taken into police protection; of the steps that the officer has taken under this section, the reasons for taking them and the further steps that may be taken with respect to the child. This element of informing the child, parent and/or relevant carers of what is happening and why is also a vital part of the protective process.

Where the child was taken into police protection by being removed to accommodation which is not provided by or on behalf of a local authority or as a refuge (under s. 51), the officer must, as soon as is reasonably practicable after taking a child into police protection, make sure that the child is moved to accommodation provided by the local authority. Every local authority must receive and provide accommodation for children in police protection where such a request is made (s. 21).

The 'Initiating Officer' and the 'Designated Officer' must not carry out these two separate roles (Home Office Circular 17/2008). The Circular also states that a police station is not 'suitable accommodation' and children should not be brought to a police station except in exceptional circumstances, such as a lack of immediately available local authority accommodation, and then only for a short period. *On no account* should a child who has been taken into police protection be taken to the cell block area of a police station.

When considering action under s. 46, it is possible that the child may already be the subject of an Emergency Protection Order (EPO) applied for by a local authority or authorised body under s. 44.

In considering the proper approach under these circumstances, the Court of Appeal has held that:

- There is no express provision in the Act prohibiting the police from invoking s. 46 where an EPO is in place and it is not desirable to imply a restriction which prohibits a constable from removing a child under s. 46 where the constable has reasonable cause to believe that the child would otherwise be likely to suffer significant harm.
- The s. 46 power to remove a child can therefore be exercised even where an EPO is in force in respect of the child.
- Where a police officer knows that an EPO is in force, he/she should not exercise the power of removing a child under s. 46, unless there are compelling reasons to do so.
- The statutory scheme accords primacy to the EPO procedure under s. 44 because removal under that section is sanctioned by the court and involves a more elaborate, sophisticated and complete process of removal than under s. 46.
- Consequently, the removal of children should usually be effected pursuant to an EPO, and s. 46 should only be invoked where it is not reasonably practicable to execute an EPO.
- In deciding whether it is practicable to execute an EPO, the police should always have regard to the paramount need to protect children from significant harm.
- Failure to follow the statutory procedure may amount to the police officer's removal of the child under s. 46 being declared unlawful.

(*Langley* v *Liverpool City Council and Chief Constable of Merseyside* [2005] EWCA Civ 1173.)

1.13.4.1 Designated Officer

The reference at s. 46(3)(e) of the Act to a 'designated officer' is a reference to the appropriate officer designated for that police station for the purposes of this legislation by the relevant chief officer of police. This is a key role in ensuring the effective use of the statutory framework set up for the protection of children in these circumstances. The responsibility for ensuring that the case is inquired into by the designated officer, together with the other responsibilities under s. 46(3) and the responsibility for taking steps to inform people under s. 46(4), clearly rest with the police officer exercising the power under s. 46.

The designated officer must inquire fully and thoroughly into the case; he/she must also do what is reasonable in all the circumstances for the purpose of safeguarding or promoting the child's welfare (having regard in particular to the length of the period during which the child will be so protected) (s. 46(9)(b)).

Where a child has been taken into police protection, the designated officer shall allow:

- the child's parents;
- any person who is not a parent of the child but who has parental responsibility for the child;
- any person with whom the child was living immediately before being taken into police protection;
- any person in whose favour a contact order is in force with respect to the child;
- any person who is allowed to have contact with the child by virtue of an order under s. 34; and
- any person acting on behalf of any of those persons;

to have such contact (if any) with the child as, in the opinion of the designated officer, is both reasonable and in the child's best interests (s. 46(10)).

The designated officer may apply for an 'emergency protection order' under s. 44 (s. 46(7)). Such an order allows the court to order the removal of the child to certain types of accommodation and to prevent the child's removal from any other place (including a hospital) where he/she was being accommodated immediately before the making of the order (s. 44(4)). An emergency protection order gives the applicant 'parental responsibility' for the child while it is in force. It also allows the court to make certain directions in relation to contact with the child and a medical or psychiatric assessment. Section 44A allows the court to make an order excluding certain people from a dwelling house where the child lives and to attach a power of arrest accordingly.

While the designated officer can apply for an emergency protection order without the local authority's knowledge or agreement (see s. 46(8)), there should be no reason why, given proper multi-agency cooperation and a well-planned child protection strategy, this situation would come about.

On completing the inquiry into the case, the designated officer must release the child from police protection *unless he/she considers that there is still reasonable cause for believing that the child would be likely to suffer significant harm if released* (s. 46(5)).

While a child is in police protection, neither the officer concerned nor the designated officer will have parental responsibility for the child (s. 46(9)(a)).

When a local authority is informed that a child is in police protection, they have a duty to make 'such enquiries as they consider necessary to enable them to decide whether they should take any action to safeguard' the child (s. 47(1)(b)). A court may issue a warrant for a constable to assist a relevant person to enter premises in order to enforce an emergency protection order.

1.13.4.2 **Contravention of Protection Order or Police Protection**

OFFENCE: **Acting in Contravention of Protection Order or Power Exercised under s. 46—*Children Act 1989, s. 49***

- Triable summarily • Six months' imprisonment

The Children Act 1989, s. 49 states:

(1) A person shall be guilty of an offence if, knowingly and without lawful authority or reasonable excuse, he—
  (a) takes a child to whom this section applies away from the responsible person;
  (b) keeps such a child away from the responsible person; or
  (c) induces, assists or incites such a child to run away or stay away from the responsible person.

(2) This section applies in relation to a child who is—
  (a) in care;
  (b) the subject of an emergency protection order; or
  (c) in police protection,

  and in this section 'the responsible person' means any person who for the time being has care of him by virtue of the care order, the emergency protection order, or section 46, as the case may be.

KEYNOTE

Where a child is taken in contravention of s. 49, the court may issue a 'recovery order' under s. 50. The order, which is also available where a child is missing or has run away, requires certain people to produce the child to an authorised person (which includes a constable (s. 50(7)(b)) or to give certain information about the child's whereabouts to a constable or officer of the court (s. 50(3)). It can authorise a constable to enter any premises and search for the child.

Under s. 102 of the 1989 Act, a court may issue a warrant to enter premises in connection with certain provisions of the Act which regulate children's homes, foster homes, child-minding premises and nursing homes for children. Section 102 allows for constables to assist any person in the exercise of their powers under those provisions. It makes allowances for a constable to be accompanied by a medical practitioner, nurse or health visitor (s. 102(3)).

1.13.4.3 **Disclosure of Information Regarding Child**

Where a child is reported missing, problems can arise once the child is discovered to be safe and well but one of the parents wants the police to disclose the whereabouts of the child. This situation arose in *S* v *S (Chief Constable of West Yorkshire Police Intervening)* [1998] 1 WLR 1716 and the Court of Appeal provided some clarification of the issues. In that case, the mother left home with her three-year-old child after a marriage breakdown. The father reported the child's absence to the police who found the child and her mother in a refuge. At the request of the mother, the police advised the father that both she and the child were safe but refused to disclose their whereabouts. The father applied 'without notice' (i.e. without telling the police) to the county court which then made an order under s. 33 of the Family Law Act 1986, requiring the police to disclose the information. The chief constable was granted leave to intervene and, following another order from the court to disclose the child's whereabouts, the chief constable appealed. The Court of Appeal held that it was only in exceptional circumstances that the police should be asked to divulge the whereabouts of a child under a s. 33 order. Their primary role in such cases should continue to be finding missing children and ensuring their safety.

However, the court went on to say that, in such cases:

- The police are *not* in a position to give 'categoric assurances' of confidentiality to those who provide information as to the whereabouts of a child. The most they could say is that, other than by removing the child, it would be *most unlikely* that they would have to disclose the information concerning the child's whereabouts.
- An order under s. 33 provides for the information to be disclosed to the court not to the other party or his/her solicitor.
- An order under s. 33 should not normally be made in respect of the police without their being present (*ex parte*).

Note that the provision of information by police officers in relation to civil proceedings involving children is governed by regulations; specific advice should therefore be sought before disclosing any such information.

1.14 Theft and Related Offences

1.14.1 Introduction

Many offences contained in this chapter are very common and you will be aware of the physical, emotional and financial cost to victims of offences such as theft, burglary and robbery. The prevalence and impact that these offences have on society as a whole can leave no doubt as to their importance.

1.14.2 Theft

OFFENCE: **Theft—*Theft Act 1968, s. 1***

- Triable either way • Seven years' imprisonment on indictment • Six months' imprisonment and/or a fine summarily

The Theft Act 1968, s. 1 states:

(1) A person is guilty of theft if he dishonestly appropriates property belonging to another with the intention of permanently depriving the other of it; and 'thief' and 'steal' shall be construed accordingly.

KEYNOTE

The final line of s. 1 is important and states that the words '"thief" and "steal" shall be construed accordingly'. This means that in any Theft Act 1968 offence where the words 'thief' and/or 'steal' are used (such as in the Theft Act 1968 offence of robbery (s. 8) or handling stolen goods (s. 22)), the 'thief' is the person who commits the theft offence and 'steal' means to commit theft. All of the elements of the theft offence must be present to '*steal*'. The definition of robbery (s. 8) tells us that 'A person is guilty of robbery if he steals'. If an element of theft has not been satisfied then the defendant will not commit theft and will not 'steal'. No 'steal' = no robbery.

Where the property in question belonged to D's spouse or civil partner, a prosecution for theft may only be instituted against D by or with the consent of the DPP (s. 30(4)). This restriction must also apply to charges of robbery or of burglary by stealing etc. but does not apply to other persons charged with committing the offence jointly with D; nor does it apply when the parties are separated by judicial decree or order or under no obligation to cohabit (s. 30(4)(a)). Theft from businesses (classed as 'theft from a shop') involving first-time offenders who are not substance misusers and where the value of the goods stolen is less than £100 can be dealt with by way of fixed penalty notice.

'Low-value shoplifting' (defined by s. 22A of the Magistrates' Courts Act 1980 as shoplifting where the value of the stolen goods does not exceed £200) may become triable summarily; however, the decision relating to mode of trial cannot be made until the defendant appears before a magistrates' court to answer a charge (*Candish* v *DPP* [2022] EWHC 842 (Admin)). Consequently, this 'mode of trial' issue would not impact on how a person is dealt with if arrested for a theft offence that fitted the definition of 'low-value shoplifting'. Section 176(6) of the Anti-social Behaviour, Crime and Policing Act 2014 provides that certain powers conferred by the Police and Criminal Evidence Act 1984 on the police and others in respect of indictable offences remain available in respect of low-value shoplifting, notwithstanding that it is reclassified as summary only. The powers concerned include a power of arrest exercisable by a person other than a constable (e.g. a store detective), powers enabling police officers to enter and search premises and vehicles in various circumstances for the purposes of searching for evidence in connection with an investigation or arresting individuals suspected of committing offences, and powers enabling a magistrate to authorise such entry and search. Section 176(5) amends s. 1 of the Criminal Attempts Act 1981 to provide that it is an offence to attempt to commit low-value shoplifting.

1.14.2.1 Dishonestly

If a person cannot be shown to have acted 'dishonestly', he/she is not guilty of theft. The decision as to whether or not a defendant was dishonest is a question of fact for the jury or magistrate(s) to decide. Whilst there is no statutory definition of the term 'dishonestly', the 1968 Act does deal with the issue by setting out a number of specific circumstances where the relevant person will *not* be treated as dishonest and one circumstance where a person *may* be dishonest.

The Theft Act 1968, s. 2 states:

(1) A person's appropriation of property belonging to another is not to be regarded as dishonest—
- (a) if he appropriates the property in the belief that he has in law the right to deprive the other of it, on behalf of himself or of a third person; or
- (b) if he appropriates the property in the belief that he would have the other's consent if the other knew of the appropriation and the circumstances of it; or
- (c) (except where the property came to him as trustee or personal representative) if he appropriates the property in the belief that the person to whom the property belongs cannot be discovered by taking reasonable steps.

KEYNOTE

In all three instances, it is the person's *belief* that is important.

Right in Law

- X is owed £100 by Y. Y tells X that he will not give him the money so X, *honestly believing that he has a right in law to do so*, takes £100 cash from Y's wallet as payment for the debt. It does not matter that there is no actual right in law for X to behave in this way; the honestly held belief by X that he does have a right in law means that he is not dishonest. The belief *need not even be reasonable*, only honestly held, and could be based on a 'mistake'. If, in the above example, X took Y's pedal cycle (worth £700) as payment for the debt, *honestly believing* that he had a right in law to do so, then X would not be dishonest if he/she honestly believed he/she had a right in law to take the pedal cycle as payment for the debt. This would also include the situation where the person acts on the basis of belief in the legal right of another. So if X, acting for the benefit of Y, took property from Z (wrongly but honestly believing that Y was entitled to it), X would not be dishonest.

Consent

- Under s. 2(1)(b), the person appropriating the property must believe both elements, i.e. that the other person would have *consented* had he/she known of the appropriation *and the circumstances of it.* For example, a person is about to run out of time on a street parking meter and needs £5 to park for the next hour or risk incurring a fine. Believing that a work colleague would consent in this situation, the person takes £5 belonging to the colleague from a change jar on the colleague's desk. If the person *honestly believes the work colleague would consent to the taking and the circumstances of it*, this would not be dishonest. If the person knew that the work colleague would not approve, this would be dishonest.

Lost

- Under s. 2(1)(c), the belief has to be in relation to the likelihood of *discovering* the 'owner' by taking reasonable steps. The nature and value of the property, together with the attendant circumstances, will be relevant. The chances of finding the owner of a valuable, monogrammed engagement ring found after a theatre performance would be considerably greater than those of discovering the owner of a can of beer found outside a football ground. Again, it is the defendant's *honest belief* at the time of the appropriation that is important here, not that the defendant went on to take reasonable steps to discover the person to whom the property belongs.

- Trustees or personal representatives cannot rely on s. 2(1)(c). This is because a trustee or personal representative can never be personally entitled to the property in question (unless the trust or will states that is the case) as if the beneficiary cannot be found, the person entitled to the property in question (now effectively 'ownerless goods') is the Crown.

The Theft Act 1968, s. 2 states:

> (2) A person's appropriation of property belonging to another may be dishonest notwithstanding that he is willing to pay for the property.

KEYNOTE

If a person appropriates another's property, leaving money or details of where he/she can be contacted to make restitution, this will not of itself negate dishonesty (*Boggeln* v *Williams* [1978] 1 WLR 873). The wording of s. 2(2) gives latitude to a court where the defendant was willing to pay for the property. The sub-section says that such an appropriation *may* be dishonest, not that it *will always* be dishonest.

EXAMPLE

X wants to buy some milk and sees an unattended milk float displaying a sign, 'Milk—£1 for 2 Litres'. X waits for several minutes but nobody in charge of the milk float appears, so X leaves £1 on the float and takes a 2-litre container of milk. The fact that the milk is for sale and X left payment would be convincing evidence to suggest that X is not dishonest.

The conclusion may be different if Y wants to own a painting that is on display in a museum. Y has made several approaches to buy the painting but has been told that the painting is not for sale. Y knows the painting is worth £10,000 and decides to take the painting from the museum, leaving a cheque for £10,000 in its place. Just because Y is willing to pay the market value for the painting does not mean to say that he is not dishonest.

1.14.2.2 Dishonesty: Case Law

Where 'dishonesty' needs to be considered but s. 2 of the Theft Act 1968 is of no assistance (s. 2 will not cater for every circumstance), the magistrates/jury will consider 'dishonesty' in the same way that it is considered in civil cases.

The test for dishonesty in civil cases was set out in *Barlow Clowes International (in liq)* v *Eurotrust International Ltd* [2006] 1 All ER 333 and *Royal Brunei Airlines Sdn Bhd* v *Tan* [1995] 3 All ER 97.

KEYNOTE

The Test for Dishonesty

When dishonesty is in question, the magistrates/jury will first have to ascertain the actual state of the individual's knowledge or belief as to the facts (this does not have to be a reasonable belief—the question is whether the belief is genuinely held). Once his/her actual state of mind as to knowledge or belief is established, the question of whether his/her conduct had been honest or dishonest is to be determined by the magistrates/jury by applying the (objective) standards of ordinary decent people. There is no requirement that the defendant had to appreciate that what he/she had done was, by those standards, dishonest.

The test has a role for the state of mind of the defendant (in relation to the facts) but there is no requirement for him/her to appreciate the dishonesty of his/her actions.

Taking this approach means that to prove dishonesty, a prosecutor need only place before a court facts of what the defendant did and thought and then invite the court to hold that he/she was dishonest according to the standards of ordinary decent people.

1.14.2.3 Appropriates

The Theft Act 1968, s. 3 states:

Any assumption by a person of the rights of an owner amounts to an appropriation, and this includes, where he has come by the property (innocently or not) without stealing it, any later assumption of a right to it by keeping or dealing with it as owner.

KEYNOTE

The owner of property has many rights in relation to it—the right to sell it, to give it away or to destroy it are just *some* examples. 'Appropriation' does not envisage that a person assumes *all* of those rights, just *one* of them would suffice for 'appropriation' to occur.

While damaging or destroying property is clearly an act of 'appropriation' (*R* v *Graham* [1997] 1 Cr App R 302), it does not follow that an act of destruction of property is also thereby automatically theft of that property. *Dishonestly* causing the destruction of property can itself amount to an offence of theft (*R* v *Kohn* (1979) 69 Cr App R 395) but this does not make theft an appropriate charge where D merely smashes V's car window by throwing a brick through it. Criminal damage would be the appropriate charge on such facts as there is clearly no 'dishonesty' present in such an act.

It is important to note that there can be an 'appropriation' without any criminal liability and appropriation itself does not amount to an offence of theft; it simply describes one of the elements of the criminal conduct that must exist before a charge of theft can be made out. An appropriation requires no mental state on the part of the appropriator. It is an objective act.

Where an appropriation takes place and is accompanied by the other elements of the offence, there will be a theft.

Appropriation under s. 3(1) envisages a physical act (*Biggs* v *R* (2003) 12 December, unreported).

When and where the particular act amounting to an appropriation took place is of importance when bringing a charge of theft (and in other offences such as robbery and aggravated burglary).

The decision of the House of Lords in *R* v *Gomez* [1993] AC 442 significantly developed the meaning of 'appropriation'. Following an earlier case (*Lawrence* v *Metropolitan Police Commissioner* [1972] AC 626), Lord Keith disagreed with the argument (made in *Gomez*) that an act expressly or impliedly authorised by the owner of the property in question can never amount to an 'appropriation' and pointed out that the decision in *Lawrence* was a direct contradiction of that proposition. The House of Lords upheld the convictions for theft in *Gomez* and accepted that there are occasions where property can be 'appropriated' for the purposes of the Theft Act 1968, *even though the owner has given his/her consent or authority.*

A number of issues come from this decision:

- *Taking or depriving.* It is not necessary that the property be 'taken' in order for there to be an appropriation, neither need the owner be 'deprived' of the property. Similarly, there is no need for the defendant to 'gain' anything by an appropriation.
- *Consent.* It is irrelevant to the issue of appropriation whether or not the owner consented to that appropriation. This is well illustrated in *Lawrence*, the decision followed by the House of Lords in *Gomez*. In *Lawrence*, a tourist gave his wallet full of unfamiliar English currency to a taxi driver for the latter to remove the correct fare. The driver in fact helped himself to ('appropriated') far more than the amount owed. It was held that the fact that the wallet and its contents were handed over freely (with consent) by the owner did not prevent the taxi driver's actions from amounting to an 'appropriation' of it.
- *Interfering with goods.* Simply swapping the price labels on items displayed for sale in a shop *will* amount to an 'appropriation'. This is because to do so, irrespective of any further intention, involves an assumption

of one of the owner's rights in relation to the property (the right to put a price on property). If that appropriation were accompanied by the other elements of the offence, then theft is committed.

- *More than one appropriation.* There may be an appropriation of the same property on more than one occasion. However, once property has been *stolen* (as opposed to merely appropriated), that same property cannot be stolen again by the same thief (*R* v *Atakpu* [1994] QB 69). Appropriation can also be a continuing act; that is, it can include the whole episode of entering and ransacking a house and the subsequent removal of property (*R* v *Hale* (1979) 68 Cr App R 415).

In *R* v *Hinks* [2001] 2 AC 24, the House of Lords was asked to rule on whether a person could 'appropriate' property belonging to another where the other person made her an absolute gift of property, retaining no proprietary interest in the property or any right to resume or recover it. In that case, the defendant had befriended a middle-aged man of limited intelligence who had given her £60,000 over a period of time. The defendant was charged with five counts of theft and, after conviction, eventually appealed to the House of Lords. Their lordships held that:

- in a prosecution for theft, it was unnecessary to prove that the taking was without the owner's consent (as in *Lawrence*);
- it was immaterial whether the act of appropriation was done with the owner's consent or authority (as in *Gomez*); and
- *Gomez* therefore gave effect to s. 3(1) by treating 'appropriation' as a neutral word covering 'any assumption by a person of the rights of an owner'.

The essence of the decision by the House of Lords in *Hinks* is that even though a person obtains good title to property under civil law (the gift), they can still be convicted of theft as the circumstances of the gift-giving are dishonest.

If a person, having come by property, innocently or not, without stealing it, later assumes any rights to it by keeping it or treating it as his/her own, then he/she 'appropriates' that property (s. 3(1)).

KEYNOTE

A later assumption of the rights of an owner amounts to 'appropriation' and could lead to an offence of theft.

EXAMPLE

X is shopping in a large department store and has placed several items in his shopping basket. Thinking about other things, X absent-mindedly walks out of the store without paying for the goods. Once outside the store, X realises what he has done but as the store alarm has not activated and nobody has noticed X leaving the store without paying, X decides to keep the goods and walks away from the store. X initially came by the goods innocently but his later assumption of the rights of an owner means he has now 'appropriated' the goods and in the circumstances commits theft.

An exception to these circumstances is provided by the Theft Act 1968, s. 3 which states:

> (2) Where property or a right or interest in property is or purports to be transferred for value to a person acting in good faith, no later assumption by him of rights which he believed himself to be acquiring shall, by reason of any defect in the transferor's title, amount to theft of the property.

KEYNOTE

If a person buys a car in good faith and gives value for it (i.e. purchases it from a car dealer believing the car dealer owns the car and has every right to sell it and they purchase it at a reasonable price) but then discovers it has been stolen, a refusal to return it to the original owner would not, without more, *attract liability for theft*. Without s. 3(2), the retention of the vehicle would be caught by s. 3(1). This narrow exemption does not mean, however, that the innocent purchaser gets good title to the car (*National Employers' Mutual Insurance Association Ltd* v *Jones* [1990] 1 AC 24), nor would it provide a defence if the stolen goods are a gift and the 'donee' (recipient) subsequently discovers that they had been stolen (the 'donee' will not have given 'value' for the property).

1.14.2.4 Property

The Theft Act 1968, s. 4 states:

(1) 'Property' includes money and all other property, real or personal, including things in action and other intangible property.

(2) A person cannot steal land, or things forming part of land and severed from it by him or by his directions, except in the following cases, that is to say—

(a) when he is a trustee or personal representative, or is authorised by power of attorney, or as liquidator of a company, or otherwise, to sell or dispose of land belonging to another, and he appropriates the land or anything forming part of it by dealing with it in breach of the confidence reposed in him; or

(b) when he is not in possession of the land and appropriates anything forming part of the land by severing it or causing it to be severed, or after it has been severed; or

(c) when, being in possession of the land under a tenancy, he appropriates the whole or part of any fixture or structure let to be used with the land.

For purposes of this subsection 'land' does not include incorporeal hereditaments; 'tenancy' means a tenancy for years or any less period and includes an agreement for such a tenancy, but a person who after the end of a tenancy remains in possession as statutory tenant or otherwise is to be treated as having possession under the tenancy, and 'let' shall be construed accordingly.

(3) A person who picks mushrooms growing wild on any land, or who picks flowers, fruit or foliage from a plant growing wild on any land, does not (although not in possession of the land) steal what he picks unless he does it for reward or for sale or other commercial purpose. For purposes of this subsection 'mushroom' includes any fungus, and 'plant' includes any shrub or tree.

(4) Wild creatures, tamed or untamed, shall be regarded as property; but a person cannot steal a wild creature not tamed nor ordinarily kept in captivity, or the carcase of any such creature, unless either it has been reduced into possession by or on behalf of another person and possession of it has not since been lost or abandoned, or another person is in course of reducing it into possession.

KEYNOTE

Money

Coins and banknotes are property (*R* v *Davis* (1988) 88 Cr App R 347). 'Money' does not include cheques or credit balances held in banks and building societies (but see below).

Personal Property

Personal property includes tangible personal property which might be described as 'things in possession'. The TV in your house, the settee you sit on etc. are all examples of 'personal' property.

Things in Action and Other Intangible Property

Under s. 4(1) 'things in action' would include patents, company shares and trademarks and other things which can only be enforced by legal action as opposed to physical possession. Other intangible property would include software programs and perhaps credits accumulated on store loyalty cards. Confidential information, such as the contents of an examination paper, is not intangible property *per se* (*Oxford* v *Moss* (1979) 68 Cr App R 183). However, if those contents were written on a piece of paper, the paper itself would be 'real' property. It has been accepted by the Court of Appeal that contractual rights obtained by buying a ticket for the London Underground may amount to a 'thing in action' (*R* v *Marshall* [1998] 2 Cr App R 282).

Cheques and Credit Balances

Cheques will be property as they are pieces of paper ('personal' property albeit of very little value). The contents of a bank or building society account, however, are also a 'thing in action' that can be stolen provided the account is in credit or within the limits of an agreed overdraft facility (*R* v *Kohn* (1979) 69 Cr App R 395). Reducing the credit balance in one account and transferring a like sum into your own account amounts to an 'appropriation' of property within the meaning of s. 1. This principle (set out in Kohn) was reaffirmed in *R* v *Williams (Roy)* [2001] 1 Cr App R 23 by the Court of Appeal.

Land

Under s. 4(2), you cannot generally steal land. However, there are three exceptions to this general rule:

(1) Trustees or personal representatives or someone in a position of trust to dispose of land belonging to another, can be guilty of stealing it if, in such circumstances, they dishonestly dispose of it.

EXAMPLE

Two company employees are asked by the company directors to sell land belonging to the company. The value of the land is £10,000 an acre. The company employees sell the land to each other for £1,000 an acre. The company employees are in a position of trust and have 'breached the confidence reposed in them' and commit theft of the land.

(2) Persons not in possession of the land may commit theft in a variety of ways. This may be accomplished by severing fixtures, plants, topsoil etc. from the land or by appropriating such property after it has been severed. If X decides to take an established and cultivated rosebush from the garden of his neighbour by ripping it out of the ground and then planting it in his own garden, this would be theft as the rosebush has been severed from the land (see below for wild plants). This would not include a person who dishonestly moves a boundary fence so as to appropriate some part of a neighbouring property as the land has not been 'severed'.

(3) Tenants can steal land but only fixtures and structures let to be used with the land. Examples of 'fixtures' would be a fireplace or the kitchen sink; a structure might be a greenhouse or a garden shed which is fixed to the land. A tenant cannot steal land such as topsoil or a rosebush growing in the garden of the rented premises as these things are not 'fixtures or structures'.

Things Growing Wild

Things growing wild on any land are 'property' and could be stolen by a person not in possession of the land if he/she severed and appropriated them. However, s. 4(3) of the Act tells us that a person who picks mushrooms, flowers, fruit and foliage growing wild on any land will not commit theft by so doing, unless the picking is done for reward, sale or other commercial purpose. If the whole plant is removed, this is theft as it is not 'picking' (this is not the case when a 'whole' mushroom is removed from the earth as the way mushrooms are harvested is to remove them entirely from the earth). Likewise, sawing through the trunk of a tree growing wild is not picking and would be theft. It is arguable that if the person does not have such a purpose at the time of the picking, any later intention to sell the fruit etc. may not bring it within the provisions of s. 4(3). If the mushroom, flower etc. is cultivated, it will be theft to pick it wherever it is growing.

Wild Creatures

Section 4(4) states that all wild creatures are 'property' whether they are tamed (your dog or cat) or untamed but ordinarily kept in captivity (a lion in a zoo). Wild creatures that are not tamed or ordinarily kept in captivity are not classed as property unless they have been reduced into possession or are in the process of being so reduced. For example, X shoots a rabbit on land belonging to Y (with Y's permission to be there and shoot). Z takes the rabbit from X—Z commits theft. If the rabbit is lost or abandoned after it has been reduced into possession or killed then it cannot be 'stolen'.

1.14.2.5 What is not Property?

'Identity theft' is a misleading phrase as adopting another person's characteristics and using his/her administrative data (such as National Insurance number) is not theft of the information as this 'confidential information' is not 'property' for the purposes of the Theft Act 1968.

Human bodies (dead or alive) are not property ('there is no property in a corpse' (*Doodeward* v *Spence* (1908) 6 CLR 406)). However, a body or body parts are capable of being stolen if they have acquired different attributes by virtue of the application of skill (such as dissection or preservation techniques for exhibition or teaching purposes). An Egyptian mummy would be the property of the museum it was kept in. This principle was upheld by the Court of Appeal in *R* v *Kelly* [1999] QB 621, after the conviction of two people involved in the theft of body parts from the Royal College of Surgeons. The court upheld the convictions for theft on the grounds that the process of *alteration* (amputation, dissection and preservation) which the body parts had undergone did make them 'property' for the purposes of the 1968 Act.

Fluids taken from a living body are property, so a motorist has been convicted of stealing a specimen of his own urine provided by him for analysis (*R* v *Welsh* [1971] RTR 478). The same rule would clearly apply to a blood sample.

Electricity is not property and cannot be stolen—it is the subject of a specific offence (abstracting electricity) under s. 13 of the Theft Act 1968.

1.14.2.6 Belonging to Another

The Theft Act 1968, s. 5 states:

(1) Property shall be regarded as belonging to any person having possession or control of it, or having in it any proprietary right or interest (not being an equitable interest arising only from an agreement to transfer or grant an interest).

(2) Where property is subject to a trust, the persons to whom it belongs shall be regarded as including any person having a right to enforce the trust, and an intention to defeat the trust shall be regarded accordingly as an intention to deprive of the property any person having that right.

KEYNOTE

Property can be 'stolen' from any person who has possession, control or a proprietary right or interest in that property. In one case where the defendant recovered his own recently repaired car from a street outside the garage where the repairs had taken place, he was convicted of stealing the car which at the time 'belonged to' the garage proprietor who had possession of it (*R* v *Turner (No. 2)* [1971] 1 WLR 901). In determining whether or not a person had 'possession' of property for the purposes of s. 5(1), the period of possession can be finite (i.e. for a given number of hours, days etc.) or infinite (*R* v *Kelly* [1999] QB 621).

It is not necessary to show who does own the property, only that it 'belongs to' someone other than the defendant. An example of how this principle operates can be seen in a case where the two defendants went diving in a lake on a golf course, recovering sacks of 'lost' balls which it was believed they were going to sell. This activity was carried out without the permission of the golf club which owned the course. Although the defendants argued that the balls had been abandoned by their owners, the Crown had shown that they were 'property belonging to another' (the golf club) and therefore the convictions were safe (*R* v *Rostron; R* v *Collinson* [2003] EWCA Crim 2206).

Charitable trusts are enforceable by the Attorney-General and an appropriation of the trust property by a charitable trustee will amount to theft from the Attorney-General. Where money is given to charity collectors, it becomes the property of the relevant charitable trustees at the moment it goes into the collecting tin (*R* v *Dyke* [2001] EWCA Crim 2184). If s. 5(2) did not exist, those charitable trustees could take the donation to the charity and do what they wished with it, including placing the charitable funds in their own bank account.

When a cheque is written, it creates a 'thing in action'. That thing in action belongs only to the payee (the 'payee' is the person to whom the cheque is made payable). Therefore a payee of a cheque cannot 'steal' the thing in action which it creates (*R* v *Davis* (1989) 88 Cr App R 347).

You must show that the property belonged to another *at the time of the appropriation*. Where a defendant decides not to pay for goods *after* property passes to him/her (e.g. people refusing to pay for meals after they have eaten or deciding to drive off having filled their car with petrol), the proper charge is found under the

Fraud Act 2006 (see chapter 1.14) or by charging with the offence of making off without payment. If ownership of the property had passed to the defendant *before* he/she appropriated it (e.g. by virtue of the Sale of Goods Act 1979; *Edwards* v *Ddin* [1976] 1 WLR 942), then this element of theft would not be made out and an alternative charge should be considered.

1.14.2.7 Obligations Regarding Another's Property

The Theft Act 1968, s. 5 states:

(3) Where a person receives property from or on account of another, and is under an obligation to the other to retain and deal with that property or its proceeds in a particular way, the property or proceeds shall be regarded (as against him) as belonging to the other.

KEYNOTE

'Obligation' means a legal obligation not a moral one (*R* v *Hall* [1973] QB 126). Whether or not such an obligation exists is a matter of law for a trial judge to decide (*R* v *Dubar* [1994] 1 WLR 1484).

Instances under s. 5(3) most commonly involve receiving money from others to retain and use in a certain way (e.g. travel agents taking deposits, solicitors holding funds for mortgagees or pension fund managers collecting contributions (*R* v *Clowes (No. 2)* [1994] 2 All ER 316)). The Court of Appeal has held that one effect of s. 5(3) is that property can be regarded as belonging to another even where it does not 'belong' to that person on a strict interpretation of civil law (*R* v *Klineberg* [1999] 1 Cr App R 427). In that case, the defendants collected money from customers in their timeshare business and told the customers that their deposits would be placed with an independent trustee. Instead, the defendants paid the sums into their company account, thereby breaching the 'obligation' under s. 5(3) to deal with the money in a particular way.

Section 5(3) would also include, say, the owner of a shopping centre who invites shoppers to throw coins into a fountain which will be donated to charity; if the owner did not deal with those coins in the way intended (e.g. keeping the money), the provisions of s. 5(3) may well apply.

1.14.2.8 Obligation to Restore Another's Property

The Theft Act 1968, s. 5 states:

(4) Where a person gets property by another's mistake, and is under an obligation to make restoration (in whole or in part) of the property or its proceeds or of the value thereof, then to the extent of that obligation the property or proceeds shall be regarded (as against him) as belonging to the person entitled to restoration, and an intention not to make restoration shall be regarded accordingly as an intention to deprive that person of the property or proceeds.

KEYNOTE

Where extra money is mistakenly credited into an employee's bank account, the employee will be liable for stealing the extra money if he/she dishonestly keeps it (*Attorney-General's Reference (No. 1 of 1983)* [1985] QB 182 where a police officer's account was credited with money representing overtime which she had not actually worked).

Section 5(4) only applies where someone *other than the defendant* has made a mistake. Such a mistake can be a mistake as to a material fact; whether or not a mistake as to law would be covered is unclear.

The obligation to make restoration is a *legal* one and an unenforceable or moral obligation will not be covered by s. 5(4). An example of a *moral* obligation can be found in the case of *R* v *Gilks* [1972] 1 WLR 1341, when a relief manager at a betting shop mistakenly paid out winnings against the wrong horse. The Court of Appeal held that the defendant did not owe a legal obligation to return the money because the bookmaker could not have sued on a gaming transaction and therefore s. 5(4) did not apply—the obligation to return the money in this case was a *moral* one as in 1972 gambling debts were not legally enforceable (they are now—Gambling Act 2005 in force since 1 September 2007).

1.14.2.9 Intention of Permanently Depriving

If you cannot prove an intention permanently to deprive, you cannot prove theft (*R* v *Warner* (1970) 55 Cr App R 93).

If there is such an intention at the time of the appropriation, giving the property back later will not alter the fact and the charge will be made out (*R* v *McHugh* (1993) 97 Cr App R 335).

In certain circumstances, s. 6 may help in determining the presence or absence of such an intention.

The Theft Act 1968, s. 6 states:

> (1) A person appropriating property belonging to another without meaning the other permanently to lose the thing itself is nevertheless to be regarded as having the intention of permanently depriving the other of it if his intention is to treat the thing as his own to dispose of regardless of the other's rights; and a borrowing or lending of it may amount to so treating it if, but only if, the borrowing or lending is for a period and in circumstances making it equivalent to an outright taking or disposal.

KEYNOTE

The key feature of s. 6(1) is the intention to treat 'the thing' as one's own to dispose of regardless of the other's rights. An example of such a case would be where property is 'held to ransom' (*R* v *Coffey* [1987] Crim LR 498). If X kidnaps a dog belonging to Y and tells Y that the dog will be returned in exchange for £500, the conclusion to be drawn is that if the ransom is not paid, the dog will not be returned, i.e. there is an intention to permanently deprive.

The borrowing or lending of another's property is specifically caught within s. 6(1). If a person takes property from his/her employer (e.g. carpet tiles) and uses it in a way which makes restoration unlikely or impossible (e.g. by laying them in his/her living room), s. 6(1) will apply (*R* v *Velumyl* [1989] Crim LR 299).

If X is given a football season ticket by Y to use for one match but then X holds on to the season ticket for several matches knowing that this was not part of the arrangement and against the wishes of Y, s. 6(1) would help to prove the required intention to permanently deprive because the circumstances of the borrowing make it equivalent to an outright taking.

In a case involving robbery, the defendants took the victim's personal stereo headphones from him and broke them in two, rendering them useless before returning them to him. The Administrative Court held that a person who took something and dealt with it for the purpose of rendering it useless in this way demonstrated the intention of treating that article as his/her own to dispose of. The court did not accept the argument that the property had to be totally exhausted before s. 6 applied and held that the magistrates had been wrong to accept the submission of no case to answer on this point (*DPP* v *J* [2002] EWHC 291 (Admin)). Therefore, the deliberate breaking of an item of property will amount to the 'intention to permanently deprive'; however, unless this action is accompanied by the other theft elements, it will be criminal damage. Note that in this case the offence dealt with was robbery so that the other elements of theft were plainly satisfied when the defendant initially took the property.

The Theft Act 1968, s. 6 states:

> (2) Without prejudice to the generality of subsection (1) above, where a person, having possession or control (lawfully or not) of property belonging to another, parts with the property under a condition as to its return which he may not be able to perform, this (if done for purposes of his own and without the other's authority) amounts to treating the property as his own to dispose of regardless of the other's rights.

KEYNOTE

Section 6(2) deals with occasions such as pawning another's property. In pawning the property, the defendant parts with the property on the basis that he/she might be able to recover it (there could never be certainty of recovery). So, there is a possibility that the defendant may not be able to do so, i.e. that he/she will be unable to meet the conditions under which he/she parted with another person's property. In such a case, s. 6(2) would help in proving an intention permanently to deprive.

1.14.3 Robbery

OFFENCE: **Robbery—*Theft Act 1968, s. 8***

- Triable on indictment • Life imprisonment

The Theft Act 1968, s. 8 states:

(1) A person is guilty of robbery if he steals, and immediately before or at the time of doing so, and in order to do so, he uses force on any person or puts or seeks to put any person in fear of being then and there subjected to force.

KEYNOTE

The Theft Element of the Offence

For there to be a robbery, there must be a theft; so if there is no theft, then there can be no robbery. The word 'steal' in the offence relates to the offence under s. 1 of the Theft Act 1968 and, therefore, if *any* element of theft cannot be proved, the offence of robbery will not be made out. For example, in *R* v *Robinson* [1977] Crim LR 173, D, who was owed £7 by P's wife, approached P, brandishing a knife. A fight followed, during which P dropped a £5 note. D picked it up and demanded the remaining £2 owed to him. Allowing D's appeal against a conviction for robbery, the Court of Appeal held that the prosecution had to prove that D was guilty of theft, and that he would not be (under the Theft Act 1968, s. 2(1)(a)) if he believed that he had a right in law to deprive P of the money, even though he knew that he was not entitled to use the knife to get it, i.e. there was no dishonesty (but **see para. 1.14.4** for blackmail).

The Robbery Time Frame

Section 8(1) requires that the force must be used or the threat made 'immediately before or at the time' of the theft. There is no guidance as to what 'immediately before' means. Clearly, if the force used or threatened is *after* the offence of theft has taken place, there will be no robbery; however, theft can be a continuing offence. This was decided in *R* v *Hale* (1979) 68 Cr App Rep 415, where the Court of Appeal stated that appropriation is a continuing act and whether it has finished or not is a matter for the jury to decide. From the robbery perspective, *Hale* decides that where D had assumed ownership of goods in a house, the 'time' of stealing is a continuing process. It does not end as soon as the property is picked up by the defendant and can be a continuing act so long as he/she is in the course of removing it from the premises. So, if D uses or threatens force to get away with the property (while still in the house, for example), a robbery is committed. This would not be the case if the defendant used force outside the house as there must come a time when the appropriation ends. The issue may be resolved by asking the question, 'Was D still on the job?' (*R* v *Atakpu* [1994] QB 69).

In Order to Do So

The use or threat of force must be 'in order' to carry out the theft. Force used in any other context means the offence is not committed, for example:

- Two men are fighting outside a pub. One man punches the other in the face and the force of the blow knocks the man out. As the injured man falls to the floor, his wallet drops out of his jacket pocket and onto the pavement. His opponent decides that he will steal the wallet. *No robbery is committed in these circumstances because the force is used for a purpose other than to steal.*

The question to ask in such circumstances is 'Why has the force been used and/or threatened?' If the answer is anything other than 'to enable the defendant to commit theft', then there is no offence of robbery.

Force

A small amount of force used in order to accomplish a theft may change that theft into a robbery. For example, in *R* v *Dawson* (1977) 64 Cr App R 170 the defendant and two others surrounded their victim. One of the attackers 'nudged' the victim and, while he was unbalanced, another stole his wallet. In *Dawson*, the court declined to define 'force' any further than to say that juries would understand it readily enough. In line with general principles of *actus reus* (criminal conduct), the force used by the defendant must be used voluntarily. Therefore, the accidental use of force such as when a pickpocket, in the process of stealing a wallet from his victim on a train, is pushed into his victim by the train jolting on the railway line would not be a robbery.

On Any Person

The force used to accomplish a robbery need not be used against the owner or possessor of the property. For example, a gang of armed criminals use force against a security guard in order to overpower him and steal cash from the bank he is standing outside and guarding.

Use of Force on Property

Force does not actually have to be used 'on' the *person*, i.e. on the actual body of the victim. It may be used indirectly, for example on something that the victim is carrying and thereby transferring the force to the person. This was the case in *R* v *Clouden* [1987] Crim LR 65, where the Court of Appeal dismissed an appeal against a conviction for robbery when the defendant had wrenched the victim's shopping basket from her hand and ran off with it. However, in *P* v *DPP* [2012] EWHC 1657 (Admin), it was held that snatching a cigarette from the hand of the victim was incapable of amounting to robbery. Mitting J stated that 'It cannot be said that the minimum use of force required to remove a cigarette from between the fingers suffices to amount to the use of force against that person'. In this case, there was no evidence of direct physical contact between the victim and the thief.

The Fear of Force

Where only the *threat* of force is involved, the intention must be to put a person in fear for *him/herself*; an intention to put someone in fear for another is not enough (*R* v *Taylor* [1996] 10 Archbold News 2). This may seem at odds with the approach to the actual use of force in the offence of robbery (in that force can be used against a third party who is unconnected with the property subject to the theft).

EXAMPLE

A man enters a betting shop and approaches the cashier. Without saying a word, he passes a note to the cashier that simply says, 'Look to your left'. The cashier looks and sees the man's accomplice standing several feet away and pointing a knife at the back of one of the shop's customers. The customer is oblivious to the actions of the man's accomplice. The man passes a second note to the cashier that says, 'Give me the money in the till or else he gets it!' The cashier, fearing for the customer, hands over the contents of the betting shop till. This is not robbery as the cashier cannot fear force for the betting shop customer. However, whilst there is no robbery there would be an offence of blackmail (Theft Act 1968, s. 21).

Let us say that instead of handing the contents of the betting shop till over to the offender, the cashier shakes her head and refuses to hand over any money. At this point, the man signals to his accomplice who shouts at the customer 'Look here!' The customer turns around and can clearly see the knife in the hand of the accomplice pointing towards him and fears force for himself. The man speaking to the cashier repeats his demand and the cashier hands over the contents of the betting shop till. This is a robbery as the customer fears force for himself.

In a final variation of this example, let us once again say that instead of handing the contents of the betting shop till over to the offender after the note demanding money is passed to her, the cashier shakes her head and refuses to hand over any money. At this point, the man signals to his accomplice who pulls the customer's head backwards and drags the knife across the side of the customer's throat causing a small cut. The customer screams in terror and at this point the cashier concedes to the man's demand and hands over the till contents. At this point in time, a robbery is committed as force is actually being used (albeit on a third party).

General Points

Any threats to use force at some time in the future (even by a matter of minutes) would constitute an offence of blackmail. Threats to use force at some place other than the location of the offence fall into the same category. This effectively excludes threats made via the telephone in all but the most improbable of situations.

1.14.4 Blackmail

OFFENCE: **Blackmail—*Theft Act 1968, s. 21***

- Triable on indictment • 14 years' imprisonment

The Theft Act 1968, s. 21 states:

(1) A person is guilty of blackmail if, with a view to gain for himself or another or with intent to cause loss to another, he makes any unwarranted demand with menaces; and for this purpose a demand with menaces is unwarranted unless the person making it does so in the belief—

(a) that he has reasonable grounds for making the demand; and

(b) that the use of the menaces is a proper means of reinforcing the demand.

(2) The nature of the act or omission demanded is immaterial, and it is also immaterial whether the menaces relate to action to be taken by the person making the demand.

KEYNOTE

The phrase 'with a view to' has been held (albeit under a different criminal statute) by the *Court* of Appeal to be less than 'with intent to' (*R* v *Zaman* [2002] EWCA Crim 1862). In Zaman, the court accepted that 'with a view to' meant simply that the defendant had something in his contemplation as *something that realistically might occur*, not that he necessarily intended or even wanted it to happen. Clearly, this is a very different test from 'intent'. In the above offence, then, it appears that the state of mind needed to prove the first element is that the defendant contemplated some gain for him/herself or for another as being realistically likely to flow from his/her actions. The alternative is an 'intent' to cause loss.

There is no requirement for dishonesty or theft and the offence is aimed at the making of the demands rather than the consequences of them.

1.14.4.1 Meaning of Gain and Loss

Section 34 of the 1968 Act states:

(2) For the purposes of this Act—

(a) 'gain' and 'loss' are to be construed as extending only to gain or loss in money or other property, but as extending to any such gain or loss whether temporary or permanent; and—

(i) 'gain' includes a gain by keeping what one has, as well as a gain by getting what one has not; and

(ii) 'loss' includes a loss by not getting what one might get, as well as a loss by parting with what one has; . . .

KEYNOTE

Keeping what you already have can amount to a 'gain'. Similarly, not getting something that you might expect to get can be a 'loss'.

For example, a person makes unwarranted demands with menaces with a view to getting a sports fixture cancelled and avoiding losing money that he/she has bet on the outcome of that fixture. Here the intention of keeping what the defendant already had (the money at risk on the bet) amounts to 'gain' as defined under s. 34(2). Similarly, the intention of preventing others getting what they might have got (their winnings or the club's earnings) could amount to a 'loss'.

A blackmailer need not be seeking any kind of material profit. In *R* v *Bevans* (1988) 87 Cr App R 64, the defendant, who was crippled with arthritis, went to a doctor, produced a gun and demanded a pain-killing morphine injection, threatening to shoot the doctor if he did not comply; this was held to be blackmail as the drug involved was a form of property.

Note that a demand for sexual favours would not constitute an offence of blackmail as those sexual favours are not 'money or other property'.

1.14.4.2 Criminal Conduct

The offence of blackmail is complete when the demand with menaces is made. As a result, it is extremely difficult, if not impossible, to have an offence of attempted blackmail as the defendant will either be preparing to make the demand or will have made it. It does not matter whether the demands bring about the desired consequences or not. If a demand is made by letter, the act of making it is complete when the letter is posted. The letter does not have to be received (*Treacy* v *DPP* [1971] AC 537).

The Court of Appeal has held that words or conduct which would not intimidate or influence anyone to respond to the demand would not be 'menaces'. As such, the term requires threats and conduct of such a nature and extent that a person of normal stability and courage might be influenced or made apprehensive so as to give in to the demands (*R* v *Clear* [1968] 1 QB 670).

Menaces will therefore include threats but these must be significant *to the victim*. If a threat bears a particular significance for a victim (such as being locked in the boot of a car to someone who is claustrophobic), that will be enough provided the defendant was aware of that fact. If a victim is particularly timid and the defendant knows it, that timidity may be taken into account when assessing whether or not the defendant's conduct was 'menacing' (*R* v *Garwood* [1987] 1 WLR 319).

In the converse situation, where an apparently serious threat fails to intimidate the victim at all, the offence is still committed. For example, if X approaches Y and threatens to break Y's legs unless Y gives X £50 but Y is unconcerned by the threat, this would still constitute blackmail as a threat to break someone's legs would influence a person of normal stability and courage.

1.14.4.3 Unwarranted?

If a defendant raises the issue that his/her demand was reasonable and proper, you will have to prove that he/she did not genuinely believe:

- that he/she had reasonable grounds for making the demand; and
- that the use of the particular menaces employed was not a proper means of reinforcing it.

The defendant's *belief* will be subjective and therefore could be entirely unreasonable. Whilst that is the case, such a subjective belief is subject to restriction. In *R* v *Harvey* (1981) 72 Cr App R 139, the defendant was convicted of kidnapping, malicious wounding, false imprisonment and blackmail. The charges arose out of an incident where he had been sold a substance that he falsely believed to be cannabis and in an attempt to get his money back he had made threats to kill, maim and rape. The defendant appealed on the basis that the judge's summing-up on the blackmail charge in relation to what were 'proper' threats was wrong. The judge had said, 'This is a matter of law. It cannot be a proper means of reinforcing the demand to make threats to commit serious offences.' The appeal was dismissed and the conviction upheld. The question of the defendant's belief should be left to the jury. The word 'proper' in s. 21(1) of the Theft Act 1968 had a wide meaning and *no act which was not believed to be lawful could be described as 'proper'*. In the present case, the judge's direction was not strictly correct, but no jury could hesitate before deciding that the defendant believed his threats to be 'proper'.

1.14.5 Burglary

There are two forms of burglary—s. 9(1)(a) and s. 9(1)(b).

1.14.5.1 Section 9(1)(a)

OFFENCE: **Burglary—*Theft Act 1968, s. 9***

• Triable on indictment if 'ulterior offence' is so triable, or if committed in dwelling and violence used; otherwise triable either way • 14 years' imprisonment if building/part of building is dwelling • Otherwise 10 years' imprisonment on indictment • Six months' imprisonment and/or a fine summarily

The Theft Act 1968, s. 9 states:

(1) A person is guilty of burglary if—
  (a) he enters any building or part of a building as a trespasser and with intent to commit any such offence as is mentioned in subsection (2) below; or . . .

(2) The offences referred to in subsection (1)(a) above are offences of stealing anything in the building or part of a building in question, of inflicting on any person therein any grievous bodily harm and of doing unlawful damage to the building or anything therein.

KEYNOTE

Enters

The Theft Act 1968 does not define the term 'entry' and so we are left to resolve the meaning of this term by reference to case law and the decisions of the courts. The common law rule was that the insertion of any part of the body, *however small*, was sufficient to be considered an 'entry'. So where D pushed in a window pane and the forepart of his finger was observed in the building, that was enough (*R* v *Davis* (1823) Russ & Ry 499). This approach was narrowed considerably in *R* v *Collins* [1973] QB 100, where it was said that entry needed to be 'effective and substantial'. The ruling in *Collins* was rejected by the Court of Appeal in *R* v *Brown* [1985] Crim LR 212, where it was stated that the 'substantial' element was surplus to requirements and that entry need only be 'effective'. Whether an entry was 'effective' or not was for the jury to decide. So the decision of the court in *Brown* appears to be the current accepted approach to defining the term; entry must therefore be 'effective'.

An 'effective' entry does not mean that the defendant has to enter a building or part of a building to such a degree that the ulterior offence, which he/she is entering with the intention to commit (the theft, grievous bodily harm or criminal damage), can be committed (*R* v *Ryan* [1996] Crim LR 320). Nor does it mean that the defendant must get his/her whole body into the building. In *Brown*, the defendant had his feet on the ground outside the building with the upper half of his body inside the building as he searched for goods to steal; this was held to be an entry. In *Ryan*, the defendant, who had become trapped by his neck with only his head and right arm inside the window, was held to have 'entered' the building. In *Brown*, the Court of Appeal stated that it would be astounding if a smash-and-grab raider, who inserted his hand through a shop window to grab goods, was not considered to have 'entered' the building.

At common law, the insertion of an instrument would constitute entry as long as the instrument was inserted to enable the ulterior offence to take place, e.g. a hook inserted into premises to steal property or the muzzle of a gun pushed through a letterbox with a view to cause grievous bodily harm. Insertion of an instrument merely to facilitate entry, e.g. using a coat hanger to open a window lock, *would not* be entry. Although there is no recent authority on the issue, it is likely that this line of reasoning in relation to the use of instruments in burglary is still acceptable.

Entry must be deliberate and not accidental.

Ultimately, whether the defendant has entered a building or not will be a question of fact for the jury or magistrate(s).

Trespasser

To be guilty of the offence of burglary, the defendant must know or be reckless as to the fact that they are entering as a trespasser (i.e. they must know they are entering without a right by law or with express or implied permission to do so) or be reckless as to that fact. Sometimes a defendant may have general permission to enter a building or part of a building for a legitimate purpose; however, the true intention of the defendant when entering is not for that legitimate purpose but in order to steal or commit grievous bodily harm or to cause criminal damage. As these intentions invariably form no part of the permission to enter the building or part of it, any entry in such circumstances means that the defendant becomes a trespasser the moment he/she enters the building or part of the building. In such circumstances, the exceeding of the granted permission places the defendant in a position of being a trespasser from the outset.

EXAMPLE

X has a key to Y's home and has permission from Y to enter Y's home at any time and sleep in one of the bedrooms. Intending to steal from Y's home, X uses the key to get into Y's house. This means that X has committed a burglary under s. 9(1)(a) at Y's house. Y did not give X the keys to the house so that he could steal.

This example is very similar to the circumstances in *R* v *Jones and Smith* [1976] 1 WLR 672, where the defendant was convicted of burglary when he took two televisions from his father's home. He had a key to the premises and was free to come and go as he liked but when he entered his father's house (using the key) accompanied by a friend at 3 am and stole the television sets, he committed burglary as it was his intention to steal as such an intent voids the general permission to enter.

1.14.5.2 Building

The Theft Act 1968, s. 9 states:

(4) References in subsections (1) and (2) above to a building . . . which is a dwelling, shall apply also to an inhabited vehicle or vessel, and shall apply to any such vehicle or vessel at times when the person having a habitation in it is not there as well as at times when he is.

KEYNOTE

Building

A building is generally considered to be a structure of a permanent nature (*Norfolk Constabulary* v *Seekings and Gould* [1986] Crim LR 167), although a substantial portable structure with most of the attributes of a building can be a 'building' for the purposes of burglary. For example, in *B & S* v *Leathley* [1979] Crim LR 314 a portable container measuring 25 ft by 7 ft by 7 ft and weighing three tons, which had occupied the same position for three years and was connected to mains electricity and which was due to remain in the same position for the foreseeable future, was considered to be a building for the purposes of burglary. An unfinished house can be a building for the purposes of burglary (*R* v *Manning* (1871) LR 1 CCR 338), although at what precise point a pile of building materials becomes an 'unfinished house' and therefore a building or part of a building would be a question of fact for the jury to decide. Tents and marquees are considered to fall outside the term, even if the tent is someone's home (the Criminal Law Revision Committee intended tents to be outside the protection of burglary).

The effect of s. 9(4) is to include *inhabited* vehicles and vessels (such as house boats or motor homes) within the term. A canal boat that is not inhabited is not a building as, whilst it may be capable of habitation, it is not being lived in.

Part of a Building

People may commit burglary when, although they are in one part of a building with legitimate access, they enter another part of it as a trespasser.

- A tenant of a block of flats has a key that provides access to a communal foyer of the block of flats. He uses the key to enter the foyer (*entering a building and plainly not a trespasser at this stage*). Instead of entering his own flat, he forces entry to a neighbour's flat by breaking down the neighbour's door that can be accessed via the communal foyer (*moving from one part of a building to another in the process and certainly a trespasser at this stage*).

The Court of Appeal decided that it is for the jury to decide whether an area physically marked out is sufficiently segregated to amount to 'part of a building'. In *R* v *Walkington* [1979] 1 WLR 1169, the defendant walked behind a movable sales counter in a shop with the intention to steal and was found guilty of burglary as this was held to be 'part of a building'. A 'No Entry' sign or a rope could mark off one part of a building from another.

1.14.5.3 Intentions at the Time of Entry

The intentions at the time of entry (not before or after) must be as follows:

- Stealing. This means an intention to commit theft under s. 1 (and 'thief' and 'steal' will be construed accordingly). It will not include abstracting electricity because electricity is not 'property' for the purposes of theft (*Low* v *Blease* [1975] Crim LR 513), neither will it include taking a conveyance (no intention to permanently deprive). The property which the defendant intends to steal must be in a building or part of a building.
- Inflicting grievous bodily harm. In proving an intention to commit grievous bodily harm under s. 9(1)(a), it is not necessary to prove that a wounding/grievous bodily harm offence was actually committed (*Metropolitan Police Commissioner* v *Wilson* [1984] AC 242). The offence in question in respect of a burglary under s. 9(1)(a) is of grievous bodily harm contrary to s. 18 of the Offences Against the Person Act 1861.
- Causing unlawful damage. This includes damage not only to the building but to anything in it (**see chapter 1.16**).

1.14.5.4 Conditional Intent

Provided the required intention can be proved, it is immaterial whether or not there is anything 'worth stealing' within the building (*R* v *Walkington* [1979] 1 WLR 1169). The same will be true if the person to whom the defendant intends to cause serious harm is not in the building or part of the building at the time (**see also para. 1.3.4**).

1.14.5.5 Section 9(1)(b)

OFFENCE: **Burglary—*Theft Act 1968, s. 9***

• Triable on indictment if 'ulterior offence' is so triable, or if committed in dwelling and violence used; otherwise triable either way • 14 years' imprisonment if building/part of building is a dwelling • Otherwise 10 years' imprisonment on indictment • Six months' imprisonment and/or a fine summarily

The Theft Act 1968, s. 9 states:

(1) A person is guilty of burglary if—

...

(b) having entered any building or part of a building as a trespasser he steals or attempts to steal anything in the building or that part of it or inflicts or attempts to inflict on any person therein any grievous bodily harm.

KEYNOTE

This type of burglary involves a defendant's behaviour *after* entering a building or part of a building as a trespasser.

The defendant must have entered the building or part of a building as a trespasser; it is not enough that the defendant subsequently became a trespasser in that part of the building by exceeding a condition of entry (e.g. hiding in the public area of a shop during opening hours until the shop closed). However, where a person has entered a particular building (such as a shop) lawfully and without trespassing, if he/she later moves to *another part* of the building as a trespasser, this element of the offence will be made out.

EXAMPLE

D enters a public house near closing time with a friend who buys him a drink from the bar. D's entry onto that part of the premises has been authorised by the implied licence extended to members of the adult public by the publican and therefore D is not a trespasser. D then goes into the lavatories to use them as such. At this point, he has entered another part of a building but again his entry is made under the implied licence to customers wishing to use the lavatories. While inside the lavatory area, D decides to hide until after closing time in order to avoid buying his friend a drink.

Once the publican has shut the pub for the night, D becomes a trespasser in the lavatory. This is because he is not supposed to be there, i.e. he has no express or implied permission or lawful right to be in the lavatory after the pub has closed. While D is a trespasser at this point in time, if he went on to steal from the lavatory he would not commit burglary because he did not enter the lavatory as a trespasser, he became one at a later stage by exceeding a condition of entry. It is essential, for an offence of burglary to occur, that the defendant has entered the building or part of a building as a trespasser. D then leaves the lavatory and walks into the lounge area. Now D has entered a part of a building as a trespasser. Having no particular intention at this point, however, D has still not committed an offence of burglary.

On seeing the gaming machines in the lounge, D decides to break into them and steal the money inside. At this point, although he has two of the required intentions for s. 9(1)(a) (an intention to steal and an intention to cause unlawful damage), those intentions were formed after his entry into the lounge. Therefore, D has not committed burglary under s. 9(1)(a). Because he has not stolen/attempted to steal or inflicted/attempted to inflict grievous bodily harm on any person therein, D has not committed burglary under s. 9(1)(b) either.

D then breaks open a gaming machine in order to steal the cash contents. At this point, he commits burglary under s. 9(1)(b). This is because, having entered a part of a building (the lounge) as a trespasser (because the pub is closed and D knows that to be the case), he attempts to steal. If he simply caused criminal damage to the machine without an intention of stealing the contents, D would not commit this offence because causing unlawful damage is only relevant to the offence under s. 9(1)(a).

Unlike s. 9(1)(a), there are only two further elements to the offence under s. 9(1)(b): the subsequent attempted theft of anything in the building or part of it, or the subsequent inflicting/attempted inflicting of grievous bodily harm to any person therein. The assault offences in question in respect of a burglary under s. 9(1)(b) are grievous bodily harm contrary to s. 18 or s. 20 of the Offences Against the Person Act 1861.

It has been suggested that if, having entered a building or part of a building as a trespasser, the defendant commits an offence of criminal damage, this will be an offence under s. 9(1)(b) of the Act as to damage or destroy something is also to steal it. *This is not the case.* If a person enters in such circumstances and causes criminal damage, there is little argument that such an activity would satisfy part of the offence of theft, i.e. appropriating property (**see para. 1.14.2.4**), but where is the 'dishonesty'? In addition, this would clearly be an unwarranted extension of the burglary offence under s. 9(1)(b) of the Theft Act 1968. If Parliament wanted such activity to be caught by the legislation, it would have included the offence of criminal damage within the definition of burglary under s. 9(1)(b).

1.14.6 Aggravated Burglary

OFFENCE: **Aggravated Burglary—*Theft Act 1968, s. 10***

- Triable on indictment • Life imprisonment

The Theft Act 1968, s. 10 states:

(1) A person is guilty of aggravated burglary if he commits any burglary and at the time has with him any firearm or imitation firearm, any weapon of offence, or any explosive; ...

KEYNOTE

An aggravated burglary is committed when a person commits an offence of burglary (either a s. 9(1)(a) or a s. 9(1)(b)) and at the time he/she has with him/her a WIFE.

- **W**—Weapon of offence
- **I**—Imitation firearm
- **F**—Firearm
- **E**—Explosive

At the Time

These words require consideration of the type of burglary the defendant is charged with. The moment at which a burglary under s. 9(1)(a) is committed is at the point of entry, therefore it is essential that the defendant has the WIFE with him/her when entering a building or part of a building with the intention of committing one of the trigger offences under s. 9(1)(a). If that is the case, the defendant commits aggravated burglary. The moment at which a burglary under s. 9(1)(b) is committed is when the defendant steals, inflicts grievous bodily harm on any person or attempts to do either. If the defendant has the WIFE with him/her when committing or attempting to commit either offence, an aggravated burglary is committed.

EXAMPLE

A person (X) enters the kitchen of a house as a trespasser intending to steal property. At the point of entry, X does not have any WIFE item with him, so at this point in time X has committed a s. 9(1)(a) burglary. While X is in the kitchen, the occupier of the house enters the kitchen and disturbs him. X picks up a carving knife (not intending to steal it but intending to hurt the occupier with it if necessary) and threatens the occupier with it. At this point, the carving knife becomes a weapon of offence (intended to cause injury and because of the concept of 'instant arming' (see below)) but this is not an aggravated burglary as X has not committed or attempted to commit theft or to inflict GBH. The occupier rushes towards X who stabs the occupier, inflicting GBH in the process. This is a s. 9(1)(b) burglary and at the time of its commission X has a WIFE item with him; as a result, this becomes an aggravated burglary.

Has with Him

'Has with him' is more restrictive than the term 'possession'. It will require the defendant to have some degree of *immediate control* of the item (*R* v *Pawlicki* [1992] 1 WLR 827) and will normally (but not exclusively) be the same as 'carrying' (*R* v *Klass* [1998] 1 Cr App R 453) although the defendant need not actually have the WIFE item *on his/her person* to be in *immediate control* of it. It is also essential that the individual has knowledge of the presence of the WIFE item. So if a burglary is committed by a single offender who knows he/she has a bayonet in his/her coat pocket when the offence is committed, the issue of aggravated burglary is clear. However, what of the situation where two offenders commit such a burglary? Liability depends on knowledge.

EXAMPLE

X and Y decide to commit a burglary together. X is concerned about being disturbed during the burglary and decides to take a knuckleduster (a weapon of offence *per se* as it is made for causing injury) along with him when the burglary takes place; he does not tell Y about the knuckleduster. When X and Y enter the building, they intend to burgle; both commit a s. 9(1)(a) burglary. As X has a knuckleduster with him at the time, X commits an aggravated burglary. However, Y does not commit the aggravated offence because he has no knowledge of the existence of the WIFE item. If X had told Y about the knuckleduster, then Y would have the required knowledge and would be deemed to have it with him so both would be guilty under s. 10 (*R* v *Jones* [1979] CLY 411).

Therefore, if the defendant has no knowledge of the WIFE item, he/she does not commit the aggravated offence.

If several people are charged with the offence of aggravated burglary, it must be shown that one of the defendants who actually entered the building or part of a building had the weapon with him/her. The offence is not committed if the WIFE item was being carried by a person who *did not* enter the building (*R* v *Klass* [1998] 1 Cr App R 453). In *Klass*, the court considered the example of an armed getaway driver who remains in a car outside the building while his colleagues burgle a nearby house. The fact that the driver has, for example, a weapon of offence with him would not mean that an aggravated burglary, rather than a burglary, has been committed.

It is important to note that the aggravated offence is committed due to the presence of the WIFE when the s. 9(1)(a) or s. 9(1)(b) burglary is carried out. It is irrelevant that the defendant had the item with him/her for some other purpose unconnected with the burglary offence.

Instant Arming

Ordinary items can, instantaneously, change into weapons of offence; it is the intention of the person to use an item in a particular way that allows this to take place. In *R* v *Kelly* (1993) 97 Cr App R 245, the defendant entered a building using a screwdriver to facilitate entry. When he was confronted, he prodded the person confronting him in the stomach with the screwdriver. At that moment, the screwdriver instantly became a weapon of offence and the defendant was later convicted of aggravated burglary.

1.14.6.1 Firearm/Weapon of Offence/Explosive

The Theft Act 1968, s. 10 goes on to state:

(1) ... and for this purpose—
  (a) 'firearm' includes an airgun or pistol, and 'imitation firearm' means anything which has the appearance of being a firearm, whether capable of being discharged or not, and
  (b) 'weapon of offence' means any article made or adapted for use for causing injury to or incapacitating a person, or intended by the person having it with him for such use; and
  (c) 'explosive' means any article manufactured for the purpose of producing a practical effect by explosion, or intended by the person having it with him for that purpose.

Weapon of Offence

This includes:

- items *made* for causing injury, e.g. a bayonet or a knuckleduster;
- items *adapted* for causing injury, e.g. a screwdriver that has been sharpened at the tip;
- items *intended* for causing injury, e.g. an ordinary cutlery knife. The cutlery knife is certainly inoffensive in everyday use but if the defendant *intends* to use it to injure, it will fall into this category;
- items *made, adapted or intended* to incapacitate a person, e.g. handcuffs, rope, CS spray and chloroform.

The defendant must not only know of the presence of the weapon but also that it is a weapon of offence (this element of the offence does not apply to weapons of offence *per se* (they are what they are) but only to items adapted or intended to cause injury/incapacitate).

Note that the defences of lawful authority or reasonable excuse in relation to the possession of an offensive weapon appear not to apply to the offence of aggravated burglary.

Imitation Firearm

This includes anything which has the appearance of being a firearm, whether capable of being discharged or not (but note that this will not include the defendant's fingers pointed at someone under a coat to resemble a firearm (*R* v *Bentham* [2005] UKHL 18)).

Firearm

This does not relate to the definition under the Firearms Act 1968. Indeed, the term is not defined other than to include airguns and air pistols.

Explosive

This would cover explosives such as TNT and items such as grenades as they are both manufactured to produce a practical effect by explosion. It also covers an item intended by the person having it with him/her for such a purpose, potentially bringing home-made devices or substances into the equation. The issue in relation to fireworks has yet to be firmly resolved by the courts, although they may well be excluded from the definition as fireworks are, by and large, manufactured to produce a pyrotechnic rather than practical effect by explosion and have been described as 'things that are made for amusement' (*Bliss* v *Lilley* (1862) 32 LJMC 3).

1.14.7 Taking a Conveyance without Consent

OFFENCE: **Taking a Conveyance without the Owner's Consent—*Theft Act 1968, s. 12***

- Triable summarily • Six months' imprisonment and/or a fine

The Theft Act 1968, s. 12 states:

> Subject to subsections (5) and (6) below, a person shall be guilty of an offence if, without having the consent of the owner or other lawful authority, he takes any conveyance for his own or another's use or, knowing that any conveyance has been taken without such authority, drives it or allows himself to be carried in or on it.

KEYNOTE

Taking a conveyance without consent (usually referred to as TWOC) is a summary only offence and as such there can be no 'attempt' (Criminal Attempts Act 1981, s. 1(1) and (4)).

As a summary offence, s. 12(1) proceedings are ordinarily subject to the time limit of six months from the day when the offence was committed (s. 127 of the Magistrates' Courts Act 1980). However, this restriction has caused significant problems in cases where the analysis of forensic evidence has been needed. As a result, the Vehicles (Crime) Act 2001 extended the time limit for s. 12(1) offences. Where there is a certificate setting out the date on which sufficient evidence came to the knowledge of the person responsible for commencing the prosecution, proceedings should be commenced within six months of the date specified. This is subject to the proviso that such proceedings shall not be commenced after the end of the period of three years beginning with the day on which the offence was committed.

Once a conveyance has been 'taken', it cannot be 'taken' again by the same person before it has been recovered (*DPP* v *Spriggs* [1994] RTR 1). However, where the original taker abandons the conveyance, it may be 'taken' again by a further defendant and the original taker may be responsible for further offences arising out of its use before it is recovered.

The person taking the conveyance must do so intentionally, i.e. not simply by moving it accidentally (*Blayney* v *Knight* (1974) 60 Cr App R 269).

1.14.7.1 Consent of the Owner

Any 'consent' given must be true consent if the defendant is to avoid liability.

This area of the law has been subject to some rather unusual decision-making in the courts, one of which relates to consent. Consent, even if obtained by a deception, is still a valid consent. *This will be the case unless the deception is one where identity is an issue.*

EXAMPLE

John Smith (who does not possess a driving licence) is walking along the street when he finds a driving licence in the name of Paul Grey. Smith takes the driving licence and visits a car hire company and asks to hire a car for a day. The assistant at the reception of the car hire company asks Smith for a driving licence and Smith produces the licence he found in the street (in the name of Paul Grey). The assistant photocopies the licence and asks for the fee of £100 which Smith pays. The assistant hands over a set of car keys and Smith drives away in the car (intending to return it later that day).

The above scenario *would not* represent an offence of TWOC; this is because the assistant has handed over a set of keys to Smith and consented to Smith taking the car. The relevant deception here relates to the possession of the driving licence, *not to the name on the driving licence*. The assistant would have handed over the keys to the car if the name on the driving licence was 'Bugs Bunny'; identity is not an issue (*Whittaker* v *Campbell* [1984] QB 318).

Where consent is obtained by misrepresentation as to the purpose or destination of the journey, that misrepresentation has been held not to negate the consent given. So where D falsely represented to the owner of a car that he needed to drive it from Bedlington to Alnwick to sign a contract and was given the vehicle by the owner, he did not commit the offence when he drove it to Burnley instead. Once again, identity is not an issue when such consent is given (*R* v *Peart* [1970] 2 QB 672).

If, after a lawful purpose had been fulfilled, the defendant did not return the car but drove it off on his own business, the offence is committed as the defendant is going beyond the limits of the consent that had been given by the owner (*R* v *Phipps* (1970) 54 Cr App R 300).

1.14.7.2 Lawful Authority

A police officer removing a vehicle which is obstructing traffic after an accident, council workers removing a vehicle parked in contravention of parking restrictions or an agent of a finance company repossessing a vehicle would be examples of such lawful authority.

1.14.7.3 Takes

You must show that the conveyance was moved. It does not matter by how little the conveyance is moved but simply starting the engine is not enough (*R* v *Bogacki* [1973] QB 832) nor is hiding in a car or doing anything else in it while it is stationary. A conveyance is taken even if it is put onto another vehicle to do so (*R* v *Pearce* [1973] Crim LR 321, where a rubber dinghy was put on the roof rack of a car and taken away).

1.14.7.4 Conveyance

The Theft Act 1968, s. 12(7) states:

> (a) 'conveyance' means any conveyance constructed or adapted for the carriage of a person or persons whether by land, water or air, except that it does not include a conveyance constructed or adapted for use only under the control of a person not carried in or on it, and 'drive' shall be construed accordingly ...

KEYNOTE

This definition includes cars, motor cycles, boats or aircraft.

The definition does not extend to hand carts or animals used as conveyances as neither are constructed or adapted for the carriage of persons.

Pedal cycles are expressly excluded by virtue of s. 12(5) of the Act. It is a separate summary offence (punishable with a fine) for a person, without having the consent of the owner or other lawful authority, to take a pedal cycle for his/her own or another's use, or to ride a pedal cycle knowing it to have been taken without such authority (Theft Act 1968, s. 12(5)). The defence under s. 12(6) also applies to pedal cycles.

1.14.7.5 For His Own or Another's Use

The conveyance must be taken for the taker's or someone else's ultimate use *as a conveyance*. So standing at the rear of a conveyance and pushing it around a corner to hide it as a practical joke satisfies the first part ('taking') but not the second 'for his own or another's use as a conveyance' (*R* v *Stokes* [1983] RTR 59). This is because although the defendants may have 'taken' the conveyance, it did not 'convey' them, i.e. they were not *in it* or *on it* and it did not move them (convey); further, they did not take it so that someone could ultimately use it as such. If the practical joker pushed the car round a corner in order for a friend to then get into it and start it out of earshot and drive it to a further location, the offence would be committed at the time of pushing the car (it is being 'taken' to be used as a conveyance in the future).

When a person got into a Land Rover that was blocking his path and released the handbrake, allowing the vehicle to coast for several metres, it was held that his actions satisfied both elements (*R* v *Bow* (1977) 64 Cr App R 54). This is because getting into (or onto) a conveyance and moving it necessarily amounts to *taking it for use as a conveyance*, therefore the motives of the defendant in doing so are irrelevant. In the rubber dinghy example (**see para. 1.14.7.3**), the dinghy was ultimately going to be used as a conveyance by someone in the future.

1.14.7.6 Allow to be Carried

The person who commits this offence *must know* that the conveyance has been taken without the consent of the owner or other lawful authority; 'suspecting' the conveyance has been taken would not be enough. Further, the conveyance must *actually move* when the person drives it or allows him/herself to be carried in or on it (the same as the 'take' element of the offence).

1.14.7.7 Defences

The Theft Act 1968, s. 12(6) states:

> (6) A person does not commit an offence under this section by anything done in the belief that he has lawful authority to do it or that he would have had the owner's consent if the owner knew of his doing it and the circumstances of it.

It is essential that this belief exists at the time of the taking. It is not enough if the owner says, later, that he would have consented had he known (*R* v *Ambler* [1979] RTR 217). The defence is available in answer to all forms of the offence under s. 12 (including allowing to be carried).

1.14.8 Aggravated Vehicle-taking

OFFENCE: **Aggravated Vehicle-taking—*Theft Act 1968, s. 12A***

- Triable either way • If the accident under s. 12A(2)(b) caused death 14 years' imprisonment, otherwise two years' imprisonment and/or a fine on indictment
- Six months' imprisonment and/or a fine summarily

The Theft Act 1968, s. 12A states:

(1) Subject to subsection (3) below, a person is guilty of aggravated taking of a vehicle if—
  (a) he commits an offence under section 12(1) above (in this section referred to as a 'basic offence') in relation to a mechanically propelled vehicle; and
  (b) it is proved that, at any time after the vehicle was unlawfully taken (whether by him or another) and before it was recovered, the vehicle was driven, or injury or damage was caused, in one or more of the circumstances set out in paragraphs (a) to (d) of subsection (2) below.

(2) The circumstances referred to in subsection (1)(b) above are—
  (a) that the vehicle was driven dangerously on a road or other public place;
  (b) that, owing to the driving of the vehicle, an accident occurred by which injury was caused to any person;
  (c) that, owing to the driving of the vehicle, an accident occurred by which damage was caused to any property, other than the vehicle;
  (d) that damage was caused to the vehicle.

KEYNOTE

In addition to the above sentences, where a person is convicted of aggravated vehicle-taking, disqualification from driving (for a minimum of 12 months) is obligatory, endorsement of licence is obligatory and the penalty points which may be imposed for the offence are 3 to 11. The fact that the person concerned did not drive the vehicle at any particular time or at all is not a special reason to avoid obligatory disqualification (Road Traffic Offenders Act 1988, s. 34).

Before this offence is made out, there must first of all be an offence under s. 12(1) which includes an offence of 'being carried', and the conveyance involved must be a 'mechanically propelled vehicle' (see *General Police Duties*, chapter 3.19).

You need only prove that *one* of the consequential factors occurred before the vehicle was recovered (*Dawes* v *DPP* [1995] 1 Cr App R 65); namely that, between the vehicle being taken and its being recovered:

- it was driven dangerously on a road/public place;
- owing to the driving of it, an accident occurred by which injury was caused to anyone or damage was caused to any other property; or
- damage was caused to it.

'Dangerous driving' will require the same proof as the substantive offence (see *General Police Duties*, chapter 3.21).

A vehicle will be 'recovered' once it has been restored to its owner or other lawful possession or custody (s. 12A(8)). This would include occasions where a vehicle has come into the possession of the police.

The word 'accident' for the purposes of the offence of aggravated vehicle-taking is not defined by the Theft Act 1968. Therefore a broad interpretation of the word is taken rather than any restricted form (such as that under s. 170 of the Road Traffic Act 1988). So, for example, if a s. 12(1) offence was committed in relation to a mechanically propelled vehicle and, after it was taken and before it was recovered, there was an 'accident' where the only person injured was the driver of the mechanically propelled vehicle, this would amount to an offence of aggravated vehicle-taking.

In *R* v *Hughes* [2013] UKSC 56, the Supreme Court held that in cases of causing death by driving when uninsured (s. 3ZB of the Road Traffic Act 1988) the defendant must be proved to have done something more than merely drive his/her vehicle on the road so that it was there to be involved in a fatal accident. It must be proved that the defendant did or omitted to do something else that contributed in a more than minimal way to the death. There must, in other words, be something more than mere 'but for' causation. The same approach is taken in respect of aggravated vehicle-taking. On a charge of aggravated vehicle-taking, the Crown must prove some act or omission in the control of the mechanically propelled vehicle which involves some element of fault on the part of the driver, whether amounting to careless or inconsiderate driving or not, and which contributed in some more than minimal way to the outcome. In *R* v *Taylor* [2016] 1 WLR 500, the defendant was charged with taking a truck without consent, and that 'owing to the driving of the vehicle, an accident occurred by which [death] was caused'. But although the truck was involved in a fatal collision with a scooter while the defendant was driving it, the fault was *entirely that of the scooter rider*, so the defendant could not be said to have 'caused' the latter's death. There must be a direct causal connection between the driving and the death, injury and/or damage.

Damage to the vehicle does not include damage caused by breaking into it in order to commit the 'basic offence'. This is because damage caused at this point will be caused before the vehicle has been 'taken' and so, at that stage, the 'basic offence' will not have been carried out.

1.14.8.1 Defence to Aggravated Vehicle-taking

The Theft Act 1968, s. 12A states:

(3) A person is not guilty of an offence under this section if he proves that, as regards any such proven driving, injury or damage as is referred to in subsection (1)(b) above, either—
  (a) the driving, accident or damage referred to in subsection (2) above occurred before he committed the basic offence; or
  (b) he was neither in nor on nor in the immediate vicinity of the vehicle when that driving, accident or damage occurred.

KEYNOTE

'Immediate vicinity' is not defined but will be a question of fact for the jury/magistrate(s) to determine in each case.

1.14.9 Interfering with Vehicles

OFFENCE: **Interfering with Vehicles—*Criminal Attempts Act 1981, s. 9***

• Triable summarily • Three months' imprisonment and/or a fine

The Criminal Attempts Act 1981, s. 9 states:

(1) A person is guilty of the offence of vehicle interference if he interferes with a motor vehicle or trailer or with anything carried in or on a motor vehicle or trailer with the intention that an offence specified in subsection (2) below shall be committed by himself or some other person.

(2) The offences mentioned in subsection (1) above are—
  (a) theft of the motor vehicle or trailer or part of it;
  (b) theft of anything carried in or on the motor vehicle or trailer; and
  (c) an offence under section 12(1) of the Theft Act 1968 (taking and driving away without consent);

and, if it is shown that a person accused of an offence under this section intended that one of those offences should be committed, it is immaterial that it cannot be shown which it was.

(3)–(4) ...

(5) In this section 'motor vehicle' and 'trailer' have the meanings assigned to them by section 185(1) of the Road Traffic Act 1988.

KEYNOTE

The term 'interference' is not defined.

For the definition of a motor vehicle, see *General Police Duties*, chapter 3.19.

A 'trailer' means a vehicle drawn by a motor vehicle (s. 185(1)(c) of the Road Traffic Act 1988).

1.14.10 Going Equipped

OFFENCE: **Going Equipped for Stealing etc.—*Theft Act 1968, s. 25***

• Triable either way • Three years' imprisonment on indictment • Six months' imprisonment and/or a fine summarily

The Theft Act 1968, s. 25 states:

(1) A person shall be guilty of an offence if, when not at his place of abode, he has with him any article for use in the course of or in connection with any burglary or theft.

KEYNOTE

Place of Abode

A person's place of abode means where he/she resides; it does not include his/her place of business (unless, presumably, they are one and the same place) (*R* v *Bundy* [1977] 1 WLR 914). If a person lives in a vehicle then that vehicle will be regarded only as his/her 'place of abode' if it is parked at the place where the person 'abides' or intends to 'abide' (*Bundy*). Therefore, if a person is found in his/her vehicle away from such a site and at the time has with him/her articles as described under s. 25, this offence is committed.

Has with Him

'Has with him' is a narrower requirement than 'possession' and, as with aggravated burglary, generally means that defendants must have the article within their *immediate control*. It would suffice if defendants had the article within their immediate control in their car or bag, at their workplace or on their person.

Article

'Article' can mean almost any physical object, such as a bunch of skeleton keys (*R* v *Metcalfe* [1971] Crim LR 112) or a torch and screwdriver (*R* v *Harrison* [1970] Crim LR 415). The indictment in *Ellames* referred to a 'sawn-off shotgun, a wig, three woollen hats, two masks, a pair of goggles, a boiler suit, a motor vehicle, two containers and a quantity of ammonia, gloves and shot-gun cartridges'. 'Article' would appear not to include animate objects, e.g. a trained monkey (*Daly* v *Cannon* [1954] 1 WLR 261).

In the Course or in Connection With

The offence is directed against acts preparatory to the offences of burglary (contrary to s. 9 of the Theft Act 1968), theft (contrary to s. 1 of the Theft Act 1968) and taking a conveyance (contrary to s. 12 of the Theft Act 1968). 'Theft' includes theft with force which would amount to robbery (firearms or imitation firearms kept for the purpose of a robbery or aggravated burglary come within the scope of s. 25 but more obviously come within the provisions of the Firearms Act 1968 (**see chapter 1.7**)).

You do not need to prove that persons having the article with them intended to use it themselves and it will be enough to show that they intended it to be used by someone for one of the purposes in s. 25(1) (*R* v *Ellames* [1974] 1 WLR 1391). Simply being a passenger in a car where such an article is found is not enough to prove the offence (*R* v *Lester* (1955) 39 Cr App R 157). The articles must be for some *future use*; it is not enough to show that the defendant had articles that *had been used* in the course of, or in connection with, one of the proscribed offences.

If you can prove that the article was made, adapted or intended for burglary or theft, that fact will be evidence that the person had it with him/her for that purpose (s. 25(3)).

The power of search under s. 1 of the Police and Criminal Evidence Act 1984 applies to this offence (**see** ***General Police Duties*****, chapter 3.3**).

1.14.11 Handling Stolen Goods

OFFENCE: **Handling Stolen Goods—*Theft Act 1968, s. 22***

• Triable either way • 14 years' imprisonment on indictment • Six months' imprisonment and/or a fine summarily

The Theft Act 1968, s. 22 states:

(1) A person handles stolen goods if (otherwise than in the course of the stealing) knowing or believing them to be stolen goods he dishonestly receives the goods, or dishonestly undertakes or assists in their retention, removal, disposal or realisation by or for the benefit of another person, or if he arranges to do so.

KEYNOTE

Handling can only be committed otherwise than in the course of stealing. The 'stealing' referred to is the time whereby the original goods became 'stolen' in the first place.

If 'goods' are not 'stolen goods', there is no handling. Whether they are so stolen is a question of fact for a jury or magistrate(s). If the goods have yet to be stolen, s. 22 would not apply and the offence of conspiracy should be considered (*R* v *Park* (1988) 87 Cr App R 164).

It is sensible, before examining the activities associated with this offence, to consider what is being 'handled'—what are 'goods' and 'stolen goods'?

1.14.11.1 Meaning of 'Goods' and 'Stolen Goods'

Goods

The Theft Act 1968, s. 34(2)(b) states:

> 'Goods', except insofar as the context otherwise requires, includes money and every other description of property except land, and includes things severed from the land by stealing.

KEYNOTE

A 'thing in action' (see para. 1.14.2.5) is 'goods' because it falls within 'every other description of property'.

Stolen Goods

The Theft Act 1968, s. 24 states:

> (1) The provisions of this Act relating to goods which have been stolen shall apply whether the stealing occurred in England or Wales or elsewhere, and whether it occurred before or after the commencement of this Act, provided that the stealing (if not an offence under this Act) amounted to an offence where and at the time when the goods were stolen; and references to stolen goods shall be construed accordingly.
>
> (2) For purposes of those provisions references to stolen goods shall include, in addition to the goods originally stolen and parts of them (whether in their original state or not),—
>
> (a) any other goods which directly or indirectly represent or have at any time represented the stolen goods in the hands of the thief as being the proceeds of any disposal or realisation of the whole or part of the goods stolen or of goods representing the stolen goods; and
>
> (b) any other goods which directly or indirectly represent or have at any time represented the stolen goods in the hands of a handler of the stolen goods or any part of them as being the proceeds of any disposal or realisation of the whole or part of the stolen goods handled by him or of goods so representing them.
>
> (3) But no goods shall be regarded as having continued to be stolen goods after they have been restored to the person from whom they were stolen or to other lawful possession or custody, or after that person and any other person claiming through him have otherwise ceased as regards those goods to have any right to restitution in respect of the theft.
>
> (4) For purposes of the provisions of this Act relating to goods which have been stolen (including subsections (1) to (3) above) goods obtained in England or Wales or elsewhere either by blackmail or subject to subsection (5) below, by fraud (within the meaning of the Fraud Act 2006) shall be regarded as stolen; and 'steal', 'theft' and 'thief' shall be construed accordingly.
>
> (5) Subsection (1) above applies in relation to goods obtained by fraud as if—
>
> (a) the reference to the commencement of this Act were a reference to the commencement of the Fraud Act 2006, and
>
> (b) the reference to an offence under this Act were a reference to an offence under section 1 of that Act.

The Theft Act 1968, s. 24A states:

> (8) References to stolen goods include money which is dishonestly withdrawn from an account to which a wrongful credit has been made, but only to the extent that the money derives from the credit.

KEYNOTE

Goods Stolen Outside England and Wales

Under s. 24(1), a person can still be convicted of handling if the goods were stolen outside England and Wales but only if the goods were taken under circumstances which amounted to an offence in the other country.

Proceeds of Stolen Property

Under s. 24(2), goods will be classed as stolen only if they are the property which was originally stolen or if they had at some time represented the *proceeds* of that property in the hands of the thief or a 'handler'.

Therefore if a mobile phone is stolen by X, and sold to Y (an unsuspecting party who is neither the thief nor a 'handler') who then part-exchanges it for a new one at a high street retailer, the first mobile phone will be 'stolen' goods (the original stolen property is 'stolen goods') but the new mobile phone in the hands of Y will not be 'stolen goods'. If Z (the first person buying the original stolen mobile phone) *knew* or *believed* that it was stolen, the mobile phone will be treated as stolen goods in the hands of Z.

Stolen Goods Ceasing to be 'Stolen'

Under s. 24(3), once goods have been restored to lawful possession they cease to be stolen. This situation does not cause problems when police officers recover stolen property and then wait for it to be collected by a handler (*Houghton* v *Smith* [1975] AC 476) as the Criminal Attempts Act 1981 and the common law rulings on 'impossibility' (see chapter 1.3) mean that a defendant could be dealt with in a variety of ways:

- Theft—collecting the property will be an 'appropriation'.
- Handling—an *arrangement* to come and collect stolen goods will probably have been made while they were still 'stolen'.
- Criminal attempt—the person collecting the goods has gone beyond merely preparing to handle them.

What are Stolen Goods?

Goods gained through offences such as robbery or burglary will be 'stolen' as theft is an intrinsic element of both offences—such goods are 'stolen'.

Section 24(4) states that apart from the goods described in subss. (1) to (3) (stolen goods, proceeds of goods in the hands of the thief and the 'handler' etc.), goods obtained by fraud and blackmail are included in the definition of 'stolen goods'. The reference to fraud is to the general offence of fraud under s. 1 of the Fraud Act 2006 (s. 24(5)).

Section 24A(8) provides that if a wrongful credit has been made to an account and money is dishonestly withdrawn from that account (money which derives from the wrongful credit), then that money is 'stolen goods' (see para. 1.14.12).

Property Outside the Scope of s. 21 or s. 24A(8)?

If the property in question appears to represent the proceeds of an offence that falls outside the scope of s. 24 or s. 24A(8), it may be possible to consider charges under the 'money laundering' provisions (see para. 1.14.14).

No Conviction Required for the 'Origin' Offence

There is no need to prove that the thief, blackmailer etc. has been convicted of the primary offence before prosecuting the alleged handler, neither is it always necessary to identify who that person was.

1.14.11.2 Handling—*Mens Rea* and *Actus Reus*

Mens Rea

The defendant must *know* or *believe* the goods to be stolen. Turning a blind eye to the facts 'can be capable, depending on the circumstances, of providing evidence going to prove knowledge or belief' (*Martin Edward Pace & Simon Peter Rogers* v *R* [2014] EWCA Crim 186). Suspicion will not be enough (*R* v *Griffiths* (1974) 60 Cr App R 14).

Knowledge or belief that the goods were stolen is not enough; the goods must be handled dishonestly. Here, dishonesty will be determined as per the decision in *Barlow Clowes* and *Royal Brunei Airlines* (**see para. 1.14.2.3**).

Actus Reus

The offence of handling stolen goods has many facets. Therefore to charge a defendant without specifying a particular form of handling is not bad for duplicity (*R* v *Nicklin* [1977] 1 WLR 403). However, the offence can be divided for practical purposes into two parts:

- *receiving/arranging to receive* stolen goods, in which case the defendant acts for his/her own benefit; and
- *assisting/acting for the benefit of another* person, in which case that assistance to another or benefit of another must be proved.

KEYNOTE

Receiving

This form of the handling offence is committed at the point the 'stolen goods' are received. However, receiving does not require the physical reception of goods and can extend to exercising control over them. Things in action, such as bank credits from a stolen cheque, can be 'received'.

'Arranging to receive' would cover circumstances which do not go far enough to constitute an attempt; that is, actions which *are* merely preparatory to the receiving of stolen goods may satisfy the elements under s. 22 even though they would not meet the criteria under the Criminal Attempts Act 1981.

Assisting/Acting for Another's Benefit

Assisting or acting for the benefit of another can be committed by misleading police officers during a search (*R* v *Kanwar* [1982] 1 WLR 845).

Disposing of the stolen goods or assisting in their disposal or realisation usually involves physically moving them or converting them into a different form (*R* v *Forsyth* [1997] 2 Cr App R 299).

If the only person 'benefiting' from the defendant's actions is the defendant, this element of the offence will not be made out (*R* v *Bloxham* [1983] 1 AC 109). In *Bloxham*, the appellant bought and part-paid for a car which he subsequently discovered to be stolen. He then sold the car at a slight loss and was convicted of handling in respect of this sale, the allegation being that he 'realised' the car for the benefit of the buyer. The House of Lords reversed this decision holding that the mischief at which the Act was aimed was the actions of those who knowingly received from the thief or facilitated the disposal of stolen goods. A purchaser of goods purchased in good faith who sells the goods after discovering they have been stolen *does not come within the ambit of the section*, even if the transaction could be described as a disposal or realisation for the benefit of the person to whom they sell it. The phrase 'by or for the benefit of another' limits the reach of the law to the situation where the handler acts *on another's behalf* in removing, disposing, realising or retaining goods (the possession of the stolen property would now be caught by s. 329 of the Proceeds of Crime Act 2002 (**see para. 1.14.14.6**) and the sale of the vehicle by fraud by false representation (s. 2 of the Fraud Act 2006, **see para. 1.15.4**). Similarly, if the only 'other' person to benefit is a co-accused on the same charge, the offence will not be made out (*R* v *Gingell* [2000] 1 Cr App R 88).

1.14.11.3 Power to Search for Stolen Goods

The Theft Act 1968, s. 26 states:

(1) If it is made to appear by information on oath before a justice of the peace that there is reasonable cause to believe that any person has in his custody or possession or on his premises any stolen goods, the justice may grant a warrant to search for and seize the same; but no warrant to search for stolen goods shall be addressed to a person other than a constable except under the authority of an enactment expressly so providing.

(2) ...

(3) Where under this section a person is authorised to search premises for stolen goods, he may enter and search the premises accordingly, and may seize any goods he believes to be stolen goods.

(4) …

(5) This section is to be construed in accordance with section 24 of this Act; and in subsection (2) above the references to handling stolen goods shall include any corresponding offence committed before the commencement of this Act.

KEYNOTE

Section 26 provides a general power to search for and seize stolen goods, whether identified in the search warrant or not, and magistrates are entitled to act on material provided by the police that gives rise to a reasonable belief that stolen goods will be found (*R Cruickshank Ltd* v *Chief Constable of Kent Constabulary* [2002] EWCA Civ 1840).

1.14.11.4 Evidence and Procedure on a Charge of Handling

Section 27 of the Theft Act 1968 allows for the admissibility of previous misconduct and states:

(3) Where a person is being proceeded against for handling stolen goods (but not for any offence other than handling stolen goods), then at any stage of the proceedings, if evidence has been given of his having or arranging to have in his possession the goods the subject of the charge, or of his undertaking or assisting in, or arranging to undertake or assist in, their retention, removal, disposal or realisation, the following evidence shall be admissible for the purpose of proving that he knew or believed the goods to be stolen goods—

- (a) evidence that he has had in his possession, or has undertaken or assisted in the retention, removal, disposal or realisation of, stolen goods from any theft taking place not earlier than 12 months before the offence charged; and
- (b) (provided that seven days' notice in writing has been given to him of the intention to prove the conviction) evidence that he has within the five years preceding the date of the offence charged been convicted of theft or of handling stolen goods.

KEYNOTE

This provision applies to all forms of handling (*R* v *Ball* [1983] 1 WLR 801) but it can only be used where handling is the *only offence* involved in the proceedings.

The evidence is admissible solely for the purpose of proving the defendant knew or believed the goods to be stolen goods and not any other purpose (*R* v *Duffus* [1994] 158 JP 224).

It should be noted that the provisions under s. 27(3)(a) and (b) are *separate*—for example, evidence could be introduced regarding a defendant's conviction for theft three years preceding the offence charged (under s. 27(3)(b)). There is no need for the element under s. 27(3)(a) to be present *as well as* that theft conviction.

1.14.11.5 Proof that Goods were Stolen

The Theft Act 1968, s. 27 states:

(4) In any proceedings for the theft of anything in the course of transmission (whether by post or otherwise), or for handling stolen goods from such a theft, a statutory declaration made by any person that he dispatched or received or failed to receive any goods or postal packet, or that any goods or postal packet when dispatched or received by him were in a particular state or condition, shall be admissible as evidence of the facts stated in the declaration, subject to the following conditions—

- (a) a statutory declaration shall only be admissible where and to the extent to which oral evidence to the like effect would have been admissible in the proceedings; and

(b) a statutory declaration shall only be admissible if at least seven days before the hearing or trial a copy of it has been given to the person charged, and he has not, at least three days before the hearing or trial or within such further time as the court may in special circumstances allow, given the prosecutor written notice requiring the attendance at the hearing or trial of the person making the declaration.

KEYNOTE

Section 27(4) allows for evidence to be admitted proving that goods 'in the course of transmission' have been stolen. They allow for a statutory declaration by the person dispatching or receiving goods or postal packets as to when and where they were dispatched and when or if they arrived and, in each case, their state or condition (e.g. if they had been opened or interfered with). The declaration will only be admissible in circumstances where an oral statement would have been admissible *and* if a copy has been served on the defendant at least seven days before the hearing and he/she has not, within three days of the hearing, served written notice on the prosecutor requiring the attendance of the person making the declaration.

This section is to be construed in accordance with s. 24 generally (s. 27(5)).

1.14.12 Retaining a Wrongful Credit

OFFENCE: **Dishonestly Retaining a Wrongful Credit—*Theft Act 1968, s. 24A***

• Triable either way • 10 years' imprisonment on indictment • Six months' imprisonment and/or a fine summarily

The Theft Act 1968, s. 24A states:

(1) A person is guilty of an offence if—
(a) a wrongful credit has been made to an account kept by him or in respect of which he has any right or interest;
(b) he knows or believes that the credit is wrongful; and
(c) he dishonestly fails to take such steps as are reasonable in the circumstances to secure that the credit is cancelled.
(2) References to a credit are to a credit of an amount of money.
(2A) A credit to an account is wrongful to the extent that it derives from—
(a) theft;
(b) blackmail;
(c) fraud (contrary to section 1 of the Fraud Act 2006); or
(d) stolen goods.
[Subsections (3) and (4) repealed by the Fraud Act 2006.]
(5) In determining whether a credit to an account is wrongful, it is immaterial (in particular) whether the account is overdrawn before or after the credit is made.
(6) ...
(7) Subsection (8) below applies for purposes of provisions of this Act relating to stolen goods (including subsection (2A) above).
(8) References to stolen goods include money which is dishonestly withdrawn from an account to which a wrongful credit has been made, but only to the extent that the money derives from the credit.
(9) 'Account' means an account kept with—
(a) a bank;
(b) a person carrying on a business which falls within subsection (10) below; or
(c) a person falling within any of paragraphs (a) to (j) of the definition of 'electronic money issuer' in regulation 2(1) of the Electric Money Regulations 2011.
(10) A business falls within this subsection if—
(a) in the course of the business money received by way of deposit is lent to others; or
(b) any other activity of the business is financed, wholly or to any material extent, out of the capital of or the interest on any money received by way of deposit.
(11) References in subsection (10) above to a deposit must be read with—
(a) section 22 of the Financial Services and Markets Act 2000;
(b) any relevant order under that section; and

(c) Schedule 2 of that Act;

but any restriction on the meaning of deposit which arises from the identity of the person making it, is to be disregarded.

(12) For the purposes of subsection (10) above—

(a) all the activities which a person carries on by way of business shall be regarded as a single business carried on by him; and

(b) 'money' includes money expressed in a currency other than sterling.

KEYNOTE

The wrongful credit to an account can occur in two ways: it may come from the circumstances outlined under s. 1 of the Fraud Act 2006 or it may come from one of the dishonest sources set out in s. 24A(2A).These offences will generally be restricted to transactions involving the crediting of accounts held with financial institutions.

There is a requirement for dishonesty which will be determined as per the decision in *Barlow Clowes* and *Royal Brunei Airlines* (**see para. 1.14.2.3**). However, there is no requirement for any deception.

The effects of s. 24A(8) are that *money* derived from credit received under s. 24A of the Theft Act 1968 may amount to stolen goods.

EXAMPLE

- If the proceeds of a theft by A are paid into his/her bank account, they are stolen goods because they represent the stolen goods in the hands of the thief (s. 24(4)).
- If they are then transferred into B's bank account, they cease to be stolen goods. This is because the 'thing in action' (the credit balance) created by the transfer in B's name is a different 'thing in action' from the one originally created by A (*R* v *Preddy* [1996] AC 815).
- As such, the credit balance in B's name has never represented the proceeds of the theft *in the hands of the thief.*
- But if B retains the wrongful credit made to his/her account, then he/she commits the s. 24A offence if he/she dishonestly retains it, knowing or believing it to be derived from one or other of those offences.
- If B withdraws money from the credited account, that money then, by virtue of s. 24A(8), becomes stolen goods once more.

This offence is also unusual in that the *actus reus* not only can be satisfied by an 'omission', but necessarily involves an omission or a failure to act (i.e. retaining something does not involve a positive act).

1.14.13 Making Off without Payment

OFFENCE: **Making Off without Payment—*Theft Act 1978, s. 3***

• Triable either way • Two years' imprisonment on indictment • Six months' imprisonment and/or a fine summarily

The Theft Act 1978, s. 3 states:

(1) Subject to subsection (3) below, a person who, knowing that payment on the spot for any goods supplied or service done is required or expected from him, dishonestly makes off without having paid as required or expected and with intent to avoid payment of the amount due shall be guilty of an offence.

(2) For purposes of this section 'payment on the spot' includes payment at the time of collecting goods on which work has been done or in respect of which service has been provided.

(3) Subsection (1) above shall not apply where the supply of the goods or the doing of the service is contrary to law, or where the service done is such that payment is not legally enforceable.

KEYNOTE

This offence is often committed by motorists who drive off without paying for petrol, diners who run off after a meal and 'punters' who jump out of taxi cabs (*DPP* v *Ray* [1974] AC 370; *Edwards* v *Ddin* [1976] 1 WLR 942; *R* v *Brooks* (1983) 76 Cr App R 66). Some problems can arise in cases of alleged theft where the ownership in the property has passed to the defendant before the act of appropriation; this offence offers a solution to some such cases.

Occasions where the supply of goods or services is contrary to law or is not legally enforceable, e.g. prostitution, are excluded (s. 3(3)). Making off without payment after the provision of an unlawful service, or one for which payment is not legally enforceable, would not then be caught by s. 3. If there is doubt as to whether the defendant has actually 'made off' from the spot, then he/she can be charged with attempting the offence.

There must be an intention to *avoid* payment; delaying payment due or making someone wait for payment is not enough. In *R* v *Vincent* [2001] 1172 EWCA Crim 295, the Court of Appeal acknowledged a 'loophole' in s. 3. This loophole might be illustrated as follows:

- A person checks into an hotel and runs up a bill.
- The person deceives the proprietor into agreeing that the bill will be settled at some later date (as opposed to on departure).
- Having gained that agreement, the person checks out of the hotel and never makes any payment.

In such a situation, there was no longer an expectation of payment at the time when the person checked out of the hotel. This expectation had been removed by the agreement; the fact that the agreement had been obtained dishonestly did not reinstate the expectation of payment on departure. The offence under s. 3 is a simple and straightforward one which applies to a limited set of circumstances only (which were not covered by the above facts). The limited scope of this offence would suggest that alternative charges of theft and/or fraud should be considered.

If the person driving or running away from the garage, restaurant, taxi cab etc. does so because he/she feels aggrieved at the service received or is in dispute with the supplier, then the question of fraud should be considered against the standards of ordinary, decent people (per the decision in *Barlow Clowes* and *Royal Brunei Airlines* (see para. 1.13.2.3).

1.14.14 Proceeds of Crime

1.14.14.1 Proceeds of Crime Act 2002

The offences and powers under the Proceeds of Crime Act 2002 are connected with day-to-day criminality and are relevant to all police officers. This section provides an overview of the three principal offences relating to 'money laundering' created by s. 327 (concealing criminal property), s. 328 (arrangements in relation to criminal property) and s. 329 (acquisition, use and possession of criminal property) of the Act. To begin with, we examine the concepts of 'criminal conduct' and 'criminal property'.

1.14.14.2 Criminal Conduct

The Proceeds of Crime Act 2002, s. 340 states:

> (2) Criminal conduct is conduct which—
> (a) constitutes an offence in any part of the United Kingdom, or
> (b) would constitute an offence in any part of the United Kingdom if it occurred there.

Section 340(4) states that it is immaterial:

- who carried out the criminal conduct;
- who benefited from it;
- whether the conduct occurred before or after the passing of the Act.

So criminal conduct not only includes the behaviour of the defendant but also of any other person. Effectively, this states that *any offence*, committed by *any person, anywhere* at all and at *any time* is 'criminal conduct'. As a consequence of s. 340, a conviction can be obtained under the Proceeds of Crime Act even if the prosecution cannot specify the offence or offences that gave rise to the proceeds or identify the person(s) responsible for the offence(s).

1.14.14.3 Criminal Property

The Proceeds of Crime Act 2002, s. 340 states:

> (3) Property is criminal property if—
> (a) it constitutes a person's benefit from criminal conduct or it represents such a benefit (in whole or in part and whether directly or indirectly) and,
> (b) the alleged offender knows or suspects that it constitutes or represents such a benefit.

KEYNOTE

The offences under ss. 327, 328 and 329 are often referred to as 'money laundering'. Note that the definition of 'property' *does not just relate to money.* Section 340(9) of the Act defines property as *all* property *wherever* situated and includes:

- money;
- all forms of property, real or personal, heritable or movable; and
- things in action and other intangible or incorporeal property.

(Incorporeal property relates to property or an asset that does not have value in material form, such as a right or a patent.)

The *mens rea* relating to criminal property and therefore to all three offences is knowing or *suspecting.* Dishonesty is not required. In *R* v *Da Silva* [2006] EWCA Crim 1654, the Court of Appeal upheld the conviction, concluding that the word 'suspect' meant that the defendant had to think that there was a possibility, which was more than fanciful, that the relevant facts existed. A vague feeling of unease would not suffice. The fact the suspicion alone will suffice means that proving such offences is remarkably less burdensome for the prosecution than the potential alternative to such offences, a charge of handling stolen goods where the defendant must be proved to know or believe that goods are stolen goods.

1.14.14.4 Concealing Criminal Property

OFFENCE: **Concealing Criminal Property—*Proceeds of Crime Act 2002, s. 327***

- Triable either way • 14 years' imprisonment on indictment and/or a fine
- Six months' imprisonment and/or a fine summarily

The Proceeds of Crime Act 2002, s. 327 states:

> (1) A person commits an offence if he—
> (a) conceals criminal property;
> (b) disguises criminal property;
> (c) converts criminal property;
> (d) transfers criminal property;
> (e) removes criminal property from England and Wales and Scotland or from Northern Ireland.
> (2) But a person does not commit such an offence if—
> (a) he makes an authorised disclosure under section 338 and (if the disclosure is made before he does the act mentioned in subsection (1)) he has the appropriate consent;
> (b) he intended to make such a disclosure but had a reasonable excuse for not doing so;
> (c) the act he does is done in carrying out a function he has relating to the enforcement of any provision of this Act or of any other enactment relating to criminal conduct or benefit from criminal conduct.

(3) Concealing or disguising criminal property includes concealing or disguising its nature, source, location, disposition, movement or ownership or any rights with respect to it.

KEYNOTE

There is an overlap between offences of concealing criminal property and handling stolen goods. However, whereas handling only occurs 'otherwise than in the course of stealing' and 'by or for the benefit of another', the offence under s. 327 can potentially be committed *during the commission of an offence and for the benefit of the thief.* On a literal reading of s. 327, a thief who conceals, disguises or sells property that he/she has just stolen may thereby commit offences under that section because the definition of criminal property applies to the laundering of an offender's own proceeds of crime as well as those of someone else.

The offence can be committed in a variety of ways. In *R* v *Fazal* [2010] 1 WLR 694, D allowed his bank account to be used by a friend to launder money, and it was held that he was guilty of converting criminal property (contrary to s. 327(1)(c)) whenever such monies were deposited in, retained in or withdrawn from the account.

In *R* v *Pace* [2014] EWCA Crim 186, the Court of Appeal rejected the argument that on a charge of attempting to commit the offence under s. 327(1)(c), it would be sufficient for the prosecution to prove that D merely suspected the property in question to be criminal property. Suspicion of this kind suffices for the substantive offence (as it does for all such offences under ss. 327 to 329) but it cannot, said the court, suffice for an attempt.

Section 327(2) creates several defences to charges under s. 327.

1.14.14.5 Arrangements in Relation to Criminal Property

OFFENCE: **Arrangements in relation to Criminal Property—*Proceeds of Crime Act 2002, s. 328***

- Triable either way • 14 years' imprisonment on indictment and/or a fine
- Six months' imprisonment and/or a fine summarily

The Proceeds of Crime Act 2002, s. 328 states:

(1) A person commits an offence if he enters into or becomes concerned in an arrangement which he knows or suspects facilitates (by whatever means) the acquisition, retention, use or control of criminal property by or on behalf of another person.

KEYNOTE

This offence will often be apt for the prosecution of those who launder on behalf of others. This could catch persons who work in financial or credit institutions, accountants etc., who in the course of their work facilitate money laundering by or on behalf of other persons and also family members (husband/wife, partner etc.). The natural and ordinary meaning of s. 328(1) was that the arrangement to which it referred must be one which related to property which was criminal property at the time when the arrangement began to operate on it. To say that it extended to property which was originally legitimate but became criminal only as a result of carrying out the arrangement was to stretch the language of the section beyond its proper limits (*R* v *Geary (Michael)* [2010] EWCA Crim 1925).

Section 328 includes the same defences against committing the offence as those included in s. 327(2).

1.14.14.6 Acquisition, Use and Possession of Criminal Property

OFFENCE: **Acquisition, Use and Possession of Criminal Property—*Proceeds of Crime Act 2002, s. 329***

- Triable either way • 14 years' imprisonment on indictment and/or a fine
- Six months' imprisonment and/or a fine summarily

The Proceeds of Crime Act 2002, s. 329 states:

(1) A person commits an offence if he—
 (a) acquires criminal property;
 (b) uses criminal property;
 (c) has possession of criminal property.

KEYNOTE

A thief who uses or retains possession of property that he/she has just stolen (this being criminal property as defined in s. 340) must therefore be guilty of an offence under s. 329(1)(b) or (c), the maximum penalty for which is twice that for basic theft. It does not follow that such a charge would be appropriate.

This offence is committed where a person knows or suspects that the property which is acquired etc., constitutes or represents his/her own or another's benefit from criminal conduct; the same defences against committing the offence apply as in s. 327.

An additional defence exists under s. 329(2)(c) which states that a person will not commit the offence if he/she acquired or used or had possession of the property for adequate consideration (e.g. being paid a proper market price of £3,000 to fix a roof). The effect of the defence in s. 329(2)(c) is that persons, such as trades people, who are paid for ordinary consumable goods and services in money that comes from crime are not under any obligation to question the source of the money. However, the defence is not available to a defendant who provides goods or services knowing or suspecting that those goods or services will help a person *to actually carry out criminal conduct.*

The coincidence between an offence of handling stolen goods and those described from the Proceeds of Crime Act 2002 might provide a dilemma as to which offence to charge. In such a situation, CPS guidance states that if it is possible to charge money laundering or handling stolen goods, then money laundering may be more appropriate if 'either a defendant has possessed criminal proceeds in large amounts or in lesser amounts, but repeatedly and where assets are laundered for profit'. However, a money laundering charge should only be considered where proceeds are more than *de minimis* (about minimal things) in any circumstances where the defendant who is charged with the underlying offence has done more than simply consume the proceeds of crime.

1.15 Fraud

1.15.1 Introduction

The Fraud Act 2006 provides a general offence of fraud which can be committed in three ways (by false representation, by failing to disclose information and by abuse of position). It also deals with offences of obtaining services dishonestly and possessing, making and supplying articles for use in fraud. In addition to the offence of fraud, there is a series of closely related offences which deal with the falsification of documents or other 'instruments'.

1.15.2 Fraud

OFFENCE: **Fraud—*Fraud Act 2006, s. 1***

- Triable either way • 10 years' imprisonment and/or a fine on indictment
- Six months' imprisonment and/or a fine summarily

The Fraud Act 2006, s. 1 states:

(1) A person is guilty of fraud if he is in breach of any of the sections listed in subsection (2) (which provide for different ways of committing the offence).
(2) The sections are—
  (a) section 2 (fraud by false representation),
  (b) section 3 (fraud by failing to disclose information), and
  (c) section 4 (fraud by abuse of position).

KEYNOTE

The essence of these fraud offences is in the *conduct and ulterior intent* of the defendant. This means that a defendant's unsuccessful 'attempt' to commit the offence of fraud may amount to the commission of the substantive offence, effectively excluding the possibility of an offence under the Criminal Attempts Act 1981.

1.15.3 Gain and Loss

Fraud offences under ss. 2, 3 and 4 are all committed when the defendant carries out the *actus reus* of the offence intending to 'make a gain for himself or another' and/or 'to cause loss to another'. As the 'gain' and 'loss' elements are essential to these offences, it is useful to examine their meaning before looking at the specific offences.

The Fraud Act 2006, s. 5 states:

(1) The references to gain and loss in sections 2 to 4 are to be read in accordance with this section.
(2) 'Gain' and 'loss'—
  (a) extend only to gain and loss in money or other property;
  (b) include any such gain or loss whether temporary or permanent; and
  'property' means any property whether real or personal (including things in action and other intangible property).
(3) 'Gain' includes a gain by keeping what one has, as well as getting what one does not have.
(4) 'Loss' includes a loss by not getting what one might get, as well as a loss by parting with what one has.

KEYNOTE

It is important to note that the 'gain' and 'loss' relate only to *money and other property*. The definition of property includes intellectual property.

In all of the offences under ss. 2, 3 and 4, the 'gain' and/or 'loss' *do not actually have to take place.*

1.15.4 Fraud by False Representation

The Fraud Act 2006, s. 2 states:

(1) A person is in breach of this section if he—
  (a) dishonestly makes a false representation, and
  (b) intends, by making the representation—
    (i) to make a gain for himself or another, or
    (ii) to cause loss to another or to expose another to the risk of loss.

(2) A representation is false if—
  (a) it is untrue or misleading, and
  (b) the person making it knows that it is, or might be, untrue or misleading.

(3) 'Representation' means any representation as to fact or law, including a representation as to the state of mind of—
  (a) the person making the representation, or
  (b) any other person.

(4) A representation may be express or implied.

(5) For the purposes of this section a representation may be regarded as made if it (or anything implying it) is submitted in any form to any system or device designed to receive, convey or respond to communications (with or without human intervention).

KEYNOTE

Dishonestly

'Dishonestly' in s. 2(1)(a) refers to the test of dishonesty as per the decision in *Barlow Clowes* and *Royal Brunei Airlines* (see para. 1.14.2.3). The same test applies to ss. 3 and 4 of the Act.

Representation

A representation is false if it is untrue or misleading *and* the person making it knows this is or knows this might be the case; an untrue statement made in the honest belief that it is in fact true, would not suffice. The words 'or might be' involve a subjective belief of the person making the representation. Where a defendant makes a false representation knowing that it is false or might be, the offence of fraud is complete.

The representation may be express or implied and can be communicated in words or conduct. There is no limitation on the way in which the representation must be expressed, so it could be written, spoken or posted on a website.

A representation may be implied by conduct. For example, a person dishonestly misusing a credit card to pay for items hands the card to a cashier without saying a word. By handing the card to the cashier, the person is falsely representing that he/she has the authority to use it for that transaction. It is immaterial whether the cashier accepting the card for payment is deceived by the representation as the cashier's state of mind plays no part in the commission of the offence.

Any representation made must be one as to fact or law, so a broken promise is not in itself a false representation. However, a statement may be false if it misrepresents the current intentions or state of mind of the person making it or anyone else. For example, D visits V's house and tells V that he needs emergency work carried out on his roof. D states that he is in a position to do the work immediately but only if V pays him £1,000 there and then. V gives D the money and D then leaves without carrying out the work; the truth of the matter was that D had never intended to carry out the work. Such a 'promise' by D would amount to an offence as it involved a false representation, i.e. he never intended to keep the promise.

A representation may be *proved* by inference. Where an elderly person has paid D vastly more for a job or product (such as gardening work) than it was worth, it may be open to a court or jury to *infer* that D must dishonestly have misrepresented the value of that job or product, even if there is no direct evidence of any such misrepresentation (*R* v *Greig* [2010] EWCA Crim 1183). When an unidentified imposter presented himself to take a driving theory test in D's name, it could be inferred that D was complicit in any false representations made by that person with a view to gaining a pass certificate in his name (*Idrees* v *DPP* [2011] EWHC 624 (Admin)).

The offence is complete the moment the false representation is made. The representation need never be heard or communicated to the recipient and, if carried out by post, would be complete when the letter is posted (*Treacy* v *DPP* [1971] AC 537).

Phishing

The offence is committed by someone who engages in 'phishing' (the practice of sending out emails in bulk, usually purporting to represent a well-known brand in the hope of sending victims to a bogus website that tricks them into disclosing bank account details).

Machines

The offence of fraud applies to cases where the representation is made to a machine (for example, where a person enters a number into a 'chip and PIN' machine) (s. 2(5)).

1.15.5 Fraud by Failing to Disclose

The Fraud Act 2006, s. 3 states:

> A person is in breach of this section if he—
> (a) dishonestly fails to disclose to another person information which he is under a legal duty to disclose, and
> (b) intends, by failing to disclose the information—
> (i) to make a gain for himself or another, or
> (ii) to cause loss to another or to expose another to a risk of loss.

KEYNOTE

The term 'legal duty' has not been defined but will include duties under oral contracts as well as written contracts. The Law Commission's *Report on Fraud* dealt with the concept of legal duty and stated that duties might arise:

- from statute;
- where the transaction is one of the utmost good faith;
- from the express or implied terms of a contract;
- from the custom of a particular trade or market; or
- from the existence of a fiduciary relationship between parties.

The legal duty to disclose information will exist if:

- the defendant's actions give the victim a cause in action for damages; or
- if the law gives the victim the right to set aside any change in his/her legal position to which he/she may have consented as a result of the non-disclosure.

A fiduciary relationship is one relating to the responsibility of looking after someone else's money in a correct way. Examples of such behaviour would include solicitors failing to share vital information with a client in the context of their work relationship, in order to carry out a fraud upon that client, or if a person intentionally failed to disclose information relating to a heart condition when making an application for life insurance. Where recipients of benefits dishonestly fail to disclose income etc. that they are legally required to disclose, fraud by failing to disclose is an appropriate charge (*R* v *El-Mashta* [2010] EWCA Crim 2595).

1.15.6 Fraud by Abuse of Position

The Fraud Act 2006, s. 4 states:

(1) A person is in breach of this section if he—
  (a) occupies a position in which he is expected to safeguard, or not to act against, the financial interests of another person,
  (b) dishonestly abuses that position, and
  (c) intends, by means of the abuse of that position—
    (i) to make a gain for himself or another, or
    (ii) to cause loss to another or to expose another to a risk of loss.

(2) A person may be regarded as having abused his position even though his conduct consisted of an omission rather than an act.

KEYNOTE

The 'position' that the defendant occupies may be the result of an assortment of relationships. The Law Commission explained the meaning of 'position' at para. 7.38 of the *Report on Fraud*:

> The necessary relationship will be present between trustee and beneficiary, director and company, professional person and client, agent and principle, employee and employer, or between partners. It may arise otherwise, for example within a family, or in the context of voluntary work, or in any context where the parties are not at arm's length.

The term 'abuse' is not defined by the Act.

Liability for the offence could develop from a wide range of conduct, for example:

- an employee of a software company uses his position to clone software products with the intention of selling the products on;
- an estate agent values a house belonging to an elderly person at an artificially low price and then arranges for the agent's brother to purchase the house;
- a person who is employed to care for a disabled person and has access to that person's bank account, abuses that position by transferring funds to invest in a high-risk business venture of his own.

The offence can also be committed by omission, for example:

- an employee fails to take up the chance of a crucial contract in order that an associate or rival company can take it up instead of and at the expense of the employer.

1.15.7 Possession or Control of Articles for Use in Frauds

OFFENCE: **Possession or Control of Articles for Use in Frauds—*Fraud Act 2006, s. 6***

- Triable either way • Five years' imprisonment and/or a fine on indictment
- Six months' imprisonment and/or a fine summarily

The Fraud Act 2006, s. 6 states:

(1) A person is guilty of an offence if he has in his possession or under his control any article for use in the course of or in connection with any fraud.

KEYNOTE

What is an 'Article'?

The Fraud Act 2006, s. 8 states:

(1) For the purposes of—
  (a) sections 6 and 7, and
  (b) the provisions listed in subsection (2), so far as they relate to articles for use in the course of or in connection with fraud, 'article' includes any program or data held in electronic form.

(2) The provisions are—

(a) section 1(7)(b) of the Police and Criminal Evidence Act 1984 (c 60),

(b) ...

(c) ...

An 'article' can be anything whatsoever. For the purposes of ss. 6 and 7 of the Act, an 'article' includes any program or data held in electronic form. Examples of cases where electronic programs or data could be used in fraud are:

- a computer program that generates credit card numbers;
- a computer template that can be used for producing blank utility bills;
- a computer file that contains lists of other people's credit card details.

The offence under s. 6 can be committed *anywhere at all*, including the home of the defendant. It is committed when the defendant has articles in his/her possession and also when the defendant has them in his/her control, so the defendant may be some distance away from the articles and still commit the offence. The s. 6 offence applies to 'any fraud' which will therefore include *all fraud offences* under the 2006 Act. However, the offence is only committed in respect of *future* offences and not offences that have already taken place (*R* v *Sakalauskas* [2014] 1 All ER 1231). The offence can be committed if possession or control is to enable *another to* commit an offence of fraud.

1.15.8 Making or Supplying Articles for Use in Frauds

OFFENCE: **Making or Supplying Articles for Use in Frauds—*Fraud Act 2006, s. 7***

- Triable either way • 10 years' imprisonment on indictment and/or a fine
- Six months' imprisonment and/or a fine summarily

The Fraud Act 2006, s. 7 states:

(1) A person is guilty of an offence if he makes, adapts, supplies or offers to supply any article—

(a) knowing that it is designed or adapted for use in the course of or in connection with fraud, or

(b) intending it to be used to commit, or assist in the commission of, fraud.

KEYNOTE

For the definition of an 'article', see para. 1.15.7.

This offence ensures that any activity in respect of the making, supplying etc. of any 'article' for use in fraud offences is an offence. Making an 'offer to supply' would not require the defendant to be in possession of the 'article'. Examples of such behaviour include:

- a person makes a viewing card for a satellite TV system, enabling him/her to view all satellite channels for free;
- the same person then offers to sell similar cards to work colleagues although he/she has only made the one prototype card and does not actually have further cards to sell;
- a number of the person's work colleagues express an interest in buying the cards, so the person makes a dozen more cards and then actually supplies them to those work colleagues.

1.15.9 Obtaining Services Dishonestly

OFFENCE: **Obtaining Services Dishonestly—*Fraud Act 2006, s. 11***

- Triable either way • Five years' imprisonment and/or a fine on indictment
- Six months' imprisonment and/or a fine summarily

The Fraud Act 2006, s. 11 states:

(1) A person is guilty of an offence under this section if he obtains services for himself or another—
  (a) by a dishonest act, and
  (b) in breach of subsection (2).
(2) A person obtains services in breach of this subsection if—
  (a) they are made available on the basis that payment has been, is being or will be made for or in respect of them,
  (b) he obtains them without any payment having been made for or in respect of them or without payment having been made in full, and
  (c) when he obtains them, he knows—
    (i) that they are being made available on the basis described in paragraph (a), or
    (ii) that they might be, but intends that payment will not be made, or will not be made in full.

KEYNOTE

Unlike the other Fraud Act 2006 offences, the offence under s. 11 is not a conduct crime; it is a *result crime* and requires the *actual obtaining* of the service. However, the offence does not require a fraudulent representation or deception. Someone would commit this offence if, intending to avoid payment, he/she slipped into a concert hall to watch a concert without paying for the privilege. The offence can be committed where the defendant intends to avoid payment or payment in full but the defendant must know that the services are made available on the basis that they are chargeable, i.e. services provided for free *are not covered* by the offence.

If D sneaks aboard a lorry or a freight train and obtains a free ride, D would commit no offence under s. 11 because the haulage company or freight train operator does not provide such rides, even for payment.

The terms 'service' and 'obtaining' are not defined by the Act. The fact that 'service' is not defined means that in the situation where a person obtains the 'services' of a prostitute (an illegal service) without intending to pay him/her, the s. 11 offence can be committed.

1.15.10 False Accounting

OFFENCE: **False Accounting—*Theft Act 1968, s. 17***

• Triable either way • Seven years' imprisonment on indictment • Six months' imprisonment and/or a fine summarily

The Theft Act 1968, s. 17 states:

(1) Where a person dishonestly, with a view to gain for himself or another or with intent to cause loss to another,—
  (a) destroys, defaces, conceals or falsifies any account or any record or document made or required for any accounting purpose; or
  (b) in furnishing information for any purpose produces or makes use of any account, or any such record or document as aforesaid, which to his knowledge is or may be misleading, false or deceptive in a material particular;

  he shall [commit an offence].
(2) For purposes of this section a person who makes or concurs in making in an account or other document an entry which is or may be misleading, false or deceptive in a material particular, or who omits or concurs in omitting a material particular from an account or other document, is to be treated as falsifying the account or document.

KEYNOTE

This section creates two offences: destroying, defacing etc. accounts and documents; and using false or misleading accounts or documents in furnishing information. A record or account need not necessarily be a document. In *Edwards* v *Toombs* [1983] Crim LR 43, it was held that a turnstile meter at a soccer stadium was a record and thus within the scope of the section.

An offence under s. 17 can be committed by omission as well as by an act. Failing to make an entry in an accounts book, altering a till receipt or supplying an auditor with records that are incomplete may, if accompanied by the other ingredients, amount to an offence.

There is no requirement to prove an intention permanently to deprive but there is a need to show dishonesty as per the decision in *Barlow Clowes* and *Royal Brunei Airlines* (**see para. 1.14.2.3**). The requirement as to gain and loss is the same as for blackmail (**see para. 1.14.4**).

The misleading, false or deceptive nature of the information furnished under s. 17(1)(b) must be 'material' to the defendant's overall purpose, i.e. the ultimate gaining or causing of loss. Such an interpretation means that the defendant's furnishing of information need not relate directly to an accounting process and could be satisfied by lying about the status of a potential finance customer (*R* v *Mallett* [1978] 1 WLR 820).

Where the documents falsified are not intrinsically 'accounting' forms, such as insurance claim forms filled out by policyholders, you must show that those forms are treated for accounting purposes by the victim (*R* v *Sundhers* [1998] Crim LR 497). An application for a mortgage or a loan to a commercial institution is a document required for an accounting purpose, the rationale being that applications for a mortgage or a loan to commercial institutions will, if successful, lead to the opening of an account which will show as credits in favour of the borrower, funds received from the borrower and as debits paid out by the lender to, or on behalf of, the borrower (*R* v *O and H* [2010] EWCA Crim 2233).

1.16 Criminal Damage

1.16.1 Introduction

The prevalence of offences of criminal damage is well documented and damage in all forms has a harmful effect on the environment, the community and the economy.

1.16.2 Simple Damage

OFFENCE: **Simple Damage—*Criminal Damage Act 1971, s. 1(1)***

- Triable either way • 10 years' imprisonment on indictment
- Six months' imprisonment and/or a fine summarily

OFFENCE: **Racially or Religiously Aggravated—*Crime and Disorder Act 1998, s. 30(1)***

- Triable either way • 14 years' imprisonment and/or a fine on indictment
- Six months' imprisonment and/or a fine summarily

The Criminal Damage Act 1971, s. 1 states:

(1) A person who without lawful excuse destroys or damages any property belonging to another intending to destroy or damage any such property or being reckless as to whether any such property would be destroyed or damaged shall be guilty of an offence.

KEYNOTE

Although triable either way, if the value of the property destroyed or the damage done is less than £5,000, the offence is to be tried summarily (Magistrates' Courts Act 1980, s. 22). If the damage in such a case was caused by fire (arson), this rule will not apply.

The fact that the substantive offence is, by virtue of the value of the damage caused, triable only summarily does not make simple damage a 'summary offence' for all other purposes. If it did, you could only be found guilty of attempting to commit criminal damage if the value of the intended damage was more than £5,000 (because the Criminal Attempts Act 1981 does not extend to summary offences) (**see chapter 1.3**). Therefore, where a defendant tried to damage a bus shelter in a way that would have cost far less than £5,000 to repair, his argument that he had only attempted what was in fact a 'summary offence' was dismissed by the Divisional Court (*R* v *Bristol Magistrates' Court, ex parte E* [1999] 1 WLR 390).

The Theft Act 1968 states that where the property in question belonged to D's spouse or civil partner, a prosecution for unlawful damage may only be instituted against D by or with the consent of the DPP (s. 30(4)). This restriction does not apply to other persons charged with committing the offence jointly with D; nor does it apply when the parties are separated by judicial decree or order or under no obligation to cohabit (s. 30(4)(a)).

Where the damage caused is less than £300, the offence can be dealt with by way of fixed penalty notice.

If the offence involves only the painting or writing on, or the soiling, marking or other defacing of, any property by whatever means, the power to issue a graffiti notice may apply (under s. 43 of the Anti-social Behaviour Act 2003).

The racially or religiously aggravated form of this offence is triable either way irrespective of the cost of the damage.

1.16.2.1 Destroy or Damage

The terms 'destroy' or 'damage' are not defined. 'Destroying' property suggests that it has been rendered useless but there is no need to prove that 'damage' to property is in any way permanent or irreparable.

Whether an article has been damaged will be a question of fact for each court to determine on the evidence before it. Defacing of a pavement by an artist using only water-soluble paint (*Hardman* v *Chief Constable of Avon and Somerset* [1986] Crim LR 330) and graffiti smeared in mud can amount to damage, even though it is easily washed off (*Roe* v *Kingerlee* [1986] Crim LR 735). In *R* v *Fiak* [2005] EWCA Crim 2381, the defendant had been arrested and placed in a police cell which he flooded by stuffing a blanket down the cell lavatory and repeatedly flushing. The defendant argued that there was no evidence that the blanket or the cell had been 'damaged'; the water had been clean and both the blanket and the cell could be used again when dry. The Court of Appeal disagreed and held that while the effect of the defendant's actions in relation to the blanket and the cell was remediable, the reality was that the blanket could not be used until it had been dried and the flooded cell was out of action until the water had been cleared. Therefore both had sustained damage for the purposes of the Act. This case illustrates that putting property temporarily out of use, even for a short time and in circumstances where it will revert to its former state of its own accord, may fall within the definition of 'damage'.

1.16.2.2 Property

Property is defined in the 1971 Act by s. 10 which states:

> (1) In this Act 'property' means property of a tangible nature, whether real or personal, including money and—
> (a) including wild creatures which have been tamed or are ordinarily kept in captivity and any other wild creatures or their carcasses if, but only if, they have been reduced into possession ... or are in the course of being reduced into possession; but
> (b) not including mushrooms growing wild on any land or flowers, fruit or foliage of a plant growing wild on any land.

KEYNOTE

This definition is similar to the definition of 'property' for the purposes of theft (see chapter 1.13) but there are some differences, e.g. 'real' property (i.e. land and things attached to it) can be damaged even though it cannot be stolen, whereas intangible property (such as copyright) can be stolen but cannot be damaged. Trampling flower beds, digging up cricket pitches, chopping down trees in a private garden and pulling up genetically modified crops could potentially amount to criminal damage.

Pets or farm animals are property for the purposes of this Act. Cases of horses being mutilated would, in addition to the offence of 'cruelty' itself, amount to criminal damage.

1.16.2.3 Belonging to Another

Section 10 states:

> (2) Property shall be treated for the purposes of this Act as belonging to any person—
> (a) having the custody or control of it;
> (b) having in it any proprietary right or interest (not being an equitable interest arising only from an agreement to transfer or grant an interest); or
> (c) having a charge on it.

KEYNOTE

This extended meaning of 'belonging to another' is similar to that used in the Theft Act 1968. One result is that if a person damages his/her own property, he/she may still commit the offence of simple criminal damage if that property also 'belongs to' someone else.

1.16.2.4 Lawful Excuse

Section 5 of the Criminal Damage Act 1971 provides for two occasions where a defendant may have a 'lawful excuse'. These can be remembered as 'permission' (s. 5(2)(a)) and 'protection' (s. 5(2)(b)). Both involve the belief of the defendant.

1.16.2.5 Permission

A person shall be treated as having lawful excuse under s. 5(2):

(a) if at the time of the act or acts alleged to constitute the offence he believed that the person or persons whom he believed to be entitled to consent to the destruction of or damage to the property in question had so consented, or would have so consented to it if he or they had known of the destruction or damage and its circumstances ...

EXAMPLE

An elderly motorist asks you to help him get his keys out of his partner's car as he had locked them inside. You tell the motorist that the car may be damaged as a result of your efforts but the motorist tells you that is alright and to go ahead. Section 5(2)(a) would provide a statutory defence to any later charge of criminal damage by the owner. The main element here would be that you believed you had the consent of the motorist (who is someone you believed to be entitled to consent to that damage) to damage the vehicle in these circumstances.

1.16.2.6 Protection

A person shall be treated as having lawful excuse under s. 5(2):

(b) if he destroyed or damaged or threatened to destroy or damage the property in question or, in the case of a charge of an offence under section 3 above, intended to use or cause or permit the use of something to destroy or damage it, in order to protect property belonging to himself or another or a right or interest in property which was or which he believed to be vested in himself or another, and at the time of the act or acts alleged to constitute the offence he believed—
   (i) that the property, right or interest was in immediate need of protection; and
   (ii) that the means of protection adopted or proposed to be adopted were or would be reasonable having regard to all the circumstances.

KEYNOTE

A 'right or interest in property' includes any right or privilege in or over land, whether created by grant, licence or otherwise (s. 5(4)).

Key features of this defence are the immediacy of the need to protect the property and the reasonableness of the means of protection adopted. This defence has attracted the most attention of the courts in cases involving demonstrators claiming to be acting in furtherance of their political beliefs. In a case involving 'peace campaigners', it was held that the threat presented by a possible nuclear attack in the future did not excuse the carrying of a hacksaw for cutting through the perimeter fence of an airbase (*R* v *Hill* (1989) 89 Cr App R 74).

This defence also applies to the offence of having articles for causing damage (see para. 1.16.6).

Belief

It is immaterial whether a 'belief' was justified as long as it was honestly held (s. 5(3)). Although this test is supposed to be an *objective* one, the evidence will be based largely on what was going through a defendant's mind at the time. In *Jaggard* v *Dickinson* [1981] QB 527, the defendant had broken a window to get into a house. Being drunk at the time, she had got the wrong house but the court accepted that her belief (that it was the right house and that the owner would have consented) had been honestly held, and that it did not matter whether that belief was brought about by intoxication, stupidity, forgetfulness or inattention. That is not to say, however, that *any* honestly held belief will suffice. An example of someone claiming, unsuccessfully, a defence under both s. 5(2)(a) and (b) can be seen in *Blake* v *DPP* [1993] Crim LR 586. There the defendant was a vicar who wished to protest against Great Britain's involvement in the Gulf War. In order to mark his disapproval, the defendant wrote a quotation from the Bible in ink on a pillar in front of the Houses of Parliament. He claimed:

- he was carrying out God's instructions and had a lawful excuse based on his belief that God was the person entitled to consent to such damage and that God had in fact consented or would have done so (s. 5(2)(a)); and
- he had damaged the property as a reasonable means of protecting other property located in the Gulf from being damaged by warfare (s. 5(2)(b)).

The Divisional Court did not accept either proposition, holding that in the first case a belief in God's consent was not a 'lawful excuse' and, in the second case, that the defendant's conduct was too remote from any immediate need to protect property in the Gulf States. The test in relation to the defendant's belief appears then to be largely subjective (i.e. what was/was not going on in the defendant's head at the time) but with an objective element in that the judge/magistrate(s) must decide whether, on the facts as believed by the defendant, his/her acts were capable of protecting property.

Taking a different tack, peace campaigners in *R* v *Jones (Margaret)* [2004] EWCA Crim 1981 argued that their fear of the consequences of war in Iraq, which they claimed to be illegal, prompted them to conspire to cause damage at an airbase and that such fear amounted both to duress (as to which, **see para. 1.4.6**) and lawful excuse under s. 5(2)(b). The Court of Appeal held that a jury would be entitled to consider some of the subjective beliefs of the defendants in determining the reasonableness of their actions.

In *R* v *Kelleher* [2003] EWCA Crim 3525, a demonstrator at the Guildhall Gallery knocked the head off a statue of Baroness Thatcher claiming that he acted in fear for his son's future which had been placed in jeopardy by the joint actions of the US and UK governments, and for which Baroness Thatcher was partly responsible. His appeal against conviction brought under s. 5(2)(b) failed.

Section 5(5) allows for other general defences (**see chapter 1.4**) at criminal law to apply in addition to those listed under s. 5.

It is not an offence to damage your own property unless there are aggravating circumstances. This is the case even if the intention in doing so is to carry out some further offence such as a fraudulent insurance claim (*R* v *Denton* [1981] 1 WLR 1446).

1.16.3 Aggravated Damage

OFFENCE: **Aggravated Damage—*Criminal Damage Act 1971, s. 1(2)***

- Triable on indictment • Life imprisonment

The Criminal Damage Act 1971, s. 1 states:

(2) A person who without lawful excuse destroys or damages any property, whether belonging to himself or another—
   (a) intending to destroy or damage any property or being reckless as to whether any property would be destroyed or damaged; and
   (b) intending by the destruction or damage to endanger the life of another or being reckless as to whether the life of another would be thereby endangered;
   shall be guilty of an offence.

KEYNOTE

The aggravating factor in this offence is the intention of endangering life or recklessness as to whether life is endangered. The life endangered must be that of another (not the life of the defendant).

The reference to 'without lawful excuse' does not refer to the statutory defences under s. 5, which are not applicable here, but to general excuses such as self-defence or the prevention of crime.

You must show that the defendant either intended or was reckless as to the following consequences:

- the damage being caused; and
- the risk of endangering the life of another.

Where a defendant fired a gun through a window pane, he was clearly reckless as to the damage his actions would cause. However, the court felt that even though two people were standing behind the window and they were obviously put in some danger, it was the missile which endangered their lives and not the result of the damage. Therefore the court held that the defendant was not guilty of this particular offence (*R* v *Steer* [1988] AC 111). In *R* v *Webster and Warwick* [1995] 2 All ER 168, damaging the windscreen of a car or ramming a car was held to be capable of endangering life as a result of the damage.

It is the damage which the defendant intended or was reckless about which is relevant, rather than the actual damage that happens to be caused (this could turn out to be minor damage). In *R* v *Dudley* [1989] Crim LR 57, trivial damage was caused but the conviction was upheld since the defendant created a risk of much more serious damage which was capable of endangering life.

1.16.4 Arson

OFFENCE: **Arson—*Criminal Damage Act 1971, s. 1(3)***

- Triable either way • Life imprisonment on indictment • Where life is not endangered Six months' imprisonment and/or a fine summarily

The Criminal Damage Act 1971, s. 1 states:

(3) An offence committed under this section by destroying or damaging property by fire shall be charged as arson.

KEYNOTE

When 'simple' or 'aggravated' damage is caused and the destruction or damage is caused by fire, the offence will be charged as 'arson'. The restrictions on the mode of trial for simple damage under s. 1(1) do not apply to cases of arson. Aggravated damage caused by arson is triable only on indictment and carries a maximum penalty of life imprisonment.

Criminal liability for either gross negligence or unlawful act manslaughter may arise from an offence of arson. In *R* v *Willoughby* [2004] EWCA Crim 3365, the defendant enlisted the help of another man in burning down a public house on which the defendant owed money. Having poured petrol around the inside of the building, the defendant set fire to it, killing the other person and injuring himself in the process. The defendant was convicted of both arson and manslaughter. The Court of Appeal held that by convicting the defendant of arson, the jury had showed that they were sure that he (on his own or jointly) had deliberately spread petrol by being reckless or with the intention that the premises would be destroyed. Provided that such conduct had been the cause of the death, the jury were therefore also bound to convict the defendant of manslaughter.

1.16.5 Threats to Destroy or Damage Property

OFFENCE: **Threats to Destroy or Damage Property—*Criminal Damage Act 1971, s. 2***

• Triable either way • 10 years' imprisonment on indictment • Six months' imprisonment and/or a fine summarily

The Criminal Damage Act 1971, s. 2 states:

A person who without lawful excuse makes to another a threat, intending that that other would fear it would be carried out,—

(a) to destroy or damage any property belonging to that other or a third person; or

(b) to destroy or damage his own property in a way which he knows is likely to endanger the life of that other or a third person;

shall be guilty of an offence.

KEYNOTE

The key element is the defendant's intention that the person receiving the threat fears it will be carried out. So there is no need to show that the other person actually feared or believed that the threat would be carried out or that the defendant intended to carry it out; nor does it matter whether the threat was even capable of being carried out.

EXAMPLE

If a person, enraged by a neighbour's inconsiderate parking, shouts over the garden wall, *'When you've gone to bed I'm going to pour paint stripper over your car!'*, the offence will be complete, provided you can show that the person making the threat intended the neighbour to fear it would be carried out.

Where a group of protestors staged a protest in the pods of the London Eye and threatened to set fire to themselves, their conduct was held to be capable of amounting to a threat to damage the property of another (as a consequence of setting themselves on fire) contrary to s. 2(a) (*R* v *Cakmak* [2002] EWCA Crim 500).

In *Cakmak*, the court held that the gist of the offence under s. 2(a) was the making of a threat and that any such threat had to be considered objectively.

Whether:

- there has been such a threat to another;
- the threat amounted to 'a threat to damage or destroy property';
- the defendant had the necessary state of mind at the time;

are all questions of fact for the jury to decide (per *Cakmak*).

While not usually enough to amount to the substantive offence under s. 2, a person's conduct which represents a threat to damage property may be relevant in triggering police action. In *Clements* v *DPP* [2005] EWHC 1279 (Admin), several protestors left a public highway, crossed a ditch and approached the perimeter fence of an RAF base. The defendant ignored a police warning to return to the road and the police attempted to restrain the protestors in order to prevent criminal damage to the fence. After a scuffle, the defendant was subsequently convicted of assaulting a police constable in the execution of his duty (as to which, **see para. 1.10.7.2**). The key issues at trial were whether the police officer had acted in the course of his duty and the extent to which the officer had reasonable grounds to believe that the defendant would cause criminal damage. The Divisional Court held that the officer had to consider the whole event in context and at the relevant time a political protest was ensuing; the defendant had deliberately left the public highway and refused to return to it; he had no legitimate reason to approach the fence; and it was plainly reasonable for the police officer to believe that he could cause criminal damage to the fence.

The defence to criminal damage under s. 5(2) ('permission'—see para. 1.16.2.5) *does not* apply where the accused knows that the threatened damage is likely to endanger life.

1.16.6 Having Articles with Intent to Destroy or Damage Property

OFFENCE: **Having Articles with Intent to Destroy or Damage Property—*Criminal Damage Act 1971, s. 3***

- Triable either way • 10 years' imprisonment on indictment • Six months' imprisonment and/or a fine summarily

The Criminal Damage Act 1971, s. 3 states:

> A person who has anything in his custody or under his control intending without lawful excuse to use it or cause or permit another to use it—
> (a) to destroy or damage any property belonging to some other person; or
> (b) to destroy or damage his own or the user's property in a way which he knows is likely to endanger the life of some other person;
> shall be guilty of an offence.

KEYNOTE

This offence covers anything which a defendant has 'in his custody or under his control', a broader term than 'possession'. This offence applies to graffiti 'artists' carrying aerosols and advertisers with adhesives for sticking illicit posters.

The key element is intention. This time the required intention is that the 'thing' be used to cause criminal damage to another's property or to the defendant's own property in a way which the defendant knows is likely to endanger the life of another.

Just as it is not an offence to damage your own property in a way which endangers no one else, neither is it an offence to have something which you intend to use to cause damage under those circumstances.

EXAMPLE

If the owner of a 10-metre high conifer decides to trim the top with a chainsaw and a ladder, putting himself, but no one else, at considerable risk, he commits no offence either by causing the damage or by having the chainsaw. If he intends to fell the tree in a way which he realises will endanger the life of his neighbours or passers-by, then he may commit the offence under s. 3(b).

Such articles are 'prohibited' articles for the purposes of the power of stop and search under s. 1 of the Police and Criminal Evidence Act 1984 (see *General Police Duties*, chapter 3.3).

A conditional intent (an intent to use something to cause criminal damage if the need arises) will be enough (*R* v *Buckingham* (1976) 63 Cr App R 159).

There is a statutory power to apply to a magistrate for a search warrant under s. 6 of the Criminal Damage Act 1971 for anything that could be used or is intended to be used to destroy or damage property.

The Criminal Damage Act 1971, s. 6 states:

> (1) If it is made to appear by information on oath before a justice of the peace that there is reasonable cause to believe that any person has in his custody or under his control or on his premises anything which there is reasonable cause to believe has been used or is intended for use without lawful excuse—
> (a) to destroy or damage property belonging to another; or
> (b) to destroy or damage any property in a way likely to endanger the life of another,
> the justice may grant a warrant authorising any constable to search for and seize that thing.

(2) A constable who is authorised under this section to search premises for anything, may enter (if need be by force) and search the premises accordingly and may seize anything which he believes to have been used or to be intended to be used as aforesaid.

1.16.7 Contamination or Interference with Goods

OFFENCE: **Contamination or Interference with Goods—*Public Order Act 1986, s. 38(1)***

- Triable either way • 10 years' imprisonment and/or a fine on indictment
- Six months' imprisonment and/or a fine summarily

The Public Order Act 1986, s. 38 states:

(1) It is an offence for a person, with the intention—
  (a) of causing public alarm or anxiety, or
  (b) of causing injury to members of the public consuming or using the goods, or
  (c) of causing economic loss to any person by reason of the goods being shunned by members of the public, or
  (d) of causing economic loss to any person by reason of steps taken to avoid any such alarm or anxiety, injury or loss,

  to contaminate or interfere with goods, or make it appear that goods have been contaminated or interfered with, or to place goods which have been contaminated or interfered with, or which appear to have been contaminated or interfered with in a place where goods of that description are consumed, used, sold or otherwise supplied.

(2) It is also an offence for a person, with any such intention as is mentioned in paragraph (a), (c) or (d) of subsection (1), to threaten that he or another will do, or to claim that he or another has done, any of the acts mentioned in that subsection.

(3) It is an offence for a person to be in possession of any of the following articles with a view to the commission of an offence under subsection (1)—
  (a) materials to be used for contaminating or interfering with goods or making it appear that goods have been contaminated or interfered with, or
  (b) goods which have been contaminated or interfered with, or which appear to have been contaminated or interfered with.

(4) ...

(5) In this section 'goods' includes substances whether natural or manufactured and whether or not incorporated in or mixed with other goods.

(6) The reference in subsection (2) to a person claiming that certain acts have been committed does not include a person who in good faith reports or warns that such acts have been, or appear to have been, committed.

KEYNOTE

'Goods' includes 'natural' goods (e.g. fruit and vegetables) or 'manufactured' goods (e.g. shampoo or disinfectant).

Section 38 creates two offences. The first involves the contamination of, interference with or placing of goods with the intentions set out at s. 38(1)(a)–(d). An example of this offence is the case of *R* v *Cruikshank* [2001] EWCA Crim 98, where the offender pleaded guilty to contaminating food in a supermarket by inserting pins, needles and nails into various items. He persisted in this behaviour for three months and some minor injuries were incurred by customers who bought the contaminated products.

The reference to 'in a place' in s. 38(1) should not be interpreted restrictively. For example, if X contaminated a jar of honey with shards of glass and then placed that contaminated jar of honey in the clothing aisle of a large supermarket (that also sold jars of honey), the offence *would* be committed. The contaminated jar of honey would not have to be placed right next to other jars of honey in the supermarket or even in the same aisle where jars of honey are sold—placing it in the clothing aisle of the supermarket would be placing it '*in a place* where goods of that description are consumed, used, sold or otherwise supplied'. If the contaminated jar of honey was placed in a shop that only sold bathroom tiles, the offence *would not* be committed.

Section 38(2) involves the making of threats to do, or the claiming to have done, any of the acts in s. 38(1) with any of the intentions set out at s. 38(1)(a), (c) or (d). It is difficult to see how a threat or claim made with the intention of causing injury to the public (s. 38(1)(b)) would not also amount to an intention to cause them alarm or anxiety but the legislation clearly excludes it.

Section 38(6) allows for people to communicate warnings in good faith where such acts appear to have been committed.

Where threats to contaminate goods are made, there may also be grounds for charging blackmail. A good example of threats to commit this offence and the overlap with blackmail is the case of *R* v *Witchelo* (1992) 13 Cr App R (S) 371, where the defendant, a police officer, was sentenced to 13 years' imprisonment after obtaining £32,000 from food producers to whom he had sent threatening letters.

Index

A

Abduction of children
connected persons 1.13.2.1, 1.13.2.2
defences 1.13.2.2, 1.13.2.4
unconnected persons 1.13.2.3, 1.13.2.4
Abstracting electricity 1.14.2.5
Abuse of position
fraud 1.15.6
sexual offences involving children 1.12.8
Accessories
definition 1.2.8
joint enterprise 1.2.8.2
parasitic accessory liability 1.2.8.2
state of mind 1.2.8.1
'Act of God' 1.2.7
Actual bodily harm 1.10.6.3
Actus reus
accessories
definition 1.2.8
joint enterprise 1.2.8.2
parasitic accessory liability 1.2.8.2
state of mind 1.2.8.1
automatism 1.2.3
causal link/ chain of causation 1.2.6
coincidence with *mens rea* 1.2.4
corporate liability 1.2.9
definition 1.2.1
handling stolen goods 1.14.11.2
intervening act 1.2.7
omissions 1.2.5
principal offender 1.2.8
vicarious liability 1.2.10
voluntary act 1.2.2
Aggravated offences *see also* **Racially aggravated offences; Religiously aggravated offences**
burglary 1.14.6
criminal damage 1.16.3
vehicle-taking 1.14.8
Aiding and abetting
accessorial liability 1.2.8
Air weapons
airsoft guns 1.7.2.1
exemptions 1.7.4, 1.7.7.4
Ammunition
definition 1.7.2.3
list of prohibited ammunition 1.7.7.1
possession 1.7.7.2, 1.7.7.3
possession without certificate 1.7.4.2
purchasing 1.7.7.2
Anonymity: sexual offences 1.12.2
Appropriation 1.14.2.3
Arrest
assault with intent to resist 1.10.7.1
lawful arrest 1.4.5.2
Arson 1.16.4
Assault
battery or 1.10.4, 1.10.6.1
common assault 1.10.4, 1.10.6.1
conditional threats 1.10.2.4
consent
key points 1.10.5
legitimate consent to risk of injury 1.10.5.1
sado-masochistic injuries 1.10.5.2
serious harm for sexual gratification 1.10.5.3
definition 1.10.2
immediate threat 1.10.2.2
mental elements 1.10.2.1
sexual offences
by penetration 1.12.4.1
by touching 1.12.4.3
definition of the term 'sexual' 1.12.4.2
definition of the term 'touching' 1.12.4.4
specific offences
assault occasioning actual bodily harm 1.10.6.3
assault on constables 1.10.7.2
assaults on emergency workers 1.10.6.2
common assault and battery 1.10.6.1
obstructing a police officer 1.10.7.3
wounding or causing grievous bodily harm with intent 1.10.6.5
wounding or inflicting grievous bodily harm 1.10.6.4
with intent to resist arrest 1.10.7.1
words or other communication 1.10.2.3
Assisting an offence
definition 1.3.2
misuse of drugs 1.6.13
Attempts 1.3.4
acts which are more than merely preparatory 1.3.4.1
mens rea 1.3.4.2
Automatism
general defence 1.2.3
voluntariness and 1.2.2–1.2.3

B

Basic intent 1.1.2.1–1.1.2.2
Battery
assault or 1.2.7, 1.10.4
definition 1.10.3
racially aggravated offences 1.10.6.1
specific offences 1.10.6.1
Belief: *mens rea* 1.1.8
Blackmail
criminal conduct 1.14.4.2
gain and loss required 1.14.4.1
statutory provisions 1.14.4
unwarranted demands 1.14.4.3
Bladed weapons *see* **Weapons**
Breast-feeding
voyeurism 1.12.18.3
Brothels 1.12.15.4
Burglary
aggravated burglary 1.14.6
'at the time' 1.14.6
buildings 1.14.5.2
conditional intent 1.14.5.4
entry 1.14.5.1
'has with him' 1.14.6
instant arming 1.14.6
intentions at the time of entry 1.14.5.3
statutory provisions 1.14.5.1, 1.14.5.5
taking a conveyance without consent (TWOC) 1.14.7
Theft Act 1968 (s. 9(1)(b)) 1.14.5.5
trespassers 1.14.5.1

C

Cannabis
classification 1.6.2.2
cultivation 1.6.8
medicinal use 1.6.10
Causation 1.2.6
Causing sexual activity without consent 1.12.5
conclusive presumptions 1.12.3.6
Child Arrangements Orders 1.13.2.1
Children
abduction
connected persons 1.13.2.1, 1.13.2.2
defences 1.13.2.2, 1.13.2.4
unconnected persons 1.13.2.3, 1.13.2.4
age of criminal responsibility 1.4.7
causing death of a child or vulnerable adult 1.5.5
cruelty towards 1.13.3
familial child sex offences 1.12.9
inciting a child family member to engage in sexual activity 1.12.9.2
sexual activity with a child family member 1.12.9.1
police powers
contravention of protection order or police protection 1.13.4.2
designated officers 1.13.4.1
disclosure of information regarding child 1.13.4.3
emergency protection orders 1.13.4
statutory provisions 1.13.4
police protection 1.13.1
sexual exploitation 1.12.11
causing, inciting, arranging or facilitating the sexual exploitation of children 1.12.11.2
information about guests at hotels 1.12.11.3
paying for the sexual services of a child 1.12.11.1
sexual offences involving
abuse of position of trust 1.12.8
arranging or facilitating commission of child sex offences 1.12.7.6
causing a child to watch a sex act 1.12.7.4
causing or inciting a child to engage in sexual activity 1.12.7.2
child sex offences committed by children or young persons 1.12.7.5
familial child sex offences 1.12.9
indecent photographs 1.12.10.1–1.12.10.5
meeting a child following sexual grooming 1.12.7.7
offences outside the UK 1.12.13
possession of a paedophile manual 1.12.12

Children (*cont.*)
possession of prohibited images 1.12.10.5
sexual activity in presence of a child 1.12.7.3
sexual activity with a child 1.12.7.1
sexual communication with a child 1.12.7.8
sexual exploitation 1.12.11
statutory provisions 1.12.6
special guardian 1.13.2.1
Common assault 1.10.4
racially aggravated offences 1.10.6.1
religiously aggravated offences 1.10.6.1
specific offences 1.10.6.1
Common law
conspiracy to defraud 1.3.3.2
homicide 1.5.1
Community Protection Notices 1.6.12
Compulsory labour *see* **Modern slavery**
Conditional consent 1.12.3.3
lies about fertility 1.12.3.3
Conditional intent 1.14.5.4
Conditional threats 1.10.2.4
Consent
assault
key points 1.10.5
legitimate consent to risk of injury 1.10.5.1
sado-masochistic injuries 1.10.5.2
serious harm for sexual gratification 1.10.5.3
negating 1.12.3.3
rape
conclusive presumptions 1.12.3.6
conditional consent 1.12.3.3
evidential presumptions 1.12.3.5
presumptions generally 1.12.3.2, 1.12.3.4
sexual offences generally 1.12.1
Conspiracy
agreement 1.3.3.1
common law conspiracy to defraud 1.3.3.2
statutory 1.3.3.1
Contamination or interference with goods 1.16.7
Continuing acts 1.2.4
Corporate liability 1.2.9
Corpse, theft of 1.14.2.5
Counselling a criminal act 1.2.8
Crime, prevention of 1.4.5.2
Criminal conduct *see* ***Actus reus***
Criminal damage
aggravated damage 1.16.3
arson 1.16.4
contamination or interference with goods 1.16.7
having articles with intent to destroy or damage property 1.16.6
key concepts
belonging to another 1.16.2.3
destroy or damage 1.16.2.1
property 1.16.2.2
lawful excuses
belief 1.16.2.6
permission 1.16.2.4, 1.16.2.5
protection 1.16.2.4, 1.16.2.6
racial or religiously aggravated 1.16.2
simple damage 1.16.2
spouses and civil partners 1.16.2
threats to destroy or damage property 1.16.5

D

Defences *see* **General defences; Special defences**
Deprivation of liberty offences *see also* **Modern slavery**
false imprisonment 1.11.2
introduction 1.11.1
kidnapping 1.11.3
Diminished responsibility 1.5.3.1
Disclosure of information
child protection 1.13.4.3
fraud by failure to disclose 1.15.5
Dishonesty
case law 1.14.2.2
definition 1.14.2.1
fraud 1.15.4
mens rea 1.1.6
***Doli incapax* 1.4.7**
Drugs
assisting or inducing offences outside the UK 1.6.13
cannabis
classification 1.6.2.2
cultivation 1.6.8
medicinal use 1.6.10
classification
cannabis 1.6.2.2
examples 1.6.2
temporary class drug orders 1.6.2.1
Community Protection Notices 1.6.12
defences
conditional belief about drug in question 1.6.9.3
general defence under s. 28 1.6.9
lack of knowledge about drug in question 1.6.9.2
lack of knowledge of some alleged fact 1.6.9.1
incitement 1.6.14
injecting others 1.6.4
intoxicating substances 1.6.17
occupiers of premises 1.6.11
police powers 1.6.16
entry, search and seizure 1.6.16.1
obstruction 1.6.16.2
possession
controlled drugs 1.6.3.7
custody or control 1.6.3.1
defence to unlawful possession 1.6.3.8
elements 1.6.3
joint possession 1.6.3.3
knowledge of possession 1.6.3.2
points to prove 1.6.3.4
quality 1.6.3.5
quantity 1.6.3.6
regulated possession 1.6.10
with intent to supply 1.6.5
production of a controlled drug 1.6.7
psychoactive substances 1.6.17
regulated possession and supply 1.6.10
supply
aggravating factors 1.6.4.2
controlled drugs 1.6.4.1
definition 1.6.4
offering to supply 1.6.4.1
possession with intent to supply 1.6.5
regulated supply 1.6.10
supply of articles 1.6.6
travel restriction orders 1.6.15
Duress
of circumstances 1.4.4
general defence 1.4.3
Duty to act 1.2.5

E

'Eggshell skull' rule 1.2.7
Emergency Protection Orders (EPO) 1.13.4
contravention of 1.13.4.2
Emergency workers: assaults on 1.10.6.2
aggravating factors 1.10.6.2
assault occasioning actual bodily harm 1.10.6.2
malicious wounding/GBH 1.10.6.2
wounding/GBH with intent 1.10.6.2
Encouraging an offence 1.3.2, 1.3.2.1
Encouraging or assisting suicide 1.5.6, 1.5.6.1
Explosives
aggravated burglary 1.14.6.1
Exposure 1.12.18.1

F

Failure to disclose 1.15.5
False accounting 1.15.10
False imprisonment 1.11.2
False representation
dishonesty test 1.15.4
fraud by 1.15.4
machines 1.15.4
phishing 1.15.4
representation 1.15.4
stolen vehicles 1.14.11.2
Firearms *see also* **Weapons**
accessories 1.7.2.1
aggravated burglary 1.14.6.1
air weapons
airsoft guns 1.7.2.1
exemptions 1.7.7.4
ammunition
definition 1.7.2.3
list of prohibited ammunition 1.7.7.1
possession 1.7.7.2, 1.7.7.3
possession without certificate 1.7.4.2
purchasing 1.7.7.2
categories 1.7.3
component parts 1.7.2.1
criminal use
intent to commit indictable offence or resist arrest 1.7.9.4
possession while committing a Schedule 1 offence 1.7.9.5
possession with intent to cause fear of violence 1.7.9.2
possession with intent to endanger life 1.7.9.1
using firearm to resist arrest 1.7.9.3
using someone to mind a weapon 1.7.9.6
deactivation 1.7.2.2
definition 1.7.2.1
general exemptions 1.7.8
antiques as ornaments or curiosities 1.7.8
authorised firearms dealers 1.7.8
authorised lending and possession of firearms for hunting 1.7.8
police permit holders 1.7.8
sporting purposes 1.7.8
visitors' permits 1.7.8
having firearm/imitation firearm in public place 1.7.10.1
historic interest 1.7.7.4
imitation firearms
aggravated burglary 1.14.6.1
converting 1.7.6
definition 1.7.2.4

in public place 1.7.10.1
offences 1.7.6, 1.7.6.1
key legislation 1.7.1
lethal barrelled weapons 1.7.2.1
pest control 1.7.7.4
police powers
power to demand documentation 1.7.11.1
statutory provisions 1.7.11
possession or acquisition by convicted persons 1.7.12
prohibited weapons 1.7.2.1
accessory 1.7.2.1
definition 1.7.7
exemptions 1.7.7.4
list of 1.7.7.1
possession 1.7.7.2, 1.7.7.3
purchasing 1.7.7.2
relevant component part 1.7.2.1
restrictions on transfer 1.7.5
trade transactions by person not registered as firearms dealer 1.7.5
section 1 firearm
conversion of weapons 1.7.4.1
definition 1.7.4
possession without certificate 1.7.4.2
sale or transfer to person prohibited by s. 21 1.7.12.1
shortening 1.7.4.3
shortened weapons 1.7.4.3
shot pistols 1.7.7.4
slaughter or humane killing of animals 1.7.7.4
starter pistols 1.7.7.4
trespassing with firearms 1.7.10.2
buildings 1.7.10.2
land 1.7.10.2
war trophies 1.7.7.4
Forced labour *see* **Modern slavery**
Foresight 1.1.2
using a false instrument with intent 1.3.4.1
Fraud
see also False accounting
abuse of position 1.15.6
failure to disclose 1.15.5
false representation 1.15.4
gain and loss as essential elements 1.15.3
making or supplying articles for use in 1.15.8
obtaining services dishonestly 1.15.9
possession or control of articles for use in 1.15.7
statutory provisions 1.15.2
types of fraud 1.15.1

G

General defences 1.4.1
defence of others 1.4.5
human rights 1.4.5.1
reasonable force 1.4.5.3–1.4.5.4
defence of property
human rights 1.4.5, 1.4.5.1
reasonable force 1.4.5.2–1.4.5.5
drugs offences 1.6.9
duress 1.4.3
of circumstances 1.4.4
inadvertence 1.4.2
infancy 1.4.7
intoxication: voluntary or involuntary 1.1.2.2
mistake 1.4.2
police officers 1.4.6
reasonable force
assisting lawful arrest 1.4.5.2, 1.4.5.3
'householder' cases 1.4.5.4, 1.4.5.5
prevention of crime 1.4.5.2, 1.4.5.3
self-defence
human rights 1.4.5, 1.4.5.1
reasonable force 1.4.5.2–1.4.5.4
vs special defences 1.4.1, 1.5.3
Going equipped 1.14.10
'article', meaning of 1.14.10
'has with him' requirement 1.14.10
'in the course or in connection with' 1.14.10
place of abode 1.14.10
Grievous bodily harm 1.10.6.4, 1.10.6.5
Gross negligence manslaughter 1.5.4.2
Gun crime *see* **Firearms**

H

Handling stolen goods 1.14.11
assisting/acting for another's benefit 1.14.11.2
evidence and procedure 1.14.11.4
goods stolen outside England and Wales 1.14.11.1
meaning of 'goods' and 'stolen goods' 1.14.11.1
mens rea and *actus reus* 1.14.11.2
no conviction required for 'origin' offence 1.14.11.1
proceeds of stolen property 1.14.11.1
proof 1.14.11.5
receiving/arranging to receive 1.14.11.2
search powers 1.14.11.3
statutory provisions 1.14.11
Homicide
causing death of a child or vulnerable adult 1.5.5
common law 1.5.1
encouraging or assisting suicide 1.5.6, 1.5.6.1
involuntary manslaughter
definition 1.5.4
manslaughter by gross negligence 1.5.4.2
manslaughter by unlawful act 1.5.4.1
murder
definition 1.5.2
malice aforethought 1.5.2.1
solicitation of 1.5.7
year and a day rule 1.5.2.2
voluntary manslaughter
diminished responsibility 1.5.3.1
loss of control 1.5.3.2
special defences 1.5.3
suicide pact 1.5.3.3
Human rights
self-defence and defence of property 1.4.5, 1.4.5.1
Human trafficking 1.11.4.2
see also **Modern slavery**

I

'Identity theft' 1.14.2.5
Imitation firearms
aggravated burglary 1.14.6.1
definition 1.7.2.4
in public place 1.7.10.1
offences 1.7.8
Impossibility 1.3.5
Inadvertence 1.4.2
Incomplete offences
attempts 1.3.4
acts which are more than merely preparatory 1.3.4.1
mens rea 1.3.4.2
conspiracy
agreement 1.3.3.1
common law conspiracy to defraud 1.3.3.2
statutory 1.3.3.1
definition 1.3.1
encouraging or assisting crime 1.3.2, 1.3.2.1
impossibility 1.3.5
Indecent photographs
disclosing or threatening to disclose private sexual photographs/ films 1.12.20–1.12.20.2
photographs of children 1.12.10
criminal proceedings 1.12.10.3
definition 1.12.10.1, 1.12.10.2
marriage and other relationships 1.12.10.3, 1.12.10.4
possession of indecent photograph of child 1.12.10.4
possession of prohibited images of children 1.12.10.5
pseudo-photographs 1.12.10.2
possession of extreme pornographic images 1.12.19
Infancy 1.4.7
Intent
attempts 1.3.4.2
mens rea 1.1.2
specific and basic 1.1.2.1–1.1.2.2
Intervening act 1.2.7
Intoxication
mistaken belief 1.1.2.2
psychoactive and intoxicating substances 1.6.17
voluntary or involuntary 1.1.2.2
Involuntary manslaughter
definition 1.5.4
manslaughter by gross negligence 1.5.4.2
manslaughter by unlawful act 1.5.4.1

J

Joint enterprise 1.2.8.2
Joint possession 1.6.3.3

K

Kerb-crawling 1.12.15.5
Khat 1.6.3.7
Kidnapping 1.11.3
Knives 1.8.9
defences 1.8.9.3
publications relating to 1.8.9.4
sale to persons under 18 1.8.9.1
unlawful marketing 1.8.9.2
'Knowing': ***mens rea*** **1.1.7**

L

Lawful arrest 1.4.5.2
Liability
accessories
definition 1.2.8
joint enterprise 1.2.8.2
parasitic accessory liability 1.2.8.2
state of mind 1.2.8.1
corporate liability 1.2.9
vicarious liability 1.2.10
Loss of control 1.5.3.2

M

Making off without payment 1.14.13
Malice 1.1.4
Malice aforethought 1.5.2.1
Manslaughter
intoxication 1.1.2.2
involuntary
definition 1.5.4
manslaughter by gross negligence 1.5.4.2
manslaughter by unlawful act 1.5.4.1
voluntary
diminished responsibility 1.5.3.1
loss of control 1.5.3.2
special defences 1.5.3
suicide pact 1.5.3.3
Mens rea
accessories 1.2.8.1
attempts 1.3.4.2
'basic' intent 1.1.2.1, 1.1.2.2
belief 1.1.8
burglary 1.14.5.3, 1.14.5.4
coincidence with *actus reus* 1.2.4
definition 1.1.1
dishonesty 1.1.6
handling stolen goods 1.14.11.2
inadvertence and mistake 1.4.2
intent 1.1.2
intoxication 1.1.2.2
'knowing' 1.1.7
malice 1.1.4
manslaughter by unlawful act 1.5.4.1
negligence 1.1.9
recklessness
awareness 1.1.3.1
definition 1.1.3
different crimes and nature of risk 1.1.3.3
reasonableness 1.1.3.2
'specific' intent 1.1.2.1–1.1.2.2
strict liability and 1.1.10
theft 1.14.2.9
transferred *mens rea* 1.1.11
'wilfully' 1.1.5
Mentally disordered persons
sexual offences against 1.12.14
causing or inciting a person with a mental disorder to engage in sexual activity 1.12.14.3
causing person with mental disorder to watch sexual act 1.12.14.5
definition of 'mental disorder' 1.12.14.1
sexual activity in presence of a mentally disordered person 1.12.14.4
sexual activity with mentally disordered person 1.12.14.2
Mistake 1.4.2
Misuse of drugs *see* **Drugs**
Modern slavery
human trafficking 1.11.4.2
slavery, servitude and forced or compulsory labour 1.11.4.1
statutory provisions 1.11.4
Motor vehicles
aggravated vehicle-taking 1.14.8
interfering with 1.14.9
taking without consent (TWOC) 1.14.7
Murder
definition 1.5.2
malice aforethought 1.5.2.1
solicitation of 1.5.7
year and a day rule 1.5.2.2

N

Negligence 1.1.9
Non-fatal offences against the person *see also* **Assault; Modern slavery; Sexual offences**
battery 1.10.3, 1.10.4
false imprisonment 1.11.2
kidnapping 1.11.3
strangulation 1.10.9
suffocation 1.10.9
threats to kill 1.10.8

O

Obstructing a police officer 1.10.7.3
Obtaining services dishonestly 1.15.9
Offences against the person *see* **Non-fatal offences against the person**
Offensive weapons *see* **Weapons**
Omissions 1.2.5
Outraging public decency 1.12.18.1

P

Paedophile manuals 1.12.12
Parasitic accessory liability 1.2.8.2
Police officers
assault on 1.10.7.2
obstructing 1.10.7.3
use of force 1.4.6
Police powers
child protection
contravention of protection order or police protection 1.13.4.2
designated officer 1.13.4.1
disclosure of information regarding child 1.13.4.3
emergency protection orders 1.13.4
statutory provisions 1.13.4
drugs 1.6.16
firearms offences
power to demand documentation 1.7.11.1
statutory provisions 1.7.11
Pornography
photographs of children 1.12.10.1–1.12.10.4
possession of extreme pornographic images 1.12.19
possession of prohibited images of children 1.12.10.5
'revenge porn' 1.12.20–1.12.20.2
Position of trust 1.12.8
Possession offences
articles for use in frauds 1.15.7
drugs
controlled drugs 1.6.3.7
custody or control 1.6.3.1
defence to unlawful possession 1.6.3.8
elements 1.6.3
intent to supply 1.6.5
joint possession 1.6.3.3
knowledge of possession 1.6.3.2
points to prove 1.6.3.4
quality 1.6.3.5
quantity 1.6.3.6
regulated possession 1.6.10
firearms
possession or acquisition by convicted persons 1.7.12
possession while committing a Schedule 1 offence 1.7.9.5
possession with intent to cause fear of violence 1.7.9.2
possession with intent to endanger life 1.7.9.1
prohibited weapons or ammunition 1.7.7.2, 1.7.7.3
Preparatory acts
attempts 1.3.4.1
sexual offences
administering substance with intent 1.12.16.1
committing criminal offence with intent to commit a sexual offence 1.12.16.2
trespass with intent to commit sexual offence 1.12.16.3
Prevention of crime 1.4.5.2
Principal offender 1.2.8
Proceeds of crime
acquisition, use and possession of criminal property 1.14.14.6
arrangements in relation to criminal property 1.14.14.5
concealing criminal property 1.14.14.4
criminal conduct 1.14.14.2
criminal property 1.14.14.3
statutory provisions 1.14.14.1
Procuring a criminal act 1.2.8
Property
appropriation 1.14.2.3
belonging to another 1.14.2.6
definition 1.14.2.4
excluded items 1.14.2.5
intention of permanently depriving 1.14.2.9
obligation regarding 1.14.2.7
obligation to restore 1.14.2.8
Property offences *see* **Criminal damage; Theft**
Prostitution
brothels and keeping a disorderly house 1.12.15.4
causing, inciting or controlling prostitution 1.12.15.2
definition of a prostitute 1.12.15.1
paying for sexual services of a prostitute subjected to force 1.12.15.3
soliciting 1.12.15.5
Psychoactive substances 1.6.17
Public decency, outraging 1.12.18.1
Public lavatory, sexual activity in 1.12.18.4

R

Racially aggravated offences
assault occasioning actual bodily harm 1.10.6.3
categories 1.9.2
common assault and battery 1.10.6.1
definition 1.9.3
hostility
definition 1.9.3.3
demonstration of 1.9.3.2
motivation by 1.9.3.5
timing of 1.9.3.1
key legislation 1.9.1
membership of racial groups 1.9.3.8
other factors 1.9.3.9
racial groups 1.9.3.6
victim 1.9.3.4
wounding or inflicting grievous bodily harm 1.10.6.4

Rape
consent
conclusive presumptions 1.12.3.6
conditional consent 1.12.3.3
evidential presumptions 1.12.3.5
presumptions generally 1.12.3.2, 1.12.3.4
criminal conduct 1.12.3.1
statutory provisions 1.12.3
Reasonable excuse 1.8.2.2
Reasonable force
assisting lawful arrest 1.4.5.2, 1.4.5.3
'householder' cases 1.4.5.4, 1.4.5.5
prevention of crime 1.4.5.2, 1.4.5.3
Reasonableness 1.1.3.2
Recklessness 1.1.3
awareness 1.1.3.1
different crimes and nature of risk 1.1.3.3
reasonableness 1.1.3.2
'specific' or 'basic' intent 1.1.2.1
Reflexive actions 1.2.2
Religiously aggravated offences
assault occasioning actual bodily harm 1.10.6.3
categories 1.9.2
common assault and battery 1.10.6.1
definition 1.9.3
hostility
definition 1.9.3.3
demonstration of 1.9.3.2
motivation by 1.9.3.5
timing of 1.9.3.1
key legislation 1.9.1
membership of religious groups 1.9.3.8
other factors 1.9.3.9
religious groups 1.9.3.7
victim 1.9.3.4
wounding or inflicting grievous bodily harm 1.10.6.4
'Revenge porn' 1.12.20–1.12.20.2
Robbery 1.14.3 *see also* **Theft**
fear of force 1.14.3
force 1.14.3
'in order to do so' 1.14.3
on any person 1.14.3
theft element of the offence 1.14.3
time frame 1.14.3
use of force on property 1.14.3

S

Sado-masochistic injuries 1.10.5.2
School premises
defences 1.8.5.4
having article with blade or point on school premises 1.8.5.2
having offensive weapon on school premises 1.8.5.3
offences and powers relating to 1.8.5
power of entry 1.8.5.5
power of staff members to search pupils for prohibited items 1.8.5.6
threatening with article with blade or point or offensive weapon 1.8.5.1
Secondary parties *see* **Accessories**
Self-defence
'householder' cases 1.4.5.4
human rights 1.4.5, 1.4.5.1
intoxication 1.1.2.2
police officers 1.4.6
use of force
prevention of crime and lawful arrest 1.4.5.2
reasonable force 1.4.5.3
Servitude *see* **Modern slavery**
Sexual gratification
consent to assault 1.10.5.3
Sexual offences *see also* **Rape**
activity in a public lavatory 1.12.18.4
against people with a mental disorder 1.12.14
causing or inciting a person with a mental disorder to engage in sexual activity 1.12.14.3
causing person with mental disorder to watch sexual act 1.12.14.5
definition of 'mental disorder' 1.12.14.1
sexual activity in presence of mentally disordered person 1.12.14.4
sexual activity with mentally disordered person 1.12.14.2
anonymity 1.12.2
assault
by penetration 1.12.4.1
definition of the term 'sexual' 1.12.4.2
touching 1.12.4.3, 1.12.4.4
causing sexual activity without consent 1.12.5
conclusive presumptions 1.12.3.6
consent
conclusive presumptions 1.12.3.6
conditional consent 1.12.3.3
evidential presumptions 1.12.3.5
presumptions generally 1.12.3.2, 1.12.3.4
disclosing or threatening to disclose private sexual photographs/ films 1.12.20–1.12.20.2
exposure 1.12.18.1
familial child sex offences 1.12.9
inciting a child family member to engage in sexual activity 1.12.9.2
sexual activity with a child family member 1.12.9.1
gender neutral language 1.12.1
involving children 1.12.7
abuse of position of trust 1.12.8
arranging or facilitating commission of child sex offences 1.12.7.6
causing a child to watch a sex act 1.12.7.4
child sex offences committed by children or young persons 1.12.7.5
exploitation 1.12.11
familial child sex offences 1.12.9
indecent photographs 1.12.10.1–1.12.10.5
meeting a child following sexual grooming 1.12.7.7
offences outside the UK 1.12.13
possession of a paedophile manual 1.12.12
possession of prohibited images 1.12.10.5
sexual activity in presence of a child 1.12.7.3
sexual activity with a child 1.12.7.1
sexual communication with a child 1.12.7.8
under 13 1.12.6
outraging public decency 1.12.18.1
overlap between offences 1.12.1
possession of extreme pornographic images 1.12.19
preparatory offences
administering substance with intent 1.12.16.1
committing criminal offence with intent to commit a sexual offence 1.12.16.2
trespass with intent to commit sexual offence 1.12.16.3
prostitution
brothels and keeping a disorderly house 1.12.15.4
causing, inciting or controlling prostitution 1.12.15.2
definition of a prostitute 1.12.15.1
paying for sexual services of a prostitute subjected to force 1.12.15.3
soliciting 1.12.15.5
sex with an adult relative 1.12.17
sexual exploitation of children 1.12.11
causing, inciting, arranging or facilitating the sexual exploitation of children 1.12.11.2
information about guests at hotels 1.12.11.3
paying for the sexual services of a child 1.12.11.1
'upskirting' 1.12.18.3
voyeurism 1.12.18.2, 1.12.18.3
Sexually transmitted infections (STIs) 1.10.6.4
Shoplifting 1.14.2
Shot pistols 1.7.7.4
Slavery *see* **Modern slavery**
Slaughter of animals
possession of a firearm or ammunition 1.7.7.4
Solicitation of murder 1.5.7
Soliciting 1.12.15.5
Special defences
voluntary manslaughter 1.5.3
vs general defences 1.5.3
Special Guardian Orders 1.13.2.1
Sporting events
possession of a firearm or ammunition 1.7.7.4
State of mind *see* ***Mens rea***
Statutory conspiracy 1.3.3.1
Stolen goods *see* **Handling stolen goods**
Strangulation 1.10.9
Strict liability 1.1.10
possession of a firearm or ammunition 1.7.7.3
Suicide
encouraging or assisting 1.5.6, 1.5.6.1
pact 1.5.3.3
Suffocation 1.10.9
Supply of drugs *see* **Drugs**

T

Taking a conveyance without consent (TWOC) 1.14.7
allow to be carried 1.14.7.6, 1.14.7.7
consent of the owner 1.14.7.1
conveyance 1.14.7.4
defences 1.14.7.7
for his own or another's use 1.14.7.5
lawful authority 1.14.7.2
statutory provisions 1.14.7
'takes' 1.14.7.3
Temporary class drug orders 1.6.2.1
Theft *see also* **Burglary; Fraud; Robbery**
aggravated vehicle-taking 1.14.8
appropriates 1.14.2.3
belonging to another 1.14.2.6
dishonesty
case law 1.14.2.2

Theft (*cont.*)
definition 1.14.2.1
test for 1.14.2.2
going equipped 1.14.10
handling stolen goods
assisting/acting for another's benefit 1.14.11.2
'by or for the benefit of another' 1.14.11.2
evidence and procedure 1.14.11.4
false representation 1.14.11.2
goods stolen outside England and Wales 1.14.11.1
meaning of 'goods' and 'stolen goods' 1.14.11.1
mens rea and *actus reus* 1.14.11.2
proceeds of stolen property 1.14.11.1
proof 1.14.11.5
receiving/arranging to receive 1.14.11.2
search powers 1.14.11.3
statutory provisions 1.14.11
stolen vehicles 1.14.11.2
low-value shoplifting 1.14.2
making off without payment 1.14.13
non-property 1.14.2.5
proceeds of crime acquisition, use and possession of criminal property 1.14.14.6
arrangements in relation to criminal property 1.14.14.5
concealing criminal property 1.14.14.4
criminal conduct 1.14.14.2
criminal property 1.14.14.3
statutory provisions 1.14.14.1
property
appropriation 1.14.2.3
belonging to another 1.14.2.6
cheques 1.14.2.4
credit balances 1.14.2.4
definition 1.14.2.4
excluded items 1.14.2.5
intangible 1.14.2.4
intention of permanently depriving 1.14.2.9
land 1.14.2.4
money 1.14.2.4
obligation to restore 1.14.2.8
obligations regarding 1.14.2.7
personal 1.14.2.4
things in action 1.14.2.4
things growing wild 1.14.2.4
wild creatures 1.14.2.4
retaining a wrongful credit 1.14.12
robbery 1.14.3
statutory provisions 1.14.2
'Thin skull' rule 1.2.7
Threats
assault
conditional threats 1.10.2.4
immediate threat 1.10.2.2
words or other communication 1.10.2.3
threats to kill 1.10.8
weapons
offensive weapons in public 1.8.3
with article with blade or point or offensive weapon 1.8.5.1
Trafficking, human 1.11.4.2
see also **Modern slavery**
Transferred *mens rea* 1.1.11
Travel restriction orders
drug trafficking 1.6.15
Trespass
burglary 1.14.5.1
with firearms 1.7.10.2
with intent to commit sexual offence 1.12.16.3
with weapon of offence 1.8.6

U

Unlawful act manslaughter 1.5.4.1
Upskirting 1.12.18.3
Use of force
defence of property
prevention of crime and lawful arrest 1.4.5.2
reasonable force 1.4.5.3, 1.4.5.4
police officers 1.4.6
self-defence
prevention of crime and lawful arrest 1.4.5.2
reasonable force 1.4.5.3

V

Vehicles
aggravated vehicle-taking 1.14.8
defence to 1.14.8.1
interfering with 1.14.9
stolen 1.14.11.2
taking without consent (TWOC) 1.14.7
Vicarious liability 1.2.10
Victims
actions by 1.2.7
racially or religiously aggravated offences 1.9.3.4
'thin skull' rule 1.2.7
Voluntary act 1.2.2
Voluntary intoxication 1.1.2.2
loss of control 1.2.3
Voluntary manslaughter
diminished responsibility 1.5.3.1
loss of control 1.5.3.2
special defences 1.5.3
suicide pact 1.5.3.3
Voyeurism 1.12.18.2, 1.12.18.3
breast-feeding 1.12.18.3
Vulnerable adults
causing or allowing death or serious physical harm 1.5.5

W

War trophies
possession of a firearm or ammunition 1.7.7.4
Weapons *see also* **Firearms**
considerations 1.8.1
having bladed or pointed article in public place 1.8.4
defences 1.8.4.1
having offensive weapons in public place 1.8.2
'adapted' 1.8.2.5
'has with him' 1.8.2.3
'intended' 1.8.2.5
lawful authority 1.8.2.1
'made' 1.8.2.5
no proof of intention to use required 1.8.2.5
not a reasonable excuse 1.8.2.2
offensive weapon, definition 1.8.2.5
public place, definition 1.8.2.4
reasonable excuse 1.8.2.2
knives 1.8.9
defences 1.8.9.3
publications relating to 1.8.9.4
sale to persons under 18 1.8.9.1
unlawful marketing 1.8.9.2
manufacture and sale of weapons 1.8.7
weapons covered by s. 141 1.8.7.1
possession of offensive weapons in private 1.8.8
school premises 1.8.5
defences 1.8.5.4
having article with blade or point on school premises 1.8.5.2
having offensive weapon on school premises 1.8.5.3
power of entry 1.8.5.5
power of staff members to search pupils for prohibited items 1.8.5.6
threatening with article with blade or point or offensive weapon 1.8.5.1
threatening with offensive weapon in public 1.8.3
trespassing with weapon of offence 1.8.6
'Wilfully' 1.1.5
Wounding or causing grievous bodily harm with intent 1.10.6.5
Wounding or inflicting grievous bodily harm 1.10.6.4
Wrongful credits 1.14.12

Y

Year and a day rule 1.5.2.2